SEXUALITY AND THE CHRISTIAN BODY

Their Way into the Triune God

Eugene F. Rogers, Jr

First published 1999

BR
115
.H6
R64
1999

2 4 6 8 10 9 7 5 3 1

Blackwell Publishers Ltd
108 Cowley Road
Oxford OX4 1JF
UK

Blackwell Publishers Inc.
350 Main Street
Malden, Massachusetts 02148
USA

British Library Cataloguing in Publication Data

A CIP catalogue record for this book is available from the British Library.

Library of Congress Cataloging-in-Publication Data

Rogers, Eugene F.
    Sexuality and the Christian body : their way into the triune God /
Eugene F. Rogers, Jr.
        p.   cm. — (Challenges in contemporary theology)
    Includes bibliographical references and index.
    ISBN 0-631-21069-5 (alk. paper). ISBN 0-631-21070-9 (pbk).
    1. Homosexuality—Religious aspects—Christianity.   2. Trinity.
I. Title.   II. Series.
BR115.H6R64   1999
233'.5—dc21   98-33149
                                                                                    CIP

Typeset in 10½ on 12½ pt Monotype Bembo by Ace Filmsetting Ltd, Frome
Printed in Great Britain by MPG Books, Victoria Square, Bodmin, Cornwall

This book is printed on acid-free paper

Challenges in Contemporary Theology

Series Editors: Gareth Jones and Lewis Ayres
University of Birmingham and Trinity College, Dublin

This series consists of carefully coordinated books which engage traditional theological concerns with the main challenges to those concerns. Each book is accessible to graduate students and good undergraduates as well as scholars. The series promotes prospective, critical and contentious positions as well as synthetic summaries of the major positions.

Already published

These Three Are One: The Practice of Trinitarian Theology
David S. Cunningham

After Writing: On the Liturgical Consummation of Philosophy
Catherine Pickstock

Mystical Theology: The Integrity of Spirituality and Theology
Mark A. McIntosh

Engaging Scripture: A Model for Theological Interpretation
Stephen E. Fowl

Torture and Eucharist: Theology, Politics, and the Body of Christ
William T. Cavanaugh

Sexuality and the Christian Body: Their Way into the Triune God
Eugene F. Rogers, Jr

Forthcoming
Theology and Mass Communication
Robert Dodara and John Paul Szura

The Practice of Christian Doctrine
Lewis Ayres

Alien Sex: The Body and Desire in Cinema and Theology
Gerard Loughlin

Critical Ecclesiology
Philip D. Kenneson

The Philoxenia or Hospitality of Abraham (Gen. 18) in a popularly reproduced icon, probably Greek, 16th century. The meal symbolizes at once the feasting that marks the life of the Triune God, the eucharist by which human beings anticipate it, and the eschatalogical wedding banquet at which they come to share it.

CONTENTS

ACKNOWLEDGMENTS

In some ways this book began with a Fulbright year at the Universität Tübingen in 1984–85, where I had gone to study the ecumenical theology of justification at a university that boasted a Katholische Fakultät, an Evangelische Fakultät, and an Ökumenisches Institut. There I happened on Dr Anne Jensen's seminar, Die Sakramente in Theorie und Praxis der Ostkirche, which opened up to a Protestant who had discovered in Aquinas a whole new world, a whole new world again. There, too, I read Paul Evdokimov's *Sacrement de l'amour: Le Mystère conjugale à la lumière de la tradition orthodoxe*[1] before ever it appeared in English, a work that figures heavily in these pages.

Thanks are due also to the Andrew W. Mellon Foundation; with their support I ended up at Yale, where I learned a great deal about sexuality and its way into the Triune God from Rowan Williams, then Lady Margaret Professor of Divinity at Oxford, who had come to visit Yale for a semester on the death of Hans Frei. He delivered to me a copy of "The Body's Grace," another essay that figures heavily in these pages, when it was still available only as a pamphlet reprint of a public address.[2]

There, too, I began to encounter views of Christian sexuality of enough charity and sophistication as to compel me, when I disagreed, to think through why. To those friends I owe great thanks: then to Regina Plunkett-Dowling[3]

[1] Paul Evdokimov, *Sacrement de l'amour: Le Mystère conjugale à le lumière de la tradition orthodoxe* (Paris: Éditions de l'Épi, 1952; Desclée de Brouwer, 1980).
[2] Rowan D. Williams, "The Body's Grace," 10th Michael Harding Memorial Address, pamphlet (London: Institute for the Study of Christianity and Sexuality, 1989), now reprinted in (and cited from) Charles Hefling, ed., *Our Selves, Our Souls and Bodies: Sexuality and the Household of God* (Boston: Cowley Publications, 1996), pp. 58–68.
[3] Regina Plunkett-Dowling, "A Paradox of Grace: The Gospel Call to Homosexuals," *Sojourners* 20 (July 1991): 26–8.

and Richard Hays, and later, when I had come to the University of Virginia, to signatories of "The Homosexual Movement: A Response by the Ramsey Colloquium."[4] Of those, I wish to thank especially David Novak, with whom I had wonderful long conversations and with whom it is delightful to disagree; and Robert Jenson, perhaps the most constructive theologian working in English today, who inspired, and received with constructive seriousness, a ten-page letter that first put into paragraphs the argument of a book that I had previously only sketched. I should also like to thank the sponsors of Jenson's Dogmatics Colloquium and Richard John Neuhaus's Dulles Group, who have patiently suffered and supported in their midst a theological conservative who is a social liberal on issues about which we disagree. From the members of the Dogmatics Colloquium, as well as from another group, the Duodecim Society, I have learned a great deal.

For their invitations to speak and helpful comments afterward, I wish to thank the Department of Religious Studies at Yale University, above all Marilyn McCord Adams (who arrived after I left), as well as David Kelsey, Wayne Meeks and Gene Outka; the Divinity School of Duke University, especially Stanley Hauerwas, for another invitation to speak; and the Department of Religious Studies at the University of North Carolina at Greensboro, especially Derek Krueger, Henry Levinson, Bennet Ramsey, and Pat Bowden. I am very grateful to Hauerwas for his constant support at every step, and particularly for the wonderful way in which he has put me in touch with other scholars who would prove helpful, especially David Matzko McCarthy (formerly McCarthy Matzko) and James Alison. Lee Yearley of Stanford and Sarah Coakley of the Harvard Divinity School also provided moral support in specific ways.

The University of Virginia has richly supported this project with summer grants of various sorts in 1995, 1996, 1997, and 1998, and with a "Sesqui" appointment to the Shannon Center for Research in 1996–97. During that year I have also the University of North Carolina at Greensboro to thank for an appointment as visiting scholar that allowed me to use a library and a computer away from the distractions of Charlottesville.

Anonymous readers for the National Endowment for the Humanities, the National Humanities Center, *The Journal of Religious Ethics, Modern Theology, Theological Studies,* and *Sexual Orientation and Human Rights in American Religious Discourse* provided constructive criticism and suggested improvements at earlier stages of the process. Special thanks are due to Saul Olyan and

---

[4]   "The Homosexual Movement: A Response by the Ramsey Colloquium," *First Things* 41 (March 1994): 15–20.

Martha Nussbaum for their encouragement to publish a programmatic essay in the last-named volume.

The National Humanities Center has graciously provided a fellowship for the year 1998–99: this will make it much easier to see this project through the press and get started on the next, which develops some of the constructive interventions of this essay on the role of the Holy Spirit in the triune life and the philanthropia of God. There I wish to thank particularly the Director, Robert Connor; the Chief Librarian, Alan Tuttle; and, for preparation of the bibliography, the Editorial Assistant, Karen Carroll. I am grateful also to Mary-Alice Talbot for granting a non-Byzantinist a reader's card for the library at Dumbarton Oaks.

Editors at Blackwell Publishers have been very helpful, including Martin Davies and Alex Wright, and especially Lewis Ayres of Trinity College, Dublin. Thanks to Jane Hammond Foster, my copy editor, for her conscientiousness and patience.

In addition to those mentioned above, I should like to thank Larry Bouchard, Jim Buckley, Annemarie Weyl Carr, Jim Childress, Elizabeth Clark, David Cunningham, Stephen Fowl, David Hart, George Hunsinger, Greg Jones, George Lindbeck, Dale Martin, Bruce Marshall, Charles Mathewes, Peter Ochs, Ashraf Rushdy, Michael Satlow, Kendall Soulen, Jeffrey Stout, Kathryn Tanner, Robert Wilken, and David Yeago for gifts of reading, bibliography, criticism, support, or conversation connected with larger or smaller parts of the essay. For the errors that remain I have only myself to thank. I wish to thank William Wilson Young, III for preparing the index.

I read paragraphs of this essay at the weddings of Idris McElveen and Michael Anderson, John Holloran and Rick Rees.

Finally I thank my partner, Derek Krueger, for intellectual conversation, moral support, patient endurance of my single-minded moods, and for continuing to risk the asceticism of married life.

I gratefully acknowledge permission to reuse in modified form:

"Supplementing Karl Barth on Jews and Gender: Identifying God by Anagogy and the Spirit." *Modern Theology* 14 (1998): 43–81.

"Sanctification, Homosexuality, and God's Triune Life." For Martha Nussbaum and Saul Olyan, eds. *Sexual Orientation and Human Rights in American Religious Discourse*. New York: Oxford University Press, 1998, pp. 134–60.

"The Narrative of Natural Law in Thomas's Commentary on Romans 1." *Theological Studies* 59 (1998): 254–76 .

"Aquinas on Natural Law and the Virtues in Biblical Context: Homosexuality as a Test Case." *The Journal of Religious Ethics* 27 (1999): 29–56.

INTRODUCTION

This book will, I hope, help students of Christianity to answer such questions about it as these: What is the relation of the human body to the trinitarian life of God? To the incarnate body of God's Word? To the body of the Church? To the body of Christ in the eucharist? How does human procreation relate to divine creation? How does sex relate to grace? How does nature relate to redemption and consummation? What are gay people and celibates for? What does God want with sex, anyway? Not only Christians but students of the humanities from English to philosophy, medieval studies to politics can benefit from understanding better how Christian argument about the body works.

In accordance with the aims of the series, this book addresses challenges to trinitarian Christian warrants both by gay and lesbian Christians *and* by their traditional Christian critics. By "trinitarian Christianity" I mean Christianity of a sort that exponents as various as Thomas Aquinas, Karl Barth, and Eastern Orthodox liturgy hold in common. By "challenges" I mean ones to both conservative *and* liberal conceptions of the body and of sacraments that observers see already *within* the community. Both traditional and revisionist arguments about the body have proved too easy, when insufficiently disciplined by more central doctrines in Trinity and christology, nature and grace. Together, traditionalist and revisionist arguments call for help upon those within or without the Christian community who would like to see it flourish – who would like to see it renew its resources for internal coherence; who would like to see it recover rationales for marriage and celibacy in assumption of Christians' bodies into the trinitarian life of God; or who would like to see it rediscover what God wants with the body and bodily desires for the common good. Thus I issue the challenge of this book not to one side or the other but to both sides and to all who care about or study them.

Not autobiography, apologetics, reaction, or devotion, this book addresses theology proper, offering a defense of marriage wide enough to include same-sex couples and committed celibates. Centrally concerned with Trinity, christology, hermeneutics, nature, and grace, it makes of the homosexuality debate an opportunity to rethink those things, because the debate raises profound and perennial theological issues. A sociologist has suggested that lesbian and gay theologies have, so far at least, fallen into four types: apologetic, therapeutic, ecological, and biographical.[1] I would argue that this work escapes such genres, because it seeks to recover for all those interested in the Christian community, and not just its lesbian and gay members, what it thinks sexuality is for at its best, how it interprets human bodies, what it means in affirming that God is Trinity, and whether it recognizes that the Church is (mostly) Gentile. The genre of this essay is not apologetic but (insofar as one can distinguish the two) dogmatic, where "dogmatic" means explaining to Christians and those who study them how Christianity's constructive and self-critical warrants work internally.

Although the book focuses on currently controversial issues of homosexuality, it seeks to interest not only readers concerned with that topic, but also anyone who has worried about the ways in which Christianity may be for or against the body, how marriage might be recovered from individualism for the community, how it might be revitalized as a locus of sanctification, how the Spirit relates to the interpretation of Scripture. More elementally, it is about the point of sexual desire, the scope of Christ's redemption, and the meaning of the Trinity. In order to construct my arguments, race, gender, and even Judaism (a traditional locus of Christian thought, to its peril, about "the carnal") come in as heuristic clues.

Part I seeks to re-orient the debates. The initial chapter constructs a typology of recent arguments, both to orient the reader and to expose similarities in opposing positions. It attempts to get beyond them by considering the criteria for debate among differing members of the Christian community. The second chapter considers how that community has settled disputed claims to full membership in the past, in the shape of arguments about how moral and natural disqualifications for full membership relate. The third chapter considers the community's claim that its members should exhibit holiness. Readers who find that the greater problem in the Christian community today is a lack of visible holiness among the baptized may like to read chapter 3 before chapter 2. Those who find, on the other hand, that the greater problem in the Christian community today is a lack of justice toward

---

[1]   Donald L. Boisvert, "Queering the Sacred: Notes for a Typology of Gay Spirituality," paper delivered to the American Academy of Religion Annual Meeting, November 1997.

disfavored groups should read chapters 2 and 3 as they appear. Although I could have put the chapters in reverse order, I put them this way so that the call for visible holiness would come as climax.

Part II seeks to retrieve the good in both the traditional and the prophetic arguments critiqued. It finds surprising openness to new views of nature in Aquinas, and to particularity and the work of the Spirit in Barth.

Part III takes up again in more detail and with more constructive purpose the re-orientation proposed in part I. It continues a defense of marriage, begun in part I, wide enough to include same-sex couples, opposite-sex couples, and lives of vowed celibacy, all under the same rationale. It offers deeper constructive arguments, not for the historical presence or logical necessity, but for the fittingness in the Christian tradition of married same-sex relationships. The starting places of these arguments are radically theological, or contingent on claims peculiar to Christianity. They include the relation of Trinity to creation; God's acting "contrary to" or "beyond" nature in incorporating the Gentiles into the Jewish olive tree (Rom. 11:24); God's predilection for irregular sexuality in salvation history, as in the cases of the women named in the genealogy of Jesus; and the recovery of adoption as a theologically ramified Christian practice.

As an epilogue it offers a charge for a wedding incorporating some of those elements, and suitable for both same-sex and opposite-sex couples.

Both theologians like Rowan Williams, author of "The Body's Grace"[2] and member of the editorial board of a new journal called *Theology and Sexuality*, and sociologists of culture wars like James Hunter, author of *Culture Wars*,[3] have called for rethinking these matters to get beyond the impasse on such sexual issues as orientation. The present volume furnishes an immediate example.

While some scholars have treated homosexuality in the New Testament and in Christian history,[4] on both sides they have been inconclusive and

---

[2]   Rowan Williams, "The Body's Grace," in Charles Hefling, ed., *Our Selves, Our Souls and Bodies: Sexuality and the Household of God* (Boston: Cowley Publications, 1996), pp. 58–68.

[3]   James Davison Hunter, *Culture Wars: The Struggle to Define America* (New York: Basic Books, 1991), esp. pp. 318–25.

[4]   Famously, John Boswell, *Christianity, Social Tolerance, and Homosexuality: Gay People in Western Europe from the Beginning of the Christian Era to the Fourteenth Century* (Chicago: University of Chicago Press, 1980), and *Same-Sex Unions in Premodern Europe* (New York: Villard Books, 1994). Most recently, see Mark D. Jordan, *The Invention of Sodomy in*

continued on next page

without theological depth. Meanwhile, "arguments to be found in the documents on sexual ethics produced by Protestant churches have, more often than not, [a] sort of purely occasional and scattershot quality to them."[5] Among important revisionist works, John Boswell's celebrated *Same-Sex Unions in Premodern Europe*, for example, never even poses the question: supposing the ceremonies described are sometimes used to bless same-sex households that include a sexual component – then how did Christians proceed when their liturgical practice conflicted with their high theology?

Conceptual analysis of Christian theological argument remains largely confined to popular genres.[6] Befitting the interest in and frustration with the topic of homosexuality in the Church, popular theology falls into liberal apologetics, conservative defense, and anthologies of essays on one

Christian Theology (Chicago: University of Chicago Press, 1997). For a recent New Testament study that refers to some of the literature pro and con, see Dale B. Martin, "Heterosexism and the Interpretation of Romans 1:18–32," *Biblical Interpretation* 3 (1995): 332–55.

[5] Kathryn Tanner, "Response to Max Stackhouse and Eugene Rogers," in Saul Olyan and Martha C. Nussbaum, eds, *Sexual Orientation and Human Rights in American Religious Discourse* (New York: Oxford University Press, 1998), pp. 161–8; here, p. 164.

[6] Four recent anthologies may constitute exceptions, covering among them both sides of the standard debates with some sophistication. See Jeffrey S. Siker, ed., *Homosexuality in the Church: Both Sides of the Debate* (Louisville, KY: Westminster/John Knox, 1994); Robert L. Brawley, ed., *Biblical Ethics and Homosexuality* (Louisville, KY: Westminster/ John Knox, 1996); Choon-Leong Seow, ed., *Homosexuality and Christian Community* (Louisville, KY: Westminster/John Knox, 1996); and Charles Hefling, ed., *Our Selves, Our Souls and Bodies: Sexuality and the Household of God* (Boston: Cowley Publications, 1996). Two older Catholic anthologies are of similar caliber: Robert Nugent, ed., *A Challenge to Love: Gay and Lesbian Catholics in the Church,* with an introduction by Bishop Walter F. Sullivan (New York: Crossroad, 1984); and Robert Nugent and Jeannine Gramick, eds, *Building Bridges: Gay and Lesbian Reality and the Catholic Church* (Mystic, CT: Twenty-Third Publications, 1992). Of books by single authors in the popular genres, see the works of John McNeill, *Freedom, Glorious Freedom: The Spiritual Journey to the Fullness of Life for Gays, Lesbians, and Everybody Else* (Boston: Beacon, 1995), *Taking a Chance on God: Liberating Theology for Gays, Lesbians, and Their Lovers, Families, and Friends,* with a new preface (Boston: Beacon, 1996), and *The Church and the Homosexual,* 4th edn (Boston: Beacon, 1993); and Thomas M. Horner, *Jonathan Loved David: Homosexuality in Biblical Times* (Philadelphia: Westminster, 1978). Midway between academic and popular are the books of Carter Heyward, among them *Our Passion for Justice: Images of Power, Sexuality, and Liberation* (New York: Pilgrim, 1984), *Speaking of Christ: A Lesbian Feminist Voice* (New York: Pilgrim, 1989), *Touching Our Strength: The Erotic as the Power and the Love of God* (San Francisco: Harper & Row, 1989), and *Staying Power: Reflections on Gender, Justice, and Compassion* (Cleveland, OH: Pilgrim, 1995).

or both sides. As one correspondent wrote, "My heart sank when I saw that you had sent me a proposal for yet another book on Christianity and Homosexuality."

Rigorous and comprehensive treatments are lacking. Even *Against Nature? Types of Moral Argumentation Regarding Homosexuality*[7] covers only natural law, does not seek to analyze liberal arguments critically, and treats the author's Dutch contemporaries at the expense of thinkers from Aquinas to Barth who influence the entire West. Meanwhile, a dozen pages of close, small-print bibliography in *The Lesbian and Gay Studies Reader* lists no religious studies at all.[8] Only "The Body's Grace," by Rowan Williams, begins to uncover with adequate conceptual rigor the connections between the social and high theological issues, and it is only ten pages long.

This book hopes, then, to make several contributions. It types and analyzes a wide variety of positions. It exposes similarities between opposing arguments. It considers the conceptual structure rather than the history or biblical basis of Christian arguments. It goes beyond narrow concerns to take up matters deeply ramified in Christian thought (the relation of law and virtue, between divine election and command). It contributes both to the understanding of Christian thought and to the civility of public debate.

I have described the genre of this book as "dogmatics." That designation may strike liberal readers as archaic, or conservative ones as inappropriate to the topic. It is neither, but a term of art, specifically what Karl Barth called "irregular dogmatics." "Irregular dogmatics" is:

> free discussion of the problems that arise for Church proclamation from the standpoint of the question of dogma. . . . Perhaps for specific historical reasons it will take up a specific theme and focus on it. Perhaps it will be relatively free in relation to the biblical basis or its choice of partners in discussion. Perhaps it will be more of an exposition of results, and will take the form of theses or aphorisms, and will observe only partially or not at all the distinction between dogmatics and proclamation. Perhaps it will leave much to be desired as regards the explicit or implicit distinctness of its path of knowledge. In one respect or another, or even in many or all respects, it will be, and will mean to be, a fragment, and it will have to be evaluated as such. The dogmatic work that has come down to us from the early Church, even from the pens of its most

---

[7] Pim Pronk, *Against Nature? Types of Moral Argumentation Regarding Homosexuality*, trans. John Vriend (Grand Rapids, MI: William B. Eerdmans, 1993).

[8] Henry Abelove, Michele Aina Barale, and David M. Halperin, eds, *The Lesbian and Gay Studies Reader* (New York: Routledge, 1993), pp. 653–66.

significant and learned representatives, is not for the most part regular dogmatics but irregular dogmatics in the sense described.[9]

Or it is an exercise in what Cardinal Ratzinger and the Catholic Congregation for the Doctrine of the Faith would call "the ecclesial vocation of the theologian."[10] In describing the questioning aspect of the theologian's ecclesial vocation, the document of that title avoids the word "dissent," which it reserves for "attitudes of general opposition to Church teaching which even come to expression in organized groups," "the weight of public opinion," and "the mass media."[11] Contrary to its portrayal in the popular media, the Vatican here opposes attempts to foreclose reasoned theological argument. On the contrary,

> the theologian has the duty to make known to the magisterial authorities the problems raised by the teaching in itself, in the arguments proposed to justify it or even in the manner in which it is presented. . . . His objections could then contribute to real progress and provide a stimulus to the magisterium to propose the teaching of the Church in greater depth and with a clearer presentation of the arguments. . . . [I]f the truth really is at stake it will ultimately prevail.[12]

Although I am not a Catholic, as a student of Christianity I find the "Ecclesial Vocation of the Theologian" a useful description of the sort of intellectual discipline that is likely to gain a hearing in the Christian community over the very long term. It is even a discipline that I am not alone among non-Catholics in attempting to emulate.[13] The "Letter to the Bishops of the Catholic Church on the Pastoral Care of Homosexual Persons," furthermore, explicitly invites such an exercise: "[T]he phenomenon of homosexuality, complex as it is and with its many consequences for society and ecclesial life, is a proper focus for

[9]　Karl Barth, *Church Dogmatics*, 4 vols in 13, trans. G. W. Bromiley, et al. (Edinburgh: T. & T. Clark, 1956–75), vol. I/1 (rev., 1975 trans.), p. 277. In the original, the last sentence begins a new paragraph.

[10]　Congregation for the Doctrine of the Faith, "Instruction on the Ecclesial Vocation of the Theologian," *Origins: CNS Documentary Service* 20 (1990): 120–6. I cite with both page and section numbers.

[11]　Congregation for the Doctrine of the Faith, "Ecclesial Vocation of the Theologian," p. 123, § 32.

[12]　Congregation for the Doctrine of the Faith, "Ecclesial Vocation of the Theologian," p. 123, § 32.

[13]　See for example Stanley Hauerwas (a Methodist), "Virtue, Description, and Friendship [formerly "Gay Friendship"]: A Thought Experiment in Catholic Moral Theology," *Irish Theological Quarterly* (1998): 170–84.

the Church's . . . attentive study, active concern, and honest, theologically well-balanced counsel." The Letter calls on "theologians who, . . . by deepening their reflections on the true meaning of human sexuality and Christian marriage with the virtues it engenders, will make an important contribution to this area."[14]

---

[14] Congregation for the Doctrine of the Faith, "Letter to the Bishops of the Catholic Church on the Pastoral Care of Homosexual Persons," reprinted most conveniently in Jeannine Gramick and Pat Furey, eds, *The Vatican and Homosexuality* (New York: Crossroad, 1988), pp. 1–10; here, §§2, 17. – As I revise this section, newspaper and radio reports wax sensational about a new apostolic letter from the pen of John Paul II, "Ad tuendam fidem," dated July 1, 1998 (*Origins* 28 (1998): 113, 115–16). It speaks of the "infallibility" of the definitive teachings of the ordinary magisterium. Although non-Catholic Christians, especially those in ecumenical dialogue with the Catholic Church, can scarcely be happy about the wording, the news media have missed several crucial matters of context. (1) Technically, the document only adds oaths of adherence for "those who exercise an ecclesiastical teaching ministry," that is, in Catholic institutions of certain limited sorts. The ecclesiastical teaching ministry is not the same as the ecclesial vocation of the theologian, and the existence of the one does not deny the existence of the other. (2) It would be wrong to interpret the document as in conflict with either the "Instruction on the Ecclesial Vocation of the Theologian" or the "Letter to the Bishops of the Catholic Church on the Pastoral Care of Homosexual Persons." Since "Ad tuendam fidem" aims to strengthen the teachings of the ordinary magisterium – including those on the ecclesial office of the theologian – it also strengthens, rather than undermines, those documents. (3) The word "infallibility" must not be understood in too broad a sense. It means that Catholic Christians are required to exercise the virtue of hope that infallible pronouncements will not prove so inadequate to the truth as permanently to separate them from the grace of Christ. Indeed, all Christians should hope, to put it crudely, that the Holy Spirit will preserve Catholic Christians from going to hell for believing the magisterium. Indeed, no less an authority than Thomas Aquinas usefully distinguishes between "infallible" and "irresistible" movements of the Holy Spirit. The Holy Spirit is resistible as long as human freedom lasts. But God will infallibly bring the predestined into the divine fellowship (*Summa Theologiae* , part I, question 22, article 4 [hereafter I. 22. 4] *ad* 1). Applied to the magisterium, Thomas's distinction would mean that its human ability to resist the Holy Spirit does not go away in this life, but the Spirit will also keep it from going so far astray as to thwart God's saving purpose. For more on the structure of authority in Catholicism, see Karl Rahner, *Foundations of Christian Faith: An Introduction to the Idea of Christianity*, trans. William V. Dych (New York: Crossroad, 1992), pp. 384–7, and "Magisterium and Theology," in his *Theological Investigations*, vol. 18, trans. Edward Quinn (New York: Crossroad, 1983), pp. 54–73; Francis Sullivan, *Creative Fidelity: Weighing and Interpreting Documents of the Magisterium* (New York: Paulist Press, 1996), and *Magisterium: Teaching Authority in the Catholic Church* (New York: Paulist Press, 1985); Richard R. Gaillardetz, *Teaching with Authority: A Theology of the Magisterium in the Church* (Collegeville, MN: The Liturgical Press, 1997), esp. pp. 101–28.

Because I seek in this book to exercise the ecclesial vocation of the theologian, I spend a lot of time arguing with the traditional view in two of its strongest forms – the natural law arguments associated with Thomas Aquinas, and the theologically ramified divine command arguments associated with Karl Barth. I do not force these thinkers to approve anachronistically of same-sex marriages. That would be impossible and do violence to the texts. Rather I put their objections extensively into context in order to make space around them. My engagement with them is an extended exercise in clearing room for constructive proposals. Despite the opposition of thinkers like Aquinas and Barth, revisionist proposals do not introduce the extremes of discontinuity into Christian thought that their critics might suppose. But the question of how and under what circumstances is necessarily complex. I clear space in each case on the thinker's own terms. My arguments therefore deeply engage peculiarities of Thomas and Barth, in order to make the space-clearing *internal* to each. In each I find internal resources for a surprising openness. The exercise is not easy work, but it is possible and rewarding. Some readers may find these chapters fascinating case studies in the aesthetics of theological thinking; others may scratch their heads or pull out their hair wondering why I bother with such unpromising resources or roundabout arguments. The answer is: it is the discipline of a theologian's ecclesial vocation.

Because this essay is an exercise in *irregular* dogmatics, it does not apologize for its irregularity – for taking the issue of sexuality as a way of interrogating and learning from the tradition. As Barth characterizes it, irregular dogmatics is historically conditioned; it is free in its choice of topics and conversation partners; it is fragmentary. Because this book is an exercise in irregular *dogmatics*, it does not apologize for – it glories in – its dogmatic character. That is, it delights in relating its theme to such topics as election and Trinity that may at first appear to stand at the farthest remove from sexuality. It aims to teach as much about creation, redemption, consummation, and God's covenant with Israel, as about anything else.

Definitions and Disclaimers

"Symbol" serves in Christian theology both as a word for ontological participation and as an older word for the creeds. This book is an essay in nuptial symbolics in both senses, primarily in the second, more theological sense. Therefore several disclaimers are worth stating at the outset.

1   Although extra-Christian debates about identity and constructivism

versus essentialism lie in the background, I consider them only as they appear *within* Christian discourse. I seek to discern a hermeneutics of the body *other* than Foucault's. Foucalt's is a voice so useful, so familiar, so powerful as possibly to drown the stiller, smaller voice I seek to overhear.

2   The description of normative Christian claims falls into two disciplines, theology and ethics, as separated by their boundary as they are united by their logic. This book straddles the boundary. But as it is concerned primarily with the symbolics, and only secondarily with the rules and virtues, of Christian marriage and monasticism, its overtures to ethics are partial and fragmentary. Just because it confines itself to nuptial symbolics – to trying to recover what marriage might be – it has little or nothing to say about other issues of sexual ethics, neither the celibacy of secular priests, nor sex before, beside, or after marriage. Those are worthy and complex topics, but they would change the subject.

3   I have also been trained primarily as a modernist, and I have worked my way back, first into medieval theology, and from there into earlier theology. No doubt the reader can tell. I have tried to hedge my bets this way. No part of the argument depends strictly on pre-medieval sources. Part of it depends on Paul Evdokimov, an important 20th century theologian (flourishing in Paris in the 1950s and '60s), and a subject of theological study in his own right,[15] who recovered patristic theologies of marriage through a particular, 19th century Russian lens, and with a particular, Eastern Orthodox agenda for the modern West. The only alternative to such breadth would have been the lack thereof.

4   I speak often of Jews and Gentiles, baptism and adoption. None of this is meant to be supersessionist. If I speak of "the people of God" and then of "the baptized," that is meant to limit the exposition to my field of competence, not to limit the range of the people of God. That is especially the case if it is one of the offices of baptism to wash away the Gentiles' lack of relation to the God of Israel. Furthermore, when I speak of natural birth and adoption, it is with the understanding that the distinction is meta-phorical, relative, and dialectical. Although Paul sometimes seems to use the word *huiothesia* (adoption) to distinguish Gentiles and Jews, in Romans he uses it to mean that the Gentiles gain (8:23) what the Jews

[15] See Michael Plekon, "Paul Evdokimov: A Theologian Within and Beyond the Church and the World," *Modern Theology* 12 (1996): 85–107, esp. 99–103; and Rowan D. Williams, "Bread in the Wilderness: The Monastic Ideal in Thomas Merton and Paul Evdokimov," in M. Basil Pennington, ed., *Monastic Traditions East and West: One Yet Two* (Spencer, MA: Cistercian Publications, 1976).

retain (9:4). The binding of Isaac makes him the son of both nature and grace.

5 I retain the language of "Father, Son, and Holy Spirit" in speaking of the persons of the Trinity. While I am aware of substitutions, none seem to do better the *specific* work that needs doing in this particular essay. "Creator, Redeemer, Sanctifier" need not, *pace* critics, be used in a modalist way; the Creed identifies the Father as Creator, and there need be nothing wrong with referring to the persons according to their appropriated functions while allowing their interior relations to go temporarily without saying. But just when, as here, their interior relations are part of the point, "Creator, Redeemer, Sanctifier" is not sufficient. Because the Father creates, redeems, and sanctifies, as do the Spirit and the Son, the substitution names indivisible external actions, rather than internal relations. (*Opera trinitatis ad extra indivisa sunt.*) "Source, Word, and Spirit" would do in some ways, but not when the exposition, as here, hopes constantly to ring of such biblical accounts as the baptism, transfiguration, and Last Supper of Jesus, where his calling upon the one he calls "Father" and the Father's recognition of the one he calls "My son, My beloved" seem to reveal something of the Trinity's interior exchange of prayer and gratitude. It is in order that human beings might come to join in their exchange, Christians believe, that Father, Son, and Holy Spirit, by grace the singular Mother of them all, creates, redeems, and sanctifies. My use of language for God involves an inadequate solution for a particular, pragmatic purpose, not the taking up of a position in another debate. To say much more would require a book of its own.

A matter of definition is more important. A critic has complained that "The Body's Grace," commended above, and to which we shall recur, makes no "argument."[16] As we shall see in chapter 1, the claim that one's opponents make no argument comes easily to the lips of both sides. In "The Body's Grace," Rowan Williams seems, to critics, to take the licitness of marriagelike gay and lesbian relationships as given, and go on from there. The critic thinks the essay begs the question, while others think it refreshes the debate. If one begins from some shared premises and attempts to make others attractive through disciplined elaboration in their terms, that is not a bad procedure in theology, but defines its usual method. It has been said of Karl Barth, perhaps the most important Protestant theologian since the Reformation (d. 1968), that he argued aesthetically, or by thick description:

[16] Personal correspondence.

Barth was about the business of conceptual description. He took the classical themes of communal Christian language molded by the Bible, tradition and constant usage in worship, practice, instruction and controversy, and he restated or redescribed them, rather than evolving arguments on their behalf. It was of the utmost importance to him that this communal language, especially its biblical *fons et origo*, . . . had an integrity of its own: It was irreducible. But in that case its lengthy, even leisurely unfolding was equally indispensable. . . . Barth had as it were to recreate a universe of discourse, and he had to put the reader in the middle of that world, instructing him in the use of that language by showing him how – extensively, and not only by stating the rules or principles of that discourse. . . . [I]t was of the essence of his design that it could not be stated apart from its specific unfolding without losing its force.[17]

Such a conceptual description *does* argue, if implicitly; it argues from and to coherence. Even a theologian as famous for formal deduction as Thomas Aquinas can agree. Considering how theology properly mounts arguments, Thomas insists that no way lies open to persuade an opponent who begins from different premises – except to start from one's own and treat the opponent's generously as *solubilia argumenta*, difficulties to be overcome.[18]

The argument I offer is not so much of the kind Christian theologians sometimes offer, with definitions and entailments, givens and therefores, the sort a scholastic would have called an argument *ex necessitate*, or from necessity – although it is that in part. It is more an attempt to retell and renarrate bits of the Christian story so as to reveal the coherence of Christian thought with a practice of marriage broad enough to include gay and lesbian couples, and leaving room for vowed celibates in community, all under the same analysis. Far from a lack of argument, that procedure mounts an argument of a different sort, one the scholastics called an argument *ex convenientia*, or from fittingness, and one Geertz would call thick description. It tests the hypothesis that gay and lesbian marriage can newly suit or befit the Christian tradition. I hope to identify fresh starting places for thinking about these matters, and treat traditional ones, liberal and conservative, constructively rather than polemically, as difficulties leading to a more adequate account, as Thomas uses objections and replies. I do not argue, that is, that Christianity could not exist otherwise, but that its existence in the way I describe does make better sense of central claims about God, the community of the faithful, and their relationship. It does them greater justice.

---

[17] Hans W. Frei, "Eberhard Busch's Biography of Karl Barth," in Frei, *Types of Christian Theology,* ed. George Hunsinger and William C. Placher (New Haven, CT: Yale University Press, 1992), pp. 147–63; here, pp. 158–9.
[18] Thomas Aquinas, *Summa Theologiae* I. 1. 8.

Which traditions? I have quoted Barth, a Protestant, and Thomas, a Catholic, and spoken in Eastern Orthodox ways about sharing in God's triune life. In this my approach is ecumenically Protestant. Protestantism had its theological origin and reason for existence in a proposal about Church teaching on the justification of the unrighteous.[19] Now that parties to ecumenical dialogue have experienced remarkable convergence on the very issue that divided them at the Reformation,[20] the only excuse for further Protestant proposals about Church teaching (about married priests, ordained women, marriages for gay and lesbian couples) must be a return to their roots as prophetic or Pauline movements of the Spirit of unity, incomplete without magisterial or Petrine response from the rest of the Church. The argument is Protestant precisely in that it does not stand alone; rather, it enjoys a characteristically Protestant obligation to take from and speak to the traditions that gave it rise. It finds itself citing Thomas Aquinas as the Catholic magisterium would not; but thus it comes inevitably into conversation with Catholics, saying: can you not use Thomas this way? Similarly, it deploys Eastern Orthodox liturgy as the Orthodox would not, asking: can you not use the liturgy this way? Perhaps all branches of Christianity, like Protestantism, exist only from and for a community of the faithful larger than itself. The community of the faithful larger than any of its parts is defined first eschatologically – by what it will be in God's kingdom, and empirically only in retrospect. Christians suppose that, looking back from the eschaton, one of the temporal, empirical markers of community with God will be baptism.

(If some Christians are now coming to believe that, since the eschatological community will fulfill the promises of the God of Israel, one of the empirical markers of community with that God will turn out to have been circumcision, that is a topic for another chapter. Thus I leave unresolved the tension between speaking of "the people of God," which arguably includes Jews more surely than it does Christians, and speaking of "the baptized," since as a Christian theologian I cannot speak for anyone else. But readers should keep in mind Kendall Soulen's thesis that what baptism washes away is nothing other than Gentiles' lack of relation to the God of Israel.[21])

[19] This thesis is defended in Robert W. Jenson and Eric W. Gritsch, *Lutheranism: The Theological Movement and Its Confessional Writings* (Philadelphia: Fortress, 1976).

[20] See for example George H. Anderson, T. Austin Murphy, and Joseph A. Burgess, eds, *Justification by Faith: Lutherans and Catholics in Dialogue* VII (Minneapolis, MN: Augsburg, 1985).

[21] Personal correspondence with Kendall Soulen. More on this when we come to Karl Barth in part II.

An ecumenical procedure – one that addresses all the baptized, but here especially those in Protestant, Catholic, and Eastern Orthodox traditions – has other advantages. One is that it can begin to apply to moral disputes the experience with dogmatic disputes that has transformed late 20th century Christian theology. *Kontroverstheologie* has become *ökumenische Harmonielehre*, or the theology of controversy has become the doctrine of ecumenical harmony. "Ecumenical theology," in the sense not of generalized American nondenominational evangelicalism, but of official dialogues among Catholics, Lutherans, Calvinists, and Anglicans, is now the topic of entire journals in several languages, numerous books, and chapters in undergraduate surveys of 20th century theology. Whole bibliographies of books, both great and small, attempt to reconcile such apparently opposed theologians as Thomas Aquinas and Martin Luther, or Thomas and Barth, on precisely the points where they seem most sharply to disagree. The great theological disputes of the Reformation have been declared settled from many quarters, at least in the sense that none of the original parties to the Reformation disputes now officially regards them as any longer Church-dividing. Negotiations recur on lifting mutual anathemas and the mutual recognition of once-rival confessions. Differences that remain are not papered over but acknowledged as theological alternatives in "convergence," a technical term of *kontroverstheologische Harmonielehre.* Convergence "indicates movement towards, not arrival at. Thus, 'convergence' is not complete consensus or agreement. It also does not mean that oppositions vanish. It means that oppositions are re-located as no longer at the center of things."[22] While it is far too soon to speak of "convergence" on the matter of homosexuality in the churches, the lessons of *kontroverstheologische Harmonielehre* are beginning to be applied already in these disputes. Those lessons are at least three:

1 Catholic, Protestant, and Eastern Orthodox traditions – as well as Jewish, Aristotelian, Puritan, secular, and more – are not isolated but connected with one another, so that their arguments are deracinated and blindered on their own.
2 Church politics is best conceived theologically not as a matter of denominationalism, still less of culture wars, but of God's eschatological plan to live in community with all human beings despite their sinful desires for division.
3 A special ethics needs to be recovered for living among Christians who

---

[22] James J. Buckley, review of *Thomas Aquinas and Karl Barth*, in *The Thomist* 61 (1997): 320–35; here, p. 324.

disagree seriously about what the truth is: "the only road to integrity passes through the narrow gate of unity."[23]

One purpose of this book is to create a convergence on Christian sexuality among traditionalists and revisionists in the sense of "relocating their opposition as no longer at the center of things." The center of things, for Christians, is God's marriage with humanity in Jesus Christ. Karl Barth condensed it into a statement to which we shall often recur: "Because the election of God is real, there is such a thing as love and marriage."[24] The convergence will be weak in this sense: some readers of this book will not be persuaded, and will still disagree over whether same-sex couples qualify to represent that marriage of God and humanity. But the convergence will be strong, I hope very strong, in this sense: almost all readers of this book, traditionalist and revisionist, gay and straight, will develop a renewed and even common sense of what Christians ought by their best lights to think God uses human bodies for, and how God takes them up into the process of making human beings holy.

My first book was on the natural knowledge of God – that is, on the natural knowledge of God's existence and character supposedly inscribed, according to scriptural warrant and traditional conviction, in the surrounding cosmos – a knowledge about which Christians disagree. Specifically, that book treated Thomas Aquinas and Karl Barth, who are usually supposed to occupy opposite sides in the debate. This book also takes up Christian thinkers usually supposed to occupy opposite sides in a debate, and their debate too concerns a natural knowledge of God. This time the debate is on what one might call the natural knowledge of God's *will*, rather than God's existence and attributes. In one of its formulations that knowledge is called natural law, although other versions of a natural knowledge of God's will avoid that phrase and speak instead of the orders of creation or the biblical witness. This debate, whatever you call it, is about the natural knowledge of God's will supposedly inscribed, according to scriptural warrant and traditional conviction, in the human body – another knowledge about which Christians disagree.

[23] David S. Yeago, "The *Concordat*, Ecumenism, and Evangelical–Catholic Politics," *The Lutheran Forum* 32, 1 (1998): 42–6; here, p. 46.
[24] Karl Barth, *Church Dogmatics*, III/1, 318. The comment refers in context only to heterosexual marriage.

Part I

ORIENTATION IN THE DEBATES: SEXUALITY AND THE PEOPLE OF GOD

Chapter 1

THE POLITICS OF THE PEOPLE OF GOD

Christians have always been debating some practical issue about the body – be it the celibacy of priests, the veneration of icons, the cult of relics, the freeing of slaves, the ordination of women, or the blessing of same-sex unions.[1] Christians have also always ranked embodiment among the highest concerns of their intellectual discourse, from the election of Israel to the incarnation of God and the resurrection of the dead. Put another way, theology has used one set of terms – creation, election, incarnation, resurrection – while ethically charged postmodern discourse uses another – embodiment, race, gender, orientation. Theologians such as Karl Barth tell us that ethics and high theology ought to be closely related,[2] and anthropologists of religion such as Clifford Geertz tell us similar things about ethos and worldview, or social and intellectual practices.[3] Yet only too rarely do Christian ethicists connect

---

[1] For more detail on "marriagelike unions for gay and lesbian people" compatible with the views of this essay, see David McCarthy Matzko, "Homosexuality and the Practices of Marriage," *Modern Theology* 13 (1997): 371–97; and Rowan D. Williams, "The Body's Grace," in Charles Hefling, ed., *Our Selves, Our Souls and Bodies: Sexuality and the Household of God* (Boston: Cowley Press, 1996), pp. 58–68. For a political argument that deals with religious views, see Andrew Sullivan, *Virtually Normal: An Argument about Homosexuality* (New York: Alfred A. Knopf, 1995).

[2] "What is called ethics I regard as the doctrine of the command of God. Hence I do not think it right to treat it otherwise than as an integral part of dogmatics," Karl Barth, *Church Dogmatics*, 4 vols. in 13, trans. G. W. Bromiley, et al. (Edinburgh, T. & T. Clark, 1956–75), I/1, p. xvi.

[3] "[R]eligious symbols, dramatized in rituals or related in myths, are felt somehow to sum up, for those for whom they are resonant, what is known about the way the world is, the quality of the emotional life it supports, and the way one ought to behave while in it," Clifford Geertz, "Ethos, World View, and the Analysis of Sacred Symbols," in his *The Interpretation of Cultures* (New York: Basic Books, 1973), p. 127.

doctrines like incarnation, election, and resurrection with race, gender, and orientation.[4] My constructive proposals attempt to *renegotiate* ethos and worldview in Christianity by reference to the central symbols that connect them – where ethos includes the practices of marriage (or lack thereof) for straight, gay, and lesbian people; worldview includes what Christians believe about the world, signally dogmatics ("a critical native model"[5]); and the central symbol is the body of Christ enacted in the sacraments. Marriage and the eucharist (as well as baptism and monastic vows) tell Christians what bodies are for before God, or what they mean, by incorporating them into the body of Christ.

Many thoughtful Christians and students of Christianity experience frustration in current churchly debates about homosexuality. They may hear conservative arguments as rigorous but wrong, liberal arguments as well-meaning but weak. They may regard most books as manifestos lacking in any real theological depth. Either love is reduced to moral norms, or it knows none. Theologically inclined readers may experience the great-est frustration over arguments about committed, monogamous relationships within the Christian community that resemble childless or child-rearing heterosexual marriages. The whole issue needs rethinking. How does the Christian community think God sanctifies and upbuilds it with sexual desire?

To get a sense of the range and disarray of the debate, consider an informal typology and critique of current Christian arguments about the body, taking the lately controverted topic of homosexuality as a test case. A typology does not settle but merely surveys the debates. It is designed to be more brief than fair, and, in this case, to show that each side is better at poking holes in the other than in making a constructive case that would illuminate the ethos and worldview of Christianity as a whole. It is in the nature of the case that some of these arguments, including those that are poorly made, really reach correct conclusions, even when they prove unpersuasive.[6] I return to make constructive use of some from both sides later on. For now I need only show how both traditional and liberal religious arguments about the body sound too easy to their opponents. Those self-evident to one side seem self-evidently embar-

---

[4]   Karl Barth is, as noted, an exception to this. For reflections on the general case of how issues of social ethics and dogmatic theology relate in Christian discourse, see Kathryn Tanner, *The Politics of God: Christian Theologies and Social Justice* (Minneapolis, MN: Fortress, 1992).

[5]   Geertz, *Interpretation of Cultures*, p. 14, n. 1 and p. 15, n. 2.

[6]   Karl Rahner, "On Bad Arguments in Moral Theology," in his *Theological Investigations*, vol. 18, trans. Edward Quinn (New York: Crossroad, 1983), pp. 74–85.

rassing to the other. Liberals can make conservatives look dumb, and conservatives can make liberals look shallow. Yet conceptual analysis of the warrants adduced for *opposing* positions suggests similarities. Both sides appeal to Scripture, tradition, community, reason, and nature. I mention five liberal complaints about conservative arguments, and five conservative complaints about liberal arguments, arranged to show parallels.

How Liberals Hear Conservative Arguments

1   Liberals accuse conservatives of misreading biblical narratives. Liberals are surprised to find some conservatives still arguing in the mid 1990s that the narratives about the rape of visiting angels at Sodom and Gomorrah (Gen. 19:4–8) tell against modern, monogamous, same-sex couples.[7] One does not have to claim that the biblical authors would approve of modern same-sex couples to see that the sex of the parties is not the point of the story. Indeed, other conservatives do concede that the point of the story is as Ezekiel tells it: "Behold, this was the sin of your sister Sodom: she and her daughters had pride, surfeit of food, and prosperous ease, but did not aid the poor and needy."[8] In the liberal view, one might as well say that the story of the Fall in Genesis refers to God's special punishment of women, or that the story of Ham records God's special punishment of blacks.[9] All of these, so liberals argue, are misreadings of biblical narratives.

2   Liberals accuse conservatives of misplaced literalism. Liberals find it

[7]   For example, Richard F. Lovelace, *Homosexuality and the Church* (Old Tappan, NJ: Revell, 1978); and more recently Thomas E. Schmidt, *Straight and Narrow? Compassion and Clarity in the Homosexuality Debate* (Downer's Grove, IL: InterVarsity Press, 1995), pp. 86–99. For the inhospitality reading of the story, see Derrick Sherwin Bailey, *Homosexuality and the Western Christian Tradition* (London: Green, 1955), pp. 2–16; John McNeill, *The Church and the Homosexual,* 4th edn (Boston: Beacon, 1993), pp. 42–50; John Boswell, *Christianity, Social Tolerance, and Homosexuality: Gay People in Western Europe from the Beginning of the Christian Era to the Fourteenth Century* (Chicago: University of Chicago Press, 1980), pp. 92–7; L. William Countryman, *Dirt, Greed, and Sex* (Philadelphia: Fortress, 1988), pp. 30–2; Marvin Pope, *The Interpreter's Dictionary of the Bible, Supplementary Volume* (Nashville: Abingdon, 1976), pp. 415–17; and notes to *The Jerusalem Bible* and *The New Oxford Annotated Bible.*
[8]   Ezek. 16:49. So Richard Hays finds Ezekiel to state the meaning of the passage in "Homosexuality," chapter 16 in his *Moral World of the New Testament: Community, Cross, New Creation: An Introduction to New Testament Ethics* (San Francisco: HarperSanFrancisco, 1996), p. 381.
[9]   For that interpretation, see chapter 2 below.

hard to credit Levitical prohibitions (18:22, 20:13) because they come in the context of and seem of a piece with rules about ritual purity and distinguishing Israelites from surrounding nations.[10] They point out that other Levitical prohibitions concern the eating of pork and shellfish and the mixing of fabric in cloth. Conservatives claim that Leviticus "makes no systematic distinction between ritual law and moral law," noting that incest is also prohibited in Leviticus.[11] In the first place, liberals find the observation question-begging. Given two categories of actions included under the Hebrew word *toevah*, liberals think that all conservatives are doing is referring to incest and waiting for the like-minded reader to put gay and lesbian people into that category by association.[12] Liberals reply further that although the Hebrew text uniformly has *toevah*, "abomination," the Septuagint systematically distinguishes in translating *toevah* between ritual purity (*bdelygma*) and injustice proper (*anomia*), putting same-sex activity in the purity class.[13] And so it goes.

Liberals also find it hard to credit conservative readings of Romans 1, although here they have a much harder argument, since they cannot dismiss Pauline strictures as easily as Levitical ones.[14] Conservatives think they have a clear case: "Their women exchanged the natural use for that beyond nature, and in the same way also the men, giving up the natural use of women, were consumed with passion for one another, men committing shameless acts with men and receiving in their own persons the due penalty for their error" (Rom. 1:26-7). Liberals reply that Paul is talking about sexual excess (beyond nature, *para phusin*), which he assumes all homoerotic behavior to exemplify, even

[10] For example, Boswell, *Christianity, Social Tolerance, and Homosexuality*, pp. 98–103; Countryman, *Dirt, Greed, and Sex, passim.*

[11] Hays, "Homosexuality," p. 382.

[12] For a sociological explanation of the (warranted or unwarranted) power of such appeals, see Jeffrey Stout, "Moral Abominations," in his *Ethics after Babel: The Languages of Morals and Their Discontents* (Boston: Beacon, 1988).

[13] Boswell, *Christianity, Social Tolerance, and Homosexuality*, pp. 101–2.

[14] For an impressive account of the difficulty for Christians wanting both to honor the Bible and be open to marriagelike gay and lesbian relationships, see recently Mark D. Smith, "Ancient Bisexuality and the Interpretation of Romans 1:26–27," *Journal of the American Academy of Religion* 64 (1996): 223–56, and the rejoinders of Daniel A. Helminiak, "Ethics, Biblical and Denominational: A Response to Mark Smith," *Journal of the American Academy of Religion* 65 (1997): 855–60; and James E. Miller, "Pederasty and Romans 1:27: A Response to Mark Smith," *Journal of the American Academy of Religion* 65 (1997): 861–6. For a contrary interpretation taking into account much of the same scholarship, see Dale B. Martin, "Heterosexism and the Interpretation of Romans 1:18–32," *Biblical Interpretation* 3 (1995): 332–55.

though he cannot have the modern concept of homosexual orientation in mind.[15] Some liberals argue further that since Paul cannot have had sexual orientation in mind, his strictures against sexual activity in excess of nature ought to be (not interpreted but) applied so that it is just as "contrary to nature" for gay and lesbian people to try to go straight, leaving ruined heterosexual marriages in their wake, as it is for straight people to seek homosexual liaisons just for kicks.[16] Finally, liberals agree, conservatives are offering a misplaced literalism that fails sufficiently to acknowledge social context. It comes down to which verses in the Bible one accepts. There is no problem with interpreting I Timothy 6:1-2, but no one argues any longer on the basis of that text that slaves should obey their masters.

3   Natural law arguments are too familiar to need much explanation or exemplification. They appear among Jews and Protestants as well as among Catholics. Under the guidance of Thomas Aquinas, I consider them at length in part II. They may start either with biblical, creation-based accounts of nature, or with biological or Aristotelian accounts of procreation. According to the standard Vatican position, a homosexual person suffers an objective disorder which always leads to a moral fault should he or she exercise that disposition, since there is no possibility of procreation. Liberals complain that the New Testament never relates marriage to procreation or that Aristotle is an odd place from which to get one's natural science. In any case, they ask what infertility in straight couples is but an objective disorder, and why an infertile or postmenopausal heterosexual couple's exercise of their sexual disposition does not always count as moral fault.[17] The rejoinder that such straight couples are awaiting a biblical miracle strikes liberals as special pleading of the most ridiculous kind. If Eve can be created from a man without a woman, and Jesus born from a woman without a man, then not only straight couples may appeal to miracle.

---

[15]   Martin, "Heterosexism and the Interpretation of Romans 1:18–32," develops this view precisely in response to Hays..

[16]   E.g., Boswell, *Christianity, Social Tolerance, and Homosexuality*, pp. 107–16. Boswell argues in terms of "the *personal* nature of the pagans in question," p. 111. The argument would be stronger if he recognized that Paul is almost certainly stereotyping the *ethnic* nature of the Gentiles as a group.

[17]   See Andrew Sullivan, "Alone Again, Naturally: The Catholic Church and the Homosexual," in *The New Republic*, November 28, 1994, pp. 47, 50, 52, 54–5; here, pp. 54–5; Peter J. Gomes, "The Bible and Homosexuality: The Last Prejudice," in his *The Good Book: Reading the Bible with Mind and Heart* (New York: Avon, 1996), p. 170. Some readers may be familiar with an analogy between homosexuality and alcoholism. Liberals reject that analogy, too. I consider it in part III.

4   Liberals accuse conservatives of special pleading with the category of vocation. According to the argument from vocation, the circumstance that a person manifestly lacks a calling to heterosexual marriage, for whatever reason, may constitute a call to celibacy.[18] So far, if one has a place in one's theology for celibacy at all, so good. Everyone agrees that calls of whatever sort do not take place except through particular circumstances. Richard Hays poses the question sharply, italicizing it in the original:

> Does this mean that persons of homosexual orientation are subject to a blanket imposition of celibacy in a way qualitatively different from persons of hetero-sexual orientation? . . . The only difference – admittedly a salient one – in the case of homosexually oriented persons is that they do not have the option of homosexual "marriage." So where does that leave them? It leaves them in precisely the same situation as the heterosexual who would like to marry but cannot find an appropriate partner . . . . [19]

Liberals reply that the interesting case is when gay and lesbian people *do* find appropriate – compatible, unattached, commitment-ready – partners: the question, to them, is what *constitutes* appropriateness, and if one decides in advance that no partner of the same sex can *in principle* be appropriate, that counts as begging it. All gay people have a vocation to celibacy that some straight people also have – as if all black people had the vocation to service that some white people have, or all women had the vocation to homemaking that some men have. A liberal might observe that the argument from vocation conflates body and soul: it proceeds as if the shape, color, or desire of one's body predetermined one's vocation without any need for considering cases or interior discernment. It is as if one could read off the call of the soul from the shape of the genitals and the physiology of their response.[20]

5   Liberals also complain about appeals to tradition or the character of the community when questions of justice are at stake and deep objections have emerged.

---

[18]   For a Catholic vocation argument, see James Hannigan, *Homosexuality: Test Case for Christian Ethics* (New York: Paulist Press, 1988). For an Eastern Orthodox one, see William B. Zion, *Eros and Transformation: An Eastern Orthodox Perspective* (New York: University Press of America, 1992).

[19]   Hays, "Homosexuality," p. 402.

[20]   For a reply to vocation arguments, see M. Basil Pennington, "Vocation Discernment and the Homosexual," in Robert Nugent, ed., *A Challenge to Love: Gay and Lesbian Catholics in the Church*, with an introduction by Bishop Walter F. Sullivan (New York: Crossroad, 1984), pp. 235-44.

> Theological arguments in favor of gay marriage . . . suggest that there is less theological consensus on this issue than [many conservatives are] willing to admit. Or that if there is a factual consensus – who can deny that for most of Church history gay marriages have not been condoned? – it is susceptible to rather stringent theological criticism. The fact of agreement here does not prove that good theological arguments sustain it, anymore than the condoning of slavery or the forbidding of women's ordination for most of the Church's history needs to.[21]

Fairly or unfairly, liberals type the conservative arguments in five ways: as narratives misread, literalism misplaced, natural law immune from natural science, vocation misapplied to groups, and tradition at odds with justice.

How Conservatives Hear Liberal Arguments

Conservatives find liberal arguments just as inadequate.

1   Liberals also have their narratives that conservatives do not buy. Conservatives are shocked to see David's lament over Jonathan taken as evidence of a homoerotic relationship: "I am distressed for you, my brother Jonathan; very pleasant have you been to me; your love to me was wonderful, passing the love of women."[22] One may see this argument as the flipside of the first on the other side. Conservatives hear their opponents as misreading stories, much as liberals do.

2   Conservatives charge that liberals, in their haste to contextualize or relativize passages they regard as taken too literally, are too quick to ignore or throw them out altogether. Conservatives then feel that the Bible is at stake. As members of a community formed by a text, liberals will have a hard time, so conservatives warn them, reducing difficult texts to silence. Conservatives admonish their rivals to prefer the hermeneutics of charity to the hermeneutics of suspicion – just as liberals do. Discarding rather than reclaiming Scripture is the flipside of the second argument of the first set: that was literalism about the text that forms the community; this is ignoring the text that forms the community.

---

[21]   Kathryn Tanner, "Response to Max Stackhouse and Eugene Rogers," in Saul M. Olyan and Martha C. Nussbaum, eds, *Sexual Orientation and Human Rights in American Religious Discourse* (New York: Oxford University Press, 1998), pp. 161–8; here, p. 166.
[22]   II Sam. 1:26. For a close reading of the entire story along these lines – persuasive if one is willing to accept the premise – see Thomas M. Horner, *Jonathan Loved David: Homosexuality in Biblical Times* (Philadelphia: Westminster, 1978), pp. 26–39.

3   Conservatives hear liberals as making arguments directly from natural science not assimilated into the community's language (theology) – arguments from undigested psychology or genetics. This can represent the flipside of the third argument of the first set. On the surface at least, "God made me this way" is as much a natural theology argument as the ones on the other side. Each side, that is, expects its own experience of a heterosexual or a homosexual orientation to carry the burden of naturalness or normality to the other side. But both sides reject that move quickly, even when reason-giving goes several stages deeper – whether the deeper stages owe their provenance to Aristotle's teleology or to modern DNA research. Even if they could agree on the facts, the two sides can still disagree about how to evaluate extratheological warrants.[23]

Alternatively, this third argument can also be read as the flipside of the first argument of the first set. That was reading alien cultural norms into stories (whether of Sodom and Gomorrah, Adam and Eve, or the curse of Ham) that do not support them, so that inhospitality becomes homosexuality. This is substituting cultural or political norms alien to the communal text or tradition (such as privacy rights) without norming them theologically first.

4   Conservatives find that liberals often vitiate their arguments by applying them in the same way across distinct moral species, making the same argument in favor of gay marriage and straight remarriage after divorce. (In the West – though not in the East – remarriage after divorce may involve promise-breaking;[24] same-sex first marriage does not.) As the fourth argument of the first set showed conservatives applying vocation without regard for cases, so liberals are capable of crying "love!" without regard for cases.

---

[23]   Something like this is true even if you are skeptical, as I am, about whether the fact-value distinction goes very far down. It has its uses.

[24]   But not in the East. "If marriage is essentially a contract undertaken by two parties, it cannot be dissolved except by the death of one of the two parties, provided that the right conditions for the contract were met at the beginning. . . . If, on the other hand, the sacrament of marriage offers a gift of grace to which human beings may respond inadequately, then the possibility exists that a marriage may fail," Catharine P. Roth, introduction to John Chrysostom, *On Marriage and Family Life*, trans. Catharine P. Roth and David Anderson (Crestwood, NY: St Vladimir's Seminary Press, 1997), p. 13. "No word that is merely human ever keeps its promises," but seeks a miracle, and "[l]ove, like martyrdom, cannot be imposed on someone"; the Eastern view is that the one flesh may die, and remarriage is allowed after death: Paul Evdokimov, *The Sacrament of Love: The Nuptial Mystery in the Light of the Orthodox Tradition*, trans. Anthony P. Gythiel and Victoria Steadman (Crestwood, NY: St Vladimir's Seminary Press, 1985), pp. 156, 188 (where quotations), and 184–90.

Conservatives may find such liberal arguments assimilable to traditional heresies, which traditional Christians would then be able to reject out of hand: the claim that the body doesn't matter but the soul does smacks of Gnosticism; the claim that rules feature in Judaism or the Old Testament, but not in the New, sounds like Marcionism. Such claims reverse the fourth argument of the first set: that was the false identification of body and soul; this is their complete separation.

5 Conservatives have their own complaints about liberal uses of tradition. Liberals can cite gay or lesbian saints or biblical figures as examples, as if the weight that they carry went all the way toward settling the issue. Recent arguments such as John Boswell's about same-sex unions in premodern Europe beg or finesse questions about how Christians should adjudicate a split tradition, especially one which appears to have high theology (like Aquinas) and some popular practices (the same-sex unions) at odds. Which trumps, theory or practice? Conservatives require additional argument about how practice and theory relate in case of conflict. Similarly and perhaps most commonly, liberals appeal not so much to the biographies or experience of saints or biblical figures as to their own.[25] Conservatives who come from traditions that suspect experience in principle, or who react against individualistic phrasing, can find this version of the move the most offensive of all, anecdotal at best, solipsistic at worst.

Fairly or unfairly, conservatives can type liberal arguments in five ways, too: as narratives misread, difficult passages ignored, natural science substituted for theology, heretical regard for souls over bodies, and experience substituted for tradition.

---

[25] This is especially the case among gay people in committed partnerships in the Protestant ministry, whose heterosexual colleagues are allowed to marry. See, for example, Chris Glaser, *Uncommon Calling: A Gay Man's Struggle to Serve the Church* (San Francisco: Harper & Row, 1988), of which the most ecclesiologically interesting reflection is the introduction by John Boswell, pp. xiii–xix; and Rose Mary Denman, *Let My People In: A Lesbian Minister Tells of Her Struggles to Live Openly and Maintain Her Ministry* (New York: William Morrow, 1990). The situation is different among Catholic secular priests and religious, whose straight counterparts also take vows of celibacy; openness about one's sexuality, however, may be a necessary component to integrating it into one's celibate vocation. See Rosemary Curb and Nancy Manahan, eds, *Breaking Silence: Lesbian Nuns on Convent Sexuality* (London: Columbus Books, 1985); and Elizabeth Stuart, ed., *Chosen: Gay Catholic Priests Tell Their Stories* (London: Geoffrey Chapman, 1993). The most theologically interesting of the lot may be the autobiographical account in Sullivan, "Alone Again, Naturally," pp. 47, 50; and Peter S. Hawkins, "Counter, Original, Spare, Strange," in Charles Hefling, ed., *Our Selves, Our Souls and Bodies: Sexuality and the Household of God* (Boston: Cowley Publications, 1996), pp. 76–88.

No one could succeed in being entirely evenhanded in such a list. Partisans may regard evenhandedness as itself suspect. Some of the arguments will turn out to be true, and many of the criticisms are sound. But I have not attempted primarily to evaluate them. I have attempted to show that the thrust and counterthrust is mostly a dreary business, often theologically sterile, often engaging in *ad hoc* arguments showing special ethics at its worst, bedeviled by impatience and charges of question-begging on both sides.

Perhaps each side is even beginning to notice. A liberal laments that "Protestant moral judgments often seem . . . to be at the mercy of the diverse perspectives of their audience."[26] A conservative exclaims about a controverted word, "Faced with yet another attempt to get at the meaning of *arsenokoites* by philology, I cry: Enough! You have satisfied the curiosity of a generation!"[27]

In any case we have seen the evidence for Rowan Williams's observation:

> Ours is a time in which it is depressingly easy to make this or that issue a test of Christian orthodoxy in such a way as to make wholly suspect the theology of anyone disagreeing on the issue in question; in other words, the possibility is neglected that Christians beginning from the same premises and convictions may yet come to different conclusions about particular matters without thereby completely voiding the commonness of their starting-point. It is really a matter of having a language *in which* to disagree rather than speaking two incompatible or mutually exclusive tongues. Of late, attitudes to sexuality have come to be seen as a clear marker of orthodoxy or unorthodoxy in many circles . . . .[28]

Williams's description also explains why I find it useful to vary terms like "conservative" and "liberal," or "traditional" and "revisionist" with little distinction or, I hope, rhetorical color. Although I find cogent Andrew Sullivan's attempt throughout *Virtually Normal* to divide two camps into four, I stick to the bare two to reflect the way in which the debate divides Christians not in four but in two. The simpler dichotomy better captures a significant fact about the debate so far, which I hope nevertheless somewhat to lessen: that it is polarizing.

---

[26] Tanner, "Response," pp. 163–4.
[27] Oliver O'Donovan, "Homosexuality in the Church: Can There Be a Fruitful Theological Debate?" in Timothy Bradshaw, ed., *The Way Forward? Christian Voices on Homosexuality and the Church* (London: Hodder & Stoughton, 1997), pp. 20–36; here, p. 28.
[28] Rowan D. Williams, "Knowing Myself in Christ," in Bradshaw, ed., *The Way Forward?* pp. 12–19; here, pp. 12–13.

Along the wide spectrum of views about marriage for gay and lesbian couples, the extremes sometimes meet in claiming that gay and lesbian marriages are irredeemable, on the far right because they are gay, on the far left because they are marriages. I claim the opposite: that they can be means of redemption. More: they can be means of anticipating God's catching human beings up into that wedding feast that God celebrates in the life of the Trinity, an elevation that the tradition has had the wisdom to call consummation. The question to the right is, given that gay and lesbian people are not going to go away, what should the Church *do* with them? The question to left is, given that gay and lesbian people are part of the Church, how much should it allow their bodies to *mean*? In the context of baptism, eucharist, and (yes) monastic vows, the Spirit is now moving Christian communities to see marriage as the central symbol by which to test and renegotiate the fit of gay and lesbian bodies into the body of Christ.

In another statement to which we shall often recur, Rowan Williams puts it this way:

> The whole story of creation, incarnation, and our incorporation into the fellowship of Christ's body tells us that God desires us, *as if we were God*, as if we were that unconditional response to God's giving that God's self makes in the life of the Trinity. . . . The life of the Christian community has as its rationale – if not invariably its practical reality – the task of teaching us to so order our relations that human beings may see themselves as desired, as the occasion of joy.[29]

The question for both sides is then this: by what sort of sacramental practices can the Church best teach gay and lesbian Christians to see themselves as occasions of joy, that God desires them as if they were God?

Marriage is peculiarly suited to teaching God's desire for human beings, because it mirrors God's choosing of human beings for God's own. Karl Barth, as we have seen, has compressed it as tightly as possible: "In that the election of God is real, there is such a thing as love and marriage."[30] God's election of Israel, like marriage, involves a discipline of faithfulness in which God permits human beings to become what God sees. God's election of the mostly Gentile Church, like marriage for gay and lesbian couples, is (in Paul's metaphor) God's overturning of nature to graft wild olives onto a domestic tree, to include them, that is, in a structure (the law of the Spirit) that allows their

---

[29] Williams, "The Body's Grace," p. 59.
[30] Barth, *Church Dogmatics*, III/1, 318.

selves, their souls and bodies, to mean much more than they would by nature – to be caught up into the very life and love by which God loves God.

Secular Politics and Christian Politics: Toward an Ethics of Controversy

Reading such wearying, uncharitable stuff as the typology of arguments I presented above, one might suppose that on the issues of homosexuality, liberals and conservatives speak incommensurable discourses, or wave unintegrable fragments. One might suppose that dispute goes all the way down, that the present state of Christian argument leads from discouragement to despair.

But Christianity maintains its own, native account of argument and integration. It takes for granted that words do not carry the day, that arguers – even God's arguers, prophets especially – get rejected and killed, until God's own argument comes embodied, the Logos incarnate, and turns death to redemption. Only in Christ, so the doctrine of enhypostasis goes, does human argument make sense. The human being and thus human argument, that is, remain a collection of fragments until reintegrated in the person of God's argument.

It should therefore come to Christians as no surprise if the current debate about Christian bodies also suffers greatly from fragmentation and rejection of prophets, the arguments that they offer and enact. In the terms of a christological theory of argument, however, that is no cause for despair. Although this side of heaven Christians believe the redemption of their bodies will be incomplete, nevertheless they also believe that God's argument with the human being continues and retains its reintegrating, enhypostatic power, in the body of the Logos that is the Church.

That is where Christian arguments get settled or continue for the long term, not with words on paper, but with words embodied in the lives and witness of the faithful. Thus celibacy proved itself – and according to many Protestants is still having to prove itself – in the embodied logoi of the Syrian monks. The all-male priesthood, and the ordination of women, are fighting it out in the embodied logoi of faithful men and women priests. For the present argument to be won, for the Logos to be achieved, for the Spirit to work it out in the community – will take time, as partners give a marriage time, celibates confirm their calling over time, and God grants time to the Church. Oliver O'Donovan advises "one word of caution for those who speak and those who listen when God's word is abroad. The first, and surely the hardest demand that it makes on them is: patience."[31] The achievement of God's argument will require not only patience, the waiting for peace and justice to take their true shape in God's time, in the time God grants the Church, but also charity – space for the compassionate completing of arguments left incomplete by ignorance and suspicion. "[G]iven the persistence of the sin of others . . . as well as our own . . . there is only one way to respond to them which would not itself be sinful and domineering, and that is to anticipate heaven, and act as if their sin was not there, by offering reconciliation. [For] virtue cannot properly operate except when collectively possessed . . . ."[32]

Peace and justice of the Christian sort need not only time but also a place, that is, a community in which to be practiced. They need a polity. The question of Christian marriage for lesbian and gay couples is political primarily in the sense that all theology is political: theology is always concerned with the question of life with God; life with God is a life in community, both with God and with other human beings; and politics is at best a reflection on what life in community ought to be. Talk of God's people, of God's kingdom or house, of a heavenly city, or a new Jerusalem is all talk of an ideal polity. So Thomas Aquinas characterizes life with God not only as "friendship," "homeland," and "community," but also as "*res publica,*" a commonwealth or republic, or, more literally, a political matter.[33] In saying that life with God is a political matter, I am not commending theocracy, but observing that Christian traditions describe the beginnings and consummation of human participation in the divine life (II Peter 1:4) in political terms.

Christian marriage for lesbian and gay couples is political secondarily in that marriage, too, is a community, a little polity, a *micrabasileia,* a domestic church, a way of life under God, one of the purposes of which is to build up that larger polity under God, the community of the faithful.[34] So Bible and tradition describe God's choosing life with the community of Israel not only in terms of polity but in terms of (sometimes adulterous) marriage, as they describe also the relationship of Christ and the Church.

That is all miles away from the marriage politics that goes on when legislators debate "defense of marriage" acts – miles away in more ways than

---

[31] O'Donovan, "Homosexuality in the Church," p. 36.
[32] John Milbank, *Theology and Social Theory: Beyond Secular Reason* (Oxford: Blackwell, 1990), p. 411.
[33] *Summa Theologiae,* 1st part of the 2nd part, question 99, article 2 and question 100, articles 2 and 5 [hereafter *ST* I–II.99.2 and 100.2, 5].
[34] For discussion of and sources for this ancient Christian idea, see Evdokimov, *The Sacrament of Love,* pp. 118, 121–3.

one, and by design. Yet a theological argument that churches should recognize gay and lesbian marriages now has political consequences of the ordinary sort in election campaigns, in legislative debates, and before the courts, because religious citizens articulate positions controversial not only outside but also within their traditions.[35]

The controversies within and between the traditions have been acrimonious and deep, threatening to introduce new divisions among earthly Church polities. Only a few theologians have risen above the disputes to begin talking about how Christians should conduct themselves toward each other under circumstances of serious disagreement on moral matters.

The reinforcement of old disputes that divide churches should worry Christians even more. Ecumenical dialogues have addressed all of the theological disputes that existed at the time of the Reformation. The dialogues have typically found the Reformation disputes, if not settled, to be sort of differences that exist within one church, rather than the sort that ought to divide one church from another. Thus it is especially dispiriting to see divisions continue not just because of differences that arose after the separation (such as papal infallibility) but because of differences that are arising today (say on ordination of women or attitudes toward homosexuality), especially when they can become doctrinal matters only by reading moral matters in the most pernicious light. That is, it is not obvious that the ordination of women or of practicing homosexuals constitutes a rejection of the grace of Christ, even if it is an error, although arguments to that effect may appear in the service of division. It begins to look as if a will for separation has taken on a life of its own, and as if no amount of dialogue will help, as if new disputes always replace old.[36]

Recent disputes within the Church of England or the Evangelical Lutheran Church in America (ELCA), for example, have sometimes approached the schismatic. Similarly, some in the ELCA have recently used the attitudes toward homosexuality of certain bishops in the Protestant Episcopal Church in the United States of America as a reason for refusing a concordat that would have allowed intercommunion between the two churches. In the following

---

[35] I owe this way of putting the matter to an application to the Rhode Island Endowment for the Humanities by Saul Olyan and Martha Nussbaum.

[36] See, for example, Karl Rahner, "Pseudo-Problems in Ecumenical Discussion," in his *Theological Investigations*, vol. 18, trans. Edward Quinn (New York: Crossroad, 1983), pp. 35–53; Karl Rahner and Heinrich Fries, *Unity of the Churches: An Actual Possibility* (New York: Paulist Press and Philadelphia: Fortress, 1985); Robert W. Jenson, *Unbaptized God: The Basic Flaw in Ecumenical Theology* (Minneapolis, MN: Augsburg Fortress, 1992).

analysis, Bruce Marshall adverts to Luther's exegesis of the commandment against bearing false witness as requiring that one put the best possible construction on one's neighbor's deeds and views:

> Take, for example, the views of our neighbors, whether Episcopal or Lutheran, on homosexuality. An Episcopal Church court refused to find Bishop Righter guilty of heresy for ordaining an openly homosexual person. Is the best possible construction we [Lutherans] can put on this decision that the Episcopal Church now regards morals as completely divorced from, and irrelevant to, the apostolic faith? Or would a better construction (and therefore, if Luther reads the commandment rightly, one closer to the truth) be that the court regarded the charge as unsuited to the case, not because faith has nothing to do with morals, but because not every disciplinary matter in the Church can be settled by appeal to the central doctrines of the faith, as would be required for a charge of heresy to stick? From which sentence of the Nicene Creed, for example, can it be inferred that open homosexuals are not to be ordained?[37]

David Yeago puts the ecumenical dispute in starker terms. Certain parties within the Lutheran Church (ELCA), he claims, have been playing culture wars with matters of intercommunion, to the detriment of careful theological thinking. To those Lutherans,

> the Episcopal Church has figured essentially as an ideological enemy, corporately "soft" on homosexuality, a crucial test issue. . . . The problem with the culture-war hermeneutic, it seems to me, is that it is divisive in the wrong way, that it conforms the life of the Church to the wrong struggle. Those who follow this analysis are, I fear, in danger of doing from the right just what they accuse the revisionists of doing from the left: subordinating the Church's life to the life of the civil community, reducing the struggle for faithfulness in the Church to an extension of the cultural struggles of the nations. The terms of the culture-war analysis are not, after all, especially theological; they are borrowed from secular neo-conservatism. The friend–foe polarization and the idea of protracted conflict which are so crucial to that perspective derive from the Marxist intellectual origins of so many of the founding fathers and mothers of neo-conservatism. Shouldn't Christian theologians and pastors be a little suspicious of all this?[38]

---

[37] Bruce D. Marshall, "Can Lutherans Have Episcopal Bishops? Reflections on a Refusal of Communion," *The Lutheran Forum* 32, 1 (1998): 36–41; here, p. 40.

[38] David S. Yeago, "The *Concordat*, Ecumenism, and Evangelical–Catholic Politics," *The Lutheran Forum* 32, 1 (1998): 42–6; here, pp. 42–3.

Thus there is politics and politics. One concerns the civil polity of the United States, England, or Germany, using the languages of civil rights, religious freedom, and so on. Another polity concerns the kingdom of God, life together with God, the heavenly Jerusalem, the Church militant and triumphant. In Augustinian terms, one is the earthly city, the other the city of God. The two are not opposed, unless we adopt a Lutheran two-kingdoms doctrine of the crudest sort. Rather theologians must consider the politics of a community of which God is a member. That polity is defined in terms of its end – its beginning and its eschaton, creation and consummation.

Yeago suggests that that community is empirically identifiable through baptism:

> Ecumenism is essentially a recovery of the political significance of Baptism in the life of the Churches, a rediscovery of Baptism as the foundational, authoritative act of God by which all the baptized are irrevocably assigned and committed to one another in the same act by which they are savingly joined to Jesus Christ (cf. Gal. 3:26-28). These two dimensions of God's baptismal action cannot be neatly separated. The baptized can therefore repudiate their bonds with one another only at the gravest risk to their bond with Christ. This does not mean that conflict and division are always wrong. . . . [But o]ne thing this surely means is that analytic strategies that divide the Church into sharply opposed groups of friends and foes are ruled out from the start. Indeed, traditional Christian exegesis took Ephesians 6:12 to mean that the Church has no human foes in any ultimately serious sense.[39]

Ephesians 6:12 begins, "For we are not contending against flesh and blood." In Thomas Aquinas, the admonition tells against taking too seriously the *vices* of mere flesh and blood.[40] In the current debate, one frequently hears of opponents' vices; they are promiscuous, they are homophobic; they are self-seeking, they are ignorant, and so on. The right way to understand the

---

[39]   Yeago, "The *Concordat*, Ecumenism, and Evangelical–Catholic Politics," p. 43. See the whole section, "Baptism's Political Significance," pp. 43–4.

[40]   Thomas Aquinas, *Super epistolam ad Ephesios lectura*, ed. Raphael Cai, in *S. Thomae Aquinatis doctoris angelici Super epistolas S. Pauli lectura*, 8th rev. ed, 2 vols (Turin and Rome: Marietti, 1953). Traditionally one cites the biblical book with the Latin word *In* and the book's abbreviation: thus *In Eph.* means a commentary on Ephesians. Then come the biblical chapter and the lecture number, or the *lectio*, which does not tell the non-Thomist where Thomas is in the chapter. I cite according to the chapter on which Thomas is commenting and, for the non-specialist, verse (which Thomas did not have), followed by the Marietti paragraph number, which is more exact for the specialist, like this: *In Eph.* 6:12, ##354–5. Similarly, the Romans commentary: *In Rom.* 1:17, #95, and so on.

admonition requires reliance on the power of God to overcome human evils and disputes: "It depends not on human will or exertion, but upon God's mercy."[41] If the flesh is weak, it is also a feeble enemy.[42] The real enemies are one's *own* sins, here ascribed to demons in order that Christians not identify evil with their neighbors.[43] Nor are the demons cultural in a sense that would render the culture or our neighbor the Enemy. Responsibility for human sin remains in the will, not the demons.[44] Demons work interiorly, not exteriorly.[45] They can only cooperate with the passions, and they do so by obscuring the truth into falsehood.[46]

That returns us to Marshall's analysis, in which the falsehood that Christians have most to look out for in controversy is their own, interior tendency to ascribe evil motives to their neighbors, for that is the essence of bearing false witness against them and contravenes the eighth commandment:

> If Luther's interpretation is correct, the eighth commandment is an epistemic principle: it has to do with figuring out when we have found the truth about our neighbor. When it comes to the assessment of our neighbor's words and deeds, we should "find ways of excusing him, speak well of him, and make the best of everything" – or as it is often rendered, "put the best construction on everything" (Small Catechism I.16). This is not just a rule of etiquette. *We cannot keep this commandment by first discovering what we suppose to be the hard truth about another's words and deeds*, and then politely keeping quiet about it, or softening up the rough edges. The commandment not to bear false witness surely cannot be an injunction to dissemble. Rather, obedience to this commandment has to enter into our very effort to discern the truth about our neighbor in the first place; *we cannot suppose that we have got the truth about our neighbor's words and deeds until we are sure that we have put the best possible construction on them*. In just this sense, presumably, the apostle Paul enjoins us to speak the truth in love, and warns against "evil talk," namely that which fails to build up and give grace to those who hear (Eph. 4:15, 29). If we sense a conflict between what we want to say about our neighbor and that kindness and tenderness of heart without which we grieve the Holy Spirit (Eph. 4:30, 32), we have a sure sign that we have so far failed to find the truth, and have instead fastened onto falsehoods of our own invention.[47]

---

[41]   *In Eph.* 6:12, ##354–5, quoting Rom. 9:16.
[42]   *In Eph.* 6:12, #355.
[43]   *In Eph.* 6:12, #357.
[44]   Thomas Aquinas, *ST* I–II.80.1.
[45]   *ST* I–II.80.2.
[46]   *ST* I–II.80.2.
[47]   Marshall, "Refusal of Communion," pp. 39-40, my emphasis.

Yeago and Marshall oppose the politics of culture wars to the politics of baptism. This is surely the theologically correct move. It allows ecclesially constructed identity to control the identity that both many gay activists and many of their opponents allow modern notions of sexuality to construct for them, as opposite ends of the spectrum meet.

In particular, Christians believe that God has bound them especially together, so that, as we saw above, their "only road to integrity passes through the narrow gate of unity in obedience to Christ," whom Christians should think of in this context under the title of "The True Witness."[48] It is Christ who both binds Christians together, and tells them the truth about themselves. That truth-telling and binding together occur in the sacraments. Marriage is a sacrament of binding together that proclaims and begins to bring about the truth that a couple belongs primarily to God and the community rather than to themselves alone. The eucharist is a sacrament of binding together that tells and begins to bring about the truth that the community's enmity is overcome in feasting. What kind of binding and truth-telling does the community receive through Christ in baptism? Yeago refers us to Galatians 3:26–8:

> For in Christ Jesus you are all children of God, through faith. For as many of you as were baptized into Christ have put on Christ. There is neither Jew nor Greek, there is neither slave nor free, there is no "male and female"; for you are all one in Christ Jesus.

What does Yeago mean by quoting this passage, which has become "the *locus classicus* of the debate about gender equality"?[49] Yeago notes in passing that he tends to side with traditionalists on questions of homosexuality. To imply that baptism has anything to do with "no longer gay or straight" would sound like taking the side he opposes, a surprising move even in someone who is trying to rise above the debate.

From late antiquity until the 1970s the verse was used to mean that slaves

---

[48]   The title of a chapter in Karl Barth's *Church Dogmatics*.

[49]   Dale B. Martin, "The Life and Times of Galatians 3:28: 'No Male and Female,' " paper delivered at the University of Oslo, September 1998, p. 2 of typescript. Cf. Krister Stendahl, *The Bible and the Role of Women: A Case Study in Hermeneutics* (Philadelphia: Fortress, 1966), p. 33; Mary Hayter, *The New Eve in Christ: The Use and Abuse of the Bible in the Debate about Women in the Church* (London: SPCK, 1987), p. 134; Robin Scroggs, "Paul and the Eshatalogical Woman," *Journal of the American Academy of Religion* 40 (1972): 283–303; Elisabeth Schüssler Fiorenza, *In Memory of Her: A Feminist Theological Reconstruction of Christian Origins* (New York: Crossroad, 1983), pp. 205, 210, 213, 218, 235; and countless others.

could be baptized Christian and still remain slaves, women could be baptized
Christian and still remain subordinate; but those differences should not
divorce Christians from one another and exclude Jews, slaves, or women from
the privilege of baptism and inclusion in the community of faith with salvation
in Christ.[50] Neither traditionalists nor revisionists may read their fellow
Christians out of the community of baptism.

> [I]n this perspective, when we see that other Christians . . . are in danger of going
> wrong in some important way, that is by no means a motive to draw back lest
> they defile us, but rather a motive to seek fellowship with them all the more
> intently. . . . The false steps of others are thus to be taken as occasion for the
> communion of involvement, not grounds for terminating communion; thus we
> fulfill the law of Christ, who took the collective "false step" of the whole human
> race as the occasion to cause grace and the spirit (or maybe the Spirit) of
> gentleness to overflow and abound for all (cf. Rom. 5:12-21).[51]

Yeago's "all" includes traditionalists and revisionists alike. It is a purpose of this
book to be an occasion for the grace and Spirit of marriage to overflow and
abound for all – opposite-sex couples, same-sex couples, and single members
of the community. The traditionalists are perhaps right in this: that it is
opposite-sex couples who have perhaps above all lost sight of what marriage
might be for. My undergraduates are bemused and speechless when I ask the
question, what is marriage for? Can people have sex without marriage? Oh,
yes, they answer. Can people raise children without marriage? That, too, they
say. Then what is marriage for? They don't have any good answer. Self-
consciously gay and lesbian people have much more passionate opinions and
debates about what marriage can be for, whether they think it is for patriarchal
oppression or personal commitment. So this book hopes to be for all a
reflection on what it means for human beings of various views and sexualities
and situations that God is espoused to Israel.

The theologically correct orientation for Christians in these debates is not
gay or straight, conservative or liberal. The theologically correct orientation
in these debates is ecclesial, an orientation for the Church.

An orientation for the Church helps set an agenda for the next two chapters
in that it helps Christians to put the best possible interpretation upon the

---

[50]   For a short history of the interpretation of Gal. 3:28, see Martin, "The Life and Times
of Galatians 3:28," including egalitarian, androgynous, traditional, and ancient readings,
and including an extensive bibliography.
[51]   Yeago, "The *Concordat*, Ecumenism, and Evangelical–Catholic Politics," p. 44.

arguments of Christians holding opposed positions – helps them to avoid bearing inadvertent false witness against their neighbor. In what follows I reduce the myriad arguments to two, both based on the shape of the community. The liberal argument is that in Christ there is no gay and straight. The conservative one is that in Christ there is holiness of life. *The best construction for conservatives to put upon the liberal analogy of gender, race, and sexual identity is not that it is a civil rights argument, but that it is a baptismal argument* (chapter 2). *Similarly, the best construction for liberals to put on the conservatives' rejection of the analogy is not that it is primarily a rejection of civil rights, but that it shows primarily a desire for visible holiness* (chapter 3).

Chapter 2

THE IDENTITY OF THE PEOPLE OF GOD: CONTRARY TO NATURE

The passage from Galatians which we considered in the last chapter joins Christians both to Jesus and to each other. It deeply intertwines therefore identity and community, salvation and holiness, things that ought only to be distinguished for the purpose of binding them more tightly together. It owes nothing to modern individualism.[1] Yet typical arguments of revisionists and traditionalists tend – despite their best intentions – to stress one at the other's expense, separating gay and lesbian Christians' identity as children of God from their holiness enacted toward each other. Revisionists tend to use the baptismal trope to stress Christians' joining to Christ,[2] while traditionalists tend to use it to call for visible holiness.[3] (The idea that Galatians 3:28 recalls an original androgyny, although popular among some New Testament scholars, has the disadvantage of being difficult to render parallel with the

---

[1] For extensive argument about how Paul is concerned with the groups Jew/Gentile and not the modern dichotomy of individual human being/universal humankind, see most recently Stanley K. Stowers, *A Rereading of Romans* (New Haven: Yale University Press, 1995), pp. 2, 6, 256, 269, 306, and esp. pp. 108–9 and 284.

[2] See Marilyn Bennet Alexander and James Preston, *We Were Baptized Too: Claiming God's Grace for Lesbians and Gays*, with an introduction by Archbishop Desmond Tutu (Louisville, KY: Westminster/John Knox, 1996); and in a very sophisticated way, L. William Countryman, *Dirt, Greed, and Sex: Sexual Ethics in the New Testament and Their Implications for Today* (Philadelphia: Fortress, 1988), esp. pp. 257–8.

[3] E.g., Thomas E. Schmidt, *Straight and Narrow? Compassion and Clarity in the Homosexuality Debate* (Downer's Grove, IL: InterVarsity Press, 1995), pp. 57–9.

other members of the series and has had in any case little effect on churchly use of the passage.)[4] While both emphases yield good exegesis, each side would also improve – and be happy to improve – by uniting them.

Consider two arguments in a nutshell, which take Galatians 3:28 in opposing ways.

1   A liberal argument. In Galatians 3:28 Paul writes, "There is no longer Jew or Greek, there is no longer slave or free, there is no longer male and female; for all of you are one in Christ Jesus." In this prophetic passage, liberals see foreshadowed in religious language the great civil rights victories of the 19th and 20th centuries: against anti-Semitism, against slavery and racism, and against sexism. In perhaps the most quoted verse in the 20th-century, English-speaking world,[5] all of the other biblical passages supporting the status quo about Jews or slaves or race or gender have been overcome. And it is a corollary of the "no longer male and female" that if Paul were writing today, he would end as many inclusive liturgies in liberal churches end: "there is no longer straight and gay." As Peter Gomes, minister in the Memorial Church at Harvard University, sums it up in a chapter title, the bias against gay and lesbian people is "The Last Prejudice."[6]

2   A conservative reply. Interpretation of Paul and arguing for rights are different matters, one religious and one political. Yet argument (1) has the distinction of conflating two analogies that are both wrong. First of all, "male and female" is overcome for Paul only in a way that accords with nature. Furthermore, while civil rights are due to groups whose distinctions are natural (such as blacks and women), similar, "special" rights are not due to those whose distinctions from the majority are moral (such as thieves and homosexuals):

> Gay and lesbian advocates sometimes claim that they are asking for no more than an end to discrimination, drawing an analogy with the earlier civil rights

---

[4]   Wayne A. Meeks, "The Image of the Androgyne: Some Uses of a Symbol in Earliest Christianity," *History of Religion* 13 (1974): 165–208. Martin, "Life and Times of Galatians 3:28" surveys interpretations that cast the androgyne not as bisexual but as subsuming the female in the male. These readings have the disadvantage of allowing materials from ancient medicine to overshadow Paul's predominating concern with the first member of the series, Jew and Greek. I do not see how the androgyny thesis squares with the parallelism of the formula.

[5]   I owe this characterization to a conversation with Louis Martyn.

[6]   Peter J. Gomes, "The Bible and Homosexuality: The Last Prejudice," in his *The Good Book: Reading the Bible with Mind and Heart* (New York: Avon, 1996), p. 144.

movement that sought justice for black Americans. The analogy is unconvincing and misleading. Differences of race are in accord with – not contrary to – our nature, and such differences do not provide justification for behavior otherwise unacceptable. . . . Certain discriminations are necessary within society; it is not too much to say that civilization itself depends on the making of such distinctions (between, finally, right and wrong).[7]

Like conservatives, black people even of liberal politics often bridle at comparisons between their struggles for civil and ecclesial standing, and those of gay and lesbian Christians. So Alveda King, niece of Martin Luther King, Jr, says, "don't expect us and our children to approve of, promote or elevate sexual preference to civil rights status. What's next, civil rights status on the basis of prostitution and pedophilia?"[8] A more nuanced example appears in a popular novel. Mitchell, African-American and gay, is talking to Philip, African-American and straight. Philip says, "if you start talking about [analogies between gay and black] civil rights, you're going to have a whole lot of Black people angry." Mitchell reflects, "I did understand his concern about the civil rights tag. Even I didn't appreciate the way white homosexuals try to link the struggle African people faced in getting the rights they should've had from jump street with that of lesbians and gays (like *they* know)."[9] Blackness tends to be more or less visible and to run in families, whereas homosexuality can be more easily hidden and occurs in the context of heterosexual parents, siblings, and children. More important, homosexuals were not deported from their homeland with an astounding deathrate and enslaved, while gay men have always had the vote and economic power.

Be the dissimilarities among the two groups ever so great, the arguments used *against* blacks and gays are all too similar. One similarity in the argument against the two groups helps to explain why blacks are today, rightly or wrongly, afraid to make common cause with gay and lesbian people. The parallel in the argument against them is this: blacks were thought of by many whites as more sexually promiscuous, much as gay men are now thought of by some straight people. If one has fought the stereotype that "the African's

---

7   "The Homosexual Movement: A Response by the Ramsey Colloquium," *First Things* 41 (March 1994): 15–20; here, p. 19.
8   See Rhonda Smith, "Civil Rights Leaders Swiftly Condemn Anti-Gay Remarks," *The Washington Blade* (Aug. 29, 1997), p. 20, col. 1. I owe the citation to Ladelle McWhorter, "The Queer Concept of Minority: Homosexual Citizens in American Public Discourse," unpublished ms., p. 3, n. 5.
9   James Earl Hardy, *B-Boy Blues* (Boston: Alyson Publications, 1994), p. 114, quoted in McWhorter, "Queer Concept of Minority," pp. 4–5, n. 6.

birthright [is] sexual madness and excess," expressed in this opinion from a respected medical journal in 1903,[10] then one will naturally think twice about solidarity with people still stereotyped like this: "Promiscuity among homosexual men is not a mere stereotype, and it is not merely the majority experience – it is virtually the *only* experience."[11] Indeed, earlier medicine could be co-opted into finding black sexuality and same-sex sexuality not only parallel but intertwined. Early sexologist Edward Stevenson wrote that the male "American negro has ever been similisexual,"[12] while Dr James G. Kiernan wrote in a survey of sexology of "negro perverts who solicit men in certain Chicago cafés,"[13] and Dr F. E. Daniel, writing in the *Medico-Legal*

[10] William Lee Howard, "The Negro as a Distinct Ethnic Factor," in *Medicine* (1903), pp. 108–9, quoted in George M. Frederickson, *The Black Image in the White Mind: The Debate on Afro-American Character and Destiny 1817–1914* (New York: Harper & Row, 1971), p. 279.

[11] Schmidt, *Straight and Narrow?* p. 108. This is a book bearing positive blurbs from such respected scholars as David F. Wright and Gilbert Meilaender. If true, the tragedy Schmidt describes would seem to cry out for the social support of gay and lesbian marriage, especially since, as Paul says, "it is better to marry than to burn" – but it does not. And the corresponding reputation of lesbians for fidelity goes unmentioned. It is to be said in Schmidt's favor, however, that he accepts the burden of proof for such claims, supporting them with three pages of statistics, pp. 105–8. Schmidt does not consider the potential for tremendous bias in the fact that most statistics of the sort he cites are collected among people who frequent gay bars or read gay pornography; what statistics would one find among heterosexual readers of *Penthouse*? I suspect the war of the statistics has just begun. One must consider such evidence in light of universally acknowledged misuses of science that may look similar, and of which I give examples below. For a similar marshaling of statistics in support of the alleged promiscuity and general lawlessness of blacks, see David Christy, "Cotton Is King: Slavery in the Light of Political Economy," the title essay in E. N. Elliott, ed., *Cotton Is King and Pro-Slavery Arguments, Comprising the Writings of Hammond, Harper, Christy, Stringfellow, Hodge, Bledsoe, and Cartwright, on this Important Subject* (Augusta, GA: Pritchard, Abbott & Loomis, 1860), pp. 177–94, a report of the effect of the immigration of a "colored" population to parts of Canada. For an insufficiently critical or historically aware, but still useful study, see Simon LeVay, *Queer Science: The Use and Abuse of Research into Homosexuality* (Cambridge, MA: MIT Press, 1996). For the use of statistics against Jews, see Sander Gilman, "The Jewish Body: A Foot-Note," in Howard Eilberg-Schwartz, ed., *People of the Body: Jews and Judaism from an Embodied Perspective* (Albany, NY: State University of New York Press, 1992), pp. 223–41; here, p. 227.

[12] Edward Stevenson [Xavier Mayne], *The Intersexes: A History of Similisexualism as a Problem in Social Life* (Rome: privately printed, 1908 or 1909; reprint New York: Arno Press, 1975), pp. 638–9; see excerpts in Jonathan Ned Katz, *Gay/Lesbian Almanac: A New Documentary* (New York: Harper & Row, 1983), pp. 326–32 and 699, n. 17; here, p. 328.

[13] James G. Kiernan, "Sexology: . . . Theory of Inversion . . . Classification of

continued on next page

Journal and the *Texas Medical Journal*, advocated the castration both for those committing "sodomy . . . and habitual masturbation" and for those "of the lower classes, particularly negroes," known for "extremely common" illicit intercourse.[14] Having had to fight assumptions such as those might well render black people reluctant to make common cause with lesbian and gay people, about whom similar assumptions have prevailed, even as similarity of argument aligns the stereotypes against them. African-Americans have largely replaced a false stereotype of animal sexuality with a reputation for the greatest visible Christian holiness of any American group, a holiness that evangelical gay and lesbian Christians in the Metropolitan Community Church are trying to emulate.

Those arguments signal that the debate is now about identity – about how homosexuality is like and unlike race, gender, or class. Liberals tend to hold that the analogy is quite close; whether constructed or essential, sexual orientation is quite like race, gender, or class. Conservatives also suppose that the debate is about identity – the identity of a community conformed in holiness to the image of Christ. This focus of the debate may, indeed, represent a second wave, distinct from, if still overlapping with the arguments described in chapter 1. But it can be a more promising focus, if the baptismal identity described by Marshall and Yeago gives Christians the polity and patience to disagree.

Is it true that baptismal identity gives a more promising focus? Identity talk can be very divisive. And a great deal seems, at least, to depend upon exactly which analogy for sexual orientation holds sway. Sound-bite strategists make much of the racial analogy because genetics seems to settle the issue for many – although rarely for blacks. Furthermore, much about such political strategies is governed by fears. If queer people admit that some among them – particularly women – experience more flexible sexual affections, they fear that conservatives will say, "If it's a choice, then choose to go straight." And they also fear that if they lean on genetics as a defense against choice, conservatives will say, "If it's genetic, then it's like alcoholism, and we should fix it if we can." It sounds as if the identity debate may become more recalcitrant than

Homosexuality," *Urologic and Cutaneous Review* 20 (1916): 345–6, 348–50; in Katz, *Gay/Lesbian Almanac*, pp. 367 and 701, n. 24.

[14] Dr F. E. Daniel, "Should Insane Criminals or Sexual Perverts be Permitted to Procreate," *Texas Medical Journal* (August 1893), *Medico-Legal Journal* (December 1893), and again in *Texas Medical Journal* 27, 10 (April 1912): 369–85, as well as other places; cited from Katz, *Gay/Lesbian Almanac*, pp. 241–3. For further bibliographic details, see Katz, *Gay/Lesbian Almanac*, p. 693, n. 15.

the earlier, scattershot debates chronicled in chapter 1. But so much may not depend on getting sexual identity correctly described, after all, if the disputants agree that some other identity is primary.

Both those who argue on civil rights grounds, and those who argue on theological grounds, disagree about whether homosexual identity is more like race or more like nationality. But their disagreements work out somewhat differently. Rowan Williams and Oliver O'Donovan disagree about homosexual identity within a common community. Rowan Williams offers an ecclesially disciplined argument that sexuality might be more like race than class, or at least more like either than nationality. Williams is commenting on a line, with which he opens, from "The Saint Andrews Day Statement," a moderately conservative and theologically careful document circulating in the Church of England. The commentary is worth quoting at some length:

> "Our sexual affections can no more define who we are than can our class, race, or nationality." No more, but perhaps also no less: to acknowledge a human identity centred in, determined by Christ is not the same as saying that such an identity is, apart from Christ, abstract and unhistorical, shaped only by maleness and femaleness "called to redeemed humanity in Christ." This . . . section of the [Saint Andrew's Day Statement] raises two questions in my mind. Does it presuppose that "sexual affections" . . . are a datum of historical humanity on much the same level as race and class? If so, the analogies would be interesting to pursue – and quite complex in character. "Race" is a non-negotiable aspect of where I stand as a historical human subject; in some environments, it forecloses certain options for me (because of the way my society as a whole organises itself), and in any case it will always as a matter of bare fact be something true of me. Christians generally and black Christians in this century particularly have wanted to add that racial identity can be touched and redeemed by Christ in the sense that the particular ways of living associated with this racial and cultural history may by the grace of Christ be shown as transparent to Christ, ways of expressing and witnessing to the richness that is in him. And at the same time, there may be aspects of that culture opaque to Christ – a history of idolatry, aggression, servility, internalised assumptions of inferiority and so on, depending on whether the cultural history is or is not one of triumphant negotiation or domination of others. There is a long job of cultural discernment ahead; but we can at least say that it won't do either to say that a particular racial identity is incapable of carrying the meanings of Christ or that such an identity is epiphenomenal, a matter pretty well irrelevant to the concrete working out of what it is to be alive in Christ. Class, on the other hand, is not so straightforward. My class origins are, like my racial identity, simply a matter of bare fact. But, unlike my racial identity, my actual class position may change. . . . We couldn't say quite so easily that any class identity was in a merely static

way capable of being transparent to Christ; what is significant here is how I come to terms with the power I have, with the limits of my possibilities, with the morality of effecting change for myself or others. I suspect that one of the areas of disagreement between those who do and those who don't wish to reaffirm the Church's historical position on homosexuality could be characterised according to whether sexual orientation was seen as more like race than class or vice versa.[15]

Oliver O'Donovan, Regius Professor of Moral and Pastoral Theology, a traditionalist on sexuality, and a theologian whose loyalty, like that of his former colleague, now Bishop Williams, is primarily to the unity of the Church, describes an argument that sexual orientation is like nationality, but, again, ecclesially disciplined. According to O'Donovan, the Church consists of many communities that do not necessarily resist the grace of Christ or compromise the fundamental unity of the faithful. Small linguistic communities provide an uncontroversial example: "At Pentecost all heard the Gospel in their own language; none had to abandon their linguistic identity to hear it." It could even be a service to God to shelter such a community, and to the wider community, which needs pluriformity of witness "to fulfill its calling." "In that case an 'identity' assumed within this community would not be a stubborn element of alien loyalty which resisted Christ's identity, but a 'vocation' to serve in a distinct context and manner. Could a homosexual 'identity' become a vocation?"[16] O'Donovan's vocation argument works quite differently from the one we encountered in chapter 1. Like Williams, the author does not assume that a homosexual identity must resist Christ's identity. Nor does he spell out vocation in negative terms, as the living out of a lack. Rather he supposes that gay and lesbian people may have something positive to offer the Church at large. This is an extraordinarily interesting change from a traditionalist, especially one who finds homosexuality more like nationality than race.

Note the surprising result. Williams thinks sexuality is more like race (or at least class), while O'Donovan thinks it is more like nationality. What is not obvious from the quotations is that Williams and O'Donovan come from opposite ends of the spectrum on the issues of homosexuality in the Church. Williams and O'Donovan can, however, *sustain* their disagreement. For they

---

[15] Rowan D. Williams, "Knowing Myself in Christ," in Timothy Bradshaw, ed., *The Way Forward? Christian Voices on Homosexuality and the Church* (London: Hodder & Stoughton, 1997), pp. 12–19; here, pp. 13–14.

[16] Oliver O'Donovan, "Homosexuality in the Church: Can There Be a Fruitful Theological Debate?" in Bradshaw, ed., *The Way Forward?* pp. 20–36; here, p. 30.

share goals for a society, this time an ecclesial one. They are committed to developing a common language – the language of identity in Christ, initiated by baptism and lived out in vocation – because they are willing to put ecclesial identity first. That willingness was not a prominent feature of the earlier debates, however committed the opponents may individually have been to the Church. Williams and O'Donovan help to show that an ecclesial identity can make space and take time for debate of the sort that Marshall and Yeago describe. As long as disputants recognize that they have a community in common – and do not try to read each other out of that community – disagreements about identity need not go all the way down. Within a community, the raging fights over essentialism and constructivism do not even need to be settled, if someone like O'Donovan can see a vocation for a sexual minority that resembles the vocation of a linguistic minority.[17]

The question of how malleable or stable sexual orientations are may not, therefore, prove as important to the Christian community as it seems from outside.

The analogy of sexuality and nationality recalls a concept much more ancient and at home in Christian theology: the idea that Christianity is a kind of citizenship, indeed a change of citizenship. Christians become citizens in the City of God, and they become resident aliens here below. The sign and accomplishment of that change of citizenship is baptism.

Nevertheless, this book does, for the most part, prefer to assume a stable sexual orientation, in moderate and not in doctrinaire fashion. It does so for a *theological* reason, one in which the deliverances of natural science have been disciplined by a well-developed ecclesiology and theology of nature, however one finally evaluates them. I mean, surprisingly enough, the Catholic magisterium: it has had the courage to admit, indeed generously to insist, that there is such a thing as a constitutionally "homosexual person," made in the image of God,[18] although of course it draws different conclusions from that decision.

The "homosexual person," too, if you like, is a construction. The point is that it is a theological construction, one made by theological realists. When John Boswell, cautiously and hedged with qualifications, expressed his

---

[17]   It may not be injurious to political arguments for civil rights, either, if we remember constitutional law on alienage. See McWhorter, "Queer Concept of Minority," *passim*.

[18]   Congregation for the Doctrine of the Faith, "Letter to the Bishops of the Catholic Church on the Pastoral Care of Homosexual Persons," reprinted in Jeannine Gramick and Pat Furey, eds, *The Vatican and Homosexuality* (New York: Crossroad, 1988), pp. 1–10, *passim*.

opinion in favor of homosexual persons, he was not so much being an "evil essentialist," as a good Catholic.[19] A moderately realist, radically theological construction of homosexual persons, realist too about the power of social construction, has theological advantages. Christians, after all, have been undergoing a version of the essentialist/constructivist debate even since Jesus said over the bread of the Last Supper, "This is my body." In the Middle Ages, debates between essentialists and constructivists reached unrivaled heights of conceptual sophistication: they were then called realists and nominalists.[20] The most theologically fruitful solution to that problem – deeply ramified in Christian beliefs about creation and eschatology – is the doctrine of analogy, which will come in for more discussion in part III.

In the best commentary on the "Letter to the Bishops of the Catholic Church on the Pastoral Care of Homosexual Persons," Andrew Sullivan notes that:

> [t]o non-Catholics, the use of the term "homosexual person" might seem a banality. But the term "person" constitutes in Catholic moral teaching a profound statement about the individual's humanity, dignity, and worth: it invokes a whole range of rights and needs; it reflects the recognition by the Church that a homosexual person deserves exactly the same concern and compassion as a heterosexual person, having all the rights of a human being, and all the value, in the eyes of God.[21]

In particular, to be a "person" invokes an analogy – created and distant, but participant and ontological – in the divine persons of the Trinity. It is they who define what true personhood, unreachable by unaided human beings, really is. It is these persons – Father, Son, and Holy Spirit – who in loving each other constitute God's triune life, and it is as persons in God's image that God brings human beings to participate in the love by which God loves God. If there are such human beings as homosexual persons, then God is committed, in unmerited grace, to take their bodies – somehow – as means rather than impediments to that communion. It is a purpose of this book to explore how that might go. For Christ took a body, that human beings might participate in the divine life.[22]

---

[19]   John Boswell, "Revolutions, Universals, and Sexual Categories," in Martin Duberman, Martha Vicinus, and George Chauncey, eds, *Hidden from History: Reclaiming the Gay and Lesbian Past* (New York: New American Library, 1989), pp. 17–36.

[20]   See Boswell, "Revolutions, Universals, and Sexual Categories," p. 19.

[21]   Andrew Sullivan, "Alone Again, Naturally: The Catholic Church and the Homosexual," in *The New Republic*, November 28, 1994, pp. 47, 50, 52, 54–5; here, p. 52

[22]   Cf. II Peter 1:4.

In what follows I shall argue that the analogy between sexual orientation and race can be made convincing and enlightening – but not when it depends upon intrinsic similarities among the disfavored groups. Rather, it depends upon similarities in the ways that the favored groups *regard* the natural *and* moral status of gays and blacks, whether or not they have much in common intrinsically. What follows, therefore, is an observation neither about homosexuals (whether or not you believe such a class exists), nor about homophobes (whether or not you believe such a class exists). It is about a way in which societies often connect nature and morality in their arguments about membership. It is about how societies might recognize that tendency in themselves and construct their notions of justice to guard against it. It is about how Paul recognized the way in which his opponents connected nature and morality in the case most important to him, whether Gentiles belonged in the Christian community, and how he constructed a notion of justice that freed them from it.

What follows offers an extended analogy between the way that societies have sometimes argued about blackness, and ways that they have sometimes argued about homosexuals, with connections to the ways that the Babylonian rabbis sometimes argued about Gentiles, arguments that Paul used and overturned. This sort of analogy is dangerous, in that it can recapitulate the polarization that we observed in chapter 1. It can divide readers into two camps, the victims and the victimizers. James Alison has written that "when the 'I' sees a possible 'we' only as a dangerous and perverse 'they', then we are faced with a symmetry of evil twins which is without possible rescue. . . . We are without the possibility of a blush [of recognizing that the other has recognized us] and without the possibility of Eucharist."[23] Those who insist upon the status of the sacred victim (whether they feel victimized as homosexuals or homophobes) may refuse forgiveness, may refuse, that is, to recognize their commonality with the other. If that happens, then both participate in a mechanism of violence, its victim becoming its manipulator.[24]

The only excuse for pointing out social mechanisms such as Paul attempts to overturn is if we hold open the possibility of recognizing ourselves as complicit in them, so that we catch ourselves in Paul's rhetorical sting operation of Romans 2. After he has thoroughly stereotyped Gentile immorality in chapter 1, he catches the reader nodding her head and addresses her in the second person: "Therefore you have no excuse, O judge, whoever you are, when you judge another; for in passing judgment on another you

---

[23]   James Alison, "Theology Amongst the Stones and Dust," *Theology and Sexuality*, forthcoming; p. 13 of typescript.

[24]   Alison, "Theology Amongst the Stones and Dust," p. 7.

condemn yourself."[25] The only way for Christians to read these comparisons is not to say, "They have made these arguments," but "We have made these arguments." Christians called upon to love their enemies must recognize forces of oppression in order to see how all sides are "but brothers entrapped by forces which they do not understand, the same forces which tend to destroy us all, and before whose gods we have all, on many occasions, bent the knee."[26] Earlier we read that Christians do not contend against flesh and blood, "but against the principalities, against the powers, against the world rulers of this present darkness."[27] In Girardian fashion, Alison has identified such a power. The purpose of this analysis is clarifying the ecclesial identity that gay and lesbian Christians share with their opponents. There is therefore something much more important that both sides can learn from it, quite apart from the homosexuality debate, and that is that they are almost entirely ethnically Gentiles, and therefore especially without entitlement to the mercy of the God of Israel. Both sides also fit enough of Paul's description of Gentiles in Romans 1, if they are "full of strife."[28] Christians of whatever stripe who are inclined to read this section in the person of the victim must try to read it as one who is without excuse, as one who has participated in the mechanism of violence. They may not succeed. That is also forgivable; for the lion does not lie down with the lamb until the eschatological banquet, which comes not by human striving even of the most compassionate sort, but by the intervention of God, who as "a little child shall lead them."[29] It is the freedom, not of the lamb from the lion, nor even of the lion from the lamb, but of both from structures from which they could not free themselves. It is the freedom, not from the enemy, but from one's enmity, or, as Nietzsche and Girard would put it, from resentment. It is such structures that I attempt to describe. Paul describes them not primarily to accuse his brothers (unless he fails at this with Peter!) but to build up the community.

Galatians 3:28 begins with the pair, "In Christ there is no Jew or Gentile." It may come as a surprise to modern Christian readers that that pair is far and away the most important of the series. If the Bible, as a whole and in each of its parts, divides people into two groups, those groups are not Christians and non-Christians. Nor are they Christians and Jews. Indeed, Paul never uses the word "Christian." Rather, the two groups into which the Bible divides

[25] Rom. 2:1.
[26] Alison, "Theology Amongst the Stones and Dust," p. 15.
[27] Eph. 6:12.
[28] Rom. 1:31.
[29] Is. 11:6–9.

human beings are Jews and Gentiles (non-Jews, or "the nations"). In Genesis, the promise to Abraham is stated in terms of an inclusive division between the family of Abraham, which will become the Jews, and all the families of the earth, the Gentiles:

> Now the Lord said to Abram, " . . . I will make of you a great nation, and I will bless you, and make your name great, so that you will be a blessing. I will bless those who bless you, and the one who curses you I will curse; and by you all the families of the earth shall bless themselves."[30]

From the promise to Abraham God's blessing already relates and embraces Jews (the "great nation") and Gentiles ("all the [other] families of the earth"). And yet Genesis ties creation itself to God's history with Israel, the stage for that drama. For the whole history of Israel is measured by generations; names of fathers and sons mark out its chronology, and the "begats" of the King James Version (the plan of *toledoth*) sum up the passage of time. From Abraham to Moses and Moses to David we have not numbers of years primarily, but generations. From David to Christ forward again we have generations as the principle of connection and continuity. The generations of God's people measure God's history too. And back from Abraham we also have generations. Before Abraham was, God was at work. Before the covenant, God was preparing it, all the way back to Adam and Eve, so that Adam and Eve, as Genesis tells it, become not so much the progenitors of the human race, as the prehistory of Israel. And it does not stop with the first parents. The priestly writer of Genesis has a vision bold enough to include the creation of the world within the compass of God's history with Israel, as he says: "These are *the generations of* the heavens and the earth" (Gen. 2:4). The chronological device of the generations assimilates all created things, from the very beginning, into the history of Israel.[31] The history of Jews and Gentiles embraces nature itself, rather than the other way around.

If the Bible's theology of the patriarchs, and even of creation and the beginning (or protology), presupposes Jews and Gentiles, so does Paul's theology of the end. Protology and eschatology alike divide and unite Jews and Gentiles. At the end, God's promise to Abraham would come true not only for Jews, but also for Gentiles. The great eschatological question, for someone trained as Paul was, was this: would the Gentiles, at the end, come

---

[30] Gen. 12:1–3.
[31] Gerhard von Rad, *Old Testament Theology*, 2 vols, trans. D. M. G. Stalker (New York: Harper & Row, 1962), vol. 1, pp. 138–9.

into God's blessing *as Gentiles*, that is, uncircumcised, not keeping the law, Torah; or would they come in as converts, keeping Torah, circumcised, *as Jews*? The answer to that question preoccupies Paul's entire ministry. "Even the irenic Luke," writes Luke Timothy Johnson, "devotes five full chapters of Acts (10–15) to the account of how the community caught up with God's intentions, stumbling every step of the way through confusion, doubt, challenge, disagreements, divisions, and debate."[32]

The shocking answer was that the first alternative seemed to be coming true. God was bringing Gentiles into the worship of the God of Israel without circumcision or Torah observance. For according to Peter's vision, God inaugurates table fellowship, as at the eschatological banquet, between Jews and Gentiles, in spite of kashrut: "'What God has cleaned you must not call common.'"[33] The sign of the eschatological entry of the Gentiles into the house of God is baptism and the Spirit:

> "As I [Peter] began to speak, the Holy Spirit fell on [some Gentiles] just as on us [Jews] at the beginning. And I remembered the word of the Lord, how he said, 'John baptized with water, but you shall be baptized with the Holy Spirit.' If then God gave the same gift to them as God gave to us when we believed in the Lord Jesus Christ, who was I that I could withstand God?" When they [the circumcision party] heard this they were silenced. And they glorified God, saying, "Then to the Gentiles also God has granted repentance unto life."[34]

This caused Paul to recur to the promise to Abraham: "And the scripture, foreseeing that God would justify the Gentiles by faith, preached the gospel beforehand to Abraham, saying, 'In you shall all the nations be blessed.'"[35] The baptismal formula, "there is neither Jew nor Gentile," means therefore first of all that Gentiles may worship the God of Israel and become members of that God's kingdom, city, or holy polity, *without* becoming circumcised or observing Torah. Although Acts and Paul may have differing accounts of the conflict, and even within Paul's corpus Romans and Galatians have differing accounts of the basis on which God brings the uncircumcised in, the point is constant that God is doing something astonishing: accepting Gentiles as such, without their becoming Jews.

---

[32] Luke Timothy Johnson, "Disputed Questions: Debate and Discernment, Scripture and the Spirit," *Commonweal* (January 28, 1994): 11–13; here, p. 13.

[33] Acts 11:9. Compare Gen. 18:8, where Abraham receives the promise at a non-kosher meal (one that mixes milk and meat).

[34] Acts 11:15–18

[35] Gal. 3:8.

Almost all current Christians are, in the biblical categories, Gentiles. Christians have therefore largely forgotten, and it becomes perilously important that they should recall, that by and large *they are Gentiles*. Gentiles, who of themselves are defined as "not knowing God,"[36] come to know a God not their own, are allowed to share in the benefits of God's people, whom they are not; they are "those who are not a nation" or an "un-nation," that is, not part of the true polity of God.[37] Paul sees the coming in of the Gentiles as the very opposite of "seek and ye shall find," the shocking reversal of the politics of desert, God's eschatological fulfillment of the prophecy of Isaiah: "I have been found by those who *did not* seek me; I have shown myself to those who *did not* ask for me."[38]

The Christian tendency to reverse that movement is immense, even enormous – to imagine that they are the ones entitled. Thus an anonymous reader of a proposal for this book for the National Humanities Center still found it possible to get the point precisely backwards, as if it referred to "non-Christians and Jews, who can be grafted into the body of the Church." Paul's point is rather about non-Jews and Gentiles, who can be grafted into the vine that is Israel.[39] The anxiety that later Christians would crystallize into the chilling compound, *die Judenfrage*, the Jewish question, was for Paul really the reverse, the Gentile question. The most important thing for Christians to learn from this book is not about sexuality, but about how they should Christianly construe their relation to God, and the most important lesson to learn there is simply *that they are Gentiles*.

The formula at Galatians 3:28 confirms Paul's experience and conforms it to a baptismal practice. It is first of all a description of the eschatological community in which Gentiles become part of God's holy nation without first becoming Jews. But it is not a mere description. As Yeago indicates, it also has a regulative force. For the new community of Jews and Gentiles experiences conflicts. Paul and the Jerusalem community have split over the circumcision of Gentiles and over table fellowship with them, then reunited after Peter's vision on the baptismal basis that in Christ there is neither Jew nor Greek. The church in Galatia has also split between a circumcision party and its opponents. The very integrity of God's polity is at stake. Therefore the baptismal formula is not merely descriptive of the eschatological community, but normative; Paul deploys it as an admonition. He admonishes the community

---

[36] I Thess. 4:5 and elsewhere.
[37] Dt. 32:21, Rom. 10:19.
[38] Is. 65:1–2, Rom. 10:20.
[39] Rom. 11:17–24

also at Rom. 11:21–2: "otherwise you [Gentiles] too will be cut off." Especially to a Church composed almost entirely of Gentiles, the formula is to be taken as a warning, even a threat. If the Jew/Gentile distinction is read in the way of Paul's opponent, then there is no salvation for the Gentiles as Gentiles, but only as circumcised, as Jews. The salvation of almost all Christians, those who are not ethnically Jews and do not observe Torah, depends on taking this verse seriously, not only because it reflects on the cause of their salvation in God's gracious grafting of an unpeople into God's people, but also because it regulates relations within God's people. To take the formula otherwise is to disbelieve in God's engrafting and endanger the community – thus in two ways to endanger one's salvation.

The importance of the baptismal formula for right relation among the baptized and the integrity of the baptismal polity does not end with Jews and Gentiles, even if Paul shows no interest in the other pairs for the purpose of his argument about Gentiles in Galatia. It proceeds in parallel pairs: "For as many of you as were baptized into Christ have put on Christ. There is neither Jew nor Gentile, there is neither slave nor free, there is no male and female; for you are all one in Christ Jesus. And if you are Christ's, then you are Abraham's offspring, heirs according to the promise." You are not Christ's (Paul might continue), not acting as Abraham's offspring, not receiving Abraham's promise, if you are a Gentile who disbelieves in God's ingrafting. You are not Christ's, and not acting as Abraham's offspring, and not receiving Abraham's promise, if you are not observing table fellowship among Jews and Gentiles – or slaves and free, or men and women. For then you are not living according to the eschatological rules of God's new polity. This would seem to apply to separate table fellowships for slaves and free – or for former slaves and free. This would also seem to apply, and in the 20th century has finally been understood to apply, to that part of eucharistic fellowship that allows both men and women to initiate it as ministers or priests. In their refusal to live within the eschatological community, Paul warns, the community has tested God's patience; the ingrafting continues only "provided you continue in God's kindness to you."[40] If Christians have departed from God's kindness to them and endangered their salvation by ignoring the other members of the formula – if they took some 1,900 years to overcome the pairs slave or free, male and female – that is no argument for why they should continue to do so. God's declared hatred of feasts and sacrifices in the presence of injustice surely applies to the community that organizes itself around its founding sacrifice and consummating feast in the eucharist:

[40]   Rom. 11:22.

I hate, I despise your feasts, and I take no delight in your solemn assemblies. Even though you offer me your burnt offerings and cereal offerings, I will not accept them, and the peace offerings of your fatted beasts I will not look upon. Take away from me the noise of your songs; to the melody of your harps I will not listen.[41]

New Testament scholars have recently begun to argue that the action of the Holy Spirit among gay and lesbian couples may be analogous to the pouring out of the Spirit upon the Gentiles.[42] If so, prohibiting gay marriages may put some Christians in the same danger of forfeiting their ingrafting into Israel – which is their very salvation – as maintaining the distinction Jew/Gentile or slave/free, in a way that disbelieves in that ingrafting. Importantly for the integrity of the community, even New Testament scholars holding traditional views on homosexuality recognize that this argument is one central to Christianity's self-understanding as a redeemed community worshiping the God of Israel.[43] Failing to accept faithful, monogamous gay and lesbian marriages may deny the work of the Spirit and put Gentile Christians in danger of their salvation.[44] Marriage for gay and lesbian spouses depends upon the work of the Holy Spirit no less than baptism for the Gentiles, and disbelief in either risks blasphemy against the Spirit. If Paul himself failed to see that consequence, he also warns explicitly that the Gentile ingrafting into the community of the God of Israel is precarious and subject to reversal.[45]

---

[41]   Amos 6:21–3.

[42]   See most recently Stephen Fowl, "How to Read the Spirit and How the Spirit Reads," chapter 4 of his *Engaging Scripture* (Oxford: Blackwell, 1998), pp. 97–127, esp. 119–27. Here Fowl takes up some of the criticisms of Siker and Johnson made by Chris Seitz and Richard Hays. See earlier Johnson, "Disputed Questions"; Jeffrey S. Siker, "Gentile Wheat and Homosexual Christians: New Testament Directions for the Heterosexual Church," in Robert L. Brawley, ed., *Biblical Ethics and Homosexuality: Listening to Scripture* (Louisville, KY: Westminster/John Knox, 1996), pp. 137–51; "Homosexual Christians, the Bible, and Gentile Inclusion: Confessions of a Repenting Heterosexist," in Siker, ed., *Homosexuality in the Church: Both Sides of the Debate* (Louisville, KY: Westminster/John Knox, 1994), pp. 178–94; cf. also Marilyn McCord Adams, "Hurricane Spirit, Toppling Taboos," in Charles Hefling, ed., *Our Selves, Our Souls and Bodies: Sexuality and the Household of God* (Boston: Cowley Publications, 1996), pp. 129–41.

[43]   Richard Hays, "Homosexuality," chapter 16 in his *Moral World of the New Testament: Community, Cross, New Creation: An Introduction to New Testament Ethics* (San Francisco: HarperSanFrancisco, 1996), pp. 395–6, 398–400. Though Hays rejects the argument from Acts, he respects it and suggests criteria according to which it might succeed.

[44]   Cf. Mt. 22.

[45]   Rom. 11:21–2.

A traditionalist critic may object that "male and female" is overcome only in a way that accords with "nature," and insist on the point that began this discussion, this time in an ecclesial rather than a social mode: that while unqualified membership in the community is due to groups whose distinctions are natural (such as blacks and women), similar, "special" rights are not due to those whose distinctions are moral (as between repentant and unrepentant sinners). As we saw before, "Differences of race are in accord with – not contrary to – our nature, and such differences do not provide justification for behavior otherwise unacceptable. . . . Certain discriminations are necessary within society; it is not too much to say that civilization itself depends on the making of such distinctions (between, finally, right and wrong)."[46]

This is a perfectly sound objection in principle, and we shall return to the justice of the distinction between right and wrong in the next chapter. The question liberals want to ask, of course, is to whom does it apply? Indeed, when does it apply for Paul? Clearly, Paul applies it against those engaging in same-sex sexual activity. Paul believed that homosexual activity was against nature. But there is more to Paul than that. Paul also believed that it was against nature for the Holy Spirit to pour out on the Gentiles or for Jews to eat with them. How exactly do such distinctions work for Paul? The question gains additional weight when we reflect that the distinction of right and wrong helps define the Christian community – helps define it as holy.

"Nature" works differently for Paul than for us. For him, nature and morality can be intertwined among Gentiles, slaves, and women, and it comes as a surprise to him and to the circumcision party that holiness appears among the Gentiles, precisely because they regard the Gentiles – in what we would consider a category mistake – as *morally inferior by nature*. For "nature" applies in Paul's vocabulary not only to male and female, but also to "Jew or Greek," which is the most important case of all. And in that case, the Gentile nature proves no barrier to God's grant of holiness in the Spirit. "Jew or Gentile" is for Paul both a natural and a moral distinction. That application shows how discrimination of the good, moral sort has in fact not rarely, but *usually* been called upon to justify a discrimination of the bad sort.

Again, in what follows, the analysis does not depend the existence of objective similarities among individual blacks, homosexuals, or Gentiles. Nor does it depend upon the existence of alleged individual bigotry or psychological homophobia among the arguers. The argument has nothing to do with modern individualism at all, but everything to do with differing groups that

[46] "The Homosexual Movement," p. 19.

have more in common than they recognize. Both sides, whether we think of them as the lions or the lambs, are trying to secure the goods of society for themselves, and Christians would say that after the Fall, the attempt to secure the goods of society for one's group must inevitably (if not necessarily) lead to strife. The arguments are not about homosexuality or homophobia, but they are structures that trap both, make both victims of a failure to recognize themselves in each other, structures from which they cannot free themselves.

Crucial to the revisionist argument, properly understood, are cases in which the pairs Jew/Greek, male/female, and free/slave were all cited by their defenders as moral, not neutral distinctions. Or better, in all cases there was a natural difference that led to a moral defect. So Gentiles, women, and slaves were sometimes considered in the antique Jewish tradition to be *constitutionally* incapable of keeping the commandments, and especially at risk of moral fault.[47] That reasoning is structurally isomorphic with the current Vatican line on homosexuality, that it is a natural difference, innocent in itself, which nevertheless tends toward a moral defect.[48] In a structurally parallel argument that now strikes Americans as outrageous, some Christian slaveholders during the positive defense of slavery in the 1850s and some recent Mormons have argued that the curse of Ham explains an objective, natural disorder or constitutional fault that gives the natural difference between blacks and whites a permanent moral distinction.[49] So slavery is a "divine institution . . . not to be removed until the curse pronounced on Ham shall have been removed from his descendants."[50] Or, more mildly, slaves, women, and homosexual

---

[47] Michael L. Satlow, "'Try to Be a Man': The Rabbinic Construction of Masculinity," *Harvard Theological Review* 89 (1996): 19–41.

[48] "Although the particular inclination of the homosexual person is not a sin, it is a more or less strong tendency ordered toward an intrinsic moral evil; and thus the inclination itself must be seen as an objective disorder. Therefore special concern and pastoral attention should be directed toward those who have this condition, lest they be led to believe that the living out of this orientation in homosexual activity is a morally acceptable option. It is not." Congregation for the Doctrine of the Faith, "Letter to the Bishops of the Catholic Church on the Pastoral Care of Homosexual Persons," §3, paragraph boundary elided.

[49] See, for example, "The Priesthood and the Black," in Robert Gottlieb and Peter Wiley, *America's Saints* (New York: G. P. Putnam's Sons, 1984), pp. 177–86. See also authoritatively Bruce R. McConkie, *Mormon Doctrine*, 2nd edn (Salt Lake City, UT: Bookcraft, 1966), reprinted 1979, s.v. "Negroes." This view was overturned by special revelation to Spencer Kimball in 1978.

[50] Quoted from Brigham Young in Gottlieb and Wiley, *America's Saints*, p. 178. See also Robert E. Hood, "Ham's Children in America," chapter 7 of his *Begrimed and Black: Christian Traditions on Blacks and Blackness* (Minneapolis, MN: Augsburg Fortress, 1994),

continued on next page

persons have not, perhaps, a necessary subordination, but they do have a contingent vocation in the order of things:

> The slave . . . is an actor on the broad theater of life – and as true merit depends not so much upon the part which is assigned, as upon the propriety and dignity with which it is sustained – so fidelity in this relation may hereafter be as conspicuously rewarded as fidelity in more exalted stations.[51]

As all are called to fidelity in their station according to pro-slavery Christians, of which the fidelity of slaves (to masters) is only a particular case, so all are called to chastity in their state of life according to certain Christians, of which the chastity of gay and lesbian Christians (in celibacy) is only a particular calling. "Christians who are homosexual are called, as all of us are, to chaste life."[52]

Or consider the last of Paul's pairs in Galatians 3:28 in the context of an antique rabbinic construction of women:

> Women are consistently portrayed as lacking sexual self-control. Women are thought to have an evil inclination at least as strong as men's. According to one mishna, "A woman prefers one measure of material substance along with sex . . . to nine measures of material substance and abstinence." According to one *baraita* (tannaitic teachings outside of tannaitic documents), when plied with wine women will lose control to the point that they will sexually proposition animals. The redactor of the Babylonian Talmud even goes so far as to suggest that a woman's sexual urge can seize her, making her unaccountable for her actions.[53]

If then it was women who were less able to control their sexual desires, and now it is men, the pattern is nevertheless the same. Indeed, just as it is now often supposed, precisely by the most liberal people, that male homosexuals

---

pp. 155–80; and Thomas Virgil Peterson, *Ham and Japeth: The Mythic World of Whites in the Antebellum South*, ATLA Monograph Series (Metuchen, NJ: Scarecrow Press and The American Theological Library Association, 1978).

[51] James Henley Thornwell, *The Rights and Duties of Masters: A Sermon* (Charleston, SC: n.p., 1850), p. 44, cited in Robert M. Calhoun, *Evangelicals and Conservatives in the Early South, 1740–1861* (Columbia, SC: University of South Carolina Press, 1988), p. 163.

[52] Congregation for the Doctrine of the Faith, "Pastoral Care of Homosexual Persons," §§3, 12.

[53] Satlow, "'Try to Be a Man,'" p. 28, quoting *Mishnah Soṭah* 3.4 (ET: Ch. Albeck, *The Mishnah*, 6 vols [Tel Aviv and Jerusalem: Dvir, 1988], 3.240–1), and citing also the Babylonian Talmud, tractates *Ketubot* 65a, 51b, 54a, and *Qiddushin* 81b; cf. Judith Romney Wegner, *Chattel or Person: The Status of Women in the Mishna* (Oxford: Oxford University Press, 1988), pp. 153–62.

must be excused from their promiscuous behavior because two men together can hardly help themselves, so the rabbis prevented a man from being with two women: "Women . . . cannot prevent each other from sexual advances, because they cannot control their desires."[54] Women – like 19th and early 20th century black men, and gay men before AIDS – "are understood to be constitutionally unable to exercise self-restraint."[55] "Male homoeroticism, " – in the same way – . . . is seen [by the rabbis] as merely the embodiment of the loss of control that turns a man into a woman."[56]

Indeed the argument is so common that I think of it as "the standard argument." In some cases, it may be true that a natural distinction leads to a moral fault. But since versions and sections of this compound argument have been offered at various times about Gentiles (by Jews), Jews (by Christians), women (by the rabbis and Aquinas), blacks (by Southern Presbyterians before the Civil War), and gay and lesbian people (by the Vatican in the 1980s),[57] Paul's account of Jews and Gentiles suggests that the burden of proof must shift to those who suggest that Christians are *not* doing the same with lesbian and gay couples as they have done with black people and women. Since Christians rejected the implications of the standard argument in the baptismal cases even before Paul quoted the formula, and since they have extended its range further in the meantime, they should ask for additional proof in the case of gay and lesbian people. The burden of proof also lies on those who suggest that Christians opposed to gay and lesbian couples are motivated by malice or fear – other Gentile characteristics in Romans 1.

To be sure, conservatives find the civil rights version of the analogies of the standard argument "unconvincing and misleading." But many – even conservatives – find the baptismal version – the version based on the circumcision controversy recorded in Acts and Galatians – "richly suggestive."[58] Even if

---

[54]   Satlow, "'Try to Be a Man,'" p. 29.

[55]   Satlow, "'Try to Be a Man,'" p. 29.

[56]   Satlow, "'Try to Be a Man,'" p. 38.

[57]   For the cases of Gentiles and women, see Satlow, "'Try to Be a Man.'" For the case of Presbyterians (for example), see Earnest Trice Thompson, *Presbyterians in the South*, 3 vols, Presbyterian Historical Society Publication Series, 13 (Richmond, VA: John Knox, 1963–73), vol. 1, *1607–1861*, especially the speeches indexed under Thornwell. See also Larry E. Tise: *Proslavery: A History of the Defense of Slavery in America, 1701–1840* (Athens, GA: University of Georgia Press, 1987). For the Vatican, see Congregation for the Doctrine of the Faith, "Pastoral Care of Homosexual Persons," esp. §§3, 6. – Note that although antiquity lacked a modern-style race theory of slavery, slaves were still constitutionally incapable of keeping the law, so that a male Jew could give thanks that God had not "made" him a woman, a Gentile, or a slave.

[58]   Hays, "Homosexuality," p. 396.

conservatives do not finally buy this analogy, they may come away with a feeling of the shock of God's grace, the precariousness of their election, and the direness of their position.

In what follows I offer structural parallels drawn from different historical periods applied in different political contexts to different groups of people.[59] I offer them first of all as a re-reading of revisionist claims, turning a political argument into a theological one – one that turns on the central act of God in bringing the Gentiles to worship the One of Israel. I offer the parallels second in what we might call the hermeneutics of paraenesis. It differs from the hermeneutics of suspicion in that it does not depend first of all upon a Marxist analysis of power and class, but on a Pauline admonition about the development of community relations toward their eschatological form, illuminated by those instances universally acknowledged by the community as a whole as ones wherein it has seen itself convicted of sin and changed by the Spirit. However historically and contextually various, the parallels and their breadth arise from one of the oldest liturgical formulas known from the early Church, canonized in one of the most important warnings issued by Paul, about the single issue that motivated his entire ministry. Critics may rightly claim that Gentiles, slaves, and women suffer quite different sorts of discrimination; sometimes the principle of discrimination is visible, sometimes not; sometimes changeable, sometimes not; sometimes compatible with political power, sometimes not; sometimes bodily, sometimes not. Paul, however, makes them parallel as similar temptations against the integrity of the community, because they depend upon similar presumptions about the sort of *moral* life the parallel members, however different, are naturally capable of – presumptions that the Holy Spirit is overturning.

Let me present the standard argument in its most comprehensive form.[60]

1   In a feature of the standard argument least often appealed to in sophisticated versions, but accounting for much of its continuing power,

---

[59]   For differences in period, see, for example, Frederickson, *The Black Image in the White Mind*, *passim*; William H. Freehling "The Indirect Defense of Slavery, 1816–1833" and "The Direct Defense of Slavery, 1833–1836," parts II and III in his *Prelude to Civil War: The Nullification Controversy in South Carolina, 1816–1836* (New York: Harper Torchbooks, 1968); and more broadly, Hood, *Begrimed and Black*. For differences of religious context, see, for example, Calhoun, *Evangelicals and Conservatives in the Early South*. For similarities and differences among several related arguments, see Willard M. Swartley, *Slavery, Sabbath, War, and Women: Case Issues in Biblical Interpretation* (Scottsdale, PA: Herald Press, 1983).
[60]   In what follows I do little with Christian arguments about women. An exhaustive and persuasive discussion of the uses of the Bible on women and on gay and lesbian Christians, appears in David Matzko McCarthy, "Marriage, Equality, and Homosexuality," unpublished ms.

decline or fall narratives in Scripture purportedly reveal that God has punished certain groups. God has punished the Gentiles for their idolatry with the animal character of the ass, according to Genesis Rabbah on v. 22:5. "God punished the non-Jewish peoples by afflicting them with a loss of self-mastery that became a disposition of their very beings."[61] According to some supersessionist Christian readings of salvation history, God has punished the Jews for "rejecting" Christ. God has punished women on account of Eve's sin, according to Gen. 3:16, so that women, too, lost self-mastery, and became "biologically and morally a failed, inferior, or weak version of a man."[62] God has punished blacks as "Hamites," or descendants of Noah's son Ham, condemned to be "a slave of slaves" for uncovering his father's nakedness, according to some traditional interpretations of Gen. 9:22–5. And God has delivered up idolatrous Gentiles to homosexual acts as punishment for their idolatry so that they will die out, according to some traditional interpretations of Rom. 1:18–27.[63]

2   The standard argument proceeds by claiming that God's just punishment of the disfavored group for some narrated sin comes in the form of a natural disorder or weakness which is not yet itself a moral fault. Gentiles, Jews, women, blacks, or gays are not evil in themselves; but they are so constituted (or "oriented") that they are specially subject to temptation – in each case particularly sexual temptation.[64] "Although desire and other carnal impulses . . . threatened both men and women, only men are thought in rabbinic sources to have the ability to subdue those desires."[65] So, too, by the 1890s South Carolina governor Ben Tillman could contend that "many Negroes [had] uncontrollable sexual passions . . . stamped by heredity."[66] The argument from heredity to sexual misconduct recalls the claim that gay and lesbian people suffer from a natural disorder, which if genetic is only that much greater. Nor are such connections confined entirely to the past. As late as its July 1998 number, *Harper's Magazine* examines recent news reporting in which all cases of HIV disease occurring in Jamestown, New York, after the appearance there of a certain black, gay man were ascribed to him without

[61]   Stowers, *A Rereading of Romans*, p. 94.

[62]   Stowers, *A Rereading of Romans*, p. 95.

[63]   See the discussion of Aquinas's commentary on Romans, below. The idea that the Gentiles would simply die out first came to my attention in a conversation with Wayne Meeks.

[64]   On the purported lability of blacks, for example, see Frederickson, *The Black Image in the White Mind*, pp. 250–4 and 273–88.

[65]   Satlow, "'Try to Be a Man,'" p. 27.

[66]   Frederickson's paraphrase, *The Black Image in the White Mind*, p. 276.

convincing evidence or even much investigation. Nushawn Williams "was deemed a 'lethal lothario,' a 'sexual predator,' a 'one-man plague,' a 'monster.'" "In the story of Williams," the author concludes, "pop culture's trinity of sex, race, and danger was perfectly realized."[67]

3   The next step of the standard argument has already come into view. As members of a naturally labile group, Gentiles, Jews, women, blacks, or gays are more prone to violate natural law, or commit moral fault, although they need not. The moral fault, furthermore, is not a private one, but one that undermines society as a whole. Natural disorder (orientation) tends to moral fault (act). It was only natural, therefore, that black women then, like gay men now, should be found more promiscuous even by scholars: "there is so large a proportion of this class of females who set little value on chastity, and afford easy gratification to the hot passions of men."[68] For German Jewish soldiers in World War I, as for gay American soldiers at present, a supposed natural disorder might make them unfit for the military and thus poorer citizens – even if the concern about the use of the genitals had migrated to become one about the use of the feet. The "particular nature of the Jew's foot [was] no longer the foot of the devil but now the pathognomic [flat] foot of the 'bad' citizen [because poor soldier] of the new national state."[69] The German ethnologist Karl Hermann Burmeister wrote that blacks also suffered flat feet, but G. Muskat, a Berlin orthopedist, was more generous in arguing that flat feet were "'merely' a sign of the abuse of the foot."[70] The standard argument can marshal even science to its support, so that Jewish physicians themselves "could not dismiss these 'facts' out of hand and thus operated within these categories." The categories included "the basic truth of statistical arguments of medical science during this period," which Jewish physicians, like today's pro-gay sociologists, could dispute only at the risk of their reputations for objectivity.[71] However related, sexual nature and sexual morals go together in the standard argument, for Gentiles, Jews, blacks, and homosexuals, to render poorer soldiers and poorer citizens.

4   In the standard argument, therefore, a religious objection to equality for Gentiles, Jews, women, blacks, or gays in religion or society can claim to be based not on mere prejudice, but on the disfavored group's characteristic but

[67]   JoAnn Wypijewski, "The Secret Sharer: Sex, Race, and Denial in an American Small Town," *Harper's Magazine* 297, 1778 (1998), pp. 35–54, esp. pp. 36, 39, 46.
[68]   Chancellor Harper, "Slavery in the Light of Social Ethics," in Elliott, *Cotton Is King*, pp. 547–626; here, p. 580.
[69]   Gilman, "The Jewish Body," p. 224.
[70]   Gilman, "The Jewish Body," p. 229, his paraphrase.
[71]   Gilman, "The Jewish Body," p. 227.

freely chosen behavior, which *does* constitute a moral fault. So the enlightened physician can claim it is the misuse of the feet (considered genital markers in any case) that makes the 19th century Jew a poor soldier, as it is today the misuse of the genitals that makes the 20th century gay man a problem for military morale.

5   Sexual restrictions can therefore claim to *protect* both the religious and the labile group. Thus Jews might not marry Gentiles; Christians might not marry Jews; blacks (until 1967 in Virginia) might not marry whites – or indeed, when slaves, legally marry each other.[72] Such marriages, between males as between slaves, are held to be naturally unstable and therefore morally wrong. Thus in the 1990s we get restrictions on gay and lesbian couples marrying under the protest against "special rights"; so in the 1890s we get articles answering in the affirmative such questions as "Have American Negroes Too Much Liberty?"[73] In both cases authors might "in assessing proposed legislation" – quite properly and laudably – "keep as their uppermost concern the responsibility to defend and promote family life,"[74] while laboring under too narrow a view of who is capable of it.

Nature and morality come together, as they did in the defense of slavery: "Anatomy, physiology, history and theology . . . sustain one another."[75] Moral discrimination of the good sort, necessary for social stability, and invidious discrimination among natural kinds, transparent to God's holiness, have not remained distinct in the history of such discriminations, but have often been tangled up, because nature and morality sustain one another. To see how, substitute "exclusively heterosexual marriage" for "slavery" in this description by Eugene D. Genovese:

> The defenders of slavery believed that they had prevailed in the battle of biblical exegesis and that God was on their side. Repeatedly, they assured their readers that their highest purpose was to "to vindicate the ways of God to man." Those very words appeared often, most forcefully in the works of [Henry] Hughes and [George] Fitzhugh. Fitzhugh was fond of saying that "Nature will out!" – by

[72]   See Martha Elizabeth Hodes, *White Women, Black Men: Illicit Sex in the Nineteenth-Century South* (New Haven, CT: Yale University Press, 1997).
[73]   Charles H. Smith, "Have American Negroes Too Much Liberty?" *Forum* 16 (October, 1893): 176, 181. For discussion, see Frederickson, *The Black Image in the White Mind*, p. 273.
[74]   Congregation for the Doctrine of the Faith, "Pastoral Care of Homosexual Persons," §17.
[75]   James Sloan (Mississippi Presbyterian cleric), quoted in Peterson, *Ham and Japeth*, p. 97, and Hood, "Ham's Children in America," p. 157.

which he meant that God's will would be done. Slavery would triumph because it conformed to God's law and to the nature of man in the wake of the Fall.[76]

6   Even should one charitably find the state of the disordered a subject of pity or apparent injustice, one could still hold that the duty of those so afflicted is to do the best they can with what they have. Thus according to the standard argument it is the contingent vocation, if not the necessary nature, of gay people or women or slaves to have a special service, even if their condition is not their fault.

It is true that calls to a particular vocation usually come not by visions or voices, but by an accumulation of particular circumstances; so that being female may contribute to a vocation to motherhood, or being gay to a vocation to celibacy. As Sebastian Moore insists, "True celibates are rare."[77] Yet to make those determinations in advance and across the board does not attend to particular circumstances, but levels them out.[78] For those not called to celibacy, "Abstinence from sex represses Eros without transfiguring it."[79] Otherwise God would elect only the first born, and not second sons; or only

---

[76]   Note that the extract also raises the issue of biblical exegesis that we will revisit when we come to Thomas Aquinas. Eugene D. Genovese, *"Slavery Ordained of God": The Southern Slaveholders' View of Biblical History and Modern Politics*, 24th Annual Robert Fortenbaugh Memorial Lecture (Gettysburg, PA: Gettysburg College, 1985), p. 22. Cf. Henry Hughes, *Treatise on Sociology, Theoretical and Practical* (Philadelphia: Lippincott, Grambo, 1854 and New York: Negro Universities Press, 1968); George Fitzhugh, *Sociology for the South, or The Failure of Free Society* (Richmond, VA: A. Morris, 1854 and New York: Bert Franklin, 1965); and Fitzhugh, *Cannibals All! Or, Slaves without Masters* (Richmond, VA: A. Morris, 1857 and Cambridge, MA: The Belknap Press of Harvard University, 1988). See also Eugene D. Genovese, *A Consuming Fire: The Fall of the Confederacy in the Mind of the White Christian South* (Athens, GA: University of Georgia Press, 1999).

[77]   Sebastian Moore, *The Inner Loneliness* (New York: Crossroad, 1982), p. 62.

[78]   For detail, see M. Basil Pennington, "Vocation Discernment and the Homosexual," in Robert Nugent, ed., *A Challenge to Love: Gay and Lesbian Catholics in the Church*, with an introduction by Bishop Walter F. Sullivan (New York: Crossroad, 1984), 235–44. In general, see Moore, *The Inner Loneliness*; and L. M. Rulla, *Anthropology of the Christian Vocation*, vol. 1 (Rome: Gregorian University Press, 1986). Evdokimov also has a profound analysis of vocation, whether for marriage or monasticism, in "The Royal Priesthood of Believers," chapter 3 in his *Sacrament of Love: The Nuptial Mystery in the Light of the Orthodox Tradition*, trans. Anthony P. Gythiel and Victoria Steadman (Crestwood, NY: St Vladimir's Seminary Press, 1985), pp. 85–103, esp. pp. 97–100.

[79]   Evdokimov, *The Sacrament of Love*, p. 168.

the fertile, and not the barren; or only the righteous, and not the sinful; or only the Jews, and not the Gentiles. As Barth was fond of quoting, *Latet periculum in generalibus*: danger lurks in generalities. In the standard argument, women are called to childrearing, blacks to service, gay and lesbian people to celibacy, in each case *as a group*, whether the particulars to which God usually attends indicate that vocation, or not. In the Bible, group membership is regularly the subject of God's subversion, so that it is the deaf who hear, the blind who see, the lame who dance for joy, the barren who conceive, and the eunuch who enters the kingdom of heaven. The great student of Christian vocation, Paul Evdokimov, puts it this way: "It is possible that the most ascetic act is not renunciation of self, but total self-acceptance."[80]

The insistence on a *general* or *group* theory of vocation rather than particular cases of it can persist even when the author generously concedes the generalization's apparent injustice. For example:

> The propriety of slavery, like that of the restraints and punishments of civil government, rests on the fact that man is depraved and fallen. Such is his character, that the rights of the whole, and the greatest welfare of the whole, may, in many cases, demand the subjection of one part of society to another, even as man's sinfulness demands the subjection of all to civil government. Slavery is, indeed, but one form of the institution, *government*. . . . And this is the Scriptural account of the origin of slavery, as justly incurred by the sin and depravity of man.[81]

So one now hears (on a far different account of sin, and a far better account of human dignity) that universal homosexual celibacy is, indeed, but one form of the virtue, chastity.

Paul did not know these arguments against blacks and against lesbians and gay men. But he did know and he did reject structurally similar if not isomorphic arguments against Gentiles; and he did know and he did sometimes extend that rejection to arguments he sometimes saw as isomorphic against women and slaves. Those three groups were at least as diverse as the ones treated here, and at least as similar in the minds of those justifying discrimination against them as of the good, moral sort. That is, Paul did not know modern stereotypes about the sexual lability of blacks and gay men, but he did know those stereotypes of sexual lability applied to Gentiles, slaves, and women.

Stowers's interpretation cuts against both sides. Against liberals, he ob-

---

[80]   Evdokimov, *The Sacrament of Love*, p. 100.
[81]   Robert Lewis Dabney, quoted in Calhoun, *Evangelicals and Conservatives in the Early South*, p. 186.

serves, "I think it certain that it will not do to make Gal. 3:28 the key and then to construe that text in terms of liberal individualism and the premises of the modern state."[82] As against some traditionalists, on the other hand, Galatians 3:28 is neither a mere description innocent of paraenesis for the community, nor so universal as to apply to all human sin without particular application. In conformity with the interpretation offered here, Stowers writes, "Paul's perspective . . . is not philosophical anthropology, the human essence, but what moderns would call ethnic cultural stereotype."[83]

Not only do I propose that the standard argument has been unjustly used so often, that the burden of proof must shift. I propose that God's providential order of salvation specifically *overturns* the standard argument.

"Rabbinic sources actively associate homoerotic intercourse with Gentiles" and the proclivity toward it as an "inherent characteristic."[84] Indeed, to understand the theology of that claim we have to understand not only that God pours out the Holy Spirit on the Gentiles without requiring that they be circumcised or keep Torah, as Paul deploys the baptismal formula in Galatians. "Gentiles, like women, are portrayed by the rabbis as totally lacking the ability to control themselves."[85] Just as the rabbi Paul in Rom. 1:23–7 associates Gentile lack of control with sexual excess characterized as "worship of the creature," so too "[a]ccording to the Mishna a Jew should not leave an animal alone with a Gentile for fear of bestiality."[86] We also have to understand the famous "contrary to nature" passages in Romans. Against certain liberals, I argue that Christians may not simply cast out that passage. Against conservatives, I argue that they must not take it too narrowly. They must take it in the context of the letter as a whole, that is, in the context of Paul's preoccupation with Jews and Gentiles. That preoccupation is, for Paul, both the primary issue about God and the body, and the primary issue in eschatology. All of Paul's reflections on sex – including his rhetorical stereotyping of the Gentiles in Romans 1 as prone to homosexuality activity – are informed by his conviction that since God is calling in the Gentiles, the end is now taking place.

---

[82] Stowers, *A Rereading of Romans*, p. 284.

[83] Stowers, *A Rereading of Romans*, pp. 108–9. That Stowers's characterization comes in the exegesis of Romans 1 strengthens my reading that Paul's primary purpose is to stereotype Gentiles, not issue a ruling on modern same-sex couples.

[84] Satlow, *Tasting the Dish*, pp. 203–4.

[85] Satlow, "'Try to Be a Man,'" p. 35, citing the Babylonian Talmud, tractates *Yebamot* 103a-b (with parallels at *Horayot* 10b and *Nazir* 23b), *Quiddushin* 49b, and *Sanhedrin* 39b, 95b; and Michael L. Satlow, *Tasting the Dish: Rabbinic Rhetorics of Sexuality* (Atlanta, GA: Scholars Press, 1995), pp. 146–53.

[86] Satlow, "'Try to Be a Man,'" p. 36, with examples, citing *Mishnah 'Aboda Zara* 2.1 and 3.1.

For the Church to understand sex, it must lose a sense of entitlement and recover a sense of grace. For that reason it is crucially necessary for the Church to acknowledge its overwhelmingly Gentile nature. For only thus will it come to lose its sense of entitlement and appreciate appropriately the grace of the God of Israel.

The Gentile Church, as Kendall Soulen puts it, has no God of its own. It worships an other God, a God strange to it, the God of Israel,[87] and Gentile Christians are strangers within their gate. Gentiles, even Gentile Christians, are not God's first love, not those of whom God is jealous, not those to whom God is betrothed, with whom God has made and renewed a covenant. Gentiles are so foreign to the God of Israel that Paul can say that God acts "contrary to nature," *para phusin*, in grafting them in.[88]

A phrase more liable to provoke, the same one Paul uses earlier in the letter to describe homosexual activity, is difficult to imagine. Does Paul mean to compare God's activity to homosexual activity? Or does he at least mean to let the phrase stand, echoing, setting up unsavory comparisons in the reader's mental ear? Both the first and the second *para phusin* have to do specifically with Gentiles. The first use, like the second, distinguishes not a modern class of people, homosexuals, but a biblical class of people, Gentiles, and distinguishes them not from heterosexuals, but from Jews. In Romans 1 Paul let his readers regard same-sex sexual activity as a characteristically Gentile sin of excess, one that they could temporarily pride themselves on avoiding, until chapter 2 comes in with what Richard Hays has called Paul's "rhetorical sting operation,"[89] according to which Jews turn out also to be without excuse.

The rhetorical sting operation has a further whip of its tail in store. By Romans 11, the God of Israel has shown solidarity with those very Gentiles (as with Jewish second sons, barren women, and unwed mothers). God associates with them, eats and drinks with them; in the modern idiom we would even say that God is sleeping with the enemy – the phrase is not too strong, for God seeks to make the Jews "*jealous.*" In both cases *para phusin* more strictly means "in excess of nature";[90] Paul sees the activity that characterizes God, like the activity that characterizes the Gentiles, as excessive, profligate, prodigal.

[87] R. Kendall Soulen, "YHWH the Triune God," *Modern Theology* 15 (1999): 25–54.

[88] Rom. 11:24. I owe my attention to this passage to Richard Hays.

[89] Richard Hays, "Relations Natural and Unnatural: A Response to John Boswell's Exegesis of Romans 1," *Journal of Religious Ethics* 14 (1986): 184–215

[90] Dale B. Martin, "Heterosexism and the Interpretation of Romans 1:18–32," *Biblical Interpretation* 3 (1995): 332–55.

The sting is this: in saving the Gentiles, God shows solidarity with something of their nature, the very feature that had led the Jew Paul to distinguish himself from them: their excessive sexuality. Although the metaphor of ingrafting is agricultural, it is also one about households. It has become natural that God should love God's natural children, that is, the children of God's covenant with Israel. What has become natural is that the domestic olive – the olive of the household and economy of God – should bear domestic fruit. And yet God loves also the Gentiles: wild olives, adopted children, strange children – idol-worshippers whom God had given up to desires in excess of nature, *para phusin*. According to Paul, divine and Gentile profligacy are both *para phusin*. God saves the Gentiles by adapting to God's own purposes that apparently most offensive Gentile characteristic. Just as God saved flesh by taking it on and defeated death by dying, here God saves those who act in excess of nature by an act in excess of nature. Gentile Christians owe their very salvation to God's unnatural act. That is how much grace it is.

One meaning of God's acting *para phusin* is that God acts against the standard. If God has not acted to overturn the standard argument on Jews and Gentiles, then Gentile Christians are not saved after all. *They are not saved!* It is the wild branches that God grafts in according to Romans 11 – the Gentiles with whom Paul associated sexual license – and on the hearts of whom the Spirit writes a new law – in this case, I will argue, the law of marriage. As God grafts Gentiles, the wild branches, onto the domestic covenant of God's household with Israel, structured by the Torah of the Spirit, so God grafts gay and lesbian couples (whom detractors also associate with sexual license) by a new movement of the Spirit onto the domestic, married covenants of straight women and men.

Paul's baptismal formula requires openness to the work of the Holy Spirit in overturning the frequent religious arguments by which natural or apparently natural distinctions, such as those between Jews and Gentiles, slaves and free, men and women are judged to depend upon sexual lability. If so, then the community of the baptized must be open to the possibility that the Holy Spirit is able to pour out holiness also on gay and lesbian couples, without erasing the distinction between gay and straight, as the Holy Spirit rendered the Gentiles holy without circumcision and keeping Torah. Before Paul's overturning of the standard argument and renewed interpretation of the Bible, that was a contradiction in terms and an offense to holiness. Circumcision and Torah observance *just was* holiness for the party of James, Peter in some moods, and the early Paul. Now Paul defines holiness with an understanding new to him of what God is doing with Gentiles.

In sum, the politics of baptism requires that we take opponents' arguments in the best light. The analogy of gay and lesbian people to blacks and women is not seen in the best theological light as a political argument about rights. The best theological light on it makes it an interpretation of the baptismal charge of Galatians. Galatians 3:28 not only describes the community's eschatological polity, but it issues a warning about how to conduct community relations. Its monitory force is this: do not let social or natural distinctions so turn into moral ones that you fail to see the Holy Spirit at work. For if you do so you Gentile Christians put your own salvation, your own community membership, at risk. The admonition applies precisely where the standard argument prevails. It applies where Christians claim that natural disorder leads to moral fault that undermines society. For Paul regarded Gentiles, slaves, and women as all suffering from the constitutional inability to observe Torah. Not only is the argument structurally isomorphic with ones now used against gay and lesbian people, but Paul comes as close as a first century writer might come to applying it that way himself, when in Romans he characterizes specifically Gentile excess with same-sex activity. That stereotype he turns on its head, since it is Gentile inclusion he is arguing for. He turns it on its head, furthermore, in order to catch the reader in a trap, when at Romans 2:1 he exclaims, "Aha! you judge!" He turns it yet again, for not only does he bring the Gentiles into the closest possible association with same-sex activity, but he brings God's building up of the eschatological community *also* into the closest possible association with the metaphorically excessive sexual activity. In the salvation of the Gentiles, none other than God acts *para phusin*.

Chapter 3

THE HOLINESS OF THE PEOPLE OF GOD: MONOGAMY AND MONASTICISM

Liberals can also apply charges in a way that seeks to identify a moral fault that undermines society, as when the allegation of "homophobia" reduces traditionalists' concerns for the visible holiness of the community to mere psychopathology. That charge, too, can perpetuate rather than overturn the standard argument. Liberals are not immune to accusation and cultural stereotyping. According to Paul's overturning of the standard argument, they, too, must make common cause with the forgiven. They must recognize that gay and lesbian couples share their deepest fears with their conservative opponents: fears for the security of their marriages. Gay and lesbian couples fear that conservatives are undermining their marriages, and conservatives fear that gay and lesbian couples are undermining theirs. Only the placement of marriage itself upon a firmer footing can put their reciprocal fears to rest. Fears for family can lead to resentment, enmity, and idolatry in both cases. It was not for nothing that Jesus asked, "Who are my mother and my brothers?"[1] According to Christians, true security comes not from the marriage of one human being to another, but the marriage of God to God's people.

The familial or baptismal identity of Christians requires not just the inclusion of Gentiles, but forging them into a new vision of holiness "in Christ." That calls for a recovery of marriage for both same- and opposite-sex couples, and of monasticism, as concrete ways of building up the community or family of God and manifesting its holiness "in Christ."

---

[1] Mt. 10:37.

Luke Timothy Johnson, the New Testament scholar, puts it this way:

> The harder question, of course, is whether the church can recognize the possibility of homosexual committed and covenantal love, in the way that it recognizes such sexual/personal love in the sacrament of marriage. This is a harder question because it pertains not simply to moral attitudes or pastoral care, but to the social symbolization of the community. The issue here is analogous to the one facing earliest Christianity after Gentiles started being converted. . . . Such a witness is what the church now needs from homosexual [and heterosexual] Christians. Are homosexuality and holiness of life compatible? Is homosexual covenantal love according to "the mind of Christ," an authentic realization of that Christian identity authored by the Holy Spirit, and therefore "authored" as well by the Scripture despite the "authorities" speaking against it? The church can discern this only on the basis of faithful witness. The burden of proof required to overturn scriptural precedents is heavy, but it is a burden that has been borne before. The church cannot, should not, define itself in response to political pressure or popularity polls. But it is called to discern the work of God in human lives and adapt its self-understanding in response to the work of God.[2]

Revisionists may purport to find disingenuous the traditionalists' claim that they are really looking out for marriage and the family. But to take their opponents in the best light requires that they honor that claim. For almost all Western Christians, and many Eastern ones as well, have lost much sense of how marriage might serve the community, reflect the electing grace of God, sanctify the couple through ascetic disciplines, and participate in God's sharing of the trinitarian life.

Heterosexual divorce rates rose precipitously as homosexual men were still calling themselves "Uranians" and long before anything that might be called a gay and lesbian liberation movement even existed, so that it is above all the heterosexually married who might have much to recover about what marriage is for. After all, there is much more in the Bible against divorce – explicit commands from Jesus in three Gospels, as well as from Paul – than against homosexuality. Even the best-churched undergraduates cannot think of more for marriage to mean than the (now socially unnecessary) legitimization of sex and offspring. So Christians might well take traditionalists at their word when they say that marriage needs to be shored up. Heterosexual Christians have been such poor stewards of their almost unbelievably rich theology of marriage that they leave almost all of it to recover.

[2] Luke Timothy Johnson, "Disputed Questions: Debate and Discernment, Scripture and the Spirit," *Commonweal* (January 28, 1994): 11–13; here, 12, 13.

Perhaps, indeed, only those denied it – such as gay and lesbian people – can be sufficiently uncynical, or even romantic, about marriage, as to defend the extravagant eschatological claims about it that the Christian tradition has sometimes made – household church, participant in the love of God for the community, means of sanctification – and to brave the equally extravagant difficulties that the tradition has always claimed attend it.

If the heterosexual practitioners of Christian marriage have left almost all its riches for those denied it to recover, they have also left it – and themselves – vulnerable to critiques by old-school gay radicals crying sour grapes. On the one hand, there is a new call even among gay leaders active since the 1970s – such as Larry Kramer – for monogamy and fidelity,[3] as well as among a new, conservative, gay movement, largely unrecognized by Christian traditionalists, writing entire books in favor of gay marriage.[4] Nevertheless, as traditionalists have claimed, there is indeed much in what passes for a gay and lesbian subculture to object to. In a recent symposium on gay marriage, for example, the author Edmund White attacks the support for monogamy by such leaders of precisely that subculture as Larry Kramer, Andrew Sullivan, and Bruce Bawer:

> I would argue that monogamy is part of a pleasure-hating package being sold by aging gay leaders, now in their 50s and 60s, people who through some ghastly process of natural selection managed to survive the plague precisely because they were so dysfunctional they could never get laid. . . . I am not an

---

[3] Larry Kramer, a gay playwright, and no conservative, can now write lines such as these: "I am so sick of the literature of sex, of the soft porn of all our novels and short stories that traffic only or mostly in sex. . . . One thing our writers are not teaching us about is love. . . . We have made sex the cornerstone of gay liberation and gay culture, and it has killed us. . . . I am at the end of my patience with gays who say they're not interested in obtaining the right to legally marry. . . . Dumb, stupid, blind gays opposed to gay marriage . . . " "Sex and Sensibility," *The Advocate* 734 (May 27, 1997): 59–66.

[4] Andrew Sullivan, *Virtually Normal: An Argument about Homosexuality* (New York: Alfred A. Knopf, 1995); Bruce Bawer, *A Place at the Table: The Gay Individual in American Society* (Boston: Poseidon Press, 1993); and John Boswell, *Same-Sex Unions in Premodern Europe* (New York: Villard Books, 1994) might fall into this category; see also the articles in Andrew Sullivan, ed., *Same-Sex Marriage, Pro and Con: A Reader* (New York: Vintage Books, 1997); and in Bruce Bawer, *Beyond Queer: Challenging Gay Left Orthodoxy* (New York: The Free Press, 1996); Marshall Kirk and Hunter Madsen, *After the Ball* (New York: Plume Books, 1990); from a legal point of view before the Hawaii cases, William N. Eskridge, Jr, *The Case for Same-Sex Marriage: From Sexual Liberty to Civilized Commitment* (New York: The Free Press, 1996); and Kittredge Cherry and Zalmon Sherwood, *Equal Rites: Lesbian and Gay Worship, Ceremonies, and Celebrations* (Louisville, KY: Westminster/ John Knox, 1995).

assimilationist. I don't want to win a perfect-attendance pin at church or head up the PTA. For me, being gay seemed at first like another way of being a bohemian and later a concomitant to fighting for social justice. I wanted gays to be in the vanguard, battling against racial and economic injustice and religious and political oppression. I never thought I'd live to see the day when gays would be begging to be let back into the Christian church, which is clearly our enemy, or would chuck aside public-mindedness and take up the most narrow, creepy, selfish sort of conformism. To my ears, *monogamy* is only one more depressing word in this dispiriting vocabulary.[5]

This kind of rhetoric leads traditionalists to observe quite rightly that White has no idea what marriage is really about – it is not a failed attempt at sexual satisfaction, but a community practice of asceticism for the whole person. Against such views traditionalists observe, again with justice:

> The sexual revolution is motored by presuppositions that can and ought to be effectively challenged. Perhaps the key presupposition of the revolution is that human health and flourishing require that sexual desire, understood as a "need," be acted upon and satisfied. Any discipline of denial or restraint has been popularly depicted as unhealthy and dehumanizing.[6]

In what follows I shall propose that marriage, for the same or opposite sexes, can be a discipline of denial and restraint that liberates the human being for sanctification. The trouble with most conservative accounts is not that in denying same-sex couples the rite of marriage they would deny them true self-satisfaction, although they might. The trouble is that in denying same-sex couples the rite of marriage they would deny them true self-denial.

From the point of view of theology or Christian symbolics, however, that may be better than giving too much ground, as even conservatives sometimes can do. In a piece otherwise moving for its ability to meet a point of view with which he has little native sympathy, the traditionalist Oliver O'Donovan writes with rather an excess of charity:

> It has been widely assumed in the Church that some form of claim for homosexual marriage is *the* challenge that the gay movement presents. This,

---

[5]   Edmund White, "What Century Is This, Anyway?" *The Advocate* 762 (June 23, 1998): 55–6, 58; here, p. 58. For description and critique from a gay point of view of the title topic, see Frank Browning, *The Culture of Desire: Paradox and Perversity in Gay Lives Today*, with a new introduction by the author (New York: Vintage Books, 1994).

[6]   "The Homosexual Movement: A Response by the Ramsey Colloquium," *First Things* 41 (March 1994): 15–20; here, 16–17.

however, has been put in question recently by . . . gay Christian writers . . . who have argued . . . that marriage is not the right paradigm for homosexual relations, but that "affective friendship" is what the homosexual is fitted for. . . . This is one of those disagreements of gays among themselves that the Church has to listen attentively to. I welcome the alternative model, in that it seems to take seriously, and, indeed, to make a virtue of, an often-observed feature of male homosexual relationships, their episodic character, and so brings a rather wider range of homosexual experience into the discussion.[7]

Non toli auxilio: It is hard to see how relationships *expected* to be episodic can give the time for sanctification, can take the risk of longevity, so that "marriage is a place where, in a singular manner, our waywardness begins to be healed and our fear of commitment overcome."[8] Williams puts it more comprehensively like this:

> I can only fully discover the body's grace in taking time . . . . the more time taken the longer a kind of risk endures. There is more to expose, and a sustaining of the will to let oneself be formed by the perceptions of another. Properly understood, sexual faithfulness is not an avoidance of risk, but the creation of a context in which grace can abound because there is a commitment not to run away from the perception of another. When we bless sexual unions, . . . we do this so that they may have a certain freedom to "take time" to mature and become as profoundly nurturing as they can. . . . In other words, I believe that . . . the giving of unlimited time to each other, remains central for understanding the full "resourcefulness" and grace of sexual union. I simply don't think we would grasp all that was involved in the mutual transformation of sexually linked persons without the reality of unconditional public commitments: more perilous, more demanding, more promising.[9]

That means that marriage, gay or straight, is a kind of ascetic practice, a communal structure that frees the body to become as a means of sanctification.[10] And that brings us back to Paul's concern with the holiness of the

---

[7]   Oliver O'Donovan, "Homosexuality in the Church: Can There Be a Fruitful Theological Debate?," in Timothy Bradshaw, ed., *The Way Forward? Christian Voices on Homosexuality and the Church* (London: Hodder & Stoughton, 1997), pp. 20–36; here, p. 34.

[8] . "The Homosexual Movement," p. 17.

[9]   Rowan D. Williams, "The Body's Grace," in Charles Hefling, ed., *Our Selves, Our Souls and Bodies* (Boston: Cowley Publications, 1996), pp. 58–68; here, p. 63.

[10]   For important recent historical accounts of asceticism, see, for example, Peter Brown, *The Body and Society: Men, Women, and Sexual Renunciation in Early Christianity* (New York:

continued on next page

community. For none of the critique of the standard argument means that holiness ceases to have structure or even moral import, or that Gentiles, while not keeping Torah, may do just as they like. If holiness is available to gay and lesbian couples, it will not mean anything goes. Christians have always regarded freedom not as an empty, inclination-free spontaneity, but as a God-moved power to do oneself true good through reason. The plea of traditionalists for discrimination between right and wrong, between holy and profane, must be heeded for freedom's own sake. If the community of the baptized must be a community that takes seriously the analogy of homosexuals, slaves, women, and Gentiles, then it must also be a community defined by holiness in marriage, even the holiness that it observes in the marriage of Christ and the Church. For its election and that marriage, Barth pointed out, represent analogical levels of the same thing. The question that traditionalists and revisionists alike must reconsider is this: what is holiness, for Christians, in marriage?

In any case, it is not mere satisfaction in morally licit ways of sexual appetites. Indeed, the whole question of satisfaction of appetites puts the matter in the wrong way. The old word "consummation" is better, because it describes not only sexual union, but the final, eschatological fulfillment of God's desires for human beings.

I propose the following provisional definition, to be modified and qualified through an exegesis of Paul Evdokimov's *The Sacrament of Love*.[11] Marriage in

Columbia University Press, 1988); Richard Valantasis, "Constructions of Power in Asceticism," *Journal of the American Academy of Religion* 63 (1995): 775–822; David Brakke, *Athanasius and the Politics of Asceticism* (Oxford: Clarendon Press, 1995); and Susanna Elm, *"Virgins of God": The Making of Asceticism in Late Antiquity,* Oxford Classical Monographs (Oxford: Clarendon Press, 1994).

[11]   Paul Evdokimov, *The Sacrament of Love: The Nuptial Mystery in the Light of the Orthodox Tradition*, trans. Anthony P. Gythiel and Victoria Steadman, with a foreword by Olivier Clément (Crestwood, NY: St Vladimir's Seminary Press, 1985). For recent appreciations of Evdokimov, see Michael Plekon, "Paul Evdokimov: A Theologian Within and Beyond the Church and the World," *Modern Theology* 12 (1996): 85–107, esp. 99–103; and Rowan D. Williams, "Bread in the Wilderness: The Monastic Ideal in Thomas Merton and Paul Evdokimov," in M. Basil Pennington, ed,. *Monastic Traditions East and West: One Yet Two* (Spencer, MA: Cistercian Publications, 1976). See also the following: Evdokimov, *Woman and the Salvation of the World: A Christian Anthropology on the Charisms of Woman*, trans. Anthony P. Gythiel (Crestwood, NY: St Vladimir's Seminary Press, 1994); Boswell, *Same-Sex Unions in Premodern Europe*; Demetrios J. Constantelos, *Marriage, Sexuality, and Celibacy: A Greek Orthodox Perspective* (Minneapolis, MN: Light and Life Publishing, 1975); Sergius

continued on next page

Christianity is best understood as an ascetic practice of and for the community by which God takes sexuality up into God's own triune life, graciously transforming it so as to allow the couple partially to model the love between Christ and the Church.

First it must be said that Evdokimov's book, first published in French in 1952,[12] scarcely sees homosexuality anywhere on its horizon.[13] Furthermore, one of its main themes is the distinct and complementary, if overlapping, charisms of women and men. Indeed, Evdokimov devoted an entire book to the charisms of woman, *Woman and the Salvation of the World*, theologically deep, steeped in the tradition, beautiful in its way, which looks as dated now as it looked avant-garde in the fifties. There is much to learn from the tradition through Evdokimov, even bracketing his unconcern with homosexuality and his ontology of the female. It is nothing less than the connection Christians have made between the nuptial mystery with ascetic practice and salvation itself.

Evdokimov first positions himself above two misunderstandings of marriage, which he characterizes as typical of the Western divide between Protestant and Catholic. One can criticize Evdokimov's dichotomy in several ways: it is a stereotypical Orthodox move to *aufheben* rival branches of Christendom while calling down a pox on both their houses; Evdokimov's interpretations of individual thinkers tend to flatten them out and sometimes misrepresent them;[14] and Evdokimov does not have current contro-

---

Heitz, ed., *Der orthodoxe Gottesdienst*, vol. 1, *Göttliche Liturgie und Sakramente* (Mainz: Matthias-Grünewald, 1965); George Khodre, "A Great Mystery: Reflections on the Meaning of Marriage," trans. A. M. Moorehouse, *St Vladimir's Theological Quarterly* 8 (1964): 31–7; John Meyendorff, *Marriage: An Orthodox Perspective*, 2nd edn (Crestwood, NY: St Vladimir's Seminary Press, 1975); Waldemar Molinsky, *Theologie der Ehe in der Geschichte* (Aschaffenburg: Pattloch, 1976); Korbinan Ritzer, *Formen, Riten, und religiöses Brauchtum der Eheschließung in den christlichen Kirchen des 1. Jahrhunderts* (Münster Westfalen: Aschendorff, 1962); Alvian N. Smirensky, "The Evolution of the Present Rite of Marriage and Parallel Canonical Developments," *St Vladimir's Seminary Quarterly* 8 (1964): 38–47; William B. Zion, *Eros and Transformation: An Eastern Orthodox Perspective* (New York: University Press of America, 1992); John D. Zizioulas, *Being as Communion* (Crestwood, NY: St Vladimir's Seminary Press, 1985), pp. 49–65, and P. Viscuso, "Marital Relations in the Theology of Theodore Balsamon," *Ostkirchliche Studien* 39 (1990): 281–8.

[12] Paul Evdokimov, *Sacrement de l'amour: Le Mystère conjugale à la lumière de la tradition orthodoxe* (Paris: Éditions de l'Épi, 1952; Desclée de Brouwer, 1980).

[13] Homosexuality appears in a single line, late in the book, associated with incest and the corruption of children; Evdokimov, *The Sacrament of Love*, p. 166. Cf. also the pop psychology in Evdokimov, *Woman and the Salvation of the World*, p. 251.

[14] See, for example, the notes on Augustine and Aquinas below.

versies in mind. Such criticisms notwithstanding, it is hard to deny that, like many thinkers who paint with a broad brush, Evdokimov has captured two attitudes that do prevail among Christians. Although he wrote before the homosexuality debates, the two attitudes he identified dominate the discussion.

On the one hand, Catholicism (according to the type, if not the reality) ties marriage to procreation; on the other, Protestantism (again according to type) ties it to the control of lust. Libertine movements, including the sexual revolution, reflect the poverty of those positions: people recognize that there is more to love than procreation or control of lust and break free from narrow straits into little structure at all. "Both preservation of the species and selfish sexual pleasure reduce the partner to a mere tool and destroy his dignity."[15]

Referring to Catholics, Evdokimov argues that "certain theologians' opinions on married love are taken from zoology manuals: the couple is seen from the viewpoint of reproduction and child-rearing."[16] As evidence, Evdokimov quotes St Ambrose: "The child is the only reason for a woman to marry."[17] Evdokimov also interprets Augustine as elevating offspring to the head of the three goods of marriage offspring, fidelity, and sanctification. (He might also, more constructively to his own purpose, interpret the passage he cites as elevating sanctification to chief position.)[18] According to him, Thomas

---

[15] Evdokimov, *The Sacrament of Love*, p. 43.

[16] Evdokimov, *The Sacrament of Love*, p. 18.

[17] "Feminis haec [prolis] sola est causa nubendi," *Patrologia Latina* 15:1632B (*In Lucan*, bk. 1, ch. 45); quoted in Evdokimov, *The Sacrament of Love*, p. 22. Migne's note 52 immediately offers the Catholic tradition's qualifications of Ambrose's remark – lest anyone use it as narrowly as Evdokimov does.

[18] *The Good of Marriage*, ch. 24: *Patrologia Latina* 34:396; *Fathers of the Church*, vol. 27 (1955), pp. 47ff; and perhaps most conveniently in David G. Hunter, ed. and trans., *Marriage in the Early Church*, Sources of Early Christian Thought (Minneapolis, MN: Augsburg Fortress, 1992), pp. 120–1. One might argue that Augustine favors the sanctifying good of marriage (*sacramentum*) from the way in which he contrasts it with the other two: "The good of marriage, therefore, among all nations and peoples lies in the purpose of procreation and in the faithful preservation (*fides*) of chastity. But for the people of God the good of marriage lies also in the holiness of the sacramental bond (*sacramentum*)," and, as in the priesthood, the married "will not lose the sacramental sign of the Lord that was imposed once and for all, although it remains as a mark of judgment," even if children and chastity should pass away. Augustine goes on to say that "surely, it is better and holier in the present time not to seek after offspring in the flesh" – precisely by reference to the third criterion, holiness. (*The Good of Marriage*, ch. 24; in Hunter's translation, pp. 120–1.) Evdokimov's interpretation appears in *The Sacrament of Love*, p. 22.

Aquinas calls childbearing "most essential" in marriage.[19] "Roman Catholic canon law," holds Evdokimov, "faithfully expresses the thesis that has become classic: The primary end of marriage is procreation and the education of offspring."[20] "Scholasticism favors procreation," he concludes, "but castrates love."[21]

Protestants have no better record to boast of, in Evdokimov's analysis. They inherit the idea that marriage is primarily a remedy against lust; there is "an echo of Gnosticism in this, where 'redemption' means 'deliverance from sex.'"[22] Certain other theologians, he writes – from the monks of the Syrian desert, to their Protestant heirs, he later implies – "deem it useless to propagate the human race; they reduce marriage to the one aim of avoiding incontinence. This is why a conjugal love that is too passionate borders on adultery," or, in Protestant terms, idolatry.[23]

He might have put it in terms of Augustine's threefold good, *proles, fides, sacramentum*: the stereotypical Catholic position favors *proles* at the expense of *sacramentum*; the stereotypical Protestant position favors *fides* at the expense of *sacramentum*. The divide, however unfair to the breadth of Catholic and Protestant positions interpreted in the best light, rings true to the terms of the homosexuality debate: the traditionalist position often (but not always) centers on procreation, and the revisionist position on faithfulness, leading to idolatry of the child on the one hand and idolatry of the partner on the other, neither under God. Evdokimov sees "the preservation of the species and selfish sexual pleasure" as two forms of functionalism.[24] In both cases his

[19] "Proles est essentialissimum in matrimonio," quoted without citation at Evdokimov, *The Sacrament of Love*, p. 22. Evdokimov's reading of Aquinas is even more tendentious than his reading of Augustine. According to Supplementum 49.3 of the *Summa Theologiae*, where the quoted phrase appears, childbearing is the most essential of Augustine's three aspects only in one sense of three. In other senses, *sacramentum* is both "more essential" (*essentialius*) and "more principal" (*principialius*) than the other two.

[20] "Matrimonium finis primarius est procreatio atque educatio prolis," in Evdokimov, *The Sacrament of Love*, p. 22, citing canon 1013. This looks quite different in the light of John Paul II, for example; see the edition of his weekly audience talks developing a spirituality of marital intimacy: Mary G. Durkin, *Feast of Love: Pope John Paul II on Human Intimacy* (Chicago: Loyola University Press, 1983).

[21] Evdokimov, *The Sacrament of Love*, p. 19.

[22] Evdokimov, *The Sacrament of Love*, p. 16.

[23] Evdokimov, *The Sacrament of Love*, p. 17.

[24] Evdokimov, *The Sacrament of Love*, p. 43. Catholic authors can agree; so L. M. Rulla argues that marriage and monasticism are both instrumental to the love of God; see his *Anthropology of the Christian Vocation* (Rome: Gregorian University Press, 1986), vol. 1, pp. 275–6 and 282–4.

diagnosis rings true – Christians for and against same-sex marriage can agree – that "[t]he question of love in itself and of its meaning still remains open today, and reveals a deep malaise."[25]

The answer requires a retelling of a Christian narrative from creation to the marriage of Christ and the Church, in terms of the sacraments. In order to understand correctly what Evdokimov calls "a priestly vocation in conjugal love,"[26] Western Christians need to recover Eastern understandings of priesthood and eucharistic sacrifice as well as marriage. In the Orthodox tradition, the eucharist is not merely Protestant communion or Catholic sacrifice, but it is these things primarily as "thanksgiving," as "eucharist" suggests in Greek. In the eucharist the human being gives thanks for God's gifts, imitating and participating at a distance in the giving and thanksgiving that the divine persons do in the life of the Trinity, taking part in the eschatological feast:

> And the Lord of hosts shall make unto all people in this mountain a feast of fat things, a feast of wine, of fat things full of marrow, of wine purified from the lees.[27]

> All you that thirst, come to the waters, you that have no money, make haste, buy and eat. . . . Hearken diligently to me, and eat that which is good, and your soul shall be delighted in fatness.[28]

> "[Y]ou may eat and drink at my table in my kingdom."[29]

In making this thanksgiving and supping at this feast, the human being performs a priestly office. The life of thanksgiving not only takes up the command "in everything give thanks,"[30] but it sees that command and that feasting as present by anticipation at the creation.

But this is also a nuptial metaphor, for the eucharist is already a wedding feast: "[T]he Eucharistic banquet is the sacrament of the participation of the nations" – the Gentiles – "in this wedding feast."[31] For in the Eastern view all

---

[25] Evdokimov, *The Sacrament of Love*, p. 19.

[26] Evdokimov, *The Sacrament of Love*, p. 41.

[27] Is. 25:6.

[28] Is. 55:1–3.

[29] Lk. 22:29.

[30] I Thess. 1:18.

[31] Jean Daniélou, *The Bible and the Liturgy*, no trans. (Notre Dame, IN: University of Notre Dame Press, 1956), p. 220.

the sacraments, from baptism, which makes believers, to ordination, which makes priests, to the eucharist, which confers redemption and anticipates the eschatological supper of the lamb, participate in the never-ending giving and receiving of gifts and thanks that constitute the trinitarian way in which God is love. Marriage is not different from but of a piece with this sacramental life.

John Chrysostom does not hesitate to use the eucharistic language of the real presence of Christ also for marriage, because every marriage images the one at Cana where Christ was present turning water into wine.[32] Cyril of Alexandria likewise assimilates all marriages to the one at Cana, declaring that the "Lord comes there always to perform the same miracle."[33] Even the medieval West retains some sense of the marriage as a eucharistic, that is, sacrificial and thanksgiving, communion, so that Hugh of St Victor could write: "Conjugal love is the sacrament of the realized communion between Christ and the Church by the effect of the Incarnation."[34] Even the Catholic magisterium can get the point, Evdokimov admits, quoting the Encyclical *On Christian Marriage* of Pius XI (1930): "[love] must have as its primary purpose that husband and wife help each other in forming and perfecting themselves in the interior life, so that through their partnership in life they may advance ever more and more in virtue; . . . this mutual inward molding of husband and wife . . . can in a very real sense . . . be said to be the chief reason and purpose of matrimony."[35]

One offspring of this partnership may be the virtue of hospitality to a child, which is not only a virtue but also a joy: "St Basil observes that children add

---

[32] John Chrysostom, "In illud, propter fornicationes uxorem," *Patrologia Graeca* 51:210, in Evdokimov, *The Sacrament of Love*, p. 43. French translation as "But de mariage," in: St Jean Chrysostome, *Dialogue sur la sacerdoce, Discours sur le mariage, Lettre à une jeune veuve*, trans. Fernand Martin (Paris: Garnier Frères, 1993), pp. 131–47; here, pp. 134–5.

[33] Cyril of Alexandria, *In Joannis Evangelium* (on John 2:1–11), book II, *Patrologia Graeca* 73:224, in Evodokimov, *The Sacrament of Love*, p. 43. It is not clear that the context supports Evdokimov's interpretation. Rather, the much more interesting point seems to be that Christ's activity at Cana makes the purpose of marriage no longer principally the procreation of children but newly the witness to the resurrection, which Cyril sees foreshadowed in John's remark that the wedding feast took place "on the third day." Cf. the English translation of P. E. Pusey in Cyril of Alexandria, *Commentary on the Gospel According to S. John*, 2 vols, Library of the Fathers of the Holy Catholic Church (London: Rivingtons and Oxford: J. Parker, 1874–85; microfilm edn, Chicago: University of Chicago Library, 1969), pp. 155–8, esp. 157–8.

[34] I have been unable to find this line, quoted in Evdokimov, *The Sacrament of Love*, p. 45, but cf. *De sacr.* II, xi, 3, at *PL* 176:482.

[35] William J. Gibbon, ed., *Seven Great Encyclicals* (New York: Paulist Press, 1963), p. 84; in Evdokimov, *The Sacrament of Love*, p. 45, translation modified.

to the fullness of the nuptial union; they are *epakolouthema*, an 'appendix,' a possible but not indispensable result."[36] As Evdokimov concludes, "It is from this overflowing fullness that the child can come as fruit, but it is not procreation that determines the value of marriage."[37]

Here as elsewhere one may see a false dichotomy between marriage and monasticism. Both nuptial and monastic communities build up the greater community by exercising hospitality to the neighbor. Evdokimov argues forcefully that it is not the case that marriage is for satisfaction, monasticism for sanctification, marriage for sexuality, monasticism for celibacy. Rather both marriage and monasticism are for sanctification; both involve a commitment to living with others in which one cannot escape being transformed by their perceptions, which by the grace of God will be for the better. In both cases, "to marry, just as to become a monk, means to take an absolute risk."[38] In both cases, too, this sanctification involves a higher satisfaction, the coming to fruition of God's plan for human holiness, so that the monk, like the married, can look for a guest "worthy to be here," and hear Love say, "You shall be he."[39]

In both cases, too, there is a possibility of sexual fulfillment, if Rowan Williams is right. For him, the sexual is rather wide: it is a matter of how human beings experience the desiring perceptions of another in their bodies, and the desiring perceptions of another person are a reflex of the way in which human beings experience in their bodies that "God loves us as if we were God."[40] Thus the devotion of the body to God need not be the exception, but prove the rule. Or as someone once remarked, if Freud thought God was about sex, Augustine thought sex was about God. Williams's conception, like the Orthodox, depends upon the whole sweep of creation and redemption:

> [T]he body's grace itself only makes human sense if we have a language of grace in the first place; this in turn depends on having a language of creation and redemption. To be formed in our humanity by the loving delight of another

---

[36]   Evdokimov, *The Sacrament of Love*, p. 121, n. 29, citing Basil of Ancyra, "Liber de virginitate," ch. 37, *Patrologia Graeca* 30:745. While the translation "appendix" appears in the parallel Latin in the *PG*, and Evdokimov's interpretation will carry weight among Orthodox thinkers, critics might regard "sequel" as a better translation, and see the relation between the necessity of companionship or assistance on the one hand, and the procreation of children on the other, as parallel rather than adversative.

[37]   Evdokimov, *The Sacrament of Love*, p. 45.

[38]   Evdokimov, *The Sacrament of Love*, p. 164.

[39]   George Herbert, "Love" (III) in *The Works of George Herbert*, ed. T. E. Hutchinson (Oxford: Clarendon Press, 1941).

[40]   Williams, "The Body's Grace," p. 59. I shall have more to say about this in part III.

is an experience whose contours we can identify most clearly and hopefully if we have also learned, or are learning, about being the object of the causeless, loving delight of God, being the object of God's love for God through incorporation into the community of God's Spirit and the taking on of the identity of God's Child. It is because of our need to keep that perspective clear before us that the community needs some who are called beyond or aside from the ordinary patterns of sexual relations to put their identities directly into the hands of God in the single life. This is not an alternative to the discovery of the body's grace. All those taking up the single vocation must know something about desiring and being desired if their single vocation is not to be sterile and evasive. Their decision (which is as risky as the commitment to sexual fidelity) is to see if they can find themselves, their bodily selves, in a life dependent simply upon trust in the generous delight of God – that Other . . . whose whole life is a "being-for," a movement of gift.[41]

The conclusion is astonishing, shared by both Williams, an Anglican, and Evdokimov, Russian Orthodox: the married need the celibate to tell them what sex is really for. It is for the experience of the body as gift. It is for the taking up of human beings by means of their bodies into the life of the One whose life is a perpetual movement of gift. It is for making the other an occasion of joy, as the life of the Trinity takes the other as an occasion of joy. If married sexuality were the only bodily instance of this movement of gift and thanksgiving, Christians might suppose that sexuality reaches its goal in pleasure or procreation, and miss or bracket the way in which it refers to God, to that for which human beings were created, and that for which they will be consummated. Saints and lovers alike are souls of longing.[42]

This leads Evdokimov to the remarkable thesis that marriage and monasticism are but two forms of one ascetic vocation – "universal interiorized monasticism"[43] – in which God uses the very bodies of Christians to sanctify them.[44] "The renunciation at work in both cases is as good as the positive content the human being brings to it: the intensity of the love of God."[45] In parallel fashion, it is not only the married that enter into the world, for even "the early monastics did not seek to escape the world but to encounter it more intensively."[46]

[41] Williams, "The Body's Grace," p. 65.

[42] Evdokimov, *The Sacrament of Love*, p. 58. See also the section "Joy," pp. 127–8.

[43] For a collection of Evdokimov texts on this theme also from outside *The Sacrament of Love*, see Plekon, "Paul Evdokimov," pp. 99–105.

[44] Evdokimov, "Marriage and the Monastic State," chapter 2 in his *Sacrament of Love*, pp. 65–84.

[45] Evdokimov, *The Sacrament of Love*, p. 65.

[46] Plekon, "Paul Evdokimov," p. 100.

This ascetic calling is universal for Christians because it continues their witness to the kingdom, which is participation in God's own trinitarian life. The tendency to interpret salvation as divinization is indeed livelier in the East, but Athanasius, Augustine, and Aquinas, all agree that "God was made human that humans might be made divine,"[47] and Wesley describes what he does not name.[48] Western Christians little note that divinization is also biblical: according to II Peter 1:4, human beings "become partakers in the divine nature." Furthermore, the author follows the promise immediately with an ascetic imperative: "For this very reason make every effort to supplement your faith with virtue," which ends in love: "and virtue with knowledge, and knowledge with self-control, and self-control with steadfastness, and steadfastness with godliness, and godliness with brotherly affection, and brotherly affection with love."[49] Disputing the Western distinction between commands directed at all Christians and "evangelical counsels" of poverty, chastity, and obedience directed only at monks, Evdokimov cites Chrysostom:

> When Christ orders us to follow the narrow path, he addresses himself not only to monks but to all human beings. Likewise He orders everyone to hate his own life in the world. It follows from this that the monk and the layperson must attain the same heights . . . You are entirely mistaken if you think that there are certain things required of seculars, and others for monks. . . . And if any have been hindered by the married state, let them know that marriage is not the hindrance, but the purpose which made ill use of marriage.[50]

Thus the universal ascetic vocation of Christians makes marriage a form of

---

[47]   Athanasius, *On the Incarnation of the Word*, ch. 54; Augustine, sermon 128, "In natali Domini," no. 12, *Patrologia Latina* 39:1997; Aquinas, *ST* III.1.2c. Augustine's version goes on to the remark in a eucharistic key: "Ut panem Angelorum manducaret homo, Dominus angelorum hodie factus est homo."

[48]   I take the last line of Charles Wesley's "Love Divine, All Loves Excelling" to invoke what the others mean by divinization: "Finish then thy new creation, /Pure and spotless let us be; /Let us see thy great salvation /Perfectly restored in thee! Changed from glory into glory, /Till in heav'n we take our place, /Till we cast our crowns before thee, /Lost in wonder, love and praise."

[49]   II Peter 1:5–8.

[50]   John Chrysostom, *Adversus oppugnatores vitae monasticae* III.14, quoted in Evdokimov, *The Sacrament of Love*, pp. 66–7. A somewhat different English translation appears in *A Comparison between a King and a Monk and Against the Opponents of the Monastic Life: Two Treatises by John Chrysostom*, Studies in the Bible and Early Christianity, vol. 13, trans. David G. Hunter (Lewiston, NY: The Edwin Mellen Press, 1988), pp. 77–176; here, pp. 157ff.

monasticism. Following the lead of Chrysostom and the developments of the 19th century Russian theologian Alexander Bukharev, Evdokimov makes the monastic vows apply also to the married, where the universal interiorized vow of obedience lies in seeking God's will and grace; poverty lies in the use of all goods for spiritual gain; and chastity in faithfulness to God.[51] Liturgically, not only monks witness to the eschatological reality of the kingdom, but also the married, for – in an example of peculiarly Orthodox humor – the crowns placed on the heads of the couple to marry them in the Orthodox rite are crowns of martyrdom.[52] Earlier marriage rites even "included the monastic tonsure, signifying the common surrender of the two wills to God."[53] Ancient Russian traditions saw engagement as novitiate and dispatched the newly married to a monastic retreat.[54] Evdokimov's vision of marriage is no *égoïsme à deux* but a mutual kenosis. The married practice a special monasticism, a particular application of the dying and rebirth[55] celebrated in the baptism of all Christians.

But the universal ascetic vocation of Christians does not merely make marriage a form of monasticism. It also makes monasticism a form of marriage. Monastic traditions, both East and West, think of monasticism as a marriage to God. We have seen that this marriage to God intends no unembodied spirituality, but seeks to find in God precisely the object and return of a desire that wells up from and satisfies the body. The *Philokalia* refers to monks who sin in their hearts as losing their virginity.[56] Marriage "includes within itself the monastic state, and that is why the latter is not a sacrament."[57] They are virgins rather than the married who form the guard of honor at the wedding of the eschatological bridegroom.[58]

Ascesis, monastic or nuptial, is however not best understood as "a system of merely moral rules but a system of exercises implying spiritual gifts that is offered to every Christian life."[59] For that reason Christian life is an expansion, a straining forward (*epektasis*) into ever-greater love of God, which means that God is constantly expanding human desire for God even as God fulfills it. True

[51]   Evdokimov, *The Sacrament of Love*, p. 68, quoting Bukharev without citing him. See also pp. 83–4.
[52]   Evdokimov, *The Sacrament of Love*, p. 70.
[53]   Evdokimov, *The Sacrament of Love*, p. 68.
[54]   Evdokimov, *The Sacrament of Love*, p. 68.
[55]   Evdokimov, *The Sacrament of Love*, p. 68.
[56]   Evdokimov, *The Sacrament of Love*, p. 67.
[57]   Evdokimov, *The Sacrament of Love*, p. 67.
[58]   Mt. 25:1, Lk. 12:35, Mk. 13:34.
[59]   Evdokimov, *The Sacrament of Love*, p. 81.

desire is ever greater.[60] Marriage is a sacrament (and within it, monasticism is a sacrament) because it gives desire time and space to stretch forward (another *epektasis*) into things that are *more* desirable. Anders Nygren famously contrasts eros and agape.[61] "For Gregory of Nyssa, however, Eros flowers into Agape and love of neighbor: Eros is 'the intensity of Agape.'"[62] The bride in the Song of Songs, "wounded with love," becomes a type of Christ, whose passion shows that (as Gregory puts it) "the honored wounds of a friend are more desirable than an enemy's kiss."[63] Marriage, like monasticism, allows eros and the body to mean *more*. "Decisions about sexual lifestyle . . . are about how much we want our bodily selves to mean, rather than what emotional needs we're meeting or what laws we're satisfying."[64] Indeed marriage shares with celibacy the end of sanctifying the whole person through the body, of permitting the body something *more* to be about, something *further* to mean, something *better* to desire, until finally it gets taken up into the life in which God loves God. In this process of desiring ever more, one incidentally or intentionally gives up – lets go of, gets rid of – the petty things that one used to want, and in that way the life of ever-greater desire is one of asceticism, an asceticism in which self-control serves self-abandonment. In this way too the end of marriage and monasticism is one.

According to Chrysostom, the union of the spouses participates in the love of God no less on account of their marriage, because "they are exactly like Jesus Christ who, united to his bride the Church, was not less one with the Father."[65] Indeed, Chrysostom's formula suggests that it is precisely because of their marriage that the two participate in the trinitarian love of God for God, because it is precisely in his sacrificial love of the Church that the Son joyfully returns thanks to the Father.

[60]   Cf. Sebastian Moore, "The Crisis of an Ethic without Desire," in his *Jesus the Liberator of Desire* (New York: Crossroad, 1989), 89–93.

[61]   Anders Nygren, *Eros and Agape*, trans. Philip S. Watson (New York: Harper & Row, 1969).

[62]   "Epitetamene agape eros legetai," Gregory of Nyssa, Homily 13, "In Cantico canticorum," *Patrologia Graeca* 44:1048C, quoted in Evdokimov, *The Sacrament of Love*, p. 82. Cf. Gregory of Nyssa, *Homilies on the Song of Songs*, trans. Casimir McCambley (Brookline, MA: Hellenic College Press, 1987), p. 234, on Song of Songs 5:8.

[63]   Gregory of Nyssa, *Commentary on the Song of Songs*, Homily 13 on Song of Songs 5.8, p. 232.

[64]   Williams, "The Body's Grace," p. 64.

[65]   John Chrysostom, *Homily III on Marriage*, quoted in Evdokimov, *The Sacrament of Love*, p. 68. This is partially translated as "How to Choose a Wife," in John Chrysostom, *On Marriage and Family Life*, trans. Catharine P. Roth and David Anderson (Crestwood, NY: St Vladimir's Seminary Press, 1997), pp. 89–114.

According to Williams and Evdokimov then, it is the transforming regard of God, the indwelling of the Holy Spirit, or grace, that explains what physical desire might be about. Human beings want to be wanted. It is the purpose of Christianity to teach human beings that God loves them. Then a Christian is first in a position to understand what sex is for. Sexual desire is a bodily manifestation of my desire to be wanted, which is finally satisfied only by God's desire for me. God does not leave my body out of God's desire for me. That would be Gnostic. Instead, God can use my body in two ways to teach me that God loves me: either directly, when God's use (rapid or slow) of my bodily desires causes me to understand God's love through the mediation of a whole community of human others as my affectional commitment – then I have a vocation to serve the community, in its office of teaching human beings that God loves them, as a celibate monk; or indirectly, when my bodily desire causes me to understand God's love through the human mediation of one affectional focus – then I have a vocation to serve the community, in the same office of teaching human beings that God loves them, in marriage (for Williams, gay or straight). "What the monks attain *directly*, the spouses work out *indirectly*, and their *means* is the sacramental sphere of grace. The one through the other they look at Christ."[66] It is this transformation wrought by others in the community of God and the Church that establishes the true, sacramental, sanctifying orientation for Christians' physical desires.

Both these forms of community – monasticism and marriage – require time to complete the transformation of human beings by the perceptions of an other. Both the married and the monastic need somebody who loves them to call them on their faults from whom they cannot easily escape. The transformation is not only, or even primarily, the experience of falling in love (eros), but that is the intensity and the clue to the importance of something else: the experience of living with someone, the neighbor, who won't leave one alone (agape).

Nothing in this appropriation of marriage as universal interiorized monasticism fails to apply to coupled gay and lesbian Christians, even if neither Evdokimov nor any of the authors he cites would use it that way. Yet in a sermon on marriage as a cure for promiscuity – and therefore relevant here by extension – Chrysostom also writes: "If evil things are done, even if the custom is ancient, abolish them. If they are not evil, even if they are not customary, introduce them and establish them."[67] Indeed, if marriage is the very form of Christ's relation to the Father, marriage is the state of every human being who takes on

---

[66] Evdokimov, *The Sacrament of Love*, p. 114.
[67] John Chrysostom, "Sermon on Marriage," in *On Marriage and Family Life*, p. 85.

Christ's identity in baptism. If marriage is not about satisfaction of sexual desires, but about a mutual sanctification by ascesis, gay and lesbian Christians who desire it can hardly be accused of self-centeredness; rather they seek to participate in a particularly vivid way in the self-emptying that Christ exemplified for the Church. If marriage is not about procreation, although it promotes the virtue of hospitality to the stranger, then there too gay and lesbian Christians suffer no disadvantage, but can carry forward the great tradition of those other same-sex communities, the monasteries, in caring for the sick and the oblate. No one then complained about foundlings being raised by communities of women or men, but hospitality to oblates was the great Christian transformation of the exposure of infants in antiquity.[68] If marriage is about transforming eros into agape, then why should gay and lesbian Christians be deprived of that ascesis? "Marriage is a place where our waywardness begins to be healed and our fear of commitment overcome"[69] – that, and much more. The last remark comes in a context disputing the call of lesbian and gay couples for recognition of their marriages, yet they too need the commended healing of waywardness and overcoming of fear. No one has seriously claimed, so far as I know, that gay and lesbian Christians are any less in need of sanctification than straight ones. Gay or straight, a couple's path "is narrow, perhaps the most narrow of all, since there are two that walk upon it."[70]

Life with others can bring the rewards of its difficulties, that is, it sanctifies, whether in the community of monks or the community of marriage (straight or gay), whether the dirty diapers one is committed to changing come from one's own biological children or one's adopted children, nieces and nephews, AIDS patients or elderly parents. There are enough to go around. Sexual activity does not make sanctification any "easier" than celibacy does. As traditional marriage and childrearing are gifts of grace more than human achievements, and means of sanctification more than satisfaction, so too monogamous, committed gay and lesbian relationships are also gifts of grace, means of sanctification, upbuilding of the community of the people of God. They are means, bodily means, that God can use to catch human beings up into less and less conditioned acts of self-donation, finally into that unconditional response to God's self-donation that God's self gives in the Trinity.[71]

---

[68]   See John Boswell, *The Kindness of Strangers: The Abandonment of Children in Western Europe from Late Antiquity to the Renaissance* (New York: Vintage Books, 1990), esp. ch. 5, "A Christian Innovation: Oblation," pp. 228–55.

[69]   "The Homosexual Movement," p. 17.

[70]   Evdokimov, *The Sacrament of Love*, p. 70.

[71]   Williams's language, "The Body's Grace," p. 59.

In its argument that the Christian community needs to recover a sense of marriage as a vehicle for asceticism and sanctification, this chapter has attempted both to change the terms of the debate about marriage for gay and lesbian couples and to render marriage more significant to opposite-sex couples as well. In so doing it has provided a rejoinder to certain conservative assumptions; as Williams writes, "the *assumption* that revisionism on one question entails wholesale doctrinal or ethical relativism is dangerous for the future of reasoned Christian disagreement of a properly theological character."[72]

"Orientation in the debates" has been away from heterosexuality and homosexuality, and toward baptism and marriage; away from an individual orientation, and toward a communal orientation; away from the nature of genes, and toward the nature of Gentiles; away from an orientation to satisfaction, and toward an orientation to sanctification; away from a sexual orientation, and toward a sacramental orientation.

Yet there are other objections to the very idea that same-sex unions could qualify as ascetic practices leading to holiness, traditional objections holding that the proper asceticism for homosexual persons is that of celibacy. We shall consider the strongest two, in their most prominent defenders, at some length: natural law, from the Catholic tradition, in the person of Thomas Aquinas; and divine command, from the Protestant tradition, in the person of Karl Barth. But since this is a book in theology rather than ethics, we shall end up learning from each some surprising and at first apparently unrelated things. From Thomas's natural law arguments, we will learn something about virtue and, oddly enough, a great deal about biblical interpretation. And from Barth's divine command arguments we shall learn a great deal more about marriage and election, sexuality and Gentiles.

---

[72]   Rowan D. Williams, "Knowing Myself in Christ," in Timothy Bradshaw, ed., *The Way Forward? Christian Voices on Homosexuality and the Church* (London: Hodder & Stoughton, 1997), p. 13.

Part II

RETRIEVING TRADITIONAL ACCOUNTS: AQUINAS AND BARTH

Chapter 2 raised questions about whether two forms of discrimination, the invidious and the morally necessary, are always easy to distinguish. It is a principle of long standing in theology, however, that abuse does not take away use.[1] That is, if in the past Christian thinkers have misapplied the argument for discrimination on moral grounds, they need not therefore necessarily be misapplying it in a particular case. Some uses may be appropriate. Many citizens tend to suppose, for example, that they discriminate justly and necessarily against convicted felons serving lawful sentences, at least generally and for the most part. In part II, I consider the most important ways of locating the apparent moral evil (or "malice") in homosexual acts – arguments that they are, in fact, like evils that no one disputes, such as theft. In Thomas Aquinas (1224–74) I consider a sophisticated account recurring to natural law and the virtues. In Karl Barth (1886–1968) I consider scriptural and divine-command accounts.

Despite their opposition to homosexual acts in whatever context, however, both Thomas Aquinas and Karl Barth have something to say to all Christians and students of Christianity about how the Church can evaluate and change its biblical exegesis, and about how it regulates appeals to Christian experience and the Holy Spirit. Thomas teaches that the Bible must not be so confined to one sense as to expose the faith to ridicule or to be caused to assert something false. Barth teaches that marriage is the external ground of the covenant

---

[1]   Karl Rahner, "On Bad Arguments in Moral Theology," in his *Theological Investigations* vol. 18, XVIII, trans. Edward Quinn (New York: Crossroad, 1983), pp. 74–85.

between God and Israel, and the covenant between God and Israel is the internal ground of marriage. I consider both thinkers in fresh and nonstandard but textually compelling ways, at considerable depth, and on their own terms.

That is in some ways a dangerous strategy. Traditionalists and revisionists will both see that it requires going back to a fairly deep methodological level to uncover resources in the likes of Aquinas and Barth for extending marriage to same-sex couples. Traditionalists may regard this difficulty as special pleading, and revisionists may wonder why I bother to work with material that must seem to them so unpromising.

The first answer is necessity. Theological innovations must reinterpret and assimilate the tradition. Ignoring it is too easy and leads to deracinated proposals that will not stand the test of time.

The second answer is *convenientia*, the desideratum in theology that it ramify deeply, that it glory in the interconnections in the conceptual web that it is. *Convenientia* is an aesthetic criterion roughly comparable to elegance in mathematics. Christian thinking about sexuality becomes an opportunity for seeing in great complexity and detail how Scripture and nature, command and virtue, creation and consummation relate. We can retrieve from Barth and Aquinas, as from few others, a great deal about Christian traditions of nature, Scripture, election, and pneumatology along the way, even if we disagree about their application.

Aquinas provides a model of ecclesial exegesis, of exegesis for the community for whom the text is authoritative. The Catholic theologian Robert Sokolowski puts the point like this:

> Christ did not speak and act by himself; he spoke and acted with and toward others. And no one speaks until he has been understood; the understanding of Christ's words achieved by those who heard him and by those who thought after him after he left is the completion of the speaking of Christ.[2]

That is a hermeneutical principle of a community formed around a text and valuing its tradition. It differs both from the peculiarly modern historical–critical exegesis of the last two centuries, and from the fundamentalist exegesis of mechanical inspiration. Historical–critical and fundamentalist approaches, like many true oppositions, share certain common features: both are products

---

[2]   Robert Sokolowski, "Reading the Scriptures," chapter 10 in his *The God of Faith and Reason* (Notre Dame, IN: The University of Notre Dame Press, 1982), p. 120. I owe my attention to this quotation to Robert McSwain. For a reading of Aquinas as seeing himself in the tradition of passing on that speaking (if a little too Hegelian), see Michel Corbin, *Le Chemin de la théologie chez Thomas d'Aquin* (Paris: Beauchesne, 1974), pp. 9–112.

of the modern era; both tend toward a certain historical positivism; and both seek to confine the text to one univocal meaning. Both are influenced despite themselves by their rivalry, hermeneutical or spiritual, with modern natural science, and differ therefore greatly from modes of interpretation that arose in the Middle Ages under Latin Aristotelian notions of science, or *scientia*. *Scientia*, more like German *Wissenschaft*, could include under the same rationale both the natural sciences and many fields we now assign to arts and humanities, among them interpretation and metaphysics, as long as they proceeded from first principles. But modern science has infected both historical–critical and fundamentalist interpretation with compulsory univocity and ostensive empirical reference.[3] Premodern exegetical procedures need not conflict with historical criticism, however, since it respects human authors and asserts the truth of the biblical narratives, and it may make grateful use of historical–critical results.[4] Unlike both forms of modern exegesis, critical and

[3] These are sweeping claims. The problem can be stated most sharply with respect to the resurrection. Both fundamentalists and historical critics cease to be able to make sense of it. Historical criticism regards the resurrection, because *sui generis*, as something it cannot approach. It distinguishes therefore the Jesus of history from the Christ of faith; the crucifixion happened to the first, the resurrection to the second. But then Christians no longer have the figure narratively depicted in the gospels, the one person who died and was raised. Fundamentalists, on the other hand, attempt to prove the ostensive historical referentiality of the resurrection accounts. But proof of the resuscitation of a dead body tells Christians nothing about its significance for salvation, according (say) to Aquinas. A resuscitated body can be regarded as saving only if a believer takes the agency of that body to be the salvific agency of God. That is, not only does the resuscitation not prove the body is God's – the body of Lazarus was not God's body – but it must be God's body on independent grounds to be saving. According to Thomas, therefore, Christ himself must argue that claim to the disciples from the (Jewish) scriptures (II–II.1.4, Lk. 24:27). For additional interpretation of Thomas on this point, see Victor Preller, *Divine Science and the Science of God: A Reformulation of Thomas Aquinas* (Princeton, NJ: Princeton University Press, 1967), pp. 248–51. For a sophisticated account of how historical criticism ceased to make sense of the resurrection, see Hans W. Frei, *The Eclipse of Biblical Narrative: A Study of Eighteenth and Nineteenth Century Hermeneutics* (New Haven, CT: Yale University Press, 1974), and "Theological Reflections on the Accounts of Jesus' Death and Resurrection" and "Of the Resurrection of Christ," in his *Theology and Narrative: Selected Essays*, ed. George Hunsinger and William C. Placher (New York: Oxford University Press, 1993), pp. 45–93 and 200–6. For a briefer and more combative account, see David C. Steinmetz, "The Superiority of Pre-Critical Exegesis," in Stephen E. Fowl, ed., *The Theological Interpretation of Scripture: Classic and Contemporary Readings* (Oxford: Blackwell, 1997), pp. 26–38.

[4] So argues Otto Hermann Pesch, "Exegese des Alten Testamentes bei Thomas," in Pesch, ed., *Das Gesetz: ST I–II.90–105,* in *Die Deutsche Thomas-Ausgabe,* vol. 13 (Graz: Styria, 1977).

fundamentalist, however, premodern exegesis does not restrict the text univocally to one meaning. Rather, it allows and even demands multiple meanings of a text. This can provide room for the community that regards the text as authoritative to consider disputed questions. It also accords well with some postmodern notions about the malleability of texts, the interests of interpreters, and ways in which strong (mis)readings succeed one another. Still, in what follows, I will make no grand claims in hermeneutics, without sticking very close to Aquinas.[5] Aquinas allows us to consider controverted texts about homosexual activity from Romans 1, not in bare text, but in the context of some of the Church's most theologically sophisticated theories of nature and interpretation. In the Aquinas chapters, I develop a theory of Scripture that undergirds my use of Scripture in part III.

Similarly, Karl Barth allows us to consider controverted matters of male–female complementarity, not in facile insistence, but in the context of a highly sophisticated and often profound theology of election. In the Barth chapters I develop a pneumatology that undergirds my use of the Holy Spirit in part III.

Readers interested only in the constructive proposals may wish to skip to part III.

---

[5] For more general reflections on Aquinas's theological hermeneutics, see Eugene F. Rogers, Jr, "How the Virtues of the Interpreter Presuppose and Perfect Hermeneutics: The Case of Thomas Aquinas," *The Journal of Religion* 76 (1996): 64–81.

Chapter 4

THE STORIED CONTEXT OF THE VICE AGAINST NATURE: RETRIEVING A NARRATIVE

Thomas Aquinas dominates two approaches of the highest importance in contemporary religious ethics: natural law and the theory of virtue. Not only Catholic, but even Protestant, Jewish, and nontheistic accounts cite Thomas.[1] At the same time Thomas stands in the center of an Anglo-American resurgence of interest in virtue-theory ethics. Marriagelike homosexual relationships may lead adherents of the two approaches to rival conclusions.[2] Many natural law theorists call such relationships "unnatural,"[3] while recently

---

[1] Daniel Westberg, *Right Practical Reason: Aristotle, Action, and Prudence in Aquinas* (Oxford: Clarendon Press, 1994); David Novak, *Judaism and Natural Law* (New York: Oxford University Press, 1998); Jeffrey Stout, "Truth, Natural Law, and Ethical Theory," in Robert P. George, ed., *Natural Law Theory: Contemporary Essays* (Oxford: Clarendon Press, 1992).

[2] For specifications of "marriagelike," see among others Rowan D. Williams, "The Body's Grace," in Charles Hefling, ed., *Our Selves, Our Souls and Bodies* (Boston: Cowley Press, 1996), pp. 58–68; David Matzko McCarthy, "Homosexuality and the Practices of Marriage," *Modern Theology* 13 (1997): 371–97; Andrew Sullivan, *Virtually Normal: An Argument about Homosexuality* (New York: Alfred A. Knopf, 1995); Margaret Farley, *Personal Commitments* (San Francisco: Harper & Row, 1986); John Boswell, *Same-Sex Unions in Premodern Europe* (New York: Villard Books, 1994).

[3] E.g., David Novak, *Jewish Social Ethics* (New York: Oxford University Press, 1992), pp. 84–117; but other recent natural law thinkers are less sure; cf. Daniel Mark Nelson, *The*

continued on next page

other natural law theorists make much of genetic and cerebral evidence of homosexuality's naturalness.[4] Virtue theorists, on the other hand, may approve lesbian and gay relationships on the basis of such virtues as exclusivity and permanence, love and justice.[5] Thomas Aquinas is appealed to in all cases.

Meanwhile, a group of more theological, mostly European scholars, scarcely read by ethicists, has over the last 40 years and in three languages slowly grown to stress Thomas's commitments to biblical interpretation.[6] Conformably with Thomas's biblical commitments, the theologians have also

Priority of Prudence: Virtue and Natural Law in Thomas Aquinas and the Implications for Modern Ethics (University Park, PA: Pennsylvania State University Press, 1992), pp. 192, 122; and Pamela M. Hall, *Narrative and the Natural Law: An Interpretation of Thomistic Ethics* (Notre Dame, IN: Notre Dame University Press, 1994), pp. 124–5.

[4] Stephen J. Pope, "Scientific and Natural Law Analyses of Homosexuality: A Methodoligical Study," *The Journal of Religious Ethics* 25 (1997): 89–126; Pim Pronk, *Against Nature? Types of Moral Argumentation Regarding Homosexuality*, trans. John Vriend (Grand Rapids, MI: William B. Eerdmans, 1993); Sullivan, *Virtually Normal*.

[5] Stanley Hauerwas, "Virtue, Description, and Friendship [formerly: "Gay Friendship"]: A Thought Experiment in Catholic Moral Theology," *Irish Theological Quarterly* (1998): 170–84; McCarthy, "Homosexuality and the Practices of Marriage"; Williams, "The Body's Grace"; Farley, *Personal Commitments*.

[6] Marie-Dominique Chenu, *La Théologie comme science au XIIIͤ siècle*, 3rd rev. edn (Paris: J. Vrin, 1957); Henri de Lubac, *Exégèse médiévale: Les Quatre sens de l'écriture* (Paris: Aubier, 1964), vol. 3, pt. 2, pp. 272–302; Otto Hermann Pesch, *Thomas von Aquin: Grenze und Größe mittelalterlicher Theologie* (Mainz: Matthias Grünewald, 1988), *Die Theologie der Rechtfertigung bei Martin Luther und Thomas von Aquin: Versuch eines systematisch-theologischen Dialogs*, 2nd edn (Mainz: Matthias Grünewald, 1985), "Exegese des Alten Testamentes bei Thomas," in Pesch, ed., *Das Gesetz: ST I–II.90–105*, in *Die Deutsche Thomas-Ausgabe*, vol. 13 (Graz: Styria, 1977), and "Paul as Professor of Theology: The Image of the Apostle in St Thomas's Theology," *The Thomist* 38 (1977): 584–605; Michel Corbin, *Le Chemin de la théologie chez Thomas d'Aquin* (Paris: Beauchesne, 1974); Marc Aillet, *Lire la bible avec St Thomas: Le Passage de la lettre à la res dans la Somme théologique* (Fribourg: Éditions universitaires, 1993); Eugene F. Rogers, Jr, *Thomas Aquinas and Karl Barth: Sacred Doctrine and the Natural Knowledge of God* (Notre Dame, IN: Notre Dame University Press, 1995), "How the Virtues of the Interpreter Presuppose and Perfect Hermeneutics: The Case of Thomas Aquinas," *The Journal of Religion* 76 (1996): 64–81, "Aquinas and Barth in Convergence on Romans 1?" *Modern Theology* 12 (January 1996): 57–84, "Selections from Thomas Aquinas's *Commentary on Romans* [9–11]," translation of excerpts with an introduction, in Stephen E. Fowl, ed., *The Theological Interpretation of Scripture: Classic and Contemporary Readings* (Oxford: Blackwell, 1997), pp. 320–37; Thomas Domanyi, *Der Römerbriefkommentar des Thomas von Aquin: Ein Beitrag zur Untersuchung seiner Auslegungsmethoden*, Basler und Berner Studien zur historischen und systematischen Theologie, vol. 39 (Bern: Peter Lang, 1979); Stephen Boguslawski, translation of Aquinas's *Commentary on Romans*, in preparation.

worked out Thomas's theory about the relation of nature and grace in a way that links the two much more closely than many natural law ethicists are ready to credit.

Convergence between theologians and ethicists looks especially promising when ethicists begin to use the category of "narrative." Yet the narrative that scholars have had in mind, however useful in Thomas interpretation, derives more from quite recent notions about the narrativity of human lives,[7] than from Thomas's own claim that "it is necessary . . . that the mode of this science be narrative (*narrativus*)," which goes unmentioned.[8] The narrative Thomas speaks of is a biblical one, and the mode of his science is exegetical.

Three observations broaden the interest of ethicists' debates beyond narrower concerns with homosexual couples. First, despite their disagreements, the recent studies make it harder and harder to view Thomas's account of the natural law as a set of rules that provides a moral calculus for demonstrating right and wrong.[9] Second, appeals to natural law arise perhaps most often in cases of sexual and property ethics,[10] the very areas in which virtue-theory and natural-law ethics may come to rival conclusions. And third, the way in which Thomas locates the malice in theft and murder, for example, is qualitatively different from the way in which he locates it in discussions of homosexuality.[11] That oddity is important if one is trying to see why different moral evaluations might apply to same-sex and opposite-sex couples.

More important, issues emerge in the history of interpretation of crucial texts. Until quite recently, scholars have read Thomas's treatises on natural law and the virtues as if they comprised separate books by namesake authors and paid insufficient attention to the real or apparent tension in the source between the two approaches, and to Thomas's attempts to resolve it. Meanwhile, rich resources in Thomas's biblical commentaries are just beginning to be captured for ethical reflection. Both virtue theorists and natural lawyers tend to confine themselves to Thomas's more systematic works, particularly his last, the *Summa Theologiae*, using previous works as support.

---

[7]   Hall, *Narrative and the Natural Law*; Stephen Crites, "The Spatial Dimensions of Narrative Truth-Telling," in Garrett Green, ed., *Scriptural Authority and Narrative Interpretation* (Philadelphia: Fortress, 1987), pp. 97–118.

[8]   *In I Sent.*, prol., 5.

[9]   I am indebted to an anonymous reader for this way of stating the point.

[10]   I owe this observation to a conversation with George Lindbeck.

[11]   I am indebted to an anonymous reader for this way of stating the point. Indeed, Thomas's accounts of lying and of homosexuality may appeal similarly to a nature of language in words and in bodies, an appeal perhaps biblical in origin – but that is an essay for another day.

Yet the *Summa*'s chief warrant for arguments from natural law comes from the Bible, Romans 1:20. Thomas quotes the verse to prove that God can engage human reason to participate in God's eternal law: "The things that are of God cannot indeed be known by us in themselves; but nevertheless in their effects they are manifested to us, according to the famous passage *In Rom.* 1[:20]: 'The invisible things of God are caught sight of [*conspiciuntur*], being understood by the things that are made.'"[12] A parallel discussion appears when Thomas comments on Romans 1:19.[13] Meanwhile, the immediately preceding verse, Romans 1:18, provides Thomas with a springboard for the discussion of the virtues (of which justice is in some ways the head): "The wrath of God is revealed against all injustice."[14] Commenting on Romans leads Thomas to reflect deeply if implicitly on the relation between the two approaches, which have not yet come apart. But Thomas's *Commentary on Romans* is (as far as I know) never mentioned in discussions of the two approaches, because it is only now being translated into English, and treatments of any sort barely exist.[15]

I do not mean to imply that Aquinas offers rival accounts in the biblical commentaries and in the *Summa*, but that students of Thomas ought to attend to the commentaries precisely in order to honor the *Summa* as a theological and scripturally based document, one that takes Scripture as the source of its first principles,[16] and written for students ordinarily instructed in lectures expounding the biblical books.[17] By and large scholars have not so attended.

Romans 1, the very place where Thomas relates the two approaches in

---

[12]   *ST* I-II.93.2 *ad* 2. Thomas also quotes it more famously to prove the parallel claim that God can engage human reason to demonstrate the proposition "God exists," as well as in almost 20 more places in the *Summa*. Cf. I.12.12 *sed contra* (the general case); I.2.2 *sed contra* (the existence of God); and III.1 (the incarnation itself). For more see Eugene F. Rogers, Jr, "The Narrative of Natural Law in Aquinas's Commentary on Romans 1," *Theological Studies* 59 (1998), n. 13.

[13]   For readers following where Thomas is in Paul, I cite by biblical chapter and (anachronistically) verse; for readers following the commentary I append the Marietti paragraph number, thus: *In Rom.* 1:19, ##113–16.

[14]   Cf. *In Rom.* 1:18, ##109–12.

[15]   Rogers, "Selections from Thomas Aquinas's *Commentary on Romans* [9–11]," pp. 320–37, and *Thomas Aquinas and Karl Barth* translate bits of chapters 1 and 9–11. Stephen C. Boguslawski is now preparing a translation of the entire commentary. French and German translations are rare: Abbé Bralé, ed. and trans., *Commentaires de S. Thomas d'Aquin: Sur toutes les épitres de S. Paul* (Paris: Vivès, 1869–74); Helmut Fahsel, ed. and trans., *Des heiligen Thomas von Aquin Kommentar zum Römerbrief* (Freiberg im Briesgau: Herder, 1927).

[16]   I.1.2, 3, 8–10.

[17]   Prol.

rehearsing Paul's narrative, goes on to one of the few places where the Bible mentions what Thomas calls "the vice against nature" and what we might now anachronistically call homosexual acts (v. 1:26).[18] Quite apart from current conflict, therefore, it provides a good test case *textually* on how Thomas relates natural-law and virtue-theory ethics.

In short, natural law, the virtues, and homosexuality all show up in Thomas's *Commentary on Romans*, chapter 1. Rom. 1:18 opens a discussion of justice. Rom. 1:20 provides Thomas's chief warrant for arguments from natural law. Rom. 1:26 applies the virtues and the natural law to "the vice against nature." In ten verses Thomas tests the relation of natural-law and virtue-theory ethics. Their relation is the more complex because it depends also upon Paul as an exemplar and teacher of virtue, and upon Thomas's high regard for the Bible as a source for what counts as natural. Here Thomas deploys the language of natural law as a mode of biblical exegesis and critique, rather than a discipline of secular provenance and goals.

The results prove surprising in two ways.

First, natural law turns out to be a *dependent* or *interdependent* source of information about the good. Thomas ties it deeply to the revelation of the gospel and the life of the virtues. That is, natural law cannot be divorced from a trinitarian context. It does not belong to a natural creation that would make sense to all comers, Christian and non-Christian alike, apart from its deep implication of God's saving purpose. Natural law makes full sense only where the creation attributed to the Father is visible to fallen creatures in the light of the Son and under the tutelage of the Holy Spirit working in the heart. I will show that despite Thomas's better-known insistence that all human beings have an inalienable, rational participation in God's law just in that they have reason, after the Fall from the grace of the Garden (which was never, for Thomas, purely natural), that inalienable participation ceases to work as it ought – it ceases to lead human beings to the good. Under those conditions, Thomas's assimilation of the logic of natural reason to the incarnate Logos of the Son turns out to be no mere decoration but the heart of the matter.

Second, Thomas turns out not only to admit but to require a certain openness in interpretation when nature and Bible stand in tension. The

---

[18] For ways in which the term "homosexuality" is improper to Paul, see Dale B. Martin, "Heterosexism and the Interpretation of Romans 1:18–32," *Biblical Interpretation* 3 (1995): 332–55; for ways in which it is improper to Thomas, see Mark D. Jordan, *The Invention of Sodomy in Christian Theology* (Chicago: University of Chicago Press, 1997), pp. 1–44, 136–58. I use it cautiously here, precisely because I am trying to use Thomas to address a modern problem, one that was not his, but one on which he is often appealed to, and on which he can still offer help.

theologian must have the flexibility to reconcile them because the truth is one,[19] and in order that the faith – and its divisions – not be exposed to ridicule. That is the correlate in hermeneutics of the principle learned in chapter 1, that the community must treat rival interpretations with charity. At the end of my treatment of Thomas, therefore, I will turn to the *De potentia*, where Thomas considers how to proceed when the best accounts of nature seem to conflict with the best interpretations of the Bible.

Thomas *mentions* acts "contrary to nature" in the commentary for the most obvious reason, but one that often goes unstated: because Paul does. Thomas is attempting to follow Paul's reasoning. Thomas bases his *account* of acts contrary to nature in the Romans Commentary (unlike elsewhere?) penultimately on natural law but ultimately on the virtues of justice and gratitude. In the biblical passages that Thomas elsewhere adduces as the *warrants* for arguments about natural law and the virtues, natural law turns out to be no *independent* source of knowledge. In the Romans Commentary, Thomas relates natural law narratively to the virtues, the Bible, and the wise.

I do not mean to imply that the virtues or the natural law lack objective content, in which case they would mean merely what the wise person thinks they mean. On the contrary, they have objective content for correcting the wise. Still, Aquinas is Aristotelian enough to pepper the *Summa* with constant if often nontechnical references to the normative judgments of human beings who are better disposed toward the good than others. In the Romans Commentary, indeed, it is part of the point to show Paul as a "vessel of election," that is, to show how God is exhibiting the gospel grace of Christ through him.[20] The appeal in the Romans Commentary is first of all to Paul as teacher and exemplar, and only then to virtue and nature exemplified and taught.[21] In the *Summa* the appeal to the wise appears mostly in passing, as ubiquitous as in Aristotle's account. So in the consideration of the virtues we find that already under the rubric of the end of a human life Thomas directs attention away from the goods that just anyone might want, toward the goods of the one having an affect well disposed.[22] Similarly, everyone seeks

---

[19]   Except at the beginning of the *Summa Contra Gentiles*. Both the *Summa* (1266–73) and the Romans Commentary (1270–72) date from *after* the *Contra Gentiles* (1259–64), which diachronic scholars of Thomas distinguish from them so sharply that "la projection de la problématique de la Somme contre les Gentils sur . . . la Somme Théologique est radicalment interdite" (Corbin, *Le Chemin*, p. 705).

[20]   *In Rom.*, prol, #11.

[21]   Rogers, *Thomas Aquinas and Karl Barth*, pp. 73–95; Pesch, "Paul as Professor of Theology."

[22]   I-II.1.7 *in fin.*

beatitude, in the sense of satisfying the will, but only some seek beatitude according to that in which beatitude really consists.[23] In considering how prudence learns to find the medium in which the moral virtues consist, Aquinas repeats with Aristotle that prudence finds it "as the wise one will determine."[24] In the consideration of natural law we also find that "Many things are done according to virtue, to which nature does not at first incline, but which human beings find through the inquiry of reason to be useful for living well,"[25] where the useful is judged by the wise.[26] The appeal to those better disposed toward the good also becomes explicit when Thomas refers matters of interpretation to the *maiores in fide*, those greater in faith.[27] None of this means that there is nothing objective to find, but it does mean that appeal to the wise is part and parcel of checking one's perceptions.

Prescinding from debates about the priority or integration of intellect and will,[28] prudence and law,[29] Thomas here follows Paul in telling a story in which ignorance of natural law follows culpably from a lack of justice.[30] In the presence of injustice, it becomes a self-consuming artifact, a nonfunctional, feckless knowledge, a knowledge *manqué*. Thomas's account may therefore show more flexibility than many give it credit for, and be susceptible of different uses by those who have different ideas from his about what justice and gratitude entail. Textual resistance to such a revisionist account will arise not so much from Thomas's view of nature as from his view of Scripture. For it is in the Romans Commentary that Thomas deploys the language of natural law as a biblical, exegetical rather than secular discipline.

That characterization is not in conflict with the *Summa*, even if at first Thomas's remarks on law may sound more political and Aristotelian. The essence of law concerns the common good, and pertains to the public person who has care of the multitude and promulgates the law.[31] The pivot of the argument comes when Thomas, introducing the eternal law, defines God's providence as the prudence of a ruler.[32] The reference to prudence interdefines law and virtue. Thomas makes a deeply Aristotelian move, because

---

[23]   I–II.5.8.

[24]   *Prout sapiens determinabit*, II–II.47.7, s.c.

[25]   I–II.94.3.

[26]   *Sapientiori*, II–II.57.3 *ad 2*.

[27]   II–II.5.4.

[28]   The topic of Westberg, *Right Practical Reason*.

[29]   The topics of Hall, *Narrative and the Natural Law*, and Nelson, *Priority of Prudence*.

[30]   *In Rom*. 1:20b, #124.

[31]   I–II.90.1, 3, 4.

[32]   I–II.93.1.

"prudence" is for Aristotle the chief of the virtues. Even more interesting, the apparently Aristotelian move in fact allows Thomas eventually to introduce his consideration of *biblical* law, since it refers the care of the community to God. And it allows him to make the transition to biblical materials – especially salvation history (the Old Law) and grace (the New Law) – from more Aristotelian material on moral psychology. Virtue describes the internal springs of human action; law – eternal, natural, human, old, and new – describes God's providential activity in moving creatures back to God.[33] The New Law, or grace, overcomes the dichotomy between internal and external springs of human action, since in it God acts from outside on the heart.[34] In what follows, Thomas mops up natural law in one question and six articles, while he revels in biblical law to the extent of some 16 questions and 102 articles. In this context, natural law simply insures that God's providential activity in salvation history and the life of grace does not violate human nature, but is met by God's providential activity in creating and sustaining the human mind.

A Few Disclaimers

This chapter is first of all an exercise in metaethics, and only secondarily in special ethics, because it sets a context in which arguments about sexuality belong among larger themes about nature and grace, redemption and consummation. As such it is of interest also to those who become impatient with narrower treatments of sex. Also for that reason, Thomas's substantive claims get shorter shrift than the interrelations among his warrants.

Furthermore, I am not arguing the discovery of a Thomas who would find homosexual acts, even under marriagelike circumstances, morally good. His period would not allow that. He might even reply to my argument that if the goodness of marriagelike same-sex relationships is one of the conclusions, then there may be something wrong with the premises.

He would lean toward such a reply because for him four lines of argument seamlessly converge that have for some moderns begun to unravel. For him, the vice against nature at once instantiates the vices of injustice and ingratitude, violates natural law, contravenes the word of Scripture, and overturns the judgments of the wise (the *maiores in fide*, those greater in faith), where each point of the analysis deeply implicates the others. Thus virtue and vice are

[33] I-II.49 proemium, 90 proem.
[34] I-II.96.1.

discerned by the wise, according to their interpretation of nature, in a community formed by Scripture. The biblical text is interpreted by virtuous readers. Natural law too, although objective in the mind of God as eternal law, must be applied by the virtuous, who correct themselves by the Scriptures. The requirement that it is the *maiores in fide* who apply traditions of virtue, interpretation, and law is important, because it rules out arguments merely self-interested and not formed by charity or motivated by the good of the believing community. Thomas would resist turning one of those four against the others.

Rather than using one of the four against the other three, a contrary interpretation open to modern disagreements must, if still Thomistic, foresee or find arguable a *counter-convergence*, where once again these things come together: what counts as justice, what counts as natural, what Scripture says, and what those greater in faith discern. Of those, what Scripture says may prove the most difficult to budge. How does Thomas evaluate the interpretation of Scripture in cases of dispute, where the dispute involves what counts as nature and virtue among the faithful, or the opponent alleges error in interpretations from the past?

Thomas allows for and insists upon the presence of errors in his work – even "many" of them. In the very first question of the *Summa*, he proclaims: "The truth of God, as investigated by reason [such as natural law], proceeds among a few, over a long time, and with the admixture of many errors."[35] He insists on the presence of mistakes in what counts as virtue,[36] what counts as natural law,[37] and in the interpretation of Scripture.[38] The virtues, the natural law, and the Scriptures, none of them, singly or together, can eliminate all moral disagreement this side of heaven. To do so would be to elevate human beings to the knowledge that God enjoys. This is one of the strengths of Thomas's system: that *for theological reasons* it must allow for human learning, from the few, and over a long period of time, and with an admixture of error – of which the account offered in these pages may constitute an example.[39] In cases of dispute the proper appeal is to the virtue that regulates a community of differing people, namely justice – a characterization that would seem to follow from Thomas's account of the natural law.[40] For "the human being

---

[35] I.1.1.

[36] The point of *gnome*, I–II.57.6, esp. *ad* 2.

[37] I–II.94.4.

[38] I.46.2; cf. also I.14.13 and 57.3; I–II.112.5; and II–II.1.3 *ad* 3.

[39] Alasdair MacIntyre, *Whose Justice? Which Rationality?* (Notre Dame, IN: Notre Dame University Press, 1988), pp. 361–5.

[40] I owe the point that follows to a briefer remark by an anonymous reader.

has a natural inclination to live in society. And accordingly, those things that regard such an inclination pertain to the natural law, such as that human beings shun ignorance, so that they not offend those with whom they have to live."[41] The call to get to know one's neighbor might sound like an appeal for tolerance and open-mindedness on disputes such as we now encounter on homosexuality.

It might, were it not for Thomas's *ex professo* treatment of sins against nature.[42] There Thomas finds it a sign of human sinfulness and *culpable* ignorance that "among certain people thievery and even vices against nature were not reputed sins" – citing as authority Paul in Romans 1.[43]

Before turning to that passage, we must consider what Thomas says about vices against (*contra*) nature in the *Summa*.[44] This account is firmly embedded in a virtue account, because Thomas considers vices against nature as a species of *luxuria*. In the *Summa*, *luxuria* is the vice of the concupiscible passions opposed to chastity, therefore of sexual pleasures (*voluptas*).[45] It extends secondarily to certain other vices "pertaining to excess," and Thomas quotes the *Glossa* with approval that "*luxuria* is a certain superfluity."[46] Note therefore that although Thomas follows the Vulgate in translating *para phusin* as *contra naturam*, the species of vice under which he places it may indicate a tradition of a subtler understanding of the Greek. *Para phusin* is more strictly "beyond" or "in excess of nature,"[47] which is exactly the extended sense of *luxuria*.[48]

An apparently similar categorization continues among many conservatives to the present day; they find it hard to imagine same-sex relationships that foster self-control, faithfulness, and charity while they build up the community.[49]

The question arises whether same-sex couples need not *ipso facto* exhibit

---

[41]   I-II.94.2.

[42]   I-II.94.6.

[43]   I-II.94.6.

[44]   II-II.154.11–12.

[45]   II-II.53.1, s.c. and corpus.

[46]   II-II.53.1 *ad* 1.

[47]   For the most recent version of this argument, see Martin, "Heterosexism and the Interpretation of Romans 1:18–32."

[48]   Thomas's exegesis of *para phusin* at Rom. 11:24, #910, may also tacitly recognize that sense.

[49]   For this characterization of conservative arguments, see Kathryn Tanner, "Response to Max Stackhouse and Eugene Rogers," in Saul M. Olyan and Martha C. Nussbaum, eds, *Sexual Orientation and Human Rights in American Religious Discourse* (New York: Oxford University Press, 1998), pp. 161–8; here, p. 166.

self-seeking, or at least no more than opposite-sex couples do. I call the categorization "apparently similar," however, because Thomas never considers the case of stable same-sex couples; he only considers the vice against nature. But it is just possible that he feels the tension here, because he shifts his weight on the virtue–nature continuum, something he does not do on any other vice except lying.[50] (Thomas calls lying against nature because he thinks animals cannot lie.) Is there some underlying hermeneutics of bodies, such that in the vice against nature Thomas thinks they lie?[51] In the late 20th century West it is gay and lesbian people who are likelier to use the language of mendacious bodies. They use it of homosexually oriented people trying, against their nature, to go straight: their bodies give them the lie.

Mark Jordan notes that, except for one important phrase, there is little to call attention to the article on the vice against nature.[52] The text runs short, a quarter of the length of the one on fornication. "Nor is there any reason on the surface of the text to think that particular emphasis is being put on the sleeping together of persons of the same sex. The language used to describe it is colorless. Indeed, the very term 'sleeping together' (*concubitus*) is rather prim." Pride, Jordan notes, is gravest, primary, and ruling among the sins.[53]

The important phrase is the one in which Thomas shifts his weight toward nature, anticipating the overarching comparison of God's nature and human nature that we will find also in the Romans Commentary. It is this: "Just as the order of right reason is from the human being, so the order of nature is from God himself."[54] With that Thomas begins his attempt to explain *why* the vice against nature exhibits *luxuria* necessarily, and not just in the same circumstances that opposite-gender sex exhibits it.

Is Thomas departing, in the shift, from virtue analysis to nature analysis? Or is he identifying the two, connecting the virtue of the human being (the order of right reason) to the virtue of God (the providential and thus prudential order of nature)? I think the shift is not, after all, a sign that Thomas has smuggled in a new category. Instead, I think the categories of nature and virtue have either not yet come apart, or Thomas is refusing to let them go separate ways. For natural law is nothing other than our rational participation in God's governance of the world with the prudence of a ruler, so that here too virtue-

---

[50]   Jeffrey Stout noted this exception to me in conversation, which he had learned from Victor Preller.
[51]   I hope to explore this question in a future article.
[52]   II-II.154.12. This whole paragraph follows Jordan, *Invention of Sodomy*, pp. 145–6.
[53]   II-II.162.6–8.
[54]   II-II.154.12.

language predominates, even when nature-language connects it to other strategies for moral reflection.[55]

Thomas continues: "And therefore in sins against nature, in which the very order of nature is violated, injury is made to God himself, the Orderer of nature." Here the vice against nature becomes the greatest of the sins of *luxuria* as *emblematic* of sins against God.

"What is peculiar about this remark," notes Jordan, "is that the same syllogism can be constructed for any sin whatever. Every vice or sin is against nature, hence against God."[56] Because every vice is, as vicious, against nature, the shift would not seem to gain Thomas much ground. And yet rhetorically, it does, at least in the modern period, if not here. For in the modern period homosexuality is argued to be against nature even when it seems (*per impossibile*) to exhibit all virtue. In the 20th century, virtue and nature *have* come apart on this issue, have gone separate ways. For Thomistic analysis – indeed for Christian analysis that uses the languages of virtue and nature – that is a grave problem. It *should* be possible to give complementary (not independent) accounts, one based on virtue and one based on nature, or one internal and one external to the human act, of every vice.

Thomas gives more detail to complementary accounts in another place where he relates nature and virtue, specifically justice, to his account of sins against nature that we would now call homosexual – his *Commentary on Romans*, chapter 1. That account looks quite congenial to modern theologians and ethicists in its broad outlines of how injustice leads to vice. There is more than a germ here of what we would now call, redundantly, "social" justice, and even an opening to the insight of liberation theologians that the practice of injustice undermines one's ability to identify virtue and vice. Here, at least, the analysis of nature *depends* on the analysis of virtue, because injustice is the cause of sins against nature. Indeed, the most liberal modern criminologists might agree, that even the most heinous crimes can stem from prior injustice and abuse – the trick, of course, is agreeing which acts are crimes. Here, the more Thomas's account descends to sexual specifics, the odder it will seem to

---

[55]   The prudence of a ruler defines eternal law, I-II.93.1. For commentary, see John Bowlin, *Contingency and Fortune in Aquinas's Ethics* (New York: Cambridge University Press, 1999).

[56]   Jordan, *Invention of Sodomy*, p. 146, referring to I-II.71.2. Jordan follows up Thomas's use or (he argues) misuse of Augustine in making the vice against nature such an emblem (*Invention of Sodomy*, pp. 147–54). "Sins against nature" also appear as examples in the single question "On Natural Law," I-II.94, where they are "said to be" against nature: *dicuntur esse contra naturam* (3 *ad* 2; cf. 94.6). Note here the combination of terms that we would now distinguish: "vices against nature" combines virtue and nature analysis without a seam.

modern eyes, conservative and liberal alike. Many Christians may want to retrieve his general account of how injustice leads to vice. I am not sure anyone will want to buy his specific application of that account to the vice against nature.

According to the prologue to Aquinas's Pauline epistles, Paul's "whole teaching is the grace of Christ."[57] In the Romans Commentary as a whole the narrative is one of the grace of Christ "in itself,"[58] where "the power of gospel grace is for the salvation of all human beings,"[59] and "all human beings" are divided in good Pauline fashion into Jews and Gentiles.[60] I mention the wider context of the rest of the letter and of Aquinas's commentaries on the other Pauline epistles in order to focus on the episode of the story in which natural law appears as a character (Rom. 1:18ff), and how that story relates to Thomas's treatments of natural law in the *Summa*. Because of the context of the letter, natural law does not show up in the order of creation abstracted from God's plan to elevate it, but in the order of creation as seen precisely in the light of the gospel grace of Christ. The drama of the story consists in the surprising situation in which Paul's narrative locates natural law: here it appears bound and captive. Many read the *Summa* as portraying natural law as strong and able. But the *Summa* refers to a Pauline context narrating natural law's eclipse. What is the story of the eclipse of natural law?

The Character of Natural Law in Aquinas's Commentary on Romans 1

The Romans Commentary, chapter 1, tells among other things how injustice and ingratitude reduced the character of natural law – like nature itself – from strength to weakness and left it in need of mercy. It is, in short, a radically theological story, one that has more in common with the Good Samaritan or the Prodigal Son than with Aristotle's *Metaphysics*. Despite the presence also in the Romans Commentary of elegant distinctions and arguments for so

---

[57]   *In Rom.*, prol., #11.
[58]   "Secundum se," as opposed to the grace of Christ as head of the church (Hebrews) or the grace of Christ as present in the mystical body (the others) – so *In Rom.*, prol., #11.
[59]   "Virtutem evangelicae gratiae esse omnibus hominibus in salutem," *In Rom.* 1:18, #109.
[60]   For more on Aquinas on Jews and Gentiles in the Romans Commentary, see Steven Boguslawski, "Aquinas on Romans 9–11," Yale Ph.D. dissertation, and Rogers, "Selections," pp. 320–37.

metaphysical-sounding a proposition as "God exists," philosophical rubrics do not control there.[61] Admirers and detractors of Aquinas who regard him as making Paul "a religious interpreter of the human situation as such, a Christian student of the philosophy of religion,"[62] will be surprised. Paul is not that in Aquinas's Romans Commentary but a "vessel of election," an apostle.[63] Accordingly, Aquinas announces the topic of the entire epistle as "gratia Christi secundum se," the grace of Christ considered in itself.[64] In the same vein Aquinas characterizes the whole epistle from 1:16b to 12:1 as "show[ing] forth the power of gospel grace."[65] In short: in the Romans Commentary Aquinas reveals that it is the purpose of the natural knowledge of God's will or law, as of the natural knowledge of God's existence, *to show forth the power of the gospel grace of Christ.*

In Aquinas's commentary on Romans 1, natural law does not show the power of the gospel by its straightforward success. There it shows forth the power of the gospel by its failure. Natural law in Romans 1 is a self-consuming artifact.[66] It serves in Romans not to improve behavior, but to increase guilt. Aquinas elsewhere deploys the natural law of the Romans Commentary to explicate two features of the Old Law of the Galatians Commentary, that it "manifests infirmity" and lends the "experience of impotence."[67] Those are

---

[61]   This thesis is the burden of my *Thomas Aquinas and Karl Barth*, pp. 96–180. For support by historians and philosophers, see Jean-François Courtine, "La Métaphysique dans l'horizon scholastique," pt. I in his *Suárez et le système de la métaphysique* (Paris: Presses Universitaires de France, 1990), pp. 10–154; John Inglis, "Philosophical Autonomy and the Historiography of Mediaeval Philosophy," *British Journal for the History of Philosophy* 5 (1997): 21–53; and John Marenbon, "The Theoretical and Practical Autonomy of Philosophy as a Discipline in the Middle Ages," *Acta Philosophica Fennica* 48 (1990): 262–74.

[62]   The phrase, derogatory in context, comes from Karl Barth, *Kurze Erklärung des Römerbriefes* (Munich: Christian Kaiser, 1956); ET: *A Shorter Commentary on Romans*, no trans. (Richmond, VA: John Knox, 1959), p. 24. I discuss and counter Barth's charge in *Thomas Aquinas and Karl Barth,* pp. 73–95.

[63]   Cf. also Pesch, "Paul as Professor of Theology," pp. 584–605.

[64]   *In Rom.,* prol., #11.

[65]   "Virtutem evangelicae gratiae," *In Rom.* 1:16b, #97.

[66]   The term originates with Stanley Fish.

[67]   "First [Paul says this] because the law shows sins. Rom. 3:20: By law came the knowledge of sin. Then because it manifests human infirmity, inasmuch as the human being cannot avoid sin, except by grace, which was not given by law. . . . So the law has yielded to grace, inasmuch as it afforded the recognition of sin and the experience of its own impotence [*experientiam propriae impotentiae*]" (*In Gal.* 3:22, #174). Note that Rom. 3:20 primarily refers to the law of nature, according to *In Rom.* 3:20, #297.

other, less accustomed uses to which the *maiores in fide*, such as Paul, or Aquinas following him as commentator, may put the language of natural law.

According to the Romans Commentary, natural law moves human beings not one step closer to right action – unless it is restored by grace. Only the New Law, which is just the Holy Spirit indwelling the heart, rectifies nature.[68] This will seem a paradox to some Protestants: natural law works not by itself but by grace. Against many understandings of nature that would *oppose* it to supernatural grace, the Christian paradox is that natural law does not, in the concrete world of God's creation, work by nature alone. Even in the Garden the nature of Adam and Eve worked by grace. God might have created them purely natural, but in fact did not.[69]

That distinction is not nearly as subtle as it seems, but lies right on the surface. It is terminological as well as structural. When Thomas uses the word "natura" and its derivatives without a possessive pronoun, he means *graced* nature – nature as it concretely exists in the order that God created for elevation to friendship with God and, after the Fall, mercifully sustains with steadfastness of purpose. "Natura" bare of modifiers and therefore concretely alloyed with grace is far and away the most common usage. When Thomas wants to indicate a pure, ungraced nature, a hypothetical or remainder concept abstracted from the concrete order of God's creation, he modifies it with a possessive pronoun, as in "ex suis naturalibus," "by their *own*, i.e., unaided nature," since God's help is precisely not the human being's own; it is the human being's by grace.[70] Indeed, Latin enjoys two third person possessives, *suus* and *eius*; *suus* comes from the reflexive and means "own," "proper," even "independent." As "independent" indicates, *suus* is almost privative in force. Nature by itself is dependent on God's grace. A human being's own, independent nature is not more powerful but weaker, since God is the source of the power.

Aquinas insists on the distinction straightforwardly in this passage:

> [Paul] says [the nations] "naturally did those things that were of the law," that is, what the law commands, namely with respect to moral precepts, which are under the authority of natural reason. . . .
>
> But a problem arises because he says "naturally."

[68] *In Rom.* 1:16b, #109, interpreted in terms of *ST* II-I.106.1 and 109.3–4.

[69] I.95.1, 100.1.

[70] Perhaps this distinction – as simple as it is crucial – is well known in the literature, but I have never seen it made explicit. Since the relation of nature and grace is a point of controversy both among Catholics and between Catholics and Protestants, the terminological distinction deserves to be thoroughly checked.

> For it seems to furnish a defense for the Pelagians, who taught that human
> beings were able to observe all the precepts of the law by their own nature.
> Thus "naturally" is to be expounded as meaning *by nature reformed by grace*. . . .
> – Or "naturally" can be said to mean the natural law showing them what is
> to be done, . . . which is the light of natural reason, in which is the image of God.
> And even so it is not excluded that grace is necessary for moving the affect [since]
> grace is furthermore required for moving the affect.[71]

So in the Romans Commentary Aquinas does not imagine natural law
operating Protestant-fashion as a rival to grace; he imagines natural law shot
through with grace, if it is to operate at all.[72]

Aquinas's portrayal of natural law as lacking in grace, an awkward and pitiful
figure, hangs on a central turn of Paul's plot: "For the wrath of God is revealed
from heaven upon all impiety and unrighteousness of those human beings
who detained The Truth of God in unrighteousness" (1:18). I have capitalized
"The Truth of God" to emphasize that in Thomas's exposition it acts like a
character in a story. Indeed, Thomas explicitly identifies it as a christological
character, since "by 'the sempiternal truth' [of Rom. 1:20] is understood the
person of the Son, according to I Cor. 1:24, 'Christ is The Truth of God.'"[73]
That in turn raises several questions that Aquinas's commentary attempts to
answer about the character here called "The Truth of God," whom human
beings detained: (1) In what light does the revelation of God's wrath show The
Truth of God? (2) What was the original character of The Truth of God?
(3) Does The Truth of God include natural law? (4) How did human beings
detain it? (5) How does Aquinas portray the character it has become under
detention? (6) How does its detention affect its human captors? The answers
to these questions make natural law look much more theological (even
christological) than its proponents tend to admit, and more difficult to
deracinate for use in secular contexts.

---

[71] "Unde exponendum est *naturaliter*, id est per naturam gratia reformatam," *In Rom.*
2:14, ##215–16. – By Aquinas's tight articular structure, the role of grace in working
nature goes without saying in the *Summa*'s parallel I-II.91.2, misleading commentators
who read the treatise on law as though it stopped short of the New Law, or grace, although
Aquinas insists on the point percussively there, I-II.109.2–4. I-II.109.1, which appears to
talk about natural knowledge abstracted from grace, does so for purposes of an analysis that
explains the *character* of the necessary grace as *gratuitous*. It praises not human freedom but
God's.

[72] For a survey of the nature–grace controversy in the interpretation of Aquinas I regard
Otto Pesch as still unsurpassed, esp. for an ecumenical audience. See Pesch, *Die Theologie
der Rechtfertigung*, pp. 516–26, 606–719.

[73] *In Rom.* 1:20a, #122.

1 In what light does the revelation of God's wrath show The Truth of God?

Aquinas glosses the wrath of God as God's *vindicta*, the providential design by which God vindicates the divine purpose and justifies human beings, culminating in the cross and resurrection, by which God brings good rather than vengeance out of evil. Thus Aquinas leaves room even for Karl Barth's way of putting the matter: that Paul "sees the Gentiles as well as the Jews in the reflected light of that fire of God's wrath which is the fire of [God's] love."[74] If not, Aquinas would already have lost sight of his purpose of only a page earlier to interpret this part of Romans as a treatise on *virtus evangelicae gratiae*.[75] The narrative of the power of gospel grace – rather than some rival narrative of Aristotelian inquiry or existential development – remains the narrative that controls.

2 What was the original character of The Truth of God?

Having asserted the detention of The Truth of God, Aquinas allows it to go for a few paragraphs without saying, as he inserts a set piece on what the effective cognition of God would look like *if* the (non-Christian) Gentiles had had it.[76] The set piece depicts the human character of The Truth of God before injustice and ingratitude took it captive. It is a flashback to how natural law by grace *used to be* and by grace *will become*. Although the passage foreshadows a comeback, it reveals natural law as a has-been. It is not a picture of a character strong and healthy, or a cause in good working order, at this point in the plot.

First Aquinas makes an important distinction. He follows the rule that the only thing human beings in this life can know about God with *scientia* is which things about God they must *believe*.[77] That is, the adherence in this life of the human soul to the first truth is due not to a full possession by a finite intellect of the first principles that would allow it to render a creaturely structure adequate to divine reality. Rather that adherence arises first in the will which, *loving* God, moves the intellect to rely on the first principles enjoyed *not* by itself, but by God and the blessed in heaven.[78] An apophatic strain in Aquinas

[74] Barth, *Shorter Commentary*, p. 26.
[75] *In Rom.* 1:16b, #97.
[76] Anyone who does have effective use of the cognition of God available to nature has it not by nature alone, but by *graced* nature, or nature perfected by faith formed in love (e.g., *ST* II–II.2.2, esp. *ad* 3).
[77] Set out in II–II.9.2
[78] I.1.2–3, 8.

comes to the fore: "It is to be known with *scientia*, [or demonstrated Aristotelian knowledge based on understanding the very forms of things], therefore that one thing about God is entirely *un*known to the human being in this life, namely what God is."[79]

This *scientia* that God is unknown opens a seeming paradox: theology is a science, since it has first principles; but in this life theologians are not yet scientists, since they believe principles seen only by others (God and the blessed in heaven). What human beings know with *scientia*, paradoxically, is that they lack *scientia* about God.

Human beings lack *scientia* about God not only of such a sort that they could mount an Aristotelian deduction of God's existence from a definition known through itself and uncompromised by inference from God's effects.[80] They also lack *scientia* about God of such a sort that they could mount an Aristotelian deduction of the contents of God's will, or eternal law, from definitive principles known through themselves. In short: both the existence of God and the contents of God's will are known to human beings only inferentially from God's effects in the world.[81] Aquinas always marks the gap between God known by immediate access and by inference from effects.[82] In considering the natural knowledge of God's existence, he marks it in the *Summa* by rejecting the ontological way (from definition) and licensing the cosmological ways (from effects).[83] He marks it here in the Romans Commentary more simply

---

[79]   *In* 1:19, #114 *in fin.*; cf. also *ST* I.2.1; 12.13 *ad* 1; 14.1 *ad* 3.

[80]   I.2.1. – The usual translation of *per se nota* as "self-evident" excludes some things that Aquinas means to include; hence the stricter "known through itself" is preferable (Victor Preller, *Divine Science and the Science of God: A Reformulation of Thomas Aquinas* [Princeton, NJ: Princeton University Press, 1967], pp. 81–6).

[81]   In general, *ST* I.12.12 *ad* 2. Applied to the natural knowledge of God's existence, I.2.1. Applied to the natural knowledge of God's law, I–II.93.2 *ad* 1 and 2.

[82]   Between divine science and the science of God, see Preller, *Divine Science*. Between the theology that belongs to sacred doctrine and the theology that belongs to metaphysics, see my *Thomas Aquinas and Karl Barth*. Between technical hermeneutics and the interpreter's infused virtues, see my "Virtues of the Interpreter." Between the conjectural knowledge of merit and the (unavailable) knowledge whether one is in a state of grace, see Eugene F. Rogers, Jr, "Good Works and the Assurance of Salvation in Three Traditions: *Fides Praevisa*, the Practical Syllogism, and Merit," *The Scottish Journal of Theology* 50 (1997): 131–56. For other applications, see David Burrell on "the distinction" in *Knowing the Unknowable God* (Notre Dame, IN: Notre Dame University Press, 1986).

[83]   In an extended sense of "cosmological." Technically, Thomas is rejecting a demonstration *per causam* or *propter quid*, since human minds do not possess the intellectual correlate (a definition) of a cause for God, in favor of a demonstration *per effectum* or *quia*. See Preller, *Divine Science*, pp. 81–91.

by distinguishing God's essence which remains "entirely unknown to a human being in this life" from "the cognition of the human being, which begins from . . . sensible things."[84] He marks it terminologically by restricting the knowledge that human beings have of God on their own account to the very weak word *cognitio*, and denying them any *scientia* in divine things.[85] The discipline of sacred theology is *scientia*, in itself; but the habit that human beings have of it is not *scientia* but faith.

More important for present purposes, Aquinas marks the distinction also for natural law: the distinction falls between eternal law, to which human beings lack direct access "in itself," and natural law, which they learn from the world around them.[86] In confirmation, he then quotes the very passage now under examination in Romans 1: "[T]hose things that are of God cannot indeed be recognized by us in themselves, but they are manifested to us in their effects, according to the famous passage in Rom. 1[:20]: 'The invisible things of God are known from the things that have been made.'"[87] Aquinas then rehearses three ways of natural cognition of God's existence, reminiscent of the Five Ways of the *Summa*[88] – the *via causalitatis*, the *via excellentiae*, and the *via negationis*.[89] Note that none of these ways has anything to do with the way in which natural law is sometimes popularly imagined to be known, namely by introspection, even though Aquinas describes the natural light of reason as "indita," or "placed in" the human being. Aquinas feels no tension between affirming that placement and giving examples of arriving at natural knowledge that all involve reasoning from sense impressions.

This, then, is the original character of The Truth of God available to human beings. It is a knowledge of God's effects known through the senses in the context of grace. Why grace? Because the entire point of the set piece on nature remains "to show forth the power of gospel grace." If The Truth of God available to human beings by natural reason were available to them by reason *without grace*, then Aquinas would have undermined rather than furthered his project, incidentally departing from Paul's plot, which speaks of knowledge only in order to render ignorance culpable: "[Paul] asserts the cognition that they had of God, when he adds 'of those human beings who

---

[84]   *In Rom.* 1:19, #114 *in fin.*
[85]   II-II.9.2. Preller puts it this way: "The word *scire* is never used in connection with cognitions of God through natural reason" (*Divine Science*, p. 32). For discussion see Rogers, *Thomas Aquinas and Karl Barth,* pp. 31–9.
[86]   The phrases are *in seipso* and *in suo effectu*, I-II.93.2.
[87]   I-II.93.2 *ad* 1.
[88]   I.2.3.
[89]   *In Rom.* 1:19, #115.

detained the truth about God,' that is, the true cognition of God, 'in injustice,' as if captive.'"[90] Aquinas follows Paul to speak of the existence of knowledge precisely in order to exhibit its *captivity*. He asserts its existence for the sake of *denying* its effectiveness.

Furthermore, we have already seen that the Romans Commentary glosses "naturaliter" in exactly two ways: either as reformed by grace, or as moved by grace. Ungraced is not an option even for fallen nature. As Otto Hermann Pesch puts it:

> It is easy to overlook: the justification of the sinner is no "new" dispensation of God's, but the carrying out of God's creatorly will over against the rebellious human creature. The dimensions of nature that remain *un*disturbed are therefore to be conceived of as the effectiveness in advance [*Vorauswirksamkeit*] of the grace that saves.[91]

Readers of the commentary have little excuse, therefore, to suppose that the knowledge here described actually functions as knowledge ought. It is a self-consuming artifact in the Romans Commentary that Aquinas may *abstract* from the context of grace for temporary purposes of analysis.

3 Does The Truth of God include natural law?

In this section I answer three objections.

1   Someone might object that understanding natural law as an alias of The Truth of God appears to remove Aquinas from the discussion he does best: talk of creation, as Josef Pieper famously put it. It is true that in the entire Pauline epistles Aquinas's commentaries make less of creation as an

---

[90]   *In Rom.* 1:18, #112.

[91]   Pesch, *Die Theologie der Rechtfertigung*, p. 526. Grace is not constitutive of nature, any more than life is constitutive of a human body; but life is both a good *of* the body and a gift *to* the body, the loss of which could not be restored by the body itself. As Pesch puts it: "Original righteousness is a good *of* nature, in that it neither altered nor added to its constituents; it is a 'supernatural,' 'gracious' *gift* to nature, because it cannot be made available by nature's own power" (*Die Theologie der Rechtfertigung*, p. 489). For the first clause Pesch cites *CG* IV, ch. 52; *In Rom.* 5:12, #416; *De malo* q. 4.2 *ad* 1; and *ST* I-II.85.1. For the second clause he cites *ST* I.95.1, corpus; q. 100.1, corpus; *De malo* q. 4.1, corpus, *ca. med.*; q. 4.4 *ad* 1; q. 4.8, corpus; q. 5.1, corpus; and *CG* IV, ch. 52. For discussion see also Rogers, "Aquinas and Barth in Convergence on Romans 1?", esp. pp. 62–4, 70–1. For an interpretation of the apparent differences between the *Summa* and the *Contra Gentiles* on whether the human end is twofold or unitary, see Corbin, *Le Chemin*, pp. 697–700.

explicit *subject*, since their stated topic is "the grace of Christ,"[92] and that that is true specifically too for the Romans Commentary, in considering the power and necessity of grace for the salvation of all human beings.[93] So a superficial answer would be that the epistles simply focus more on redemption, "the grace that saves," than many of Aquinas's other works, and to concede that they offer a limited, if under-noted, perspective on his work as a whole. But a deeper answer would be that God's redeeming work in the Romans Commentary shows above all precisely God's *commitment* to creation and the divine plan to elevate it. In the Romans Commentary God loves creation by restoring it, vindicating rather than overturning the divine promise. That is so to the extent that even God's *wrath* serves the end of doing *justice* to the creature, a justice that, so far from destroying creation, perfects and elevates it.[94] It is God's *creatorly* will that God carries out.

2   Someone might object that the object here is to undermine appeals to natural law, and such an undermining, whether desirable or not, cannot be in accord with Thomas Aquinas. On the contrary, the language of natural law is one that the wise (as Aristotle would put it) or the *maiores in fide* (as Aquinas would put it) may always resort to.[95] For nothing here disputes Aquinas's claim that any human act against right reason is also objectively against the law of the nature of the human being, known particularly by God and in abbreviated form by participant human reason. It is hard to imagine cases in which the virtuous judgments of the wise would not be stable in the language of natural law. But it is easy to imagine cases in which the virtuous judgments of the wise would not be effective or persuasive in the language of natural law. Aquinas knows of such a case, and he rehearses its surprising story in following Paul in Romans 1.[96] Aquinas might also use the language of natural law to explicate the loss of virtue, but he does not, because Paul tells the story differently, as one in which the wrath of God is revealed in virtue language, "against injustice," and the language of natural law has been gagged (*ligatur*).

3   Or someone might object that since Aquinas's examples all concern natural cognition of God's existence, natural law is not in question in the

---

92   *In Rom.*, Prol., #11.
93   *In Rom.* 1:18, #109.
94   *In Rom.* 1:18, ##109–12.
95   I owe this way of putting the matter to personal correspondence with John Bowlin.
96   I owe this paragraph to a conversation with John Bowlin. See Bowlin, *Contingency and Fortune in Aquinas's Ethics*, ch.3.

Romans Commentary after all. Is natural law an alias of The Truth of God, or a different character altogether? Surrounding context indicates that God's existence does not exhaust what Aquinas has in mind under natural cognition of God. Human participation in God's will, or God's eternal law, by rational observation of human nature, also counts as a natural cognition of God. The Romans Commentary does not distinguish but assimilates speculative and practical reasoning. The usual distinction, relative and penultimate in any case, does not appear, and Aquinas follows Paul to move back and forth between them without remark.[97]

Objections notwithstanding, natural law is an alias of The Truth of God. According to Aquinas, Paul considers the natural knowledge of God not for some speculative reason but a practical one: "because certain philosophers were saying that the penalties of sinners did not come from God."[98] The celebrated "fool" of the Psalms, "who says in his heart, 'There is no God,'" is not primarily one who speculates, but one who supposes he or she can get away with some injustice because God is not watching – because it is as if "there is no God" to watch. After the passage Aquinas returns, with Paul, to moral matters – the list of vices at Romans 1:26 – and feels no need for new argument. The ignorance in question has to do no less with the knowledge of God's design than with the knowledge of God's existence – or no less with natural law than with natural theology. With respect to natural law too it is *ignorance* that follows from *injustice*. Otherwise the ignorance is not culpable.

4 What happened to natural law?

The Gentiles "detained the truth about God in unrighteousness" in two ways: first in impiety, or sin committed against God – ingratitude, primarily, indicated in the refusal to pay God proper cult; and second, in injustice proper, or sin against other human beings.[99] The result of that injustice is that the Gentiles held their knowledge captive, so that it could not form their souls as Aristotelian cognition should. This is the heart of Aquinas's teaching about natural human knowledge of God, whether about God's existence or God's

---

[97]   Aquinas at once distinguishes and compares the two numerous times: "the natural ends of a human life . . . dispose themselves in things to be done as principles naturally known in speculative matters," II-II.56.1. Cf. *ST* I-II.57.2; *ST* II-II.47.6.

[98]   *In Rom.* 1:18, #110.

[99]   *In Rom.* 1:18, #111.

will. It does not work, except by grace. It proves feckless, except by the Spirit. Human beings have culpably held it in captivity by their lack of justice. Aquinas cannot but constrain it to prove his Pauline thesis: "that the power of gospel grace was necessary for the salvation of the Gentiles, since the wisdom in which they had been confiding was not able to save them."[100]

It is detained or held captive in a precise sense: it *fails* to do what Aquinas says true knowledge of God is supposed to do – to lead human beings toward the good: "For the true cognition of God, insofar as it is in itself, leads human beings to the good. But it is bound, as if held in captivity, by the affect of injustice, by which, as Ps. 11[12]:1 has it, 'truths are diminished by the children of human beings.'"[101]

In Aquinas's mouth these Pauline moves abbreviate a whole moral psychology. In the *Summa*, one needs the intellectual virtue of prudence – skipping a number of steps – to reach the right conclusions from sense impressions, and prudence in turn is formed in Aquinas's Christian system by justice and finally the grace of charity.[102] Here Aquinas transposes that principle into Pauline language. Recall Aquinas's insistence that it takes grace to move the human affect: the affect in need of grace is here identified as that of injustice. Virtue is a necessary concomitant of effective cognition, and injustice breeds culpable ignorance.[103]

First Aquinas insists explicitly on the matter of culpable ignorance. "[W]hen one's ignorance is caused by fault, one cannot by ignorance excuse subsequent fault."[104] Injustice leads to culpable ignorance, which leads to more, still culpable, injustice.

Then Aquinas confirms that the ignorance in question is an ineffective knowledge, or one of which human beings no longer have the use: "Those having cognition of God no longer used it for good."[105] And that for two

---

[100]   *In Rom.* 1:18, #109.

[101]   *In Rom.* 1:18, #112.

[102]   This generalization, though sweeping, should be uncontroversial. Skill about things to be made does not need virtue, but use does: "In order that one may make good use of art, one needs a good will, which is perfected by moral virtue" (I-II.57.3 *ad* 2). On the application to prudence, see the next article (I-II.57.4). For the argument that the interpretation of Scripture constitutes a use of skill in need of charity, see Rogers, "The Virtues of an Interpreter." For a more complete account, see Nelson, *Priority of Prudence*, chs. 2 and 3, "The Context for Prudence" and "The Priority of Prudence," pp. 27–104.

[103]   I do not say "virtue is a *precondition* of effective cognition of God," which would fly in the face of Aquinas's doctrine of grace.

[104]   *In Rom.* 1:20b, #124.

[105]   *In Rom.* 1:21, #127.

reasons: they "subtracted from God's power (*virtus*) and knowledge," and they refused to give thanks for it, ascribing it to themselves:

> For they recognized God in two ways. In one way as the super-eminent of all, and so they owed God the glory and honor that is owed to the most excellent. They are therefore called inexcusable . . . either because they did not pay God the due cult, or because they imposed an end to God's power (*virtus*) and knowledge (*scientia*), subtracting somewhat from God's power and knowledge.
>
> Second, they recognized God as the cause of all good things. Therefore thanksgiving was owing to God in all things, which they were not, however, intending; but rather they were ascribing their good things to their own ingenuity and virtue.[106]

These then are the original sins in Aquinas's reading of the Romans narrative, the sins of subtraction and insult. In failing to pay to God the due cult, the Gentiles landed in idolatry. In imposing an end to God's power and knowledge they imagined that God would either fail to see their injustice, or prove unable to punish it.[107] In ascribing their good to themselves they showed ingratitude, or, as a later, Lutheran-sounding passage has it, a lack of fiducial faith.[108] From those original sins comes ignorance: "Next [Paul] asserts the subsequent ignorance, saying 'and [their heart] was darkened'; that is, because it was darkened, 'their heart' was made 'foolish,' that is, deprived of the light of wisdom by which the human being recognizes God truly."[109]

The pattern is complete. Impiety leads more or less automatically to idolatry: the Gentiles became mistaken about who God was.[110] Injustice and ingratitude, furthermore, have now led the Gentiles to culpable failure to use the light of wisdom by which a human being "truly" recognizes God, that is, has the *vera Dei cognitio* that "leads human beings to the good." Since the due knowledge of God is of God's eternal plan or law for their good, in which human participation is natural law, we may sum up: *They lacked the effectiveness of natural law.*

Aquinas himself puts it more strongly than that in the *reportatio*, *De duobus*

---

[106]   *In Rom.* 1:21, #127.

[107]   *In Rom.* 1:18, ##111–12.

[108]   "They became empty 'in their own thoughts' insofar as they had *fiduciam* in themselves, and not in God, ascribing their good things to themselves and not to God" (*In Rom.* 1:21, #129).

[109]   "Vere Deum cognoscit," *In Rom.* 1:21, #130.

[110]   *In Rom.* 1:23, ##132–6.

praeceptis charitatis: "The law of nature had [already] been destroyed: *Lex naturae . . . destructa erat.*"[111]

What happened to natural law? It was held captive – or, Aquinas is not afraid to say – it had been destroyed. Why do ethicists and moral theologians make so many appeals to it, if it has been destroyed and is resurrected only in the presence of saving grace? Why not rather appeal to the *New* Law, the Holy Spirit working in the heart, which alone restores it?

5 How does Aquinas portray the character that natural law has become under detention?

Part of the answer has to do with Aquinas's description of captive natural law. Aquinas exploits metaphors of subtraction in two directions. On the one hand, natural cognition has had its effectiveness taken away, so that it counts as ignorance. On the other hand, by grace it used to be effective knowledge, and by grace it can become effective again.

To understand that better, consider a parallel case. The Romans Commentary makes the same move also with a different form of cognition, that of unformed *faith*. Unformed faith is ineffective, but it continues to be called "faith." Why? Because *should God revive it*, it is the "identical" habit revived, and not another one.[112] The two versions of faith do enjoy continuity. Only they enjoy it in virtue not of the human creature, but of God's action.

Unjust knowledge is like unformed faith: a gift of God, it means that God, in withdrawing grace in punishment for sin, need not at the same time withdraw the assent of the understanding. The sinner continues to enjoy it by God's mercy. Unjust knowing does not mean that God first gave a feckless knowledge to the helpless creature and then the justice to form it as an afterthought. Unjust knowledge is a matter of a *decline* from the original justice of nature granted it by grace, not an *ascent* by unaided nature to justice before

---

[111] The context is the more familiar decline narrative of Genesis, which Aquinas refers to Romans 7:23f: "But even though God had given the human being this law, namely of nature, nevertheless the devil overseeded the human being with another law, namely that of concupiscence . . . and this is what the Apostle says in Rom. 7:23: 'I see another law in my members, opposing the law of my mind.' . . . Since therefore the law of nature had been destroyed by the law of concupiscence, it was necessary that human beings be redirected [by grace] to the works of virtue, and drawn away again from their vices"(*De duobus praeceptis charitatis*, prologue). I owe the reference to Russell Hittinger.

[112] "Idem numero," *In Rom.* 1:17, #107.

God.[113] Thus natural knowledge is cognition *manqué,* which Aquinas continues to call cognition by a sort of courtesy, in virtue of what it has been and
might be, rather than in virtue of what it has penultimately and temporarily
become at this point in the story. God's courtesy, as Julian of Norwich would
teach, is itself grace. Such "cognition," so called by courtesy, may be
assimilated into faith. For faith involves a *taking up,* or christological assumption, of nature into grace, of the light of reason into the light of the Spirit, as
the Word assumes flesh. Unlike his modern successors in natural law theory,
therefore, Aquinas appropriates natural law (as we have already seen) to the
second person of the Trinity.[114] *That* is part of the reason why Thomas seems,
in the *Summa,* to retain a higher opinion of natural law than the narrative of
the Romans Commentary recommends. The courtesy, in the Romans
Commentary as in the *Summa,* does not last long.

6 How does the detention of natural law affect its human captors?

For the narrative goes on to depict an effect not of the good that natural
knowledge might do, but of the evil that corresponds to culpable ignorance.
    I quote first of all from the Vulgate as Aquinas knows it:

> [20]Therefore they are without excuse.
> [21]Since, although they knew God, they did not so glorify God or offer thanks,
> but emptied themselves in their own thoughts, and their foolish heart was
> darkened.
> [22]For calling themselves wise, they were made stupid.
> [23]And they exchanged the glory of the incorruptible God for a likeness of the
> image of the corruptible human being and of birds and of beasts and of serpents.

Aquinas makes certain sins characteristic of what we may call *cognitio detenta*
by arguments *ex convenientia.* He finds it appropriate that the Gentiles can no
longer rely on their God-given nature when God punishes them for their
idolatry with corresponding sins: "Then when [Paul] says 'For that reason God
gave them up,' he asserts a *penalty* corresponding to such faults."[115] The fault
(the instance of culpable ignorance) is natural theology; the penalty, sins
against nature.[116] Given later usage, it may come as a surprise that *theologia*

---

[113]   That paraphrases Pesch's corresponding analysis of unformed *faith* (*Die Theologie der
Rechtfertigung,* pp. 735–7).
[114]   *ST* I–II.93.1 *ad* 2; *In Rom.* 1:20a, #122, read with 1:19, #115.
[115]   *In Rom.* 1:24, #137, my emphasis.
[116]   *In Rom.* 1:25, #142.

naturalis is a term of disapprobation also for Aquinas, as it was for Augustine and would be for Barth. It denoted a sort of Gentile theology, one of three, "which the philosophers practiced in the world."[117] Both natural theology and sins against nature exhibit culpable ignorance: the first fails to give God the due gratitude of worship, while the second fails to give God the due service of justice. For Aquinas describes the sin of impiety, accounted for in terms of virtue and the lack thereof, now for the first time in terms of nature, in order to render Paul's move: "The fault of impiety having been set forth, according to which [the Gentiles] sinned against the divine nature, [Paul] sets forth the penalty, by which namely they were reduced to this, that they should sin against their own nature."[118] This is formally an argument *ex convenientia* or from fittingness.[119] I say "formally" because Aquinas has not yet come to what a sin against human nature might consist in. It is here simply a matter of coordinating "nature" and "nature." And that to be sure is just what an argument *ex convenientia* consists in, the fitting coordination of concepts.

So nature here does not formally serve the purpose of assigning praise and blame. That belongs, analytically, to the virtues. Rather it serves an explanatory function: it serves to *connect* views about God to views about human beings, or cosmology to ethics.[120]

Note, too, that the appeal to "nature" language serves primarily a theological purpose. It serves first of all to mark a correspondence between God and creatures, and only second to explain how a lack of creaturely virtue does the creature harm, or counts as vice. It is an odd correspondence for Aquinas, since he ordinarily issues sharp disclaimers – as he does in the case of human ignorance of God's essence – about how God and creatures cannot be in the same class, especially since "nature" is a specification of "the essence of a thing considered as the source of its operation."[121] On Aquinas's own terms, this use of "nature"

---

[117]   *In Rom.* 1:20a, #122. For more, see Rogers, *Thomas Aquinas and Karl Barth*, pp. 154–6.

[118]   *In Rom.* 1:25, #142.

[119] For an interpretation of some uses of the technical phrase *ex convenientia*, see Rogers, "The Virtues of an Interpreter."

[120]   So, a Catholic anthropologist argues, concepts of nature always function. See Mary Douglas, "Institutions Are Founded on Analogy," ch. 4 in, *How Institutions Think* (Syracuse, NY: Syracuse University, 1986), pp. 45–54.

[121]   Preller's summary (*Divine Science*, p. 123) of *De ente et essentia*. For the usual disclaimer, consider this example: "God is not like material things, either according to natural genus or according to logical genus, for God is not in *any* general class. . . . Thus, through the similitudes of material things something affirmative may be known of [immaterial] angels

continued on next page

must be highly analogous, or, to put it oxymoronically, an appropriate equivocation.[122] We may state the ground of the analogy thus: "nature" explains how *God* operates creatures as their provident ruler, in the way most proper or essential to them. Aquinas reads Is. 26:12 as a prooftext for that analogous way of talking: "You have worked all our works in us, Lord."[123]

In short: in the Romans Commentary, Aquinas follows Paul to make knowledge depend upon justice. Under conditions of injustice, human knowledge fails so badly that Aquinas calls it ignorance. That may come as a surprising conclusion, not, indeed, as a reading of Paul, but as a reading of Aquinas. For it shows that Thomas Aquinas has ample structural room for some of the claims of liberation theologians, namely that injustice can hinder right knowledge of God.[124] The question then becomes: what does justice require? Our time may come to quite different conclusions from Aquinas, and different interpretations of Paul.

The Chief Role and Limits of Natural Law

The Romans Commentary, with its emphasis on injustice leading to subsequent ignorance lends support to Daniel Nelson's thesis:

> The natural-law vocabulary is not insignificant, but it does not [in the *Summa* primarily] play the role of guiding conduct, of determining right and wrong, or of providing the kind of foundational moral imperatives from which one can deduce specific judgments.
>
> What role then does it play? . . . Thomas is responding generally to an intellectual concern with causality. In this instance in particular, Thomas is concerned to explain what "moves" or "causes" the virtues and our practical deliberation: Prudence moves the virtues, and the natural knowledge of first principles through synderesis moves prudence.[125]

according to a common [logical] *ratio*, even if not by virtue of a specific [material] *ratio*: but in no way is that possible with God [*de Deo non nullo*]" (*ST* I.88.2 *ad* 4, in Preller, *Divine Science*, p. 91).

[122] Preller's phrase, *Divine Science*, p. 243.

[123] In the *sed contra* for *ST* I.8.1.

[124] If true, the claim would also count as additional evidence for Nelson's contention that prudence (which is oriented to justice) does have some priority, even to the construal of natural law (the title thesis of *The Priority of Prudence*; see esp. chs 3–4). My argument rests not, however, on the grounds of Aquinas's moral psychology, but on the grounds of Aquinas's commitment to Paul and the Bible.

[125] Nelson, *Priority of Prudence*, pp. 99–100, citing II-II.47.6.

The claim that Thomas deploys the language of natural law for purposes other than controlling widespread moral disagreement in a secular society gains additional weight in John Bowlin's study, *Contingency and Fortune in Aquinas's Ethics*, in which the main thesis is that Thomas deploys the language of natural law to answer a Stoic question. The claim that the life of the virtues leads to human flourishing is subject to a devastating critique, if one considers certain slings of fortune; death and loss come even to the virtuous, rendering their goodness fragile, perhaps too fragile for stable happiness. Is virtue productive enough of flourishing for beatitude to survive misfortune? Thomas uses natural law to describe fortune's parameters. God's providence in nature establishes contingency within limits so that it does not go all the way down. There is no wildly destructive *fortuna* as a force outside God's control. Within wide limits, contingency can even be productive of virtue, and the virtuous can flourish after all.[126]

Nelson's related thesis makes sense because, in the order of knowing, the natural moral law, like the natural physical law, is discovered by reasoning from sense impressions, which require the intellectual and moral and theological virtues for interpretation. That goes no less for the *Summa* as (we have seen) for the Romans Commentary.

1   Thomas is Aristotelian enough to suppose that human beings come to their knowledge of natural law by the same means through which they come to knowledge of anything else: through the evidence of their senses. The knowledge of God's will, or the eternal law, in which human beings participate by reason, or natural law, is no more an exception to the Aristotelian axiom that nothing is in the mind that is not first in the senses, than the natural knowledge of God's existence is.[127]

We can draw these conclusions, which go without saying in the section on natural law, from several more programmatic passages. In one, Thomas asks whether we human beings are able to recognize things about God (*cognoscere Deum*) in this life by natural reason (*per rationem naturalem*):

> [O]ur natural cognition takes its beginning from sense: whence however our natural cognition can extend itself only so far as it can be led by the hand by sensible things.[128]

---

126   Bowlin, *Contingency and Fortune in Aquinas's Ethics*, esp. chapter 3.
127   I.88.3.
128   I.12.12.

That generalization goes also for human self-knowledge. Human beings do not enjoy special access to anything created by its essence – that Thomas reserves to God. Human beings specifically do not even enjoy special access to their own essence[129] – although God grants it to the angels. Rather human beings enjoy that access to the law God's prudence has established for them, that they also enjoy for any other material thing – say their access to the law God's prudence has established for rocks. Another way of putting it is to say that for Thomas human beings' access to themselves is public, not private, subject to community interpretation, correction, and dispute.

Thus the intellect knows itself by reflection on its *acts*, not immediately but indirectly.[130] It knows itself, that is, by reflection upon instances of *completed* intellectual activity. Socrates, in Thomas's example, perceives that he has a soul because he understands something, not as introspection but as completed act. That is, he understands himself not immediately, but *through his effects*. Unlike modern hermeneuticians, Thomas takes understanding for granted in the strict sense: he starts there. The act of understanding is, like any act, the completion of a potentiality or process, an effect. Moral acts, too, are those completed events we ordinarily talk about, publicly observable, to which we *supply* intentions in order to render them intelligible:[131] *in-tentiones* are "reachings-into."[132] Intentions, too, are inferences from their effects.[133]

That is what Thomas means when he says that the intellectual soul knows itself not by its essence, but by its act, that is, its effects. "But since it is connatural to our intellect in this state of the present life that it consider material and sensible things . . . it follows that it so understands itself as it is made actual [*fiat actu*] by the species abstracted from sensible things."[134]

Here I take up again the apparent paradox noted above, that God places natural knowledge in the human being – it is *indita* – but all the *viae* given in the Romans Commentary require not introspection, but deduction from sense impressions. That placement describes the divine source or cause but

---

[129]   I.87.1.

[130]   I.88.

[131]   "Vis cognoscitiva non cognoscit aliquid actu, nisi adsit intentio" (*CG* I.55).

[132]   "Intentio, sicut ipsum nomen sonat, significat in aliquid tendere" (I-II.12.1).

[133]   As in sensory perception an *intentio* is the impression or similitude received by the mind, so too in moral perception an *intentio* is an impression or similitude received, inferentially and corrigibly, by the mind.

[134]   I.87.1 *in med.*

does not change the creaturely *character* of human reason (*ratio*) as such, which is to move discursively, or stepwise over time, from one proposition to another by composing and dividing, given the evidence of sense impressions.[135] Another way of putting it is to say that the placement in human beings of the light of natural reason is by no means the *re*placement of the mode of knowing appropriate to material creatures by the mode of knowing appropriate to God, which Thomas calls intuition.[136] The introspection sometimes imagined in cases of natural law confuses human discursiveness with divine intuition, or, at best, that of angels.[137] Knowledge by nondiscursive introspection is precisely the mode of knowledge that "rational participation" *denies* us – both because it is rational, and because it is participation.

We cannot *see* the eternal law in which the law of our nature is a rational participation, or know the law of our nature with *scientia*, until we *see ourselves in God*, a prospect Thomas reserves for the next life. Until then we can observe it only *in effectu*.

2   Crucial to the learning grounded in sense impressions is what the mind makes of them; the proper functioning of the mind, however, depends on developing the right mental habits, or the intellectual virtues. But the intellectual virtues, the chief of which is prudence, depend in turn for their right use on moral virtues,[138] specifically justice and charity.[139] Any acquisition of additional knowledge requires such a use of previous knowledge so that even the composition of a passage of prose or the deduction of a syllogism require moral virtue.[140] Therefore it is the rule for Thomas that *human beings cannot expect to come to correct conclusions on moral matters under conditions of injustice.* In this, too, Thomas offers surprising support to the more recent insights of liberation theologians, and shows the resources for a Thomistic account of prejudice – one that would seem to require a hermeneutic of charity.[141]

---

[135]   *In Rom.* 1:19, #114; I.85.5.
[136]   I.14.7.
[137]   Preller, *Divine Science*, pp. 69–80; Rogers, *Thomas Aquinas and Karl Barth*, pp. 209–10.
[138]   I-II.57.4; Nelson, *Priority of Prudence*, pp. 95–6; Rogers, "The Virtues of an Interpreter," pp. 75–80, and *Thomas Aquinas and Karl Barth*, pp. 166–80.
[139]   I-II.57.2.
[140]   I-II.57.3 *ad* 3.
[141]   Not as anachronistic as it may sound. One can also construct a critique of prejudice from the Fathers; see Frans Jozef van Beeck, "Fantasy, the Capital Sins, the Enneagram, and Self-Acceptance: An Essay in Ascetical Theology," *Pro Ecclesia* 3 (1994): 179–96.

Objection

A qualification is in order. Part of the required moral virtue – part of justice and charity – is honoring God's use of others, so that it is intellectually reckless and morally wicked to write off truth from the mind of any imperfect creature, or deny God the use of any mouth to teach, whether that of Aristotle or Baalam's ass. That is the point of several apparently contrary texts from the *Summa*. Thus sinners may teach ethics and unbelievers theology: only the wisdom that comes from study is required for teaching sacred doctrine, and not the wisdom of the Holy Spirit.[142]

For similar reasons of God's freedom, the tractate on grace does not limit the recognition of truth to the justified.[143] It teaches the necessity of grace for doing good, loving God, fulfilling the law, meriting everlasting life, growth in grace[144] – but not for cognition of truth generally.[145] Does natural cognition of truth provide an exception to the view defended here?

The contribution of the Romans Commentary to the interpretation of that well-known feature of Thomas is to put it in a different light – the light of grace on the way to glory. Natural knowledge insists upon the persistence of God's mercy, not the pride of human power. Read in conformity with the Romans narrative, it proceeds from God down, not from human beings up; it reflects the light of God's consistent purpose to consummate human creatures, rather than the light of some independently persisting creation. The constancy of God's purpose is a sign of hope; the persistence of a creature in God-abandonment would be a monstrosity. The Romans Commentary rehearses the story of how God has *not* left the Gentiles godforsaken after all. It rehearses rather the story of nature's surprising *un*godforsakenness – or of grace. Pesch's insight bears repeating, because the Romans Commentary tells it as a story: the grace of redemption is not a new dispensation of God, but the carrying out of God's creatorly will to consummate the human creature in the face of its rebellion, so that what remains undisturbed in human nature is nothing but the effectiveness in advance of the grace that saves.

The perspective of narrated grace makes cognition of truth apart from

---

[142]   I.1.6. Thus, too, "as long as the geometrician demonstrates the truth, it does not matter . . . whether she is joyful or angry" (I-II.57.3). But any *use* of the knowledge already requires "a virtue that perfects the will, such as charity or justice, [which] confers the right use of such speculative habits" (*ad* 2).

[143]   I-II.109.1.

[144]   I-II.109.2–10.

[145]   I-II.109.1.

saving grace strictly an exception that proves the rule. It is an exception in that it is the only human accomplishment of the question on the necessity of grace that appears to qualify that necessity. It proves the rule in that it exposes grace's necessity even in grace's absence. It proves that human nature is not such as to extort saving grace from God as due. Thus grace is necessary as *grace*, that is, as gratuitous, rather than as a demand of human nature itself. It proves, too, that human cognition of truth remains under the command of God's providential rule, whether that rule should crown it with sanctifying grace or not: thus the human nature moves to its act "according to the plan of God's providence." So human cognition of truth does not *escape* God's rule, any more than it extorts God's gift.

As neither extorting God's gift, nor escaping God's rule, the human cognition of truth turns out to serve not human freedom over against God, but the freedom of God over against the human being. God remains *free* to rule, and *free* to save. God remains free not to take "no" for an answer. God remains free to be *for* human beings. God remains free to *consummate* human beings. God remains free to be for human beings by involving and engaging them in their consummation, their rebellion notwithstanding. God remains free to complete what God began, to be true to God's purpose, to keep faith with God's promise. God remains free to vindicate and justify the plan and with it the rebellious creature. God remains free, even in a question on the necessity of grace, to act as the God of the Romans Commentary: as the promising God, the vindicating God, the justifying God, the faithful God, the true God. The plan God promises, persists in, vindicates, justifies, keeps faith with and remains true to is friendship with human beings – human beings who image God's *justice* and *charity*, and so *become* friends to God as God is a friend to them. God's preservation of unjust human knowing is precisely God's refusal to withdraw every benefit of original justice, so that the separation of human knowing from justice and gratitude, as the Romans Commentary narrates it, can only be exceptional, temporary, and ordered to their restoration.

Therefore it *remains* the rule for Thomas that human beings cannot expect to come to correct conclusions on moral matters under conditions of injustice – even in the breach.

Only the second person's assumption of flesh in the incarnation – only God's own, complete humanity – can restore the knowledge lost as the Holy Spirit writes the New Law upon the heart. Aquinas alludes to that restoration when he says that the Gentiles were "lacking in the third sign, that is, in the Holy Spirit"[146] – which is just a trinitarian way of pointing out natural law's

---

[146] *In Rom.* 1:20a, #122.

ineffectiveness. The intervention of God's saving humanity, too, is variously appropriate, or *conveniens*. First, Aquinas appropriates natural law to the second person of the Trinity.[147] More important, since the root problem lies in the will, or heart, which Aquinas has here called the *affectum*, so, too, must the solution be there.

In the decline narrative of the Romans Commentary Aquinas tells a story in which God allowed the causation of natural law, or God's providential movement of the Gentile heart, to fail. God's providential rule could afford the failure for reasons explained only in the story of Christ.[148] It failed because the Gentiles had imposed the obstacles of injustice and ingratitude, which had the effect for them of "subtracting somewhat from God's power and knowledge." In the *Summa*, and in the frame narrative of the Romans Commentary, the obstacle is removed and the causation of natural law restored by the intervention (*auxilium*) of operative grace. The *Summa* merely adds that God governs the world with the prudence of a ruler.[149] The deliverances of God's prudence in singular cases make up the eternal law, in which, since God's knowledge is causative,[150] natural law is an ontic as well as psychological participation, or in the realm of cases, an abridgment.[151] Both the imposition and the removal of obstacles take place in the will, which, in Augustinian fashion, remains "free" even to ignore the directions of the intellect. It is in that space where both the creature rebels and God redeems.

To sum up, natural law appears in the Romans Commentary as a character in a story – more precisely, as an alias of a character in a story. The character is "The Truth of God." Beginning *in medias res*, the story of Romans 1 opens as The Truth of God languishes in captivity. It has been "detained in unrighteousness" (1:18). It is an injured, weakened, chained character, unable to do what it should, feckless and finally pitiful. Thomas uses flashback and foreshadowing to show that character as a has-been and a wannabe.[152] How can The Truth of God be detained?

---

[147]   *In Rom.* 1:20a, #122; *ST* I-II.93.1 *ad* 2.

[148]   *ST* III.1.2–3, esp. 3 *ad* 3, quoting Rom. 5:20.

[149]   I-II.90.1 *ad* 2; a. 3–4; q. 91.1. For an elegant account, owing a similar debt to Preller, of natural law as the work of God's rulerly prudence, see Bowlin, *Contingency and Fortune in Aquinas's Ethics*, esp. part II of ch. 3, "Natural Law and Moral Diversity."

[150]   *ST* I.14.8.

[151]   *ST* I-II.91.1–2. "Abridgment" is Bowlin's word.

[152]   Or, in positive terms: just as Thomas cites scripture as license and charge to talk about the natural knowledge of God temporarily abstracted from faith for purposes of analysis, so he cites the same scripture as license and charge to talk about the natural law abstracted from virtue.

The central metaphors for the turn of plot that somewhere in the past has left The Truth of God – also known as natural law – in its pitiful detained state are those of captivity and subtraction. The Gentiles have "detained the truth of God as if held captive."[153] Human beings have "subtracted from God's power and knowledge."[154] Thus The Truth of God, also known as natural law, is unable to do what true knowledge of God (*vera Dei cognitio*) ought to do, namely lead human beings to the good.[155] That is the tragedy portrayed in Romans 1. It is confirmed elsewhere, so that in the two sermons on charity Thomas could describe natural law as "destroyed."[156]

With that, natural law arguments cease to enjoy many of the advantages that lead their modern advocates to favor them. While they do offer a source of knowledge, that knowledge is not independent of the virtues. And while natural law is universal, its universality has a theological, not secular character – it is the universality by which Christ represents all human beings to the Father.

Liberals might indeed imagine making Thomistic arguments of their own. Under conditions of injustice toward gay and lesbian people, human beings will have difficulty identifying what true virtue for gay and lesbian couples consists in, or what counts as their action in accord with nature properly understood. Christians, gay and straight, will share that difficulty. Similarly, conditions of injustice toward blacks, women, Gentiles, and so on, have prevented their detractors from perceiving their virtues – and even their true nature – in the past. While Thomas would not himself apply in that way the logic of justice and virtue that he finds in Romans 1, he notes features of the account that may encourage others to do so.

An appeal to justice and virtue, rather than nature and law, will not settle the debate. But it does shift it to the language under which Thomas governs relations among differing people – namely, that of justice.

Justice returns us to one of the rubrics under which we began: the nature of

---

[153] "Tertio [Paulus] ponit cognitionem quam de eo habuerunt, cum subdit 'hominum eorum qui veritatem Dei,' id est de Deo cognitionem, 'detinent in iniustia,' quasi captivatam. Nam vera Dei cognitio quantum est de se inducit homines ad bonum, sed ligatur, quasi captivitate detenta, per iniustitiae affectum, per quam, ut Ps. XI, 1, 'diminutae sunt veritates a filiis hominum,'" *In Rom.* 1:18, #112.

[154] "Isti ideo dicuntur inexcusabiles 'quia cum cognovissent Deum, non sicut Deum glorificaverunt,' vel quia ei debitum cultum non impenderunt, vel quia virtuti eius et scientiae terminum imposuerunt, aliqua eius potentiae et scientiae subtrahentes . . ." *In Rom.* 1:20b, #127.

[155] *In Rom.* 1:18, #112.

[156] "Destructa erat" (*De duobus praeceptis charitatis,* prol.)

justice among the baptized. Thomas is not unaware that Paul has a sting in store for those who take the condemnations at Rom. 1:26 in a certain way. The second chapter of Romans famously opens, "For you are without excuse, O one who judges! In that you judge another, you condemn yourself."[157]

Thomas comments that one of the causes of unjust judging is "usurping for oneself the judgment of hidden things, of which God alone has the judgment."[158] One of those hidden things is hidden "not only to us, but according to its own nature, the knowledge of which pertains to God alone." That is first of all the meditation of the heart.[159] The heart would certainly include what we now think of as sexual orientation. Liberals might then rightly take Thomas as warning against condemnations here. Conservatives should not assume that self-seeking rather than charity moves the hearts of same-sex couples.

But the warning applies in two other ways as well. First of all, liberals must not assume that malice moves the hearts of their opponents. And most important, no one, according to Thomas, knows his or her own heart with certainty, but God alone.[160] Any Christian short of beatitude may be holding the truth captive to injustice – even the truth about nature, and especially the truth about the nature of human hearts.

[157]   Rom. 2:1.
[158]   *In Rom.* 2:1, #174.
[159]   *In Rom.* 2:1, #175.
[160]   I-II.112.5.

Chapter 5

NATURE AND JUSTICE WHEN SCIENCE AND SCRIPTURE CONFLICT: RETRIEVING A TRADITIONAL HERMENEUTICS

In the last chapter we saw the storied context in which Thomas's Romans Commentary first comes to any practical applications of natural law, so deep is natural law embedded in the Pauline narrative. Thomas appeals to it as explanatory of Paul's assertions. In the Romans Commentary it plays a supporting role. The assertions that move the argument relate either to the narrative, or to the virtues.

What does Thomas say about the list of condemnations Paul temporarily concludes with at 1:26? Quite apart from methodology, it is central to Thomas's project to find ways for Paul to be materially *right*. Any Thomistic answer must save the text of Paul. The simplest way to save the text is to agree with it straightforwardly.

As expected, Thomas agrees with the condemnations. Human actions can run contrary to nature in several ways. The first is to counter God's nature: that is, impiety. The second is to counter human nature, also in two ways: one, against reason, or human nature proper; two, against the nature of the human species as animal.

In the first way, something can be against the nature of a human being as against the constitutive difference of the human being, which is rational. As it was in the *Summa*, so it is in the commentary: "thus all sin is said to be against the nature of the human being, to the extent that it is against right reason."[1] That is, it runs contrary to the motive or causative power of synderesis to inquire after the good to be done and the evil to be avoided,[2] or it upsets the proper functioning of human nature. This first use of natural-law language adds a new vocabulary in which the wise may describe the successes and failures of practical reasoning, while it adds no new content to the internal principles of human action. The sins of the Gentiles were perfectly describable as impiety and injustice, and their knowledge of what God had manifested to them was perfectly describable in commentary on vv. 18–19 without any reference to the vocabulary of law. Why? Because Thomas takes *Paul* to be describing the practice and knowledge of the Gentiles in terms of justice (v. 18) rather than law.

In the second way, something can be against the nature of the human being by reason of the genus, which is animal. So here it is sexuality that raises the question of *what* goods are to be done and what to be avoided. The answer follows immediately, as self-evident, that sexuality is for the good of the species. It is hard not to agree with Thomas that sexuality raises questions for human beings who must (and may) reason about it – and thus, under conditions of finitude and sin, wonder at and worry about it – rather than having instincts to follow straightforwardly.[3]

---

[1]   "[S]ic omne peccatum dicitur esse contra naturam hominis, inquantum est contra rationem rectam," *In Rom.* 1:26, #149.

[2]   Thomas speaks not in modern fashion of the sources of knowledge, but of what moves and causes it. Speculative reason is moved by beings extensive in the world through *intellectus*, or the habit of understanding that includes such formal rules as the principle of noncontradiction. Practical reason, similarly, is moved by the need to *do* things intentionally in the world through synderesis, or the habit of seeking the good and avoiding evil – a similarly formal rule. Cf. Daniel Mark Nelson, *The Priority of Prudence: Virtue and Natural Law in Thomas Aquinas and the Implications for Modern Ethics* (University Park, PA: Pennsylvania State University Press, 1992), pp. 13–14. The world "naturally" demands understanding: hence human beings seek a knowledge described as natural history. Similarly human beings "naturally" demand action. Hence human beings seek a knowledge sometimes described as natural law, but which Thomas prefers to describe in terms of prudence. "Synderesis serves the function of explaining how we begin to reason practically, but it does not provide content for our moral deliberations" (Nelson, *Priority of Prudence*, pp. 2, 97). It is thus that synderesis "moves" prudence, and prudence moves the virtues (II–II.47.6; Nelson, *Priority of Prudence*, p. 96.) The saturation of the desire to understand God's will for our nature in the beatific vision is not, on the other hand, construed as a demand, since both the desire and its fulfillment are two moments of a gift.

[3]   Thomas's way of handling sexuality in this passage might not lead one to Nelson's conclusions (*Priority of Prudence*, p. 122), but neither is it at odds with them. For an argument

continued on next page

Here Thomas does adduce the vocabulary of law. Why? Because he takes *Paul* to be referring to it, with language about an exchange of a natural use for one that is contrary to nature.[4] Thomas governs his choice of vocabulary by the usage of the text upon which he is commenting.

Note too that Thomas here suggests that procreation is a good of the species, not of individuals. If Thomas did not make that distinction, he would have more trouble accounting for the celibacy of Jesus and religious.

Thomas follows Romans to see homosexual acts as a fitting punishment for Gentile idolatry. He argues that the insult to God's nature – ingratitude and injustice – results in a detriment to human nature,[5] and furthermore that "this punishment is fitting."[6] Such fittingness makes a typical theological point for Thomas. It exhibits a coherence between human sin and God's punishment of it, in that God punishes sin by withdrawing grace,[7] resulting in a tendency toward further sin – as in the Fall itself. Even conservative modern commentators agree on this, when they are careful: "Homosexual activity, then, is not a *provocation* of 'the wrath of God' (Rom. 1:18); rather, it is a *consequence* of God's decision to 'give up' rebellious creatures to follow their own futile thinking and desires."[8] But not only that: the relation of fittingness also exhibits a coherence, between God's nature and its due on the one hand, and human nature and its due on the other. When Thomas follows Paul in the Romans Commentary, the sin against the human nature is no independent sin for Thomas. The sin against the human nature follows[9] from a sin against the divine nature. The "deformation of their [Gentile] nature . . . is according to the order of justice, because it was due that those who had done injury to God's nature, that is, to what is proper to God, by attributing it to creatures, should emerge dishonored in their

that Paul's Greek *para phusin* is better translated "beyond," *para*, rather than "contrary to" nature, see Dale B. Martin, "Heterosexism and the Interpretation of Romans 1:18–32," *Biblical Interpretation* 3 (1995): 332–55 (here, pp. 339–49), so that what Paul objects to, lacking the modern notion of desire distinguished by its object, is an extreme rather than misdirected example of undifferentiated lust (p. 342).

4   "[M]utaverunt naturalem usum in eum qui est contra naturam," *In Rom.* 1:26, ##146–50.

5   "Recedit, deducitur, decidit," #147.

6   "[H]anc poenam convenientem esse," on v. 27, #151

7   "Non impellendo in malum sed deserendo," *In Rom.* 1:26, #147.

8   Richard Hays, "Homosexuality," chapter 16 in his *Moral World of the New Testament: Community, Cross, New Creation: An Introduction to New Testament Ethics* (San Francisco: HarperSanFrancisco, 1996), p. 388; emphasis in original.

9   *Trahitur,* even *deducitur,* #147.

own nature."[10] The technical term "convenientia" plays into Thomas's hands because the Vulgate actually uses the verb: "God delivered them up to a reprobate sense, with the result that they did things that were unfit [*non conveniunt*]."[11] Thomas's account shows a deep interconnectedness and coherence, and that interconnectedness and coherence are part and parcel of it, because he argues *ex convenientia*.[12]

It is worth noting that the original sins of the Romans narrative – injustice and ingratitude against God, or failing to return to God the acts and attitudes due to God's nature – are defined *both* in terms of virtue *and* in terms of nature, in a way which also manifests a deep interconnection. "Injustice" and "ingratitude" are first of all virtue – terms; justice the chief of the cardinal virtues, and gratitude a Pauline virtue that Thomas has already noted several times in the commentary. What is new in the passage surrounding Rom. 1:26 is that Thomas also treats them in terms of nature, because it is precisely God's *virtus* or power that the Gentiles fail to acknowledge with due acts of piety and thanksgiving. So the insult to God's *virtus* results in a lack of due Gentile *virtus* – which would be precisely a participation in God's – just as the insult to God's nature results in a debility in Gentile nature.

Such correspondences are not merely matters of argumentative elegance. Thomas is not just trying to make God's punishment look theoretically appropriate. He suggests that it is appropriate in fact, a fitting solution to the problem of Gentile idolatry. By failing, through idolatry, to acknowledge the *virtus* of God's nature, nations not worshiping the God of Israel will cease to participate in the *virtus* of their own nature. As idolatry increases, so homosexual activity increases.[13] Thomas finds that so not only by logic,[14] but also according to biblical history. For "the Apostle calls the vices against nature the penalty for idolatry since they are seen to have begun at the same time as idolatry, namely in the time of Abraham, when idolatry is believed to have begun. For that reason and at that time they are first read of as having been punished in the Sodomites."[15] Idolaters will fittingly and by their own fault

[10]   "[S]ecundum iustitiae ordinem, ex qua debitum erat ut qui in Dei naturam iniuriosi fuerant, id quod est proprium sibi, creaturis attribuendo, in sui natura contumeliosi existerent," #151.

[11]   Rom. 1:28, at #155.

[12]   References to *convenientia* also occur in ##153, 155, and 156.

[13]   "Simul etiam idololatria crescente, huiusmodi vitia creverunt," #151.

[14]   "[S]atis rationabiliter," #151

[15]   "Apostolus vitia contra naturam . . . ponit idololatria poenam, quia simul cum idololatria inc[o]episse videntur, scilicet tempore Abrahae, quando creditur idol/atria

continued on next page

come to reproduce less, since from homosexual activity "generation cannot follow."[16] The practice of idolatry, Thomas suggests, fittingly results in the reduction of idolatry. Idolatrous nations, coming to lack the good of the species, will, at least by implication, die out of their own (un)nature. "Generation cannot follow" corresponds – logically and causally, since Thomas uses *deducitur* in an undifferentiated sense[17] – to "the wages of sin is death."[18] That is the *convenientia* of the *res* that corresponds for Thomas to the *convenientia* of the argument.

Not only does idolatry lead to homosexual practice, but homosexual practice of the sort Paul describes is accompanied by "all vice," *omni iniquitate*, including malice, fornication, avarice, wickedness, envy, murder, and so on, according to a vice list much studied by New Testament scholars (vv. 29–31). In commenting on the list, Thomas says that Paul "expands upon" (*exaggerat*) all vice extensively and intensively.

How does it affect the cogency of Thomas's argument if such correspondences no longer seem self-evident? Suppose homosexual couples in marriagelike relationships seem not to be delivered up to "all vice," including the other items on the list. Does not that count as evidence that they do not perhaps number among the idolaters Thomas has in mind in this passage?[19] Suppose the Catholic Church does not regard a homosexual orientation as a fitting divine punishment; or as one for Gentile idolatry, such that a nation practicing idolatry will die out. Does not such a supposition count as evidence that Christians need to renegotiate the congruity between the Pauline passage, the law of nature, and deliverances of the faithful? Suppose biblical exegetes no longer locate the sin of the Sodomites in homosexuality, but in inhospitality and violence. Suppose homosexual relations in a faithful, monogamous pairing are not or no longer connected to empirical idolatry but the empirical Church: that they build up the people of God, that they result in faith, hope, and charity – or, more to the point here, in justice, gratitude, and right worship of God. Some will object that the text answers that question: homosexual activity by definition cannot result in justice, gratitude, and right worship of God. I merely point out that if Christians disagree about those matters, the convergence Thomas seeks to

---

incoepisse. Unde et tunc primo leguntur in Sodomitis punita fuisse, ut Gen. XIX," #151. For a recent account that agrees in interpreting Paul this way, as well as for Jewish sources for that or similar ideas, see Martin, "Heterosexism and the Interpretation of Romans 1:18–32."

16   "[G]eneratio non sequi postest," #149.
17   At #147.
18   #151.
19   I am indebted to an anonymous reader for this question.

uphold becomes harder to sustain, not only in the Romans Commentary, but also in the natural law for which Rom. 1:20 serves as warrant.

Indeed, it is only the absence of such modern concerns from his audience – which is to say, the presence of much greater agreement among the wise – that can allow him to proceed with such abbreviation and dispatch. Since here, as in the *Summa*, arguments from nature cohere deeply with the virtues, the interpretation of the Bible, empirical facts about the world, and the sense of the faithful – the argument has to be reconstituted until coherence re-emerges.

Therefore, too, there can be such a thing as genuinely Thomistic disagreement, or *quaestiones disputatae*. On homosexuality, the traditional coherence can be asserted with great sophistication. And yet the interpretation of the relevant biblical texts (especially in Paul), the state of natural science, and what counts as virtue no longer cohere so obviously as they once did, but become (severally and together) topics of widespread debate – and the debate is not just in popular culture, but precisely among the wise or the *maiores in fide*. To put it starkly, we now observe a debate about whether either can serve justice, the advocates of gay couples or their opponents; whether either can be moved by the Holy Spirit writing the law, and infusing the virtue, of charity upon the heart; whether either can square with the text of the Bible interpreted according to the best deliverances of the *maiores in fide*; and whether either can occur under licit circumstances that Thomas could not imagine.

One answer, of course, and one that certainly satisfies Thomas in this passage, is to appeal to the model and teacher of virtue, Paul. In case of dispute, appeal to the text.

Thomas's respect for the text, and for its traditional and communal interpretation, is very high – much higher than scholars often give him credit for. The entire discussion of whether sacred doctrine counts as *scientia* in the first question of the *Summa Theologiae* represents a heightening of scriptural authority over the earlier systematic treatises.[20] Sacred doctrine is *scientia* in a new way. To be an Aristotelian science is to proceed from first principles. Since first principles inhere indifferently in minds and things,[21] a different Aristotelian science arises from distinct sources of light or understanding

---

[20]   This is one of the main theses of Michel Corbin, *Le Chemin de la théologie chez Thomas d'Aquin* (Paris: Beauchesne, 1974), pp. 9–112.

[21]   See Corbin, *Le Chemin*, pp. 717–18; Terrence Irwin, *Aristotle's First Principles* (New York: Oxford University Press, 1988), p. 7; Alasdair MacIntyre, *First Principles, Final Ends and Contemporary Philosophical Issues*, The Aquinas Lecture, 1990 (Milwaukee, WI: Marquette University Press, 1990), pp. 1–7; Eugene F. Rogers, Jr, *Thomas Aquinas and Karl Barth: Sacred Doctrine and the Natural Knowledge of God* (Notre Dame, IN: Notre Dame University Press, 1995), pp. 20–7.

informing things in the world. So (and this is Thomas's brilliant move) *to proceed from first principles is, on Aristotle's terms, to proceed from (small-r) revelations.* Thus sacred doctrine is not vitiated by proceeding from Revelation: rather, by proceeding from Revelation, sacred doctrine becomes *scientia par excellence.* As in both Karl Barth and Vatican II, the real aspect of the first principles is the Revelation of God's own self in Jesus Christ,[22] so that even Aristotelian demonstration becomes a penultimate and deficient case of the demonstration *par excellence,* the demonstration of the Father by the Son.[23] Question 1 of the *Summa* obviates the issue of whether sacred doctrine construed as *scientia* is more biblical or more Aristotelian. The more Thomas attends, in good Aristotelian fashion, to first principles, the more they return him to the Bible. Thus Thomas makes Aristotle a term or index of his commitment to the Bible: the more Aristotelian he is, the more biblical he is.[24]

Although the formal object of faith is God as the first truth, the material object of faith consists of enunciable propositions from Scripture well understood,[25] where "well understood" is specified by the believing community, and by those "greater in faith."[26] Unsurprisingly, Thomas did know of disputes within the believing community, among the *maiores in fide,* over the interpretation of Scripture. It was such disputes, in fact, that led to *quaestiones disputatae,* and it was disputed questions that led to *Summas.*[27] The *Summas* and disputed questions of Thomas *internalize* dispute as *the* way that human beings come to know, both in investigation and in teaching. In its institutionalization of dispute, if not in other ways, the medieval university culture may have been more open than our own.

Specifically, Thomas knew of disputes about the scriptural teaching on what should count as the law of nature.[28] The most famous of those was not about natural moral law or Aristotelian biology but about physics.[29] I mean the

---

[22] Vatican Council, *Dei Verbum* I.2.

[23] I.42.6 *ad* 2.

[24] Rogers, *Thomas Aquinas and Karl Barth*, pp. 16–70.

[25] "[I]ntellectis sane," II–II.5.3 *ad* 2.

[26] "[M]aiores in fide," II–II.5.4.

[27] Alasdair MacIntyre, *Whose Justice? Which Rationality?* (Notre Dame, IN: Notre Dame University Press, 1988), pp. 84–5.

[28] I follow Bruce D. Marshall, "Absorbing the World: Christianity and the Universe of Truths," in Marshall, ed., *Theology and Dialogue: Essays in Conversation with George Lindbeck* (Notre Dame, IN: Notre Dame University Press, 1990), pp. 69–102; here, pp. 90–7.

[29] In the 20th century we may (or may not) be accustomed to thinking that interpretations of natural physical law are more changeable than interpretations of natural moral law, or

continued on next page

one about whether the world had a beginning in time. There, not only in the *Summa*, but also in the *De potentia*, Thomas makes some broad qualifications, which he takes from Augustine, about the interpretation of Scripture with respect to natural science.[30] Unlike modern hermeneuticians, Thomas rules out harmonizing the Bible and modern science by applying a hermeneutic of suspicion either to the Bible or to the "visible created things, in which, as in a sort of book, the cognition of God may be read."[31] He requires the hermeneutic of charity that holds for truth. (Here we see requirements of the baptismal polity at work.) In the Bible there may not be anything false.[32] For the First Truth, God, is not a deceiver. Yet for that very reason interpreters ought not turn a hermeneutic of suspicion against the natural sciences either. Thus Thomas insists that readers ought to interpret the Bible in accord with the best deliverances so far of (relatively independent) natural science that prove adaptable to the text, literally "saving the circumstances of the letter, or "the way the words go."[33] Precisely if God does not deceive, either in the text or in the world, error must reside in interpretation, in what interpreters think the text – or the world – means.

When Bruce Marshall considers Aquinas's handling of the apparent tensions between Scripture and natural science, he writes that "the usefulness of this example lies partly in its utterly noncontroversial character – it has been hundreds of years since anyone worried about whether Aristotelian science could be reconciled with the plain sense of Scripture."[34] Thomas and his contemporaries, however, worried a great deal about this question (so also many theologians in our own day are worried about whether and how current science and Scripture are compatible) and devoted considerable energy and ingenuity to exhibiting the assimilative power of Christianity at just the point of conflict. In the process, Thomas made some illuminating procedural comments about how theologians should try to absorb alien truth claims into the biblical world.

---

physics than ethics, but Thomas was not. If anything, the moral law was harder to know (that is, to apply): "In speculative matter there is the same truth in all, so in principles as also in conclusions, although the truth is not recognized by all in the conclusions . . . But in matters of action, truth or practical rectitude is not the same for all individually (*quantum ad propria*) but only communally (*quantum ad communia*); and where there is the same rectitude in individual matters, it is not equally noted by all" (I-II.94.4).

[30] *ST* I.46.2, *De pot.* 4.1.

[31] *In Rom.* 1:19, #116 *in fin.*

[32] *De pot.* 4.1; cf. *ST* II-II.1.3.

[33] Marshall's translation of "salva litterae circumstantia," in "Absorbing the World," p. 93.

[34] Marshall, "Absorbing the World," p. 91.

In the attempt to reconcile the theological interpretation of Scripture and the natural scientific interpretation of the world, Aquinas can and does allow two paths: either

i)   we can revise our identification of the plain sense [of Scripture] in light of external beliefs; [or]

ii) we can revise our estimate of our external beliefs in light of the requirements of the plain sense. Both of these courses of action are in fact strategies for absorbing the world into the biblical text.[35]

Thomas plies both. In both cases he argues that apparent conflict comes from taking either the way the words go, or the way the world works, *in too narrow a sense*. What Thomas seeks is space – whether in a more capacious text, or a roomier science. In the case of the eternity of the world, Aquinas finds room in Aristotle: Aristotle need not be interpreted as requiring the eternity of the world. In the case of creation out of nothing, Aquinas finds room in Scripture: Scripture need not be interpreted as requiring creation from unformed matter.

In the first case, many 13th century theologians supposed that Aristotle's physics required the eternity of the world. All agreed that the eternity of the world was incompatible with the plain sense of Scripture. So Bonaventure, for example, thought the conflict meant Christians must reject Aristotle.[36] But Thomas hesitates to choose between the best available natural science and the plain sense of the Bible. He denies, therefore, that "Aristotle should be read as though he were really attempting to demonstrate the eternity of the world."[37] The problem arises because the best available physics cannot, contrary to the assumptions of many, even decide the issue about the eternity of the world, leaving certainty about the matter rather to faith than to natural science.[38]

So some might argue on the issue of homosexuality. The plain sense of Scripture (principally Romans 1) appears to conflict with the best deliverances of natural science in psychology and genetics. Those who follow Bonaventure will say: so much the worse for natural science. Those who follow Thomas on the eternity of the world, however, will prefer rather to honor natural science within the confines of Romans 1. They might then read the justified

---

[35]   Marshall, "Absorbing the World," p. 95.
[36]   Marshall, "Absorbing the World," pp. 95–6.
[37]   Marshall, "Absorbing the World," p. 96.
[38]   Marshall, "Absorbing the World," p. 96.

claims of contemporary psychology and genetics as either (a) still in dispute, or (b) more descriptive than normative, so that moral conclusions about what one ought to do given a homosexual orientation do not follow from those claims. In that case, the argument parallels Thomas's on the eternity of the world: natural science does not, properly interpreted, really argue the case, and therefore faith, in accord with the plain sense of Romans 1, controls. The conservative could claim that homosexual activity is never licit, and yet maintain a compatibility of the apparent plain sense of the biblical text with the best deliverances of natural reason.

That move may strike liberal critics as resembling creationist readings of the fossil record and exposing the faith to the ridicule Thomas deploys it to avoid. In that case, such critics will prefer a second strategy that Thomas offers, also to preserve the faith from ridicule.

In the second case, Aristotelian physics denies the existence of unformed matter. Yet the Vulgate of Gen. 1:2 calls the earth "inanis et vacua," which sounds very much like unformed matter, from which God would go on to make creatures. Now it is the text, rather than Aristotle, that proves capacious in Thomas's hands. Thomas rules out the interpretation "unformed matter," since "What is false can never be the literal sense of sacred scripture,"[39] and we have good reasons – specifically, Aristotelian ones – to think that "unformed matter" makes no sense. The exposition of *inanis et vacua* as "unformed," he writes, "seems deficient, since it asserts that Scripture should be understood to mean certain things the contraries of which are shown by sufficiently evident reasons."[40] Scripture must therefore mean something else.

Thomas offers two interpretations, one Augustinian (that the work of the six days was done all at once), and one Cappadocian (that without creating unformed matter, God remains free to mold the creation more determinately over time). Thomas says Augustine's reading "is more profound and better upholds Scripture against the mockery of unbelievers," while he finds the Cappadocian reading "more obvious and more in agreement with the words of the text in their surface meaning."[41] Thomas concludes that "the way the words go allows both senses."[42]

Unlike most moderns, Thomas allows both to stand, citing as a principle that "One should not want to force Scripture to have a single senses in such a way that other senses which have truth in them and can be adapted to

---

[39]   Marshall, "Absorbing the World," p. 91, translating *ST* I.1.10 *ad* 3; cf. *De pot.* 4.1.r.
[40]   *De pot.* 4.1 *ad* 5, adopting Marshall's translation, "Absorbing the World," p. 92.
[41]   *De pot.* 4.2.r, trans. Marshall, "Absorbing the World," p. 92.
[42]   *De pot.* 4.2.r, trans. Marshall, "Absorbing the World," p. 92.

Scripture by agreeing with the way the words go [*salva circumstantia litterae*] are completely excluded."[43]

So liberals might argue on the issue of homosexuality. Contemporary genetics and physics deny that homosexuality appears among certain nations for the purpose or with the result of killing them out. Rather than rejecting the biblical text as false – since that would break the rule that "what is false can never be the literal sense of sacred scripture" – Christian theologians, according to Thomas, have a positive duty to seek other senses that accord with the way the words go. Since God is the primary author of the literal sense of Scripture,[44] the Christian theologian must not limit interpretation to senses available to the human author. "Even if some true things that the [human] author does not understand are adapted [*aptentur*] by expositors to the literal sense, there is no doubt that the Holy Spirit, who is divine scripture's principal author, will have understood them."[45] It is not a defect but a virtue – a christologically necessary dignity – for the text to bear more than one sense. It is insisting upon a univocal biblical text that sets up defective interpretation in the community. And that goes not just for the spiritual senses, but for the literal sense too, since Thomas defines the literal sense as what the author – God – intends.[46]

Take two recent, possibly incompatible examples. It may be that by *para phusin* the divine author means that human beings, gay or straight, must not act against their individual natures, so that homosexually oriented men must no more test God by marrying women than heterosexually oriented individuals may test God by seeking (to them) exotic liaisons with members of the same sex.[47]

Or it may be that by *para phusin* Paul means primarily "in excess" of nature, so that promiscuous relations of whatever type are excluded; same-sex relations are taken as exemplary for excess in most cases, especially those associated with Gentile idolatry; but monogamous, lifelong same-sex households upholding the household of God and exemplifying not excess, but the love of God for God's people, do not count as excessive.[48] One might go on

---

[43] *De pot.* 4.1.r, trans. Marshall, "Absorbing the World," p. 93.

[44] *De pot.* 4.1r, *ST* I.1.10.

[45] *De pot.* 4.1 r.

[46] ST I.1.10; cf. Henri de Lubac, *Exégèse médiévale: Les Quatre sens de l'écriture* (Paris: Aubier, 1959–64), vol. 3, pt. 2, pp. 280–5.

[47] So John Boswell, *Christianity, Social Tolerance, and Homosexuality* (Chicago: University of Chicago Press, 1980), pp. 108–9.

[48] So Martin, "Heterosexism and the Interpretation of Romans 1:18–32."

to argue that the first reading is, like Augustine's on the six days, farther from the text, but more profound and more readily understandable for defending the Church against the mockery of unbelievers, while the second reading, like the Cappadocians', is "more in agreement with the words of the text in their surface meaning." Neither may be excluded (compatible with each other or not) because, as Thomas capaciously concludes, "Every *truth* which can be adapted to divine Scripture, while preserving the way the words go, *is* the sense of Scripture."[49]

That is not just a pious defense of the spiritual senses of medieval exegesis, but of the capacity of precisely the literal sense, from which all Christians can learn something about theological exegesis for the community that forms itself around a text.[50] Furthermore, it protects against a hermeneutical instance of the very same "detention of" or "subtraction from" the truth of which the Romans Commentary warns. According to the *De potentia* one may not "confine" the text (*cogere*), as according to the Romans Commentary one may not "bind" the right (*ligare*), "detain" or "subtract from" the truth (*detinere, subtrahere*). The power of God under discussion in *De potentia* is the very *virtus* or *potentia* of God from which the Gentiles had subtracted to their discredit according to the Romans Commentary.

Readers of Scripture must take care "lest anyone want to confine [*cogere*] Scripture so to one sense, that other senses be entirely excluded, that in themselves contain truth and are able to be adapted to Scripture, preserving the literal sense [*salva litterae circumstantia*]."[51] Insofar as there are interpretations of Rom. 1:26f that distinguish what Paul objects to from what gay and lesbian Christians in marriagelike unions practice, thinking in the style of Thomas does not just allow, but *requires* theologians to keep the matter open. The literal sense of Scripture becomes a *class* of readings.[52]

The surprise is not that that settles the matter. It does not. The surprise is that it gives theologians considerable room – requires giving them room. The

---

[49]   *De pot.* 4.1.r; my translation and emphasis; cf. Marshall, "Absorbing the World," p. 97.
[50]   See, for example, Hans W. Frei, "The 'Literal Reading' of Biblical Narrative in the Christian Tradition: Does It Stretch or Will It Break?," in Frei, *Theology and Narrative: Selected Essays*, ed. George Hunsinger and William C. Placher (New York: Oxford University Press, 1993), pp. 117–53.
[51]   *De pot.* 4.1.c.
[52]   Eugene F. Rogers, Jr, "How the Virtues of the Interpreter Presuppose and Perfect Hermeneutics: The Case of Thomas Aquinas," *The Journal of Religion* 76 (1996): 64–81. Frei, "The 'Literal Reading' "; Kathryn E. Tanner, "Theology and the Plain Sense," in Garrett Green, ed., *Scriptural Authority and Narrative Interpretation* (Philadelphia: Fortress, 1987), pp. 59–77; and de Lubac, *Exégèse médiévale,* vol. 3, pt. 2, pp. 284–5.

surprise is that disputants on both sides may be Thomists – not just partial Thomists, the natural-law Thomists against the virtue-theory Thomists, but integral Thomists. What counts as true and false by criteria of natural science, what counts as just and unjust, grateful and ungrateful in sexual ethics, what counts as according with the way the words go in Scripture, and what counts as exposing the faith to ridicule – those are all to a greater or lesser extent *quaestiones disputatae*, questions for the wise, or the *maiores in fide*, to decide in disputation. They are not questions that lack objective answers, but ones that the wise investigate by interpreting and reinterpreting nature and Scripture *per longum tempus*. Thomas would have the *maiores in fide* seek to learn from those both inside and outside the faith, and apply for the gifts of the Spirit in prayer, which is the highest of secondary causes, and the end of interpretation.[53] That way of putting the matter makes it harder to argue that current clashes over homosexuality ought to be regarded as Church-dividing.

---

[53] I.1.6, II–II.83 *ad* 3; *De modo studendi* #1223; Rogers, "The Virtues of the Interpreter," pp. 80–1.

Chapter 6

KARL BARTH ON JEWS AND GENDER: A PRELIMINARY CRITIQUE[1]

Karl Barth's account of homosexuality depends on his general theory of the creation of human beings as male and female. His account of the command of God on this matter is less scripturalist than it appears. In one exposition, Rom. 1:20ff offers but a confirmation of a creation-based complementarity thesis. In another exposition, typically enough, Rom. 1:20ff offers a critique of bourgeois society – and therefore even of its heterosexual norms.

Barth's general account of the creation of human beings as male and female is much deeper and more complex than so bald a statement would imply. It looks little like other complementarity theses, for two reasons.

First of all, the creation account from Genesis is richly complicated by Barth's principle that true humanity exists only in Jesus Christ. In both cases, true humanity is co-humanity (*Mitmenschlichkeit*), humanity in fellowship, whether the fellowship of man and woman or of Jesus and the disciples. Co-humanity seemed to deal the last blow to the old Christian idea that woman was deficient man. Furthermore, co-humanity, according to Barth's exegesis of Genesis, explains how the human being is in the image of God: the human being is in the image of God not individually but in community. The reception of co-humanity was very favorable; who would wish to deny that true humanity involves fellowship with others?

[1] I wish to thank Kendall Soulen, Stanley Hauerwas, George Hunsinger, Bruce Marshall, George Schner, Walter Lowe, and an anonymous reviewer for comments and criticisms on earlier versions of this chapter, and Bruce McCormack for conversation. Faults remain my own.

But the specific working out of co-humanity in a thesis about the complementarity of the sexes seemed to be a reduction. It found detractors as soon as it appeared. Detractors emerged not least because the complementarity thesis also contained an "ordering," into which "man is A" and "woman is B." According to oral legends circulating at Yale, Barth admirer Richard Niebuhr threw the volume across a room in frustration.[2]

It quickly occurred to critics to exploit the tension between true human fellowship as redeemed in Jesus, and true human fellowship as created male and female. This looked especially easy since Jesus never married. Was he then less than fully human? Surely not. One had to choose. To critics, the fellowship of Jesus should control, to the point of eliminating any constitutive role for fellowship male and female.

Yet that critique had the result of evacuating Barth's account of anything distinctive to creation; it left Barth once again all grace and no nature, contrary to his intention.

Barth's defenders then made much of a qualification. The fellowship of Jesus involves not only true humanity; it involves also true divinity. Adam and Eve in the Garden, and male and female as created, can be *with* one another. After the Fall, only Jesus can show human beings what that withness is really like.

And yet Jesus is more than a human being, so that he can also be *for* others, executing the peculiarly divine office of election in being God not only for triune fellowship, but also for human beings. Thus the representative co-humanity by which Jesus is with *and* for all human beings, is not the same as the co-humanity of Adam and Eve, who can only be *with* each other.[3] Thus the tension between the true human being as male and female and the true human being as Jesus in fellowship with his disciples seemed to be worth the risk. Barth's defenders could agree that the christological thesis controls and still demur that it does not eliminate the complementarity of male and female after all. For the complementarity of male and female provides the condition for the possibility of the restoration of human fellowship by Jesus the human being with and for others, and the elevation of human fellowship to fellowship with God. Critics may not merely chuck it out.

Part of the work of these chapters will be to rescue created co-humanity from compulsory complementarity, by doing exegesis of biblical fellowship

---

[2]   I heard the story from Hans Frei.

[3]   For an account of the difference and difficulties this makes for the ethics of the imitation of Christ, see Gene Outka, "Following at a Distance," in Garrett Green, ed., *Scriptural Authority and Narrative Interpretation* (Philadelphia: Fortress, 1987).

other than the male–female variety. Male–female complementarity may be typical of co-humanity, but it need not be essential.

Second, and even more interesting, Barth takes with utmost seriousness the great Pauline symbology according to which the love of the Son for the Church is a model for marriage between a man and a woman, and the marriage of a man and a woman represents the love of the Son for the Church. Even anthropologists can argue that human culture cannot fool with great overarching symbols without severe loss.[4] Thus the male–female complementarity goes to the heart of the love of God for human beings, which, Barth realizes, is at home in the love of God for Israel. In an amazing line that we have seen before, and to which we will return, Barth sums up: "In that the election of God is real, there is such a thing as love and marriage." The notion that a marriage is a covenant is no mere symbol or evocative language for Barth: it reveals rather the deep truth of the matter, that marriage is a type of the love of God for Israel.

Those two complications of Barth's complementarity thesis make it very strong – indeed, far and away the strongest one available. To test the suspicion that there is still something reductive about the construal of the image of God in the human being as necessarily male and female, and that there is more to be said about the singleness of Jesus, requires a different tack, one apparently indirect, even roundabout. It requires looking for heuristic clues in another place where Barth makes a binary dichotomy and unites the division in Jesus, one in which, however, the problems are much clearer, if in both cases there is more to be retrieved than rejected. Readers who recall the Pauline pairs will not be surprised: the illuminating parallel case is Barth's treatment of Jews and Gentiles.

The apparent detour through Barth's doctrine of Israel may frustrate readers who regard it as a digression from the main matter. That impression would be misleading for two reasons.

First, this chapter gives us a chance to deepen, qualify, and evaluate the more sweeping claims of chapter 2. There I deployed instances of parallel argumentation about Paul's parallel communities – Gentiles, slaves, women – to raise questions about argumentation on sexuality. I made the case that such argumentation was widespread by adducing instances from vastly different times and contexts. Here we have a chance to see how those generalizations do and do not apply in a very particular and influential case.

---

[4]   Mary Douglas, *Natural Symbols: Explorations in Cosmology*, with a new introduction by the author (New York: Routledge, 1996). Actually, Douglas goes further than that, arguing that human cultures can hardly avoid identifying their great institutions with natural forms such as sun and moon, male and female. It's no good trying to get rid of them.

This chapter furnishes an important test not only of its own claims, but also of those.

More important, readers who regard Barth's doctrine of Israel as a digression away from the theme of sexuality have yet to appreciate the strategy of this book, which is not unrelated to that of posters in the hallways of high schools that say "Sex! Now that I have your attention, computer classes begin. . . ." Unlike such posters, however, Christian views about the body are so deeply implicated in everything that Christians believe that no such strategy can really be a non sequitur. If agape can assume and transfigure eros, then an interest in sex can lead to an interest in theology. If the Church has forgotten that it is, to its impoverishment, almost entirely Gentile, then a detour from the relation of the sexes to the relation of Jews and Gentiles is not a detour at all, but a highway to Jerusalem.

Barth's doctrine of Israel, as we shall see, is even more innovative, and more problematic, than his doctrine of the human being as male and female. The two doctrines enjoy not only suggestive material connections; they also suffer from common faults and blind spots. In particular, they offer similar binary patterns, patterns that allow Barth to hide real Jews and women behind projections. Not only does engagement with such patterns help us to deconstruct Barth's argument about homosexuality. It also helps us to see when such patterns are promising and when pernicious. Such matters are important, beyond and apart from the sexuality debates, to anyone who wants to retrieve Paul's parallels, Jew/Gentile, slave/free, male/female, to think deeply about how gender and ethnicity function in high Christian theology, or to consider what Christ and the Spirit have to do with the human being.

The strategy of these chapters, therefore, is oblique by design: to get at Barth on homosexuality and gender by an internal critique of his treatment of the Jews. In the process, we get a second exercise in the theological tendency to analogize Jews and Gentiles to male and female, in which Barth unconsciously reverses Paul, since it is Jewish rather than Gentile practice that Barth polemicizes against. We get a second exercise, too, in the way in which Christian theology ramifies widely, in the way in which everything affects everything else. And we get a second exercise finally in the way in which Christian theology assimilates empirical experience to specifically Christian experience, or the world to revelation. It is probably not possible in Christianity to argue about men and women without arguing about Jews and Gentiles; but perhaps Christians can do it better. I do not regard it as a flaw that an argument about sexuality should say more about Christian theology of Israel than about sex. Rather I regard it as sign of the way in which considerations of sexuality ought not to be narrow and superficial but lead directly into the most central of Christian concerns with the body. Both sex and circumcision, after all, involve the very highest characterizations of the work of Christ in dying for the community he loves – as well as the same part of the body.

These chapters have a circular structure as befits their tracing of complex and understated hermeneutical assumptions. They proceed with a hypothetical critique of Barth's treatments of Jews and gender, a critique designed to show both the similarity of the flaws and the possibilities for retrieval. Finally they return to exegesis of biblical passages along Barthian lines – suggesting that some biblical same-sex couples can furnish better exemplars of Barthian co-humanity than Adam and Eve do.

The brevity with which I cover Barth on homosexuality will disappoint readers looking for him to say more on the subject than he says, and delight others who know that the real interest of his position is in the context and background to those remarks. Brevity is appropriate, when one considers that Barth devoted only two pages to the subject among the seven thousand pages in his *Church Dogmatics*. Yet Barth is important because he has the most theologically well developed and interesting version of the complementarity of men and women that underlies not only his short treatment of homosexuality, but the much longer and ultimately shallower treatments of countless others.

Finally, Barth leaves room by his own principles for further, even different thinking about Jews and gender, and, therefore, about homosexuality, than he records in the *Dogmatics*. Now that Marquardt, Klappert, Sonderegger, Soulen, and others have offered sympathetic critiques from a generally Barthian point of view, and Eberhard Busch has exhaustively laid to rest any *biographical* questions of Barth's relation to the Jewish people in his 1996 book, *Unter dem Bogen des einen Bundes: Karl Barth und die Juden 1933–1945*, the way lies open to carry forward Barth's *theological* critique of 19th century theology and of abstraction further into the areas of Jews and gender, and to propose constructive pneumatological and exegetical *supplements* to his thinking. Barth's thinking on women and men, like his thinking on Jews, labors, for all its promise in its time, under a defect he calls abstraction. Barth faulted Calvin for abstracting both elect human beings and the electing God from Jesus Christ, whom Barth called the elect human being and the electing God in one. Yet on the election of the *community* Barth did not entirely escape the abstraction. In the manner of Augustine's *Retractions*, Barth wrote to Marquardt toward the end of his life that he had been so busy with (theological) Israel that he had had no time for the Jews. Does Barth, as Marquardt and Sonderegger suggest, throw up, despite himself, a conceptual screen onto which he at once *projects* an abstraction ("Israel") and behind which he *hides* actual human beings ("the Jews"), a screen resistant to the blowing of the *Spirit*? Do the concepts "man" and "woman" form a similar conceptual screen, dating from Schleiermacher's dialogue *Christmas Eve*, in which men and women (like Christians and Jews) have essentially different responses to the incarnation of Jesus Christ?[5] *Das ewig Männliche* and *das ewig Weibliche*, inherited from German romanticism, seem to run afoul of Barth's trinitarian particularism, as does "Israel." Yet further application of Barth's own principles, including more attention to the Spirit, leaves him more options in his treatment of Jews and gender, and richer exegesis – including exegesis by anagogy.

Barth on Homosexuality

Although Christian attitudes toward Jews and women are hardly settled, sexual orientation is currently sometimes a louder and more controverted topic of debate. Religious people in moral quandaries about homosexuality appeal to thinkers like Barth when they want to honor their tradition in its most faithfully adequate and rationally sophisticated form. The exception proves the rule: a leading Jewish ethicist, David Novak, appeals to Barth's powerful reading of how the tradition opposes homosexual practice. He does so by claiming that Barth has in common with the rabbis the connection between homosexuality and idolatry, Paul in Romans 1 being the obvious link.[6] Oddly, the most important texts offer little support. Barth's commentary on Romans 1 leaves homosexuality alone, even when it appears (to speak anachronistically) in the text, and prefers to connect *heterosexuality* with idolatry! So he writes:

---

[5]   Friedrich Schleiermacher, *Die Weihnachtsfeier: Ein Gespräch*, ed. G. Wehnung (Basel: B. Schwage, 1953); ET: *Christmas Eve: Dialogue on the Incarnation*, trans. with an introduction and notes by Terrence N. Tice (Richmond, VA: John Knox, 1967). For more on *das Männliche* and *das Weibliche* in 18th and 19th century Germany, see Marilyn Chapin Massey, *Feminine Soul: The Fate of an Ideal* (Boston: Beacon, 1985) and the essays in Iain G. Nicol, ed., *Schleiermacher and Feminism: Sources, Evaluations, and Responses*, Schleiermacher: Studies-and-Translations, vol. 12 (Lewiston, NY: The Edwin Mellen Press, 1992), esp. Sheila Briggs on polarities in gender and epistemology in "Schleiermacher and the Construction of the Gendered Self," pp. 87–94. See more recently Patricia E. Guenter-Gleason, *On Schleiermacher and Gender Politics*, Harvard Theological Studies (Boston: Trinity Press International, 1997).

[6]   David Novak, "Before Revelation: The Rabbis, Paul, and Karl Barth," *The Journal of Religion* 71 (1991): 50–67. The argument in question occupies part II of the article. Parts I and III are quite useful.

Wherever the qualitative distinction between men and the final Omega is overlooked and misunderstood, that fetishism is bound to appear in which God is experienced in "birds and fourfooted things," and finally, or rather primarily, in "the likeness of corruptible man" – Personality, the Child, the Woman – and in the half-spiritual, half-material creations, exhibitions, and representations of man's creative ability – Family, Nation, State, Church, Fatherland.[7]

At the very place where Novak locates a connection between idolatry and homosexuality, Barth locates a connection between idolatry and certain concepts that Barth regards some as idolatrously defending – Woman (by which Barth means of course the heterosexual male's desire for Woman), even Child and Family – and he puts them in a series that ends with Fatherland.

The ethics of the section "Man and Woman" (§54.1), on the other hand, explicates the divine command in terms of the very abstractions we have been talking about, and against which Barth himself had fulminated decades earlier. Homosexuality turns out to be a matter of "a masculinity free from woman and a femininity free from man."[8] Granted, it would constitute a violation of co-humanity to uphold either "freedom from woman" or "freedom from man," which strictures would seem to rule out both permanent lesbian separatism and an all-male priesthood. But only the 19th century romantic *constructions* of *das Männliche* and *das Weibliche* actually do the work here. It is true that Barth does quote Rom. 1:25–7 in his exposition. But it does him no work outside his abstractive categories. And there is no support in his more considered commentary, no mention of homosexuality at all, even as (or especially because) he follows Paul. If this is so, the tension will make Barth's pronouncements on homosexuality at once more complicated and more interesting for his religious admirers on both sides of the current debates.[9]

---

[7] I retain the English translation of *Mensch* by "man," since the *Menschen* Barth has in mind become paradigmatically male. Karl Barth, *Der Römerbrief*, 6th edn (Munich: Christian Kaiser, 1929), "5. Abdrück der neuen Bearbeitung"; ET: *The Epistle to the Romans*, 6th edn, trans. Edwyn C. Hoskyns (New York: Oxford University Press, 1980), pp. 50–1.

[8] Karl Barth, *Die Kirchliche Dogmatik*, 4 vols in 13 (Zürich: Evangelischer Verlag/ Zollikon, 1932–70; ET: *Church Dogmatics*, 4 vols in 13, trans. G. W. Bromiley et al. (Edinburgh: T. & T. Clark, 1956–75). Hereafter cited by volume/part-volume, page: III/ 4, 166. Page references are to the English translation, occasionally modified without notice the better to reflect the German.

[9] For more by an important theologian on the application to the homosexuality debate of the Barmen Declaration and Barth's interpretation of Genesis, see Bertold Klappert, "Auf dem Weg der Gerechtigkeit ist Liebe: Gemeinschaftsgerechte Lebensformen in der Perspektive des Reiches Gottes und Seiner Gerechtigkeit. Erwägungen zum

continued on next page

Hypothetical critique

Karl Barth made remarkable and beautiful innovations in his theological accounts of Israel and of men and women. After Barth, two things had changed for Christian theology – quite apart from the Holocaust and the women's movement. The Jews could no longer be other than the people of God, and women could no longer be deficient men. As a matter of christological exegesis, Israel becomes again the chosen people of God, beside whom Gentiles retain their goyishness, and women become *constitutive* of the image of God, integral to a *co*-humanity consummated in the neighbor-love of Jesus. Author of the Barmen Declaration, the document of Christian resistance to Nazism, Barth also writes of the Jews in German in 1942:

> it is incontestable that this people as such is the people of God: the people with whom God has dealt in His grace and in His wrath; in the midst of whom He has blessed and judged, enlightened and hardened, accepted and rejected; whose cause either way He has made His own, and has not ceased to make His own, and will not cease to make His own. They are all of them sanctified by Him, sanctified as ancestors and kinsmen of the Holy One in Israel, in a sense that Gentiles are not by nature, not even the best of Gentiles, not even the Gentile Christians, not even the best of Gentile Christians. . . . [10]

It is ironic, therefore, that 50 years later Barth looks retrograde to many on just the topics on which at mid-century he led the vanguard. The question arises whether Barth's thinking on gender resembles his thinking on Jews also in this, that both accounts have yet to emerge completely – perhaps because they began to emerge so early – from a defect Barth calls abstraction, in this case an abstraction from the Spirit. Although, so far as I know, no one has put together the topics Jews, gender, and Spirit in this way, each component has already caused misgivings in Barth's admirers. Consider the following threefold critique.

1   Barth's student Friedrich Marquardt worries that (as Sonderegger summarizes it) "at times, Barth is tempted to reduce the Jews to a cipher,

Diskussionspapier 'Sexualität und Lebensformen sowie Trauung und Segnung,'" in *"Und hätte die Liebe nicht": Texte vom Mülheimer Symposion zum rheinischen Diskussionspapier "Sexualität und Lebensformen sowie Trauung und Segnung,"* ed. Evangelischen Kirche im Rheinland (Düsseldorf: Presseverband der Evangelischen Kirche im Rheinland, eV, 1997), pp. 23–119, with discussion, pp. 119–43. See recently also Graham Ward, "The Erotics of Redemption – After Karl Barth," *Theology and Sexuality* 8 (1998): 52–72.
[10]   II/2, 287.

to a mirror that reflects life, but lives none of its own."[11] Barth had faulted his own, Reformed tradition for abstracting both elect or predestined human beings and the electing God from Jesus Christ, whom he called the elect human being and the electing God in one. Yet when he turned to the election of the community he renewed the abstraction in part. It is despite himself, therefore, that Barth's rhetoric sometimes runs to *der ewige Jude*. Marquardt compiled – and showed to Barth – the following list.

> In paragraph 34 of the *Church Dogmatics*, Barth refers to the Synagogue as "the monstrous [*ungeheure*] shadow-side of Israel's history," "the disobedi-ent, idolatrous Israel of every age," "the whole of Israel on the left hand, sanctified only by God's wrath"; he says that the Synagogue is "the Synagogue of death," which, to be sure, "hears the Word and yet for and in all its hearing is still unbelieving," is "the tragic, weirdly [*unheimlich*] painful figure with blindfolded eyes," the "living petrification of the Old Testament in itself and *in abstracto*," an "organization of a humanity which again and again hastens toward an empty future." That organization, Barth states, is "the phenomenon of the unbelieving, the refractory Synagogue," which is characterized by a "vaunting lie" and its "nationalistic–legalistic Messiah-dream"; it stands there like a "spectral form"; its members are "wretched members of the Synagogue"; "the Synagogue Jews are not numbered among the obedient." Rather, the Synagogue is "the debased Israel of the Synagogue," it stands as "an enemy of God," which "has no part anymore in the fulfillment of the promise given to it," going by a "cheerless chronology," living a "carnal hope," taking a stand on "a carnal loyalty to itself," and practicing "Jewish obduracy, melancholy, caprice, and phantasy" – in short, the Synagogue cuts the figure of "a half-venerable, half-gruesome relic, of a marvelously preserved antique," the figure of "the human crone [*menschlicher Schrulle*]." (II/2, 195ff)[12]

---

[11]   The summary appears in Katherine Sonderegger, *That Jesus Christ Was Born a Jew: Karl Barth's "Doctrine of Israel"* (University Park, PA: Pennsylvania State University Press, 1992), p. 146; see also p. 61. The reference is to Friedrich-Wilhelm Marquardt, *Die Entdeckung des Judentums für die christliche Theologie: Israel im Denken Karl Barths* (Munich: Christian Kaiser, 1967), p. 317.

[12]   Marquardt, *Die Entdeckung des Judentums*, p. 335. The translation, here altered, appears in Michael Wyschogrod's (generally sympathetic) "Why Was and Is the Theology of Karl Barth of Interest to a Jewish Theologian?" in Martin Rumscheidt, ed., *Footnotes to a Theology: The Karl Barth Colloquium of 1972*, Studies in Religion Supplements (Waterloo, Ontario: Corporation for the Publication of Academic Studies in Religion in Canada, 1974), pp. 95–111; here, n. 7, pp. 110–11.

After such examples, it seems mild to ask, with Marquardt and Sonderegger:

> Israel as an environment, as mirror, mediating and reflecting another's will: are these not the terms of Idealism, subtly altered? Does Barth's treatment of Israel . . . not denigrate history, reduce history itself to the Idea, now chastely called Jesus Christ? Is the particularity of election, of Israel's election, not here eviscerated, to be refilled instead with the Christian themes of disobedience and self-reproach?[13]

Despite himself, Barth throws up a conceptual screen onto which he can at once *project* a partial abstraction ("Israel") and *hide* actual human beings ("the Jews") behind it. Worse, it is a screen that protects him from the blowing of the Spirit.

2   The concepts "man" and "woman" form a similar conceptual screen, dating from Schleiermacher's early 19th century dialogue *Christmas Eve*, in which men and women (like Christians and Jews) have different responses to Jesus Christ. *Das ewig Männliche* and *das ewig Weibliche*, binary structures inherited from German romanticism, admit of critique in terms of Barth's trinitarian particularism, much as his doctrine of Israel does.

3   Meanwhile, a consensus has developed among a large number of Barth scholars that Barth leaves room to pay more attention to the Holy Spirit. As Robert Jenson writes, "Karl Barth is the initiator and the model . . . of this century's renewal of trinitarian theology. . . . The near-unanimity is therefore remarkable, with which a recent meeting of the Karl Barth Society of North America agreed that long stretches of Barth's thinking seem rather binitarian than trinitarian."[14]

Does Barth's reticence about the Spirit, both in his treatment of Church and Synagogue and in his treatment of men and women, help to explain anything about the power of binary categories in those cases?

In what follows we take a much closer look at theological projection, in which groups of people stand for concepts, as today liberals charge that lesbian and gay people are made to stand for promiscuity and the decline of the family. Yet if Christian theology is to remain true to its Scripture and tradition, can it really

---

[13]   Sonderegger, *That Jesus Christ Was Born a Jew*, pp. 66–7, is very carefully qualified in her answers to those questions.

[14]   For a statement and diagnosis of the consensus, see Robert W. Jenson, "You Wonder Where the Spirit Went," *Pro Ecclesia* 2 (1993): 296–304. In what follows I will not rehearse that critique, but take it for granted, in order to work out the consequences for Barth's critique of abstraction and his exegesis of scripture.

do without characterizations of groups, technically known as typology? At the end I make some suggestions – only suggestions – of better ways to do that.

Initial Objection and Reply: Barth's Doctrine of Israel

Because Barth had "discovered the Jews," in Marquardt's phrase, for Christian theology, because his doctrine of election otherwise succeeded in expressing "the sum of the Gospel, because of all the words that can be said or heard it is the best,"[15] and because he stood as the author of Barmen against the Nazis and later for Israel, it is shocking to hear the tenor of Barth's rhetoric in Marquardt's list. In earlier drafts I suppressed the list as the worst Barth has to offer. I include it now because I saw that Barth himself had read and accepted it. Of the many implicit and explicit calls Barth made for improvement in his doctrine of Israel, I choose three:

1   Much farther on in the *Dogmatics*, in its last long volume (1959), Barth wrote in a different vein, blaming the Church, rather than the Synagogue, for the wound in the people of God. In a characteristic reversal, the notorious *"Judenfrage"* becomes the *"Kirchenfrage."*

> [The Church] must call [the Synagogue] by joining with it as [the Messiah's] people, and therefore with Him. No particular function can be this call, but only the life of the community as a whole authentically lived before the Jews. It need hardly be said that the life of the community as a whole neither has been nor is this call. To this day Christianity has not succeeded in impressing itself upon Israel as the witness of its own most proper reality and truth, of the fulfilled word of God in the Old Testament. It has certainly not succeeded in making it jealous, in making clear to it the nearness of the kingdom as the kingdom of the Son of David, in making Jesus of Nazareth dear and desirable and inviting to it. In this sense the Church as a whole has made no convincing impression on the Jew as a whole. It has debated with him, tolerated him, persecuted him, or abandoned him to persecution without protest. . . . This failure . . . is one of the darkest chapters in the whole history of Christianity and one of the most serious wounds in the body of Christ. Even the modern ecumenical movement suffers more seriously from the absence of Israel than of Rome or Moscow. . . . The recurrent Jewish question is the question of Christ and the Church. . . . [16]

---

[15]   II/2, 3.
[16]   IV/3/2, 878. I am grateful to Bruce McCormack for calling my attention to this passage.

2   In August 1966 Barth received a visit from Michael Wyschogrod, and proved willing, on the basis of God's trustworthiness, to entertain a question about his entire promise–fulfillment structure for construing the relation between Israel and the Church. Wyschogrod writes:

> [Barth] had been told that I was a "Jewish Barthian," and this amused him no end. . . . [A]t one point he said, "You Jews have the promise but not the fulfillment; we Christians have both promise and fulfillment." Influenced by the banking atmosphere of Basel, I replied: "With human promises, one can have the promise but not the fulfillment. The one who promises can die, or change his mind, or not fulfill his promise for any number of reasons. But a promise of God is like money in the bank. If we have his promise, we have its fulfillment and if we do not have the fulfillment we do not have the promise." There was a period of silence and then he said: "You know, I never thought of it that way."[17]

3   Most important, Barth found himself willing to accept, explicitly and without reservation, Marquardt's critique of his doctrine of Israel. He raised no objection even to Marquardt's harshest expressions. He rejected excuses. He encouraged improvements. Marquardt's book appeared in 1967. On September 5 of that year, at the very end of his life, Barth wrote Marquardt:

> I have just finished reading your book. For two and one-half days it kept me holding my breath or breathless. . . .
> You have discovered and expounded my doctrine of Israel with great skill and finesse, and historically and materially I can raise no objection. This doctrine of mine was . . . impressing and convincing to me . . . before I came to §5. . . .
> You had good cause to develop the criticism made in §5. I can only say two things, not by way of excuse, but by way of explanation.
> 1.   Biblical Israel as such gave me so much to think about and to cope with that I simply did not have the time or intellectual strength to look more closely at Baeck, Buber, Rosenzweig, etc. as you have now done in such worthy fashion.
> 2.   I am decidedly not a philosemite, in that in personal encounters with living Jews (even Jewish Christians) I have always, so long as I can remember, had to suppress a totally irrational aversion, naturally suppressing it at once on the basis of all my presuppositions, and concealing it totally in all my statements, yet still having to suppress and conceal it. Pfui! is all

---

17   Michael Wyschogrod, "A Jewish Perspective on Karl Barth," in Donald K. McKim, ed., *How Karl Barth Changed My Mind* (Grand Rapids, MI: Eerdmans, 1986), pp. 156–61; here, p. 161.

I can say to this in some sense allergic reaction of mine. . . . A good thing
that this reprehensible instinct is totally alien to my sons and other better
people than myself (including you). But it could have had a retrogressive
effect on my doctrine of Israel.

. . . May this not happen to you in the projected improvement of my first
attempt! . . .[18]

Although a critique like Marquardt's is still controversial, it need not be.[19]
I seek to extend his critique of unintended idealism from Jews to gender. I
seek, more important, to expand the appeal to particularity from Christ to the
Spirit, and to retrieve (not analogy but) *anagogy* alongside typology. (One of
the four medieval senses, anagogy "leads up," reading the Bible in light of the
eschatological community, as when "Let there be light" means "let us be led
into glory."[20]) In so doing I prefer Barth to his defenders; I hope only to deploy
a critique that Barth accepted and suggest improvements that Barth invited.
My aim is less to rehearse the critique than to cast it in such a way as to suggest
how to go on.

---

[18]   Karl Barth, *Letters 1961–1968*, ed. Jürgen Fangmeier and Hinrich Stoevesandt, trans.
Geoffrey W. Bromiley (Grand Rapids, MI: Eerdmans, 1981), letter #260, pp. 261–3.
[19]   The literature on Barth and Judaism has grown vast. Eberhard Busch, *Unter dem Bogen
des einen Bundes: Karl Barth und die Juden 1933–1945* (Neukirchen-Vluyn: Neukirchner
Verlag, 1996), has recently defended Barth against any charge of *moral* and *biographical* anti-
Semitism. Among 15 pages of closely spaced bibliography in that book, theological works
of note *other* than those treated here include Bertold Klappert, *Israel und die Kirche:
Erwägungen zur Israellehre Karl Barths* (Munich: Christian Kaiser, 1980), and "Barmen I und
die Juden," in Jürgen Moltmann, ed., *Bekennende Kirche wagen: Barmen 1934–1984*
(Munich: Christian Kaiser, 1984), pp. 59–124; H. Jansen, "Anti-Semitism in the Amiable
Guise of Theological Philo-Semitism in Karl Barth's Israel Theology Before and After
Auschwitz," in Y. Bauer, et al., eds, *Remembering for the Future* (Oxford: Oxford University
Press, 1986), pp. 72–9; Pinchas Lapide, *Jeder kommt zum Vater: Barmen und die Folgen*
(Neukirchen-Vluyn: Neukirchner Verlag, 1984); Friedrich-Wilhelm Marquardt, *Die
Juden im Römerbrief* (Zurich: Theologischer Verlag, 1971), *Die Gegenwart des Auferstandenen
bei seinem Volk Israel* (Munich: Christian Kaiser, 1983), *Von Elend und Heimsuchung der
Theologie: Prolegomena zur Dogmatik* (Munich: Christian Kaiser, 1992), and *Das christliche
Bekenntnis zu Jesus, dem Juden: Eine Christologie*, Bd. 1 (Munich: Christian Kaiser, 1990).
[20]   Thomas Aquinas, *In Gal.* 4:24a (lect. 7), #254. A translation exists: *Commentary on Saint
Paul's Epistle to the Galatians*, trans. F. R. Larcher, Aquinas Scripture Series, vol. 1 (Albany,
NY: Magi Books, 1966). Far from opposing anagogical to christological exegesis, the
example actually refers to Christ as the head glorifying the eschatological community. For
more see *Summa Theologiae* I.1.10c; *Quaestiones Quodlibetales* 7.6.2; and Henri de Lubac,
Exégèse médiévale: Les Quatre sens de l'écriture (Paris: Aubier, 1959–64).

Three Further Objections

Even as a constructive project of retrieval, the approach invites three further objections.

1 Why attempt to cover Jews and gender in the same essay? They are two very large topics, and their relation, for Barth, seems distant at best.
2 What view of reality underlies the conjunction of topics? Although the topics of Jews and gender *are* closely related in the postmodern study of oppression,[21] that connection has much to do with the evidential significance of historical and empirical reality, but little to do with the exegetical and christological warrants that define reality for Barth.
3 Why turn to pneumatological rather than christological judgments for the supplement? Despite complaints of binitarianism, Barth devoted hundreds if not thousands of pages to the Spirit. Besides, Christians with views of the Spirit *more* robust than Barth's, from the Pentecostals to the Orthodox, can hold views of Jews and women arguably *less* progressive than his.

Replies and Qualifications

"Because the election of God is real, there is such a thing as love and marriage."[22] So Karl Barth deeply and beautifully connects one doctrine, election, which has to do with the Jews, and another, human love and marriage, that has to do with gender. The connection is christological and exegetical; it arises, that is, from biblical tropes about God as the jealous lover of Israel and Christ as the bridegroom of the Church. It fulfills, therefore, Barth's requirement that theological statements should be christologically "concrete" rather than "abstract"; that is, they do not abstract the Father from

---

[21] Not necessarily incorrect, but not the basis for this argument. See, for example, the essays in Nancy A. Harrowitz and Barbara Hyams, eds, *Jews and Gender: Responses to Otto Weininger* (Philadelphia: Temple University Press, 1995); and Howard Eilberg-Schwartz, ed., *People of the Body: Jews and Judaism from an Embodied Perspective* (Albany, NY: SUNY Press, 1992), esp. Eilberg-Schwartz, Introduction and "The Problem of the Body for the People of the Book", and Sander Gilman, "The Jewish Body: A Foot-Note," pp. 1–46, 223–42. See also Katharina von Kellenbach, *Anti-Judaism in Feminist Religious Writings*, American Academy of Religion Cultural Criticism Series, no. 1 (Atlanta, GA: Scholars Press, 1994).

[22] III/1, 318.

Christ the Son to produce an uninvolved God, or the human being from Christ the *verus homo* to produce a godforsaken creature. The exegetical procedure appropriate to such claims is that of *typology*, which reads a passage as figuring Christ. The chief older mode of exegesis that Barth revives, typology defines realistic exegesis for Barth, as Christ defines the real. Since the study of oppression, on the other hand, tends to define reality historically and empirically, an attempt to address Barth on the grounds of the usual connection of Jews and gender would therefore seem, on its face, designed to fail. I offer two answers to this charge.

1   Ironically enough, it is *Barth*, according to Marquardt, who introduces natural theology into his doctrine of Israel. Defenders find the sting from Barth's portrayal of the Synagogue lessened, in that the Synagogue represents the sinfulness "only" of the human being as such. (Similarly, homosexual couples come to represent the sinfulness of unchastity as such, as the divorced and remarried had done in the past.) Yet because for Barth human pride first comes to light and is visible – empirical – in the history of the Jews, Marquardt can write that for Barth, "The Jews *are* the empirical and to this extent: [they become] the observable and effective representation of [the human] predicament; in other words, the Jews are for Barth the proof of the kernel of truth of natural theology within the revelation of grace."[23] (So gay and lesbian people, too, become the observable and effective representation of the human predicament, sin.) Marquardt says that by way of observation, not criticism: it is not only a theological and biblical, but a Barthian rationale, revealing why the empirical is strictly *appropriate* in the case of the Jews. Barth allows a "demythologization" – or remythologization – not of Jesus, but of his people. Thus Barth not once but often and in complete seriousness offers the survival of the Jews as an empirical proof of God's existence,[24] as well as of human pride. Marquardt's observation, while not intended directly as criticism, does put Barth in a bind. Either it is not appropriate to adduce the empirical history of rabbinic Judaism, "the Synagogue," or there is a great deal more evidence to consider, including "Baeck, Buber, and Rosenzweig" – in short, Jewish self-understanding.

2   Although Barth elsewhere insists that empirical reality, the evidential significance of history, and the self-understanding of groups are never the

---

[23]   Marquardt, *Die Entdeckung des Judentums*, p. 316. I owe my attention to this passage to Sonderegger, *That Jesus Christ Was Born a Jew*, p. 62, with discussion.

[24]   III/3, 209–12; Karl Barth, *Dogmatics in Outline*, trans. G. T. Thomson (London: SCM Press, 1949), p. 75.

defining object of dogmatic theology, he also refused to immunize his theology against their claims, and he did so long before the famous opening to the "little lights of creation" later in his work. The biblical system hermetically sealed off against the world is a parody of Barth, opposing his christology. Although the office of dogmatics is to test the proclamation of the Church against the Word of God, not against empirical reality or evidential history, Barth raises and answers the question, already in I/1: can *God* speak through those other signs? Yes, of course; to do so is a matter of God's freedom; and yet God does not exercise that freedom capriciously or abstractly. Rather, God exercises it according to God's own self-determination, or "concretely," that is, in a trinitarian pattern. On the pattern of the enhypostatic taking on of flesh by the Logos, the triune God *assumes* human words into the divine Word.[25] On the pattern of the founding of the Church by the Spirit, the triune God *baptizes* human speakers into the divine community. If and when, therefore, God in freedom should speak to the Church about its proclamation from empirical events or evidentiary history, God's speech does not remain *external* to God's Word, but is by definition *internal* to it – just as the incarnation confirms that human flesh is not external but internal to God, from the beginning of God's free self-determination to be God also for the human being. Empirical events and evidentiary history, should God assume them into the Word, do not break the rule that the community tests its proclamation by God's Word, but prove it. Similarly, groups whose self-understandings really call the Church to account do not break the rule that God speaks within the community, but prove that the Spirit founds the community with just such a call. Circular? Yes indeed, Barth would say, and virtuously so, insofar as the circularity of the argument traces the inner circulation, or perichoresis, of the persons of the Trinity. Thus we read:

> [T]here can be nothing to prevent God from turning even such utterance concerning Him into proclamation of His Word to us which, in its character as sanctified utterance within the Church, is at first partially or even totally concealed from us. If the Church is visible, this need not imply that we actually see it in its full compass, that the dimensions of its sphere might not be very different from what we think we know them to be. God may suddenly be pleased to have Abraham blessed by Melchizedek, or Israel blessed by Balaam or helped by Cyrus. . . . He can establish the Church anew and directly when and where and how it pleases Him. . . .

[25] For an elegant account of that pattern, see Bruce McCormack, *Karl Barth's Critically Realistic Dialectical Theology* (Oxford: Clarendon Press, 1995), chapter 8, pp. 327–74.

Hence it can never be the case that the Word of God is confined to the proclamation of the existing Church, or to the proclamation of the Church as known to us, or to the proclamation in this known Church which specially claims to be proclamation [i.e., in official or magisterial pronouncements]. Church proclamation itself, in fact, regards itself only as service of the Word of God, as a means of grace in God's free hand. Hence it cannot be master of the Word, nor try to regard the Word as confined within its own borders. . . .

God may speak to us through Russian Communism, a flute concerto, a blossoming shrub, or a dead dog. . . . [T]he boundary between the Church and the secular world can still take at any time a different course from that which we think we discern.[26]

That ecclesiology could read a great deal of lesbian and gay protest against the Church right back into it.

Nevertheless, a word from the outside is not self-validating, is not entitled to prophetic authority within the Church, until tested by exegesis. To make the test *is* the task of dogmatics, "the *wissenschaftlich* self-examination of the Christian Church with respect to the content of its distinctive talk about God."[27] The Word of God in Christ includes what survives a test against the Word of God in Scripture. The Spirit of Christ in the Church includes what survives the discernment of spirits. It is because Christ's Spirit puts down and raises up challenges to the Church's exegesis, bringing it into greater conformity with the Word, that pneumatological judgments can prove especially "open or eager to register the cantankerous details available only through discernment of public reality."[28]

That the cantankerous details of public reality urging reform of the Church's proclamation about Jews and gender may belong to movements of the Spirit emerges from their presence in the Church not only unknown to Barthians, but even in the Church known to them. For the Church to listen to the experience of Jews and women and gay and lesbian people is not necessarily just another species of illicit natural theology, but a self-examination by some churches' own, internal doctrinal norms. That God wills the continued existence of Jews as an *identifiable* people, not absorbed into the Gentile mass, is now Church

---

[26]   I/1, 54–55.

[27]   I/1, 1, *Leitsatz*.

[28]   I owe this way of putting the matter to personal correspondence from Kendall Soulen.

[29]   For a summary, see Clark M. Williamson, *A Guest in the House of Israel: Post-Holocaust Church Theology* (Louisville, KY: Westminster/John Knox, 1993), p. 37. For complete statements, see Alan Brockway, et al., *The Theology of the Churches and the Jewish People*

continued on next page

dogma for large numbers of the faithful,[29] whom Barth's doctrine must continue to interest. That homosexual persons are specially in need of pastoral care and deserving of further theological reflection is now the official position of the Catholic magisterium.[30] So moves the Spirit also within the Church known to Barthians as to excite it to test traditional views by renewed exegesis.

Several reasons outweigh the disadvantages of holding the topics of Jews and gender together.

1 The reception of Barth's views on both Jews and gender has undergone an about-face, reason enough to ask after connections. Despite Barth's confession that he was "no philosemite," no less a witness than Theodor Adorno regarded him as "grenzlos philosemitisch,"[31] while others regarded him as innovative in rendering women constitutive of co-humanity with men. Yet now critics regard him with suspicions of a rhetoric positively medieval on the Jews and hopelessly hierarchical on women.[32]

2 Critics regard the two reversals as related not accidentally but formally. Both critiques accuse Barth of throwing up a conceptual screen onto which he can project an abstraction (the Church and the Synagogue, Man and Woman) and hide real people (the Jews, men and women). Both question the *Dogmatics' Realitätsbezug*, or relation to reality. A critique Barth's defenders reject has acquired the Lukan urgency of the knocker persisting at midnight or the widow importuning the unjust judge.

3 Barth himself launched critiques of his theological predecessors with the charge of "abstraction." He made Luther and Calvin guilty of "abstraction" in their doctrine of election, Schleiermacher in his entire anthropology. Is Barth's worry the same or different? If similar, it raises the possibility of internal critique.

4 It might appear that Barth's own critique of abstraction has little in common with his detractors', since Barth defines the "real" differently. At

(Geneva: WCC Publications, 1988). For discussion of the authority and challenge of such statements for traditional Christian theology, see Kendall Soulen, *The God of Israel and Christian Theology* (Minneapolis, MN: Fortress, 1996), esp. ch. 1, pp. 1–21.

[30] Congregation for the Doctrine of the Faith, "Letter to the Bishops of the Catholic Church on the Pastoral Care of Homosexual Persons," conveniently in Jeannine Gramick and Pat Furey, eds, *The Vatican and Homosexuality* (New York: Crossroad, 1988), pp. 1–10; here, §§2, 17.

[31] Busch, *Unter dem Bogen des einen Bundes*, p. v.

[32] E.g., Rosemary Radford Ruether, *Sexism and God-Talk* (Boston: Beacon, 1983), p. 98; Elisabeth Moltmann-Wendel and Jürgen Moltmann, *Humanity in God* (New York: Pilgrim, 1983), p. 95, nn. 13 and 14.

least, it might appear so until we recall that despite the distinctively Barthian critique of the 19th century, especially Schleiermacher, Barth's treatments of Jews and gender appear to reflect examined or unexamined but formally similar 19th century Platonisms about *das ewig Weibliche* or *der ewige Jude*. Such Platonisms may fall to an extension of Barth's own Schleiermacher-critique: Jews and gender belong together because they are both matters Barth picks up out of German romanticism, especially if they are matters he greatly, but incompletely, reworks.

5   Most interesting of all, Barth perceived and elevated a deep conjunction, even a marriage between the two topics, one quite different from the conjunction discerned by historians of oppression, and one he did not regard as a theological conceit or quaint anachronism, but as an ontological feature of God's covenant with humankind richly apt for theological elaboration: as creation is the external ground of the covenant, and covenant the internal ground of creation, so the love of man for woman is the external ground of God's love for Israel, and God's love for Israel the internal ground of man's love for woman.[33]

6   That connection carries us deeply into Barth's greatest strategy for reading the Bible, namely typology. Of the four medieval senses, Barth prolifically practiced three – the literal, the typological, and the moral. One of the two disused ones, typology, he retrieved with great self-conscious satisfaction. It is the odder therefore that a work so rich in ecclesial reflection as the *Church Dogmatics* never reflects explicitly upon the other, anagogy, the ecclesial sense. Perhaps that is because it is also the eschatological sense, and Barth's eschatology went unfinished. Anagogy, seeing communities in the light of glory, proposes compatible supplements to Barth's pneumatology and exegesis.

The connection of Jews and gender lies deep in the structure of Barth's thought, in his inheritance from the 19th century and in his critique of it, in his exegetical practice and in his trinitarian concreteness. Barth always took a lively interest in politics. Those features invest a political critique with theological interest.[34]

In the following chapter I attempt to construct a better Barth by providing him with a more robust doctrine of the Spirit, one that helps set up the constructive pneumatology of part III.

---

[33]   III/1, 318.
[34]   For more, see George Hunsinger, ed., *Karl Barth and Radical Politics* (Philadelphia: Westminster, 1976).

Chapter 7

UNINTENDED ABSTRACTION IN BARTH'S DOCTRINE OF ISRAEL: RETRIEVING A DOCTRINE OF THE SPIRIT

Barth's Critique of Abstraction

Barth's critique of abstraction does not, however, attempt in the first instance to attend to "empirical" reality, or descriptions of reality undisciplined by the Word of God in Christ. Barth would not say that a theology is abstract because it favors the biblical witness to Christ over empirical descriptions, or theological "Israel" over empirical "Jews." Rather he calls a theology abstract that favors empirical descriptions over the details of the biblical narratives. The "real" world for Barth is "the strange new world within the Bible."[1] The critique of abstraction does not address the problem of *Realitätsbezug*, as reality is commonly understood; rather it addresses theology's *Realitätsbezug* precisely as *God in Christ* defines what reality is. That means that Barth's critique of abstraction centers on such topics as trinitarian doctrine and biblical narrative. It does not ignore such topics as statistics and secular history, but may absorb them magisterially, as a center takes in its periphery, because the critique of abstraction aims not to constrain but to honor God's freedom, not to impoverish exegesis but to enrich it.

[1] The famous title of a 1916 address, reprinted in Barth, *The Word of God and the Word of Man*, trans. Douglas Horton (London: Hodder & Stoughton, 1928), pp. 28–50.

Let me give an example. Barth's most famous and successful innovation in all the *Church Dogmatics* is his reformulation of the doctrine of election. Barth diagnoses traditional doctrines of election as suffering under a twofold abstraction: an unknown electing God, a *Deus absconditus* whose ways are past finding out, whose freedom abstracts from love, and whose character abstracts from the revelation in Jesus Christ; and an unknown elected human being, the object of God's caprice and therefore at sea.[2]

> *Latet periculum in generalibus*: we were forced to say this of the first error, and we must now repeat it with reference to the second. In the first case we were forced to challenge the *general* character of the proposed view of humanity. In the second, we must challenge the *general* character of the proposed concept of God.[3]

Barth cures the twofold abstraction with a singular *concreteness* or *particularity*: Jesus Christ is the electing God and the elect human being in one.[4]

> In the doctrine of predestination we have to do with the understanding both of God and of the human being *in particular*: in the *particular* relationship in which God is the true God and the human being the true human being.
>
> [The doctrine of election] must begin *concretely* with the acknowledgment of Jesus Christ as both the electing God and the elected human being.[5]

Although Barth claims never to deploy a method, he does reveal a certain evaluative and constructive *procedure* in criticizing his predecessors and defending his innovation, marked by negative words like "absolute," which goes with "general" and "abstract," and positive words like "definition" and "determination," which go with "particular." From a large number of texts in II/2 I pick out a number of features.

1   The particular attends to the story of Jesus. Not just any particularity will do. Barth inveighs against a particularity deduced "as a species from a genus,"[6] and against Calvin's "particular," i.e., empirical, interests.[7] Nor is it even a

---

2   E.g., II/2, 103–4.

3   II/2, 49, my emphasis.

4   For more, see Mary Kathleen Cunningham, *What Is Theological Exegesis? Interpretation and Use of Scripture in Barth's Doctrine of Election* (Valley Forge, PA: Trinity Press International, 1995).

5   II/2, 76, my emphasis.

6   II/2, 48.

7   II/2, 37.

christological principle or method, when the emphasis falls upon the nouns. Rather "In itself, and as such, *the particular* leads us to the general, which it includes within itself."[8] The particular is christological in a recognizable way; in Hegelian language, Christ is the concrete universal.[9] Yet Barth does not make Christ the concrete universal to pursue a Hegelian method or a Durkheimian explication, however powerful they may be. Rather he finds the Hegelian–Durkheimian insight *strictly appropriate* to the peculiar character of God.

> [T]he true God is the One whose freedom and love have nothing to do with *abstract* absoluteness or naked sovereignty, but who in His love and freedom has determined and limited Himself to be God *in particular and not in general*, and only as such to be omnipotent and sovereign and the possessor of all other perfections.[10]

We know God in the particular human being Jesus Christ as he is available to us not even in dogma but in the text. As Barth wrote to Berkouwer, "in each individual theological question I seek to orientate myself afresh – to some extent from the very beginning – not to christological dogma but to Jesus Christ himself (*vivit! regnat! triumphat!*)."[11]

2   Abstraction is at root an insufficiency in *trinitarian* thinking. While Barth explicates and defends the *knowledge* of God as particular by displaying that particularity in the biblical stories about Jesus Christ, he also explicates and elaborates the *being* of God as particular by reference to the Trinity. Thus in the doctrine of election, Barth accuses the Reformers of a *trinitarian* mistake: without intending to, they had proceeded as if the Father alone were the electing God, and not the Son.

Particularity is trinitarian not so much textually in Barth as architectonically. In fact, the only places where the Trinity becomes a subject of explicit

---

[8]   II/2, 51, my emphasis.

[9]   Or, in the language of Durkheim (who has himself learned something from Hegel about concrete universals), Barth has seen the power of Christ, the Christian totem. Barth confessed a tendency "always to Hegelianize somewhat." See Michael Welker, "Barth und Hegel: Zur Erkenntnis eines methodischen Verfahrens bei Barth," *Evangelische Theologie* 43 (1983): 307–28.

[10]   II/2, 49, my emphasis.

[11]   To Berkouwer, in Eberhard Busch, *Karl Barth: His Life from Letters and Autobiographical Texts* (Philadelphia: Fortress, 1976), p. 380, quoted in George Hunsinger, *How To Read Karl Barth: The Shape of His Theology* (New York: Oxford University Press, 1991), p. 14.

reflection in the doctrine of election warn that just as one can speak of Christ, but abstractly, so one can also speak abstractly of the Trinity.

> It is [a] temptation to think of God the Father, Son and Holy Spirit merely as a Subject . . . which differs from other such subjects only by the fact that its election is *absolutely* free. . . . God is not *in abstracto* Father, Son and Holy Ghost, the Triune God. He is so with a *definite* purpose and reference . . .[12]

Barth causes the doctrine of the Trinity to arise from "the being of God as the One who loves in freedom" (title of §28); "a correct doctrine of election" (title of §32) arises from God's self-determination to be "for the human being too the One who loves in freedom" (*Letitsatz* of §32). So "the One who loves in freedom" is the hinge that connects the two halves of the doctrine of God together, II/1 and II/2, the being of God and the correctness of a doctrine of election. And election, therefore, is simply the *application* of the trinitarian doctrine to human beings. God is the God that God is, not only for God, but also for human beings; God is Trinity not only for God or *in se* but also for *human beings*. That is what it means to be that God, the God revealed in Jesus Christ. But God's being for us is an action of the whole Trinity *ad extra*, and therefore indivisible from the Holy Spirit. Although reticence about the Holy Spirit does not in itself constitute a flaw, neither can it be wrong to elaborate the critique of abstraction in a pneumatological way. In the only place where the Spirit gets a material role in the doctrine of election, it is possible just to glimpse Barth making the same move from God *in se* to God for us, if you keep in mind that it is proper to the Spirit to glorify the love of the Father and the Son:

> [God's] glory, which in Himself, in His inner life as Father, Son, and Holy Spirit, cannot be subjected to attack or disturbance, . . . [is ordained to enter] the sphere of contradiction . . . . [Therefore, i]n the beginning it was the resolve of the *Holy Spirit* that the unity of God, of Father and Son should not be disturbed or rent by this covenant with the human being, but that it should be made the more glorious. . . .[13]

3   Theology regards the mirrorings provided by empirical reality (ordinary sense) as distinctly dim; when Barth sees clearly, he relates "empirical" reality to the Bible and sees types (correspondences to Christ). Types are precisely *not* the sorts of "abstractions" Barth inveighed against; they are the sort of concretions

---

[12]   II/2, 100, 79, my emphasis.
[13]   II/2, 169, 101, my emphasis.

that gave his theology power. They are concrete because they press this reality into the strange new world within the Bible; because they read everything as a type of Christ. To conclude, "theology regularly entails judgments about reality that go beyond or otherwise differ from what is 'empirically' available (e.g., human beings are created in the image of God)." The charge of going beyond the empirical is hardly to be avoided, short of redefining "empirical"; and it is hard to see why theologians should want to avoid it.[14]

In what follows, therefore, I do not propose that theology do without judgments that reach beyond empirical reality, and I assume with Barth that the "really real" absorbs this world into the one depicted in the Bible. Nevertheless I also propose that Barth's readings of Jews and gender have room to become *more* concrete, *more* absorbed into the Biblical text, related to Christ in a *more* complex way, specifically by his people and his Spirit. In particular, I will be proposing that Barth's critique of the 19th century insufficiently identified two of its abstractions, two of its *failures* to see reality in the mirror of Christ. It will not have escaped attentive readers of Marquardt's list that Barth accuses the Synagogue of being "a living petrification of the Old Testament in itself and *in abstracto*." Is it really in accord with Barth's doctrine that the elect people can actually succeed in "abstracting" themselves from God's self-determination to be for them – or can only theologians do that?

Furthermore, consideration of the Jews could scarcely count as natural theology if their community is still a concern or a material mode of the Spirit. Either the doctrine of Israel is worse than critics thought – it is a doctrine that there exists a group of human beings entirely natural, in hyper-Protestant opposition to grace, entirely godforsaken and Spirit-bereft – or Barth's pneumatology had grown fairly abstract. It must have grown abstract, if Barth could refrain from protest against a doctrine of Israel characterized as natural theology – even as its kernel of truth within the revelation of grace.

Unintended Abstraction in Barth's Doctrine of Elect Pairs

Barth reformulates the doctrine of election by taking up all the traditional examples of individual elect and rejected human beings and even animals,

---

[14] I am grateful to Kendall Soulen for the last two sentences of the paragraph (personal correspondence).

setting them into pairs, and referring *both*, the elected *and* the rejected member, to Jesus Christ as their typological reference, since he is elect and the rejected human being in one, the *rejected* human being *elected*. It is a glorious change of subject from the usual elect-and-reprobate division, a brilliant unasking of the question. All the things the orthodox predestinarians said are true, even about reprobation – if only they all apply first and paradigmatically not to individual human beings, but to Jesus Christ, and to others only "in him."[15]

Thus when Barth finally comes, after some 300 pages of turning the reader's attention to the election of Christ and the community, to "The Elect and the Rejected," there is no change of subject. Barth finds pairs of elect and rejected everywhere in the Bible, all pointing to the rejected one elected, Jesus Christ. There he launches a litany to recover for fiercely christocentric usage the older doctrine of twin predestination, or *praedestinatio gemina*.[16] So we hear of the following pairs: Cain and Abel, Isaac and Ishmael, Rachel and Leah, Ephraim and Manasseh, Tamar and Judah, Perez and Serah, the offering goat and the scapegoat, the slain bird and the released bird, Saul and David, the man of God of Judah and the prophet from Bethel, and finally Judas and Paul.[17] In ringing the changes upon this theme Barth is not tone-deaf. The renditions abound in subtlety and depth. The elect and the rejected are allowed to intersect and change sides, and both – Saul no less than David – are types of Jesus Christ. In a famous long, small-print excursus on Judas,[18] Barth shows Judas as one of the elect, the disciples, and insists that he has completed the three traditional parts of contrition, *contritio cordis, confessio oris, satisfactio operis*, washed out any distinction between Judas and Peter, Judas and any of us, Judas and Paul, before concluding:

> But to say this is to say all that we need to say about the general question of the divine will and intention for the rejected, the non-elect. The answer can only be as follows. [God] wills that [the non-elect human being] too should hear the Gospel, and with it the promise of his election. He wills, then, that this Gospel should be proclaimed to him. He wills that he should appropriate and live by the hope which is given him in the Gospel. He wills that the rejected should

---

15   Eph. 1:4, II/2, 110–15.
16   Also the title of Heinrich Vogel's contribution to the Barth *Festschrift* of 1936, "Theologische Aufsätze," an essay that goes unmentioned in the *Dogmatics*. See Katherine Sonderegger, *That Jesus Christ Was Born a Jew* (University Park, PA: Pennsylvania State University Press, 1992), p. 45, n. 8.
17   II/2, 354–409, 458–506.
18   II/2, 458–506.

believe, and that as a believer he should become a rejected human being elected. The rejected one as such has no independent existence in the presence of God. He is not determined by God merely to be rejected. He is determined to hear and say that he is a rejected human being elected. This is what the elect of the New Testament are – rejected human beings elected in and from their rejection, human beings in whom Judas lived, but was also slain, as in the case of Paul. They are rejected ones who as such are summoned to faith. They are rejected ones who on the basis of the election of Jesus Christ, and looking to the fact that He delivered Himself up for them, believe in their election.[19]

This gives one a taste for rich biblical exegesis, from Cain and Abel to Judas and Paul, and for relentless christocentric focus.

But it can give one a taste for *more* riches. Christocentrism works well with dialectic. It is good at resolving pairs. In spite of great detail, in spite of its ability to adduce figures like Ephraim and Manasseh, Perez and Serah, unknown to most theologians, in spite of its ability to evoke and incorporate a huge volume of biblical narrative, it has its limits. It does better with character than with plot. It does better with dialectic than with complication. It does better with individuals or groups treated individualistically, than with individuals in community. Even as it evokes and incorporates biblical narratives as no theologian has done since Luther, it also suppresses and flattens parts of them. Its subtlety is dialectical, not plotted; twofold, not circumstantial. It does not tell Christians how to talk about the *means* by which God works among others – *third* parties, *circumstances*, *communities* – to hold up the twinned pairs for display. Think of Rebecca tricking Isaac into blessing Jacob, Jonathan allying himself with David, the costuming of Tamar lying in wait for Judah, the dozens or thousands who surround and support the pairs. Barth can evoke these details – but he cannot exploit them. Or better: he cannot exploit them without referring much more often to that trinitarian person to whom Christians appropriate the movements of hearts, the providence of circum-stances, and the gathering of communities, who blows where it wills, and thus *resists* reduction into twofold categories, however skillfully plied: I mean the Spirit. Barth has whetted one's appetite for a radically theological reading of biblical narrative – whetted it in such a way that one wants more. More is readily available. It is the overplus that the Spirit supplies, never apart from the Father and the Son, but *enriching* and *celebrating* them. It is the Spirit to whom Christians appropriate the plots and turns of biblical narrative, the circum-stances and communities of biblical characters, the secondary causes that move

---

[19] II/2, 506.

their hearts in this world. Barth is richly open for this sort of elaboration, though he does not pursue it.

The Holy Spirit Can Alleviate the Unintended Abstraction

The condition for the possibility *in God* for "Jesus's existence, of the life of our brother-man," is God's life as the One who loves in freedom *in se* before being that One *also for the human being*. It is because God loves in freedom already without human beings that they can know God in Jesus as loving in freedom now for human beings, not capriciously or abstractly but by God's own trinitarian self-determination, because God *is in se* as God *does in Jesus*; because God's loving in freedom is neither externally compelled nor spontaneously arbitrary, yet mysteriously and reliably characteristic. Thus we read in the stirring *Leitsatz* to §32: "The doctrine of election is the sum of the Gospel because of all the words that can be said or heard it is the best: that God elects the human being; that God is *for the human being too* the One who loves in freedom."[20] The mystery and reliability of the One who loves in freedom is revealed, enacted, and furthered in a real history with human beings in the resurrection of Jesus. God proves free to restore the love between the Father and the Son, even in the face of death. Barth stops there – it is enough – he has explicated the doctrine of election with the doctrine of atonement. But he might have gone further. He might have completed the doctrine of election not only in terms of the second person but also in terms of the third.[21]

Precisely as God proves free to restore the love between God the Father and God the Son identified with sinful human flesh, God is free *also* to celebrate and glorify and consummate that love by *catching the human being up into it*. God's loving in freedom is not without celebration, glorification, and delight, not without the sort of communal joy that feasts and weddings grant to love. To do that is the intratrinitarian role of the Spirit. It is therefore not necessary, but it is both gracious and fitting for God to catch the human being up into it. To do *that* is the appropriated work of the Spirit.[22] God the Father is not to be separated from God the Son; classical predestinarians drove in a wedge there. And human *incorporation* into that inseparable relationship is not to be

---

[20]   II/2, 3.
[21]   Robert W. Jenson, "Predestination," in Robert W. Jenson and Carl E. Braaten, eds., *Christian Dogmatics* (Philadelphia: Fortress, 1984).
[22]   Rom. 8:11.

separated from the work of the Spirit. Although the solution is resolutely christocentric, Barth does not fail to mention the Spirit. God's being as the One who loves in freedom is explicated by the Trinity, and election simply describes the turn of the One who loves in freedom toward us human beings in Christ not without the Spirit. It is the chief end of the human being, for Barth as for the opening answer of the Westminster Confession, "to glorify God and enjoy Him forever," but that is what the Spirit does already in the Trinity.[23] So human beings can glorify God because in so doing the Holy Spirit *catches them up* into its proper work of glorifying the love between the Father and the Son.

No work of the Triune God can be without the celebration and witness of the Spirit, since then the love of the Father and the Son would be isolated, lonely, lacking in the richness that the parables of Jesus portray, like a wedding without a celebration, a marriage without a witness, a feast without a guest.[24] Nothing requires that human beings celebrate the wedding, witness the marriage, enjoy the feast; in the Spirit God enjoys all those things, already rich.[25] But by the same Spirit it is not foreign to God, but *characteristic* of God – particularly characteristic of *this* God, the one who is not without the Spirit – to catch up human beings into those things.

Thus election, too, cannot be without the Spirit, even if Barth chooses to emphasize the role of the Son. Election, too, is *for* something, for the triune life that the Spirit prepares and fulfills human beings to share. The *trinitarian* explications of particularity may remain formulaic compared to the christological ones that subdivide them, but they *leave open* room for additional explications, just as Barthian, and necessarily so.

Robert Jenson has seen this openness in Barth and proposed, not as a

---

[23] §§12, 18. In the short version of this in Barth's *Dogmatics in Outline*, trans. G. T. Thompson (London: SCM Press, 1949), Barth manages to say that the presence of the second person in the Trinity is the condition for the possibility of creation, but unaccountably not that the presence of the third person in the Trinity is the condition for the possibility of consummation. Thus we read that "In that God became human, it has also become manifest and worthy of belief that He did not wish to exist for Himself only and therefore to be alone [not lonely]" (p. 50, *Leitsatz*). And in the same place we read also that "[God] creates, sustains, and rules [creation] as the theater of his glory – and in its midst, the human being also, as the witness of His glory." We expect to read, in parallel fashion, something like this: "In that God the Spirit blows at Pentecost, it has also become manifest and worthy of belief that He does not wish to enjoy and glorify Himself only and therefore to be without a created participant and witness of it." But we do not.

[24] Cf. Mt. 3:17, 9:15, 22:2; Mk. 1:9–11; Lk. 3:21–2; Jn. 1:31–3.

[25] Barth, *Dogmatics in Outline*, pp. 53–4.

replacement of Barth's discovery that Jesus Christ is the electing God, but as its necessary complement: *the Holy Spirit is the electing God*.[26] What would that mean for Barth's biblical exegesis, especially the exegesis of all those typologized pairs?

It would mean a greater openness to the complications and details of the stories, the ways in which the Spirit moves not just pairs of people, but the communities and environments around them, to construct typological relationships, so that supporting actors and circumstances and growth and reversal and plot come into play – or, to put it into more theological language, so that one attends more to community or Church and providence and sanctification and resurrection, not just "*the* rejected" and "*the* elect." The Bible knows lots of detail and lots of characters and lots of complication that *praedestinatio gemina* washes out. I am not proposing to give up the typological majesty of Cain and Abel, sacrifice and scapegoat, Sarah and Hagar, Jacob and Esau, Leah and Rachel, David and Saul, Judas and Paul. But I am proposing that a reference to the Spirit helps Christian theologians to complicate the typology in a way at once more biblical, more communitarian or ecclesial, and more trinitarian in execution as well as in program.

When Barth neglects Spirit to concentrate on the christological references of *praedestinatio gemina*, he neglects Rebecca and Laban and Jonathan and sheers the biblical stories of half their characters and most of their circumstances, the Spirit's painful, complex work. The Spirit works among details and diversity in which Barth's pairs stand out in relief: but they do not so stand *without* the Spirit, and greater attention to the Spirit can restore theological readings of such stories, precisely in a Barthian mode, but ever new, to more biblical detail. It comes not amiss if the Spirit should use circumstances of farmers and herders to illuminate Cain and Abel; if sacrifice and scapegoat should be part of a richer communal and ritual life; if Abraham should belong to Sarah and Keturah and Hagar; if Rebecca should become the means for Jacob's receiving the promised blessing over Esau; if Laban should manipulate Leah and Rachel; if Jonathan should transfer kingship from Saul to David; and if Matthias should recede into obscurity to allow Paul to become the effective replacement for Judas.

We may sum up like this. Barth did not abhor abstraction for its own sake. Barth abhorred it just as it impugned the character of the One who loves in freedom as revealed in Jesus Christ. The Father's freedom may not be compromised by a love without reception and response. That is true both

---

[26]   That is a striking thesis of Jenson's "Predestination."

antecedently *in se*, as the Father loves the Son, and also for the human being, in the Son's appropriated work of reconciling the human being to God (through his atonement) for sharing in their love.[27] Such an abstraction would finally amount to the heresy that Jesus is not the Lord.

The same move is inalienable from the Spirit. The Father and the Son may not be abstracted from the Spirit; their love may not go unwitnessed, unblessed, uncelebrated, undelighted in. So, too, the being of the One who loves in freedom may not be abstracted from that One's gracious self-determination to be the One who loves in freedom by freeing for love.[28] That is true both antecedently *in se*, as the Spirit liberates the love of the Father and the Son for fruitfulness and joy, and also for us, in the Spirit's appropriated work of liberating us by sanctification and gathering to share in their fruitfulness and joy.[29] Such an abstraction would amount to the heresy that the *Spirit* is not the Lord.

The requisite supplements would be: to speak of God's self-determination in covenant with Israel as seriously as God's self-determination in covenant with Jesus Christ, not on a two-covenants theory, but on a one-covenant theory where the gap is stressed between the cause of the covenant in Christ's atoning work and the guarantee of the covenant to Israel in the promise to Abraham;[30] and to deploy anagogy as seriously as typology.

Unintended Abstraction in Barth's Doctrine of Israel

Barth's §34, "The Election of the Community," is remarkable for explaining to Protestants – and to a lesser extent to Christians generally – what Jews have

---

[27] §§11, 13, 33.

[28] I play on the *Leitsatz* for §12, "God the Holy Spirit," which reads: "The one God reveals Himself according to Scripture as the Redeemer, i.e., as the Lord who sets us free. As such He is the Holy Spirit, by receiving whom we become the children of God, because, as the Spirit of the love of God the Father and the Son, He is so antecedently in Himself" (I/1, 448).

[29] §§12, 67, 68. In using the language of fruitfulness I do not mean to call procreation particularly to mind; Augustine rejects the identification of the Spirit with childbearing at *De trin.* 12.8. The Spirit's work is more properly that of baptism, producing more adopted children of God.

[30] I owe the distinction between cause and guarantee to Bruce D. Marshall, "Theology of the Jewish People," in Colin E. Gunton, ed., *The Cambridge Companion to Christian Doctrine* (New York: Cambridge University Press, 1997).

never forgotten and what Christians should have been unable to miss: most of the election talk in the Bible is about an elect *community*.[31] Undergraduates typically suppose that "chosenness" (used of Israel) and "predestination" (used of individuals) are two separate things – and students are not so culpable in that supposition: generations of Christian theologians have taught and stupefied them with it. Furthermore, Barth insists with Romans 11, but against much of the Christian tradition and the particular anti-Semitism of the Nazis, that the election of Israel is secure. The Church and Israel comprise *one* elect community, the environment of the Messiah. Barth is the father of many late 20th century doctrines of Israel that improve on him,[32] yet continues to be more important than they. Even though the polemic against abstraction continues into §34, abstraction returns with alternately renewed and mitigated virulence in "The Election of the Community." Instead of the unknown human being, elect and rejected, we get an unknown human community, the human being in its "passing and coming" form. We get again an unknown God in Barth, too, one who can change his mind on the Jews, making a covenant that supersedes the old. It is another *Deus absconditus*, a God who has absconded from the covenant at Sinai. For according to Barth, although God honors Jews, God no longer honors Judaism.

To be sure, Barth thinks he has avoided the abstraction of the human being. He means Israel not as an abstraction, but as a biblical and christological concretion of the human being in its passing form. He means the Church not as an abstraction, but as a biblical and christological concretion of the human being in its coming form. Both of those communities, furthermore, are empirically identifiable. And both of them, as before, are types of Jesus Christ, who passes through death and comes again. Furthermore, Barth is *not* supersessionist in one sense, because he upholds the covenant with Abraham.[33]

---

[31]   For Jewish accounts see Michael Wyschogrod, *The Body of Faith: Judaism as Corporeal Election* (Minneapolis, MN: Fortress, 1983); David Novak, *The Election of Israel: The Idea of the Chosen People* (New York: Cambridge University Press, 1995), esp. "The Retrieval of the Biblical Doctrine," pp. 108–62.

[32]   E.g., Klappert, Marquardt, Wyschogrod.

[33]   We should be suspicious of that defense because Calvin (say) might have defended himself similarly on the doctrine that Barth marshals the critique of abstraction to demolish. Calvin might also have said that the human being in its rejected form is represented by the unregenerate, in its elect form by the true church. In spite of disclaimers in his better moments, Calvin, too, at least sometimes, thought the groups empirically identifiable, and he would certainly have had no trouble seeing them as representative of biblical types. Therefore the classical doctrine, too, Calvin might complain, was sufficiently "concrete." What Calvin would not be able to claim is that the doctrine sufficiently protects concreteness in the sense of Jesus Christ as *the* elect one.

Barth is not able successfully to claim that the doctrine of the election of the community sufficiently protects concreteness in the sense of the Holy Spirit as the electing God and the immanent electedness of human communities, or immanent in the Church.[34] And precisely because it is communities we are talking about here, one would expect Barth to talk about the Holy Spirit as the one to whom we appropriate their gathering, upbuilding, and holiness, as elsewhere he does, and does at length. But not here. As Barth is less able to particularize the community by reference to the Spirit's work, so he is less able to identify God by the Spirit's work.

What does it mean to identify God by the Spirit's work? Two things:

1   It means to identify God by God's self-commitment in covenant *not*, this time, to the human being in Jesus Christ, but to the human *community* in Israel. More broadly, the promise to Abraham was that he would be a father of many nations, by which they would bless themselves, by which, that is, they would become for one another a source not of hostility, but of mutual blessing.[35]

2   To identify God by the Spirit means, second, to identify God by scriptural exegesis not, this time, typologically focused on Jesus Christ, but anagogically focused on the perfect community, the heavenly Jerusalem, the consummation for which Christians daily pray, "thy kingdom come." To identify God by Jesus Christ is to refuse abstraction from God's concrete self-determination to be for human beings in him, and thus to practice typological exegesis. To identify God by the Holy Spirit is to refuse abstraction from God's concrete self-determination to be for Israel, and thus to practice anagogical exegesis.

It is Robert Jenson who has suggested that to identify God by the Spirit's work is to identify God by the Spirit's agency in the Church. Unfortunately, "the personal agent of this work in fact turns out at every step of Barth's argument to be *not* the Spirit, as advertised, but Christ; the Spirit is denoted invariably by impersonal terms. The Spirit is 'the power of Jesus Christ's being.'"[36] The

---

[34]   For more on the Holy Spirit immanent in the Church, see Robert W. Jenson, "You Wonder Where the Spirit Went," *Pro Ecclesia* 2 (1993): 296–304; here pp. 302–4, and *Unbaptized God: The Basic Flaw in Ecumenical Theology* (Minneapolis, MN: Augsburg Fortress, 1992), pp. 107–47.

[35]   I owe this to "The Blessing of an Other: A Proposal," chapter 5 in Kendall Soulen, *The God of Israel and Christian Theology* (Minneapolis, MN: Fortress, 1996), pp. 109–13, and also its development in Soulen, "YHWH the Triune God," *Modern Theology* 15 (1999): 25–54.

[36]   Jenson, "You Wonder Where the Spirit Went," p. 303, citing IV/3, 868, 869, 870.

Spirit is God's power, but not God's act. The sheer potentiality here echoes the sheer potentiality of the Father in Reformation doctrines of election, with similar abstraction. The abstract human being that Barth denied was unrelated to God, was not christologically defined, was indeed godforsaken, in that God had no prior commitment to that human being, or better, no prior commitment of God's own to that human being, so that God was "free" to exercise caprice. God's "relation" to the human being was not personal, but potential; it was a matter of abstract power.

If the abstraction here of Father and Son from the Spirit is similar to the abstraction there of Father from Son, then all sorts of talk of the Spirit can prove ineffective, as earlier accounts of election made Christ *not* the concretely electing God and elected human being in one, but the much-discussed instrument of the Father's caprice. Similarly, we should expect to find a community abstracted from the Spirit, as before we found a human being abstracted from the Son.

An abstraction from the Spirit would be similar to an abstraction from the Son. God's "relation" to the human community is not personal, but potential; it is a matter of abstract power. The "power" even "of Jesus Christ" is still an abstraction if not bound to "the act of a particular community." In this case, for Barth, God has a future relation to Israel, but Israel is not identifiable, since God has (for Barth) no future relation to the material community of the Synagogue. Yet the eschatological community of Jews and Gentiles must make something of the community in which circumcision and Passover are still honored, since the Church has become so Gentile as hardly ever to do so.[37] It is "the Old Testament *in abstracto*" for Barth, the "passing" form of the human being. It is, for Barth, what Jews need to be saved *from*. Precisely to the extent that Barth's "Synagogue" is *that which human beings are saved from*, it is *Spirit-bereft*, just as the rejected in the Reformed system were Christ-bereft. Barth does not say that the Spirit has ignored the Jews, to be sure. He includes them into the community of Jews and Gentiles which is the Church, humanity's coming form. Yet precisely that leaves the Synagogue an abstract absence of good, an abstract Spirit-less-ness, as the rejected were an abstract Christ-less-ness. Despite all disclaimers, that seems to be the logic of the matter, so many epicycles and protests. And yet if God knows the human being only in Christ, Barth complained, there is really no such thing as a

---

[37]   For discussion see the various views of Michael Wyschogrod, Eugene Borowitz, David Burrell, Ellen Charry, Paula Frederiksen, George Lindbeck, David Novak, and Peter Ochs in the "Symposium on 'Jewish Christians and the Torah,'" occupying *Modern Theology* 11, 2 (April 1995): 163–241.

Christ-less human being. Is there such a thing as a Spirit-less human community?

Barth wants to claim that God is free to keep faith with Jews who continue to act as Jews, because the eschatological community will consist of Jews and Gentiles. But Barth's identification of Jews who continue to *act* as Jews, who concretely keep faith with God's self-commitment to them, as humanity's "passing form" does little justice to Barth's intention, making it sound as if God is through with them after all. Soulen applies the phrase "Israel-forgetfulness": it means that God's history with Jesus so overwhelms God's history with Israel that the latter becomes *indecisive* for God's identity.[38] One would not normally say that Barth's theology suffers from Israel-forgetfulness. But does Israel's history continue to be *decisive* for the identity of God, if Israel ceases to live a life of its own, coming merely to represent or to mirror, in the terms of a German Idealism that Barth otherwise eschewed, humanity's "passing" form? Barth's Israel-anthropology sounds less general than Schleiermacher's, because it seems to be a biblical rather than an Enlightenment anthropology.[39] But is it really? Is the Holy Spirit, the bond of fidelity between Father and Son, still free to keep faith with circumcision? Is the Holy Spirit, the bond of community within the Trinity, still free to build effective community at Passover? If not, does God not pass over the community to which God was bound and abandon it (for reasons of sin), just as the Reformers' God passed over and abandoned the abstract human rejected (for reasons of sin)? If Israel's history is humanity's passing form, does its history not become something human beings are saved *from*, rather than the bearer of the consummation that human beings are saved *for*?[40] Barth intones, "Its mission as a natural community has now run its course and cannot

---

[38] Soulen, *The God of Israel*, pp. 16, 19, 31–3, 43, 51–2; for Soulen on Barth, see pp. 81–94.

[39] We have seen how Marquardt and Sonderegger tie the doctrine of Israel to unintended Hegelianism. Soulen (*The God of Israel*, p. 105) ties it to incomplete Schleiermacher-critique. Like Schleiermacher, both Barth and Rahner "are forced to make covenant history a function of the particular relationship that exists between the God-man Jesus Christ and human creation as a whole. Unfortunately, the result is that covenant history as the medium of God's consummating work tends to collapse into one of the two poles of Schleiermacher's original christocentric paradigm. In Barth's case, covenant history collapses back into the particular figure of Jesus Christ. In Rahner, it collapses into the dynamism of the human creature. In both cases, covenant history disappears as an identifiable feature of the common world. The irony of this collapse is that both theologians remain bound to Schleiermacher at precisely the point where one might have expected them to transcend him."

[40] For argument, see Soulen, *The God of Israel*, pp. 93–4, 104–6; for argument that this amounts to a kind of semi-Gnosticism, or a salvation from contingent history (rather than the created world), see pp. 16, 54–5, 82, 89, 92, 94, 109–10, 138, 159, 165, 175.

be continued."[41] If there should be no abstract piling up of sin upon the rejected human being, then should there be an abstract piling up of sin upon the rejected community, humanity's passing form? The continuing existence of Jews is emphatically God-willed for Barth, but not the continuing existence of the practices that constitute and build up and set apart the community that alone makes Jews concretely identifiable, the community of Judaism.

Barth does say, "It is not any other people, nor the totality of others, but the Jews who are the universal horizon of each and all peoples."[42] But the language of humankind's "passing form" and the relative absence of Spirit-talk prevent him from saying that as effectively as he would like.

The Holy Spirit Improves Barth's Doctrine of Israel, Because Consummation Is Especially Appropriate to the Spirit

In her marvelous book *That Jesus Christ Was Born a Jew: Karl Barth's "Doctrine of Israel,"* Katherine Sonderegger argues that the problem in Barth's doctrine of the elect community is that he conceives it on the pattern of justification.[43] One community must represent the sinner, the other the righteous; the combined community of God, the environment of Jesus Christ, represents the sinner justified, as he does. The sinner is the passing, the justified one the coming human being. Israel represents sin, the Church redemption. But such a canonical construal remains pneumatologically abstract, no matter how many supporting details one adduces.

According to George Lindbeck, the biblical witness is that the Church and Israel are types, but not of Christ: they are types of the people of God in fellowship with God at the end of time.[44] If Barth were still alive, and now had time for the Jews, he could notice the amazing (or perhaps not so amazing) fact that Jewish theologians can have the same eschatology as Paul: at the end,

---

[41]   III/2, 584, discussed in Soulen, *The God of Israel*, p. 91.

[42]   III/4, 319, discussed in Soulen, *The God of Israel*, p. 88; for a compatible, sympathetic, and nuanced account of Barth on Israel and consummation, see Soulen, *The God of Israel*, pp. 85–9.

[43]   Sonderegger, "Barth's Doctrine of Israel as the Divine Act of Justification by Grace," in *That Jesus Christ Was Born a Jew*, pp. 161–79.

[44]   George Lindbeck, "The Church," in Geoffrey Wainwright, ed., *Keeping the Faith: Essays to Mark the Centenary of Lux Mundi* (Philadelphia: Fortress, 1988), pp. 179–208. The potential of anagogy first impressed me under the article's influence, although it goes unmentioned there.

when the Messiah comes, the Gentiles will become part of the people of God without having to convert to Judaism.[45] Lindbeck suggests that the two become compatible even about "when the Messiah comes" if we recall that for Christians the Messiah comes twice[46] – or if, as Stan Stowers suggests as a reading of Romans, the one mission of the Messiah is split into two moments for the salvation of the world.[47] In any case the type of the people of God that both Israel and the Church indubitably represent (however they relate to Christ) is most easily appropriated to the concreteness of the *Spirit*. The gathering and setting apart and consummation of the community is the work of the Triune God appropriated to the Spirit.

Furthermore, precisely the continued God-willed distinction of Gentile Christians and Jews that Barth favors might lead one to this observation: that while God's history with the nations is easily parsed as a type of redemption – since God so graciously and surprisingly includes them in the one covenant with Abraham – God's biblically recorded history with Israel is less so. For Gentiles, the main plot of the biblical story is redemption, with consummation as an unexpected further benefit:[48] so the paschal benediction in the Roman order, "felix culpa, quae tantum ac talem meruit habere Redemptorem!"[49] But for Jews the main plot of the biblical story is about the community and the promises made to it; that those promises will also be kept in the face of sin is a corollary and subplot to the main movement. The doubt is never, in Judaism, about whether God will abandon them in anger over sin; doubt is rather about whether God will keep faith in the face of enemies and difficulties, from Babylon to the Holocaust, and Jews are so bold, in the Psalms, as simply to *hold God to account* for those promises.[50] For Gentiles, redemption is the plot, consummation the denouement; for Jews, consummation is the main plot, redemption the subplot, the outcome of which is

---

[45] So Novak, *The Election of Israel*, pp. 200–40.

[46] "Ultimately, however, in what for Judaism will be the First Coming and for Christianity, the Second, the church and Israel will in extension coincide," George Lindbeck, "Response to Michael Wyschogrod's 'Letter to a Friend,'" *Modern Theology* 11 (1995): 206–7.

[47] Stanley K. Stowers, *A Rereading of Romans: Justice, Jews, and Gentiles* (New Haven, CT: Yale University Press, 1994).

[48] I have learned the distinction of redemption from consummation from David Kelsey; Soulen argues a subtler application to Israel in *The God of Israel*.

[49] Attributed to Ambrose and quoted prominently by Thomas Aquinas, *Summa Theologiae* III.1.3 *ad* 3.

[50] At least, that is a thesis of Jon D. Levenson, *Creation and the Persistence of Evil: The Jewish Drama of Divine Omnipotence*, 2nd edn (Princeton, NJ: Princeton University Press, 1988).

never in real doubt. So redemption is not the right *main* model for the election of Israel, but consummation is. So, too, consummation belongs to the work Christians appropriate to the Spirit: the work of glorifying and celebrating the goodness of God, as Jews teach Christians to do, and by which Christians believe they are themselves caught up into the Spirit's office of doing that also within the trinitarian communion. Those are not two stories, much less two covenants, but two ways the Spirit excites gratitude for the blessings of Abraham in the readers of the Bible, integral because in this, too, they can become sources of mutual blessing one for the other.

To use the words in their narrower senses, this means, too, that Barth's exegesis needs supplementation with pneumatologically concrete forms in addition to typology, where "typology" means to take biblical and extrabiblical events in reference specifically to Christ. That is to admit that there is something a little funny about talking of a typology of the Spirit. But to say that Israel and the Church are types of the community of God in the world to come, and to say that the main plot of God's story with Israel is one of consummation, into which, as subplot, the Gentiles get eschatologically engrafted by redemption, is to talk about an exegetical procedure forgotten in Protestantism, even by Barth, except among the traditionally black churches: that of anagogy.

Barth's critique of prior theology, especially of the Reformation, proceeded by recovering a precritical mode of exegesis that related biblical and extrabiblical figures to Christ, namely typology. Barth might have recovered another, distinct precritical mode of exegesis for relating biblical and extrabiblical realities to their existence in and before the Triune God. There are more ways of being trinitarianly concrete than typology. Classically, anagogy related realities on earth to realities in heaven, the Church militant to the Church triumphant. Like pneumatology, anagogy does not solve problems straightforwardly. Earlier anagogical exegesis was shot through with anti-Judaism. But it provides a fitting arena for *die Anstrengung des Begriffs*. It can improve upon typology for the concrete representation of Jews and gender in theology for three reasons.

1   Typology typically relates individual figures to Christ; anagogy typically relates groups on earth to groups in heaven; although theology does need to speak of Adam and Israel as concrete types of Christ, it needs additionally to acknowledge women, men, and Jews as concrete groups. Speaking of women and men as anagogically concrete will differ from treating them as statistical cohorts; men can participate in female anagogues, such as the Church, and women can participate in male anagogues, such as Christ.

2   Typology tends to relate individual figures to Christ's work as accom-

plished once and for all; anagogy supplements typology by relating groups to the Holy Spirit's work as ongoing; and therefore anagogy is particularly appropriate when the churches wonder whether the Spirit is trying to stir them further with respect to women or Jews.

3 Typology belongs especially to the order of redemption, but anagogy especially to the order of consummation; therefore anagogy is particularly appropriate in reading Jews and Gentiles as somehow both heirs[51] to the one covenant with Abraham that through him all the nations of the earth would bless themselves, or in reading women and men in terms of the wedding of the lamb: because both those images are *eschatological* images, images of a *consummation* in which human beings, especially in the groups now marked by hostility, actually become the occasions of mutual blessing that God is in the life of the Trinity, and so come finally to share in the trinitarian life, participants by the Spirit of adoption into the divine nature.[52]

To affirm, furthermore, that prophetic words are anagogues of the last judgment – which is clearly the case in most New Testament prophecy, such as the synoptic apocalypse in Mark 13 and parallels, and in Revelation – is also to contextualize (if not deny) Barth's notion that they are types of the crucifixion, and therefore of God's justification of sinners in Christ's atoning work. As anagogues of God's judgment, they belong rather to God's call of sinners into a holy community with God, a heavenly city, a new Jerusalem. The "new Jerusalem," anagogical language *par excellence*, confirms the role of Israel in prefiguring the *consummation* of God with us. But that is what Barth would call the *coming* human being, not the passing one: his identification of Israel with the latter has rendered him tone-deaf about how Israel still has something that the Church needs.

What Jews have that Christians lack is a straightforward although not uncomplicated relation to God in the covenant, so that, as Barth insisted, they are "all of them sanctified by Him, sanctified as ancestors and kin of the Holy One in Israel, in a sense that Gentiles are not by nature."[53] Barth could do that insight more justice. The language of the passing form obscures it. Barth might have learned from Rosenzweig, too, that "Iudaios nascitur, Christianus fit," or, to put it in Pauline language, that Jews are "naturally" children of God, and Gentiles are made children of God by adoption,[54] or, more strikingly,

---

[51] Gentiles, Rom. 8:15; Jews, Rom. 9:4.
[52] Rom. 8:23; cf. Eph. 1:5, Jn. 1:12.
[53] II/2, 287.
[54] Rom. 8:15, 23.

"contrary to nature,"[55] by engrafting. Now that most Christians are Gentiles, Barth might have supposed that until the eschaton the Holy Spirit is keeping identifiable Jews apart from the Christian community so that they will not be swallowed up in Gentileness – and so that, more important, Gentile Christians will learn *that they are Goyim*.[56] Almost all Christians – Gentile ones – need to learn that life with God is *not* their due reward, not their natural possession, not theirs to demand or extort, and they can learn that perhaps best by learning that *others* have a prior claim, *others* are God's first love,[57] *others* have become (also by grace) God's quasi-natural family. Almost all Christians need to learn to see themselves as Gentiles whose baptism washes away their lack of relation to the promises of Israel.[58] They do not need to learn to see Jews as disobedient proto-Christians. If the Jews, as Barth sees, are the "horizon" of the Gentiles, and if the Gentiles, therefore, are defined in terms of their lack over against the Jews, then Barth might have spoken of the Jews, too, as humanity's coming form. That Barth does speak that way of Jewish Christians does not succeed in teaching the vast majority of Christians who are Gentiles that Gentileness, originally marked by idol worship and a lack of relationship with the God of Israel, is also humanity's passing form. What passes away for Gentiles is God's continuing threat to cut off again the engrafted branches.[59] What comes is unending life with the God of Israel. The doctrine of election is the sum of the gospel precisely if it teaches us this: that the God of Israel is for the Gentile, too, the One who loves in freedom.

The eschatological community where Christians learn to see themselves as possessing no God of their *own*, but as brought by sheer grace into the worship of the God of the Jews,[60] would lead to a doctrine of the election of the community to which the Holy Spirit *calls* us. Unlike most Protestants, Barth has a rich doctrine of vocation, which Catholics might call glorification or Orthodox deification. He might have built his doctrine of election on that model. "Predestination is the human being made usable to God by the Holy Spirit"[61] – he might have started there. Nevertheless there is one passage in which he glimpses the possibility, one passage in which he sees that the problem

---

[55]   *Para phusin*, Rom. 11:24.
[56]   On the possibility of Torah-observant Jewish Christians serving those purposes, see the various views in "Symposium on 'Jewish Christians and the Torah.'"
[57]   See Michael Wyschogrod, "Love and Election," §4 of chapter 2 in *The Body of Faith*, pp. 58–65.
[58]   I owe the clause about baptism to personal correspondence with Kendall Soulen.
[59]   Rom. 11:22.
[60]   I owe this way of putting the matter to Soulen, "YHWH the Triune God," thesis 1.2.3.
[61]   II/2, 315.

for overwhelmingly Gentile Christians is less the justification of the Jews than the vocation of the Gentiles. The reversal is typically Barthian. Would that it had come sooner. In commenting on the unity of the community of God, Barth adverts, as we have seen, to the unity to which the Spirit calls it:

> [The Church] must call [the Synagogue] by joining with it as [the Messiah's] people, and therefore with Him. No particular function can be this call, but only the life of the community as a whole authentically lived before the Jews. It need hardly be said that the life of the community as a whole neither has been nor is this call. . . . [The Church] has debated with [the Jew], tolerated him, persecuted him, or abandoned him to persecution without protest. . . . The recurrent Jewish question is the question of Christ and the Church. . . .[62]

The whole doctrine of election needs to be recast on that basis. Persecution, too, belongs to humanity's passing form, and not because it is Jewish! Two features of the passage call for comment.

On the one hand, it would make a much more promising start for the doctrine of the election of the community than the one that Barth in fact adopts, open as it is to vocation and thus, implicitly, to Spirit and anagogy, and willing, by the end, to raise the Christian question, the Church question. Under that rubric much of the doctrine of justification could still be mined, only explicitly this time as the question of "the life of the community before the Jews." That puts Jews in the position of judging, which does not avoid but revitalizes Barth's use of christocentric typology. Seeing the Jews as judges is both typologically and anagogically apt. Christians might then tremble before the prospect that Jesus Christ was not only "born" a Jew.

Beside the implicit notion that Jews judge the Church, on the other hand, stands the explicit notion that the Church calls "the Jew." Barth has still to state what the logic of his paragraph implies, that the Holy Spirit calls the Church, and that their work cannot be identified precisely when the Church stands under the judgment of another, or when one part of the community of God, the mostly Gentile Christian part, stands under the judgment of the Messiah for its sins against another part of the community of God, the Jewish part. On Barth's own grounds the call of the Spirit ought not to be identified with that of the community, when the community itself lacks the marks of the Spirit in justice and unity. When the Church finally calls "the Jew," it will be the Last Judge who comes.

[62] IV/3/2, 878.

Chapter 8

UNINTENDED ABSTRACTION IN BARTH'S ACCOUNT OF GENDER: RETRIEVING CO-HUMANITY

Unintended Abstraction in Barth's Doctrine of Co-Humanity

Barth's exegesis of the image of God in the human being as explicated by a man–woman pair occurs in the *Church Dogmatics* §41.2–3.[1] The section as a whole is very beautiful: creation is the external basis of the covenant, the covenant the internal basis of creation. Nothing is wrong with analogizing the marriage covenant with the divine–human covenant. The one flesh, says Barth, "has its frontiers in a very different beginning and end, where Yahweh and His people are together 'one flesh.'"[2] Similarly, "Love and marriage become to them in some sense irresistibly a parable and sign of the link which Yahweh has established between Himself and His people, which in His eternal faithfulness He has determined to keep, and which He for His part has continually renewed."[3] And the analogy goes in the right direction – God's love the primary analogate, human love the secondary: "Because the election of God is real, there is such a thing as love and marriage."[4]

---

[1]   III/1, 94–329.
[2]   III/1, 315.
[3]   III/1, 315.
[4]   III/1, 318.

But Barth overstates the case. So we get assertions like this: "Man is no longer single but a couple."[5] "As there is no abstract manhood, there is no abstract womanhood. The only real humanity is that which for the woman consists in being the wife of a male and therefore the wife of man."[6] Furthermore, the duality is "unequal,"[7] and in an "order" in which man is A and woman B.[8]

Barth's use of I–Thou categories begins at III/1, 290, and appears again in §45, the *Leitsatz* for which reads, "creaturely being is a being in encounter – between I and Thou, man and woman.'"[9] That I–Thou categories are made for projection Barth had certainly learned from Feuerbach's use of them to argue that the divine Thou is just a projection of human need; they form a recurrent theme of Feuerbach's *Essence of Christianity*, analyzed in Barth's introduction.[10]

It should come as no surprise, then, if Barth resists projecting the desire of man onto God, only to project the desire of man onto woman, in calling "wirklich" an Edenic man–woman pair that Genesis refrains from portraying in act. Barth takes what is essentially a phenomenological category, which in Buber's version can support an I–Thou encounter with a tree,[11] and uses it to express, import, or smuggle in a paradigm. Man and woman do not relate as I and Thou phenomenologically; they relate as a *model* of co-humanity, its "basic form."[12] "Being in encounter is (1) a being in which one man looks the other in the eye."[13] "Being in encounter consists (2) in the fact that there is *mutual* speech and hearing."[14] "Being in encounter consists (3) in that we render mutual *assistance* in the act of being."[15] "But being in encounter consists

---

[5] III/1, 308.
[6] III/1, 309.
[7] III/1, 288.
[8] III/4, 168ff.
[9] III/2, 203; esp. also 244–74.
[10] Ludwig Feuerbach, *The Essence of Christianity*, trans. George Eliot, intro. Karl Barth (New York: Harper Torchbooks, 1957); for Barth's understanding of Feuerbach's use of I–Thou categories, see the introduction (a lecture given in 1926), pp. xiii-xvi. There, too, Barth credits Feuerbach with a 19th century discovery of co-humanity: "Now this being of man exists 'only in community, it is found only in the unity of man with man – a unity that is supported only by the reality of the difference between I and Thou'" (p. xiii). In this case I leave to the reader how much the English reflects a real coincidence between *Mann* and *Mensch*, and how much "man and woman" is an improvement.
[11] Martin Buber, *I and Thou*, trans. Walter Kaufmann (New York: Charles Scribner's Sons, 1970).
[12] §45.2, esp. III/2, 250–74.
[13] III/2, 250.
[14] III/2, 252, my emphasis.
[15] III/2, 260.

(4) in the fact that all the occurrence which we have so far described as the basic form of humanity stands under the sign that it is done on both sides with gladness."[16] One may have no quarrel with those theses and yet wish to add two qualifications. First, they ought not to end up treating the I–Thou encounter, whether intentionally or surreptitiously, as if it led to a model "relationship." Second, Adam and Eve do not, in fact, act in Genesis as those in a model relationship – although others in the Bible may come closer. Adam and Eve experience their failure under precisely the categories in which Barth projects their unrecorded success – a projection, despite attempts and disclaimers aimed at "wirklichkeit," that proves almost as romantic as similar projections in Goethe or Schleiermacher or Feuerbach – precisely in their looking each other in the eye, in their mutual speaking and hearing, in their mutual assistance, and in their gladness. It is precisely in those respects that, according to the Bible, they fail as soon as they act.

In giving woman a constitutive, structural role in the human creature rather than seeing her as, say, a defective man, Barth did better than predecessors with whom he was in conversation, and even his refusal to explicate man–woman in terms of strength–weakness looks less as if he is dignifying that explanation by mentioning it, than that he is countering ideas all too current in 1940s Switzerland.

Barth and Feuerbach disagree about whether I and Thou is an intrahuman relation. So Barth's criticism of Feuerbach is that although Feuerbach is right about the need of the I for a Thou, and right that it is an intrahuman relation, Christianity nevertheless does not in fact project the Thou mistakenly onto God; it has the I–Thou relation correctly understood in the created fellowship of one human being with another, in co-humanity. So the I–Thou relation that exists in creation is not about the human being and God, but about man and woman. I agree with Feuerbach in this sense, which Barth does not deny: sex is for God, after all. The world *is* oriented to God. And I would not deny that the orientation involves human projection. The projection is, however, only partially understood as such. It is understood more fully as a eucharistic offering, as we shall see in part III. Feuerbach's materialist dictum that *der Mensch ist, was er ißt*, is not false, as Schmemann notes; but for Christians it first reveals its depth when what the human being eats is the bread of the eucharist.[17] Then it reveals that by eating the bread of the eucharist the human being begins to participate in the divine nature. The I–Thou relation is neither

[16]   III/2, 265.
[17]   Alexander Schmemann, *For the Life of the World* (New York: National Student Christian Association, 1963), p. 1.

a projection from the human onto God nor a merely intracreation event. It is a gift from God down that we may offer back up to God in a participation in the exchange of gift and gratitude that constitute the trinitarian life. Sex and marriage, as we will see in the constructive chapters of part III, also make best sense in this eucharistic pattern, which tells us what bodies are for in Christianity.[18]

I pass over much that is good and innovative in §45 of the *Dogmatics* – like Barth's decision to treat our humanity as something ontologically good from which sin cannot alienate us, or the decision to relate creation as outer to covenant as inner ground so that the two resist any attempt to separate them. Rather I go on here to pursue questions raised by Barth's own best lights. I look at biblical narratives that appear to provide richer resources for what Barth treats in §45 and that might well have led him to modify his views.

Despite the distinctions assayed in §45.1, "Jesus, Human Being for Other Human Beings," in §45.2, "The Basic Form of Humanity," Barth wanders from the christocentric focus on which in §43 he had set his gaze. §45.1 *does* do the service of reversing Feuerbach's thesis that God is the human being in a loud voice; rather God is the human being in Jesus concretely. But §45.2, despite disclaimers,[19] leaves Jesus out of the "basic form." That much shows up already in the boldface thesis statements or *Leitsätze* of the two sections:

> [§43] As the human creature [*der Mensch*] Jesus is Himself the revealing Word of God. He is the source of our knowledge of the nature of the human creature as created by God.[20]

> [§45] That the real human creature [*der wirkliche Mensch*] is determined by God for life with God has its inviolable correspondence in the fact that its creaturely being is a being in encounter – between I and Thou, man and woman. It is human in this encounter, and in this humanity it is a likeness of the being of its Creator and a being in hope in Him.[21]

A number of gaps open up in Barth's exposition. Not that we expect him to deduce the nature of the human creature simply from the humanity of God

---

[18]   Similarly, a theologian might argue, Durkheim is correct in reverse à la Wyschogrod. God is incarnate in the community, if the community is Israel.

[19]   III/2, 222–8.

[20]   III/2, 3.

[21]   III/2, 203.

in Jesus Christ: that possibility he has already excluded. Nor that we could deny him a priori the use of I–Thou or even man–woman categories. They have their proper use and service. Rather, more modest questions arise.

1   As dualistic, I–Thou categories fall short prima facie of likeness to the triunity of the creator. They pay too little attention to the work of the Holy Spirit, not easily reducible to a Thou, or even, as Barth might have learned from Schleiermacher, to the social character of God's relationships with God's creatures in Israel and the Church. Despite the suggestive bridal imagery, which serves another purpose, God's relationship to Israel and the Church resists reduction to I–Thou (in the singular) but may resemble I–Ye (in the plural). Otherwise the God-given and Spirit-consummated particularity of the biblical and post-biblical saints gets washed out. That modification would open the way for Barth to set communal, ecclesial, and anagogical rather than the surreptitiously or openly phenomenological categories of I–Thou to work. Jesus worked not only one-on-one but often, perhaps even primarily, with groups – the disciples, the crowds, the children. In the healings, one gets as close as may be to an authentically *biblical* approach to the "looking in the eye" and the "speaking and hearkening" under which Barth seeks to describe the relationship of an I and a Thou, but even there the approach to the I–Thou category is reductive: they always take place in and for the benefit also of a *larger group*. The I–Thou phenomenology tends to reduce co-humanity to co-individuality and wash out the *ecclesial* nature of the biblical healing stories, which appears signally in the story of the paralytic lowered through the roof. He gets healed and has his sins forgiven *on account of the faith of others:* "And when Jesus saw *their* faith, he said to the paralytic, 'My child, your sins are forgiven.' "[22] Among New Testament illustrations of those relationships Barth might have noticed that I–Thou categories systematically *hide* the presence of third parties and ecclesial mediation: disciples, crowds, friends. The sick are always being brought or even recommended from a distance to Jesus by *mediating others*. This is the sort of work that trinitarian thinking appropriates to the Spirit. Christ promises to be with human beings *not* each individually that we might meet him as I and Thou, but when *two or three* are *already* gathered in his name. Thus the first gap: the I–Thou phenomenology of Barth's anthropology stands in great potential tension with his commitments to Bible, Trinity, and Church.

2   The gap between an I–Thou form and its male–female instantiation yawns particularly wide because it reduces, perhaps even *resists* the pattern of

[22]   Mk. 2:5.

I–Thou relationships that both the Hebrew Bible and the New Testament typically holds out to us. Of course the I–Thou category serves not only to counter individualistic definitions of the human creature that infect the Enlightenment generally and reach their *reductio ad absurdum* in Nietzsche's Zarathustra, but also to exclude them in advance. And the man–woman division makes an elegant strong reading of the Genesis passage, taking seriously God's observation that Adam should not be alone. It proceeds, however – in rather too much faith, hope, and charity – to overlook the possibility that Adam and Eve, as soon as Genesis shows them acting and therefore being concretely, each treat the other less as Thou than as It.

In Genesis 1:26–9 God makes Adam, male and female, in God's image and gives them dominion over the rest of creation. From that passage we cannot determine whether woman and man correspond to God's image separately or together. For as soon as they act, they sin. Their "concrete" relation does not tell us about the unfallen image. They may bear the image complementarily or distributively; no unsinful action tells us. To discover how the image actually works, Barth would say, we must turn to Jesus Christ. But his example would hardly lead us to the conclusion that the co-humanity he exemplifies takes man–woman pairs as paradigm cases of I and Thou. If so, then Jesus shows us a deficient case of the image, not its fullness – which is absurd. That point holds even if one argues that it was Jesus's peculiar vocation that prevented him from marrying. The absurd conclusion would still follow that if it takes a man–woman pair to exhibit the fullness of the image, then Jesus, precisely because of his vocation, provides a deficient case of the image he came to renew. Then Jesus is a failure, not a savior.

In Genesis 2:6–8 and 15–25 we find nothing to indicate that an I–Thou relationship, if it exists, has anything to do with their sex. In 2:18 we learn that Adam needs a helper; in 2:24 that a husband and wife become one flesh; in 2:25 that the man and the woman were not ashamed. As soon as the man and the woman begin to interact, they support each other in disobedience and deceit. Indeed, the man and the woman as interacting partners do nothing – nothing at all – until Genesis 3. What the man says in recognition of the woman while she still lies there does not count as the sort of interaction Barth needs. In reading Genesis 2 apart from Genesis 3, Barth removes being from history, just as he removes Israel from history. Furthermore, Barth misses the irony that accrues to Genesis 2 in Genesis 3.[23] "One flesh" turns out, ironically enough, to suffer the gloss "eating the same fruit." Being a "fit helper" turns

---

[23]   For an account that does see the irony in the passages, cf. Phyllis Trible, "A Love Story Gone Awry," in her *God and the Rhetoric of Sexuality* (Philadelphia: Fortress, 1978).

out to mean that Eve bears the blame that also belongs to Adam. "Not being ashamed" turns out to mean having eyes still closed. This is not the Gnostic reading that the Fall was a good thing. It is the claim that Barth has missed the writer's or redactor's sense of irony and humor. The shared flesh the text names becomes that of the shared fruit. The helper becomes an accomplice. Their innocence gets explicated as closed eyes. These observations of the text do not denigrate the Edenic state, but they distance us from it with humor. Humor and irony depend upon distance and time and reflect therefore the work of the Spirit in bringing resurrection from death, good from evil, comedy from tragedy. But humor, and the Spirit, not represented in the dyad, are what Barth has missed in the story.

It is Barth's own emphasis on the phenomenology of "speaking and listening" and "looking the other in the eye" and of history (*Geschichte*) as an explication of being that alert us to these things. If Barth had turned to the concrete, biblical narratives (*Geschichten*) of human speaking and listening and of looking the other in the eye, instead of deploying them as the formal abstractions that he elsewhere deplores, he might have noticed that the very account he takes as paradigm for the I–Thou structure of actual human being employs them to mark it not as real (*wirklich*) but precisely as fallen. Granted, Barth, like Thomas, knows the value of ideal counterfactuals in theology. An analysis of the Edenic state before the Fall is licit and useful. But an analysis of the state before the Fall relies on rubrics that the biblical story reserves for the ironic display of the state *after* the Fall. Barth's rubrics of speaking and listening and looking each other in the eye describe actions that Genesis shows us only in their fallen forms. For the first conversation that Genesis records takes place between Eve and the serpent, and the first possibility it records of man's and woman's openly looking each other in the eye comes only after they have eaten the fruit and results immediately in their sewing aprons together.

Thus Genesis 2 offers only empty forms (being abstracted from history) and Genesis 3 fills them only with ironic content (history separated from true being by sin), as Genesis uses the I–Thou categories that Barth suggests. Before the Fall we have no history between Adam and Eve to tell us whether and how I–Thou categories apply; after the Fall we have evidence only that they treat each other as Its. Even before the Fall we ought to be suspicious; I–Thou categories imply that Adam and Eve are alone with each other, an isolated dyad, whereas in the story they emphatically are not. God the Spirit that broods over creation and brings it to consummation is walking in the Garden, and I–Thou categories crowd the Spirit out. Therefore the creation story offers only superficial and ironizing support for the explication of I and Thou in terms of man and woman as such. Barth would have done better to follow his own advice and see the possibility of I–Thou not in the duality of the sexes but as the condition for the variety of relationships that Jesus Christ enacted and interpreted, relationships that are explicitly surrounded by a community and filled with the Spirit, and therefore resist dyadic reduction. Barth might have seen a foreshadowing of co-humanity in community and Spirit in the creation of the two, without turning male and female into ontological categories that threaten to make the humanity of Jesus deficient. The fact that Jesus is also God, or that for Barth we do not so much imitate as follow him at a distance, or that Jesus serves typologically as bridegroom of the Church, do not grant him an exception to Barth's stronger statements, such as that the human being is "no longer single but a couple."[24] Jesus is not a couple but single. That cannot be allowed to impugn his humanity – as Barth does not intend it to do.

The Holy Spirit Improves Barth's Doctrine of Co-Humanity, Because Consummation Is Appropriate to the Spirit

Consider the following speculations, which seem, on the surface at least, to hold some promise:

1   That the helping relationship should be a mutual being-with-the-other Christians learn first from Christ. They know it, Barth might better have said, in Christ's saying that "greater love has no one than this, than to lay down life for friends." They hear its promise, looking back, not between Adam and Eve. Neither of those two lays down life for the other; rather Genesis has it that each leads the other into death. The old Adam, like the old Eve, does not foreshadow the new in being-with-the-other, but must be overcome. In fact, if we look for a typological foreshadowing of the Christ's laying down life for his friends of a covenantal sort, the Bible does not present man–woman as the paradigm pair, but Ruth's words to Naomi:

> Entreat me not to leave you or to return from following you for where you go I will go, and where you lodge I will lodge; your people shall be my people, and your God my god; where you die I will die, and there will I be buried. May the Lord do so to me and more also if even death parts me from you.[25]

That same-sex covenant, often quoted at weddings, is given priority over childbearing when the women say, "your daughter-in-law who loves you is

---

24   III/1, 308.
25   Ruth 1:16–17.

more than seven sons,"[26] and over Ruth's seduction of Boaz, when her son is attributed to her mother-in-law: "a son has been born to Naomi."[27] Like the other "irregular" conceptions picked out by the inclusion of the mothers' names in Matthew's genealogy – Tamar, Rahab, Ruth, and "the wife of Uriah" – this one foreshadows the irregular conception of Jesus, who would, like Ruth, covenant his life for his friends.

2   That the one flesh serves not merely for the production of children, but, by the rigors of communal sanctification, for the production of children of God, we might better learn from Christ's addition[28] to the "one flesh" of Genesis that *God* has joined it together. Genesis states only that the two become one flesh; in keeping with its ironic tone it *refrains* from ascribing the relationship that Adam and Eve are living out to God's doing. Christ's addition of divine agency represents the consummation of human nature that belongs less to nature as Adam and Eve exemplify it than to grace – as God, in the incarnation, proves able to use even flesh, and even sexuality, for God's own purposes, namely the sanctification, in the asceticism of a common life, of the human being.[29] Christians may recognize it, looking back, not between Adam and Eve, but perhaps in Hosea's reluctant loyalty to Gomer:

> And the Lord said to me, "Go again, love a woman who is beloved of a paramour and is an adulteress; even as the Lord loves the people of Israel, though they turn to other gods and love cakes of raisins." So I bought her for fifteen shekels of silver and a homer and a lethech of barley.[30]

To define the one flesh in terms of Adam and Eve tends to make it work straightforwardly, instead of redemptively, ecclesially, and christologically, and therefore to conceal its theological function.

3   The right use of the shame that Genesis delights in linking with its first mention of their eyes Christians might better learn from Christ's warning that "whoever is ashamed of me and of my words in this adulterous and sinful generation, of that one will the Son of humanity also be ashamed."[31] Right shame, christologically defined, is a matter of loyalty to the good in the face

---

[26]   Ruth 4:15.

[27]   Ruth 4:17.

[28]   Mt. 10:9 and parallels.

[29]   On marriage as ascetic practice, see Paul Evdokimov, *The Sacrament of Love: The Nuptial Mystery in the Light of the Orthodox Tradition,* trans. Anthony P. Gythiel and Victoria Steadman (Crestwood, NY: St Vladimir's Seminary Press, 1985), esp. pp. 65–84.

[30]   Hos. 3:1–2.

[31]   Mk. 8:38, para. Lk. 9:26.

of sin, a sort of loyalty that Adam and Eve signally fail to show. Their loyalty after having led each other into sin and blamed each other is a matter of default, not virtue. Rather Christians might recognize right shame in Jonathan's loyalty to David in the face of Saul's anger. So far from a man–woman context, Jonathan's father appears to accuse him of a homosexual relationship, one that will not result in children: "'You son of a perverse, rebellious woman, do I not know you have chosen the son of Jesse to your own shame, and to the shame of your mother's nakedness?'"[32] Thereupon Jonathan runs to David, kisses him, and takes on the role of a king's *daughter* in passing the succession to him and envisioning for himself the role of consort:

> Jonathan rose from the table in fierce anger . . . went out into the field to the appointment with David . . . and they kissed one another, and wept with one another . . . . And he said to him, "Fear not; for the hand of Saul my father shall not find you: you shall be king over Israel, and I shall be next to you."[33]

Among illustrations of I–Thou relationships in what Jesus called Scripture Barth ought to have noticed that much better examples than Adam and Eve show up between Ruth and Naomi, Hosea and Gomer, Jonathan and David – with a striking lack of mutuality in the man–woman pair, even though it may constitute the best candidate for a covenantal I–Thou relationship among the Hebrew possibilities. If we are right to find those relationships better examples of Barth's own rubrics of "looking each other in the eye," "speaking and listening," "offering mutual assistance," and doing so with gladness; if we are right to find the Genesis author humoring and ironizing the relationship between Adam and Eve; and if we are right to worry that I–Thou categories in the case of Adam and Eve, although not in the case of Jesus, tend to crowd out the community and the Spirit: then we will find the paradigmatic expression of co-humanity as man–woman unbiblical, untrinitarian, and anti-ecclesial.

The kind of abstraction Barth succeeds in avoiding is an abstraction from Christ. The kind he commits is an abstraction from the Spirit. It is the Spirit to whom we appropriate the *messiness* of biblical histories, the ways in which God's work *resists* reduction to type, in which God's grace shows greater abundance[34] and diversity[35] than Barth gives it credit for. There is *more* even

---

32   I Sam. 20:30.
33   I Sam. 20:34–5, 41; 23:17.
34   Rom. 5:12.
35   Heb. 1:1.

than Christ: the overplus is the Spirit, as John Milbank has it, "a trinitarianism *without reserve*."[36] The abstraction that Barth succeeds in overcoming still has reservations. The abstraction that remains to be overcome underplays God's work in the Spirit. Thus in the original biblical versions of the stories of *praedestinatio gemina* we read of *third* parties, not just two. Predestination always takes place concretely in a community and an environment. It is the community gathered by the Spirit; it is the environment that the Spirit creates, which is that of the Trinity projected onto creation. So, too, expressions of co-humanity. They, too, always take place in a community and an environment. They, too, in biblical stories, involve more than binary types – more than rejected–elected pairs, more than man–woman pairs – complications and concreteness that the Spirit can handle, if dialectic cannot. They, too, require the presence of others, like the witnesses at a marriage, the guests at a wedding feast, or the public at the pronouncing of a verdict, that do not fit neatly into I and Thou, but do correspond to the celebration by the Spirit of the love between the Father and the Son.

What about anagogy? Does the saying about Christ and the Church lead to theologically justified speculation about women and men as organized groups in the community of God, the way Israel and the nations do? I can think of three proposals that tend in that direction. One is Paul Evdokimov's *Woman and the Salvation of the World*; another is Hans Urs von Balthasar's *Die Personen des Spiels*; a third, by a Catholic anthropologist, is Mary Douglas's "The Gender of the Beloved."[37] But none of these is persuasive. Evdokimov trades on too many ontological stereotypes, for all he uses them in surprising and eschatologically fruitful ways. Von Balthasar treats groups again as types – the Marian type, the Petrine type – and is not eschatological enough. Douglas's suggestion that the Catholic Church should set up a counter-hierarchy to the priesthood and episcopacy, made up of women, shows no chance of being adopted. Initially, the practice of anagogy for developing an exegesis about gender looks decidedly less promising than about Jews and Gentiles, even downright dangerous.

More is to be learned by looking to the actual practice of anagogy when it

[36] John Milbank, "The Second Difference: For a Trinitarianism without Reserve," *Modern Theology* 3 (1986): 213–33.
[37] Paul Evdokimov, *Woman and the Salvation of the World: A Christian Anthropology on the Charisms of Woman*, trans. Anthony P. Gythiel (Crestwood, NY: St Vladimir's Seminary Press, 1994); Hans Urs von Balthasar, *Theodramatik: Die Personen des Spiels*, 2 vols (Einsiedeln: Johannes, 1973–83); Mary Douglas, "The Gender of the Beloved," *The Heythrop Journal* 36 (1995): 397–408.

flourished, in the Middle Ages. The prime locus of anagogy was in fact about gender: it was the Song of Songs. Furthermore, after Genesis and the Psalms, the Song of Songs was the biblical book that attracted the most commentary among the books of the Hebrew Bible.[38]

> [T]he reasons why the erotic model of the love of God so appealed to the monastic commentator of the middle ages – and the vast majority of these commentators were monks – had to do with very fundamental preoccupations of the monastic theologian . . . rooted in the monks' theological eschatology, in their sense that their life of partial withdrawal from the world situated them at a point of intersection between this world and the next, . . . between anticipation and fulfillment. This meant that the concept of love as a "yearning" or "longing" – as an *amor-desiderium*, or, in Greek, *eros*, exactly expressed what they wanted by way of a language of love.[39]

How then do the speculations of monks apply to modern women and men, especially when monastic life and its influence has so drastically declined since the Reformation? The answer lies in recovering the sense in which the household is a little church, a little ascetic community – only to be hazarded because the wider Church can save and redeem it[40] – so that marriage and monasticism share, not opposed, but the same ascetic end, sanctification by means of the body. Then marriage is not about satisfaction, but, precisely at its best, about yearning and anticipation of the satisfaction that it cannot provide. Anagogy then becomes a means for putting marriage into a new context, and recovering the insights of monasticism. Here Evdokimov has a very great deal to teach the Church.

---

[38] Denys Turner, *Eros and Allegory: Medieval Exegesis of the Song of Songs*, Cistercian Studies Series, 156 (Kalamazoo, MI: Cistercian Publications, 1995).

[39] Turner, *Eros and Allegory*, p. 20

[40] I owe the qualification to a conversation with Stanley Hauerwas.

Part III

THE WAY OF THE BODY INTO THE TRIUNE GOD

Chapter 9

CREATION, PROCREATION, AND THE GLORY OF THE TRIUNE GOD

In a wedding, the community is taken up into the work proper to the Spirit of giving praise to love: "You have been sealed with the Holy Spirit . . . you whom God has taken for God's own, to make God's glory praised."[1] Jesus says that the kingdom of heaven is like a wedding feast.[2] In fact, if Thomas Jefferson and the Unitarians are wrong, *God* is like a wedding feast, the love of two celebrated by a third. For the parable does not actually say the kingdom of heaven is like a marriage. There is too much work in most marriages for them to be like the kingdom of heaven, and they may have more in common with purgatory. The parable does not even say the kingdom of heaven is like a wedding, as if it would be complete with two. It says that the kingdom of heaven is like a wedding *feast*. Love not only desires an other; love desires a witness, a third. For this reason human lovers carve hearts with initials into tree trunks and spraypaint declarations on highway bridges. The love internal to God has an other, the Son, and does not lack for a third, either, to witness, bless, and celebrate it: this is the Holy Spirit. In a wedding, third parties celebrate, witness, bless, testify to, and delight in the love of two.

---

[1]   Eph. 1:14; for use in a nuptial context, see Paul Evdokimov, *The Sacrament of Love: The Nuptial Mystery in the Light of the Orthodox Tradition*, trans. Anthony P. Gythiel and Victoria Steadman (Crestwood, NY: St Vladimir's Seminary Press, 1985), p. 62.

[2]   Mt. 9:15, 22:1–14; cf. Lk. 14:16–24, Mt. 8:11, Lk. 13:29, 5:34, Mk. 2:18–22, Is. 62:5, Rev. 19:9. In a distinct but related metaphor, the father also bestows a ring and a feast upon the Prodigal Son, Lk. 15:22–3.

Wedding guests also guarantee and insure the love of two against times of difficulty, as the Spirit keeps faith between the Father and the Son, reuniting them after the crucifixion.[3] The celebration, blessing, and witnessing of a human wedding may catch up human beings by the Spirit into the very inner love and life of God, as the resurrection, too, by the Spirit catches up "your mortal bodies also" into the everlasting life of God.[4]

That is why the parable ends with a dire warning about one who does not celebrate. The one without a wedding garment is "cast into the outer darkness where they will weep and gnash their teeth."[5] That one cuts him or herself off from the work of the Spirit and the life of God. Meanwhile, another warning tells against those who "set a table for fortune and fill cups of mixed wine for destiny," of which the celebration of sexual conquest would provide an example, an anti-wedding feast.[6] Let those warnings stand against those on the right and on the left who deny the Spirit at same- or opposite-sex weddings.

The famous sermon is wrong that begins with God saying, "I'm lonely! I'll make me a world."[7] God is not lonely; God has perfect love and community already in the triune life. Precisely because love is incomplete à deux, it is the office of the Holy Spirit to witness, glorify, rejoice in, celebrate, and bless the love between the Father and the Son. Thus should God cause marriage to transcend itself, it can become "the eschatological representation of the kingdom."[8] Because the marriage of two is for the community, God can make "marriage a living icon of God, a 'theophany.'"[9] A marriage "is in the image of the Triune God, and the dogma of the Trinity [its] divine archetype, the icon of the nuptial community."[10] Richard of St Victor puts it this way: "When those who love mutually are of such great benevolence that, as we have said, they wish every perfection to be shared, then it is necessary, as has been said, that each with equal desire and for a similar reason seek out someone with whom to share love."[11]

---

3   Rom. 8:11.
4   Rom. 8:11 again.
5   Mt. 22:11–13. Cf. Mt. 12:31.
6   Is. 65:11–12.
7   James Weldon Johnson, "The Creation," in Johnson, *God's Trombones* (New York: Penguin, 1955), pp. 17–20; here, p. 17.
8   Evdokimov, *The Sacrament of Love*, p. 169.
9   Evdokimov, *The Sacrament of Love*, p. 118.
10   Evdokimov, *The Sacrament of Love*, p. 117.
11   Richard of St Victor, *De Trinitate* III.15 *in fin.*; translation from Richard of St Victor, *The Twelve Patriarchs, The Mystical Ark, Book Three of the Trinity*, trans. and introduction by Grover A. Zinn, Classics of Western Spirituality (New York: Paulist Press, 1979), p. 389.

Continued on next page

At the same time, the Trinity has little or nothing in it to encourage a fertility cult. Augustine rejects the image father–mother–child for the Trinity.[12] Much of the doctrine's power arises from the ambiguity and fluidity – even gender bending – of its symbolics. God as the Trinity without reference to persons can, in traditional Christian exegesis, both require masculine pronouns and be "our Mother";[13] God is Father but not male; Jesus is Mother but not female;[14] the Spirit is male, female, or neuter depending on language, and also denied to have gender. Among medieval Cistercians an abbot could be Mother, as abbot; Father, as priest; "ontologically" female, as human; and biologically male.[15] Women may be female, by biology; Father, by ordination; and female again, by traditional Christian symbolics of the human and the Church. It has even been argued that "Father" language for priests, to model power as God the Father exercises it, *requires* the ordination of women.[16] Analogy is more flexible than to require that one occupy a gender to represent it. Unlike, therefore, most uses of divine marriage, the Trinity resists sharp definitions of gender and denies the image of the fertile union of a private two.

Rather, the Trinity is a public celebration of a fluid or perichoretic three, "a dancing day." As the old carol has Jesus say of humanity, his true love, "Tomorrow shall be my dancing day": "Then down to hell I took my way / For my true love's deliverance, / And rose again on the third day, / Up to my true love and the dance. / Then up to heaven I did ascend, / Where now I dwell in pure substance / On the right hand of God, that man / May come

Referring to Richard's preference in favor of same-gendered names for the divine persons (*De Trinitate* VI.4), Marilyn McCord Adams goes farther, defending the thesis that "Way back in the twelfth century, Richard of St Victor made centuries-old trends explicit, when he represented the Holy Trinity as a paradigm 'same-sex' friendship. How could we have missed it? Father, Son, and Holy Spirit, an intimate community of lovers, the center of Christian worship for over sixteen hundred years!" in "Yes to Bless," a paper on friendship in Cicero, Aelred of Rievaulx, and Richard of St Victor, delivered to the conference "Beyond Inclusion" at All Saints' Episcopal Church, Pasadena, CA, April 1997, p. 3 of typescript.

[12]   Augustine, *De Trinitate* XII.6–7, §§8–9.

[13]   E.g., Julian of Norwich, *Showings*, trans. Edmund Colledge and John Walsh (New York: Paulist Press, 1978), the long text, ch. 59.

[14]   Julian of Norwich, *Showings*, the long text, chs 57–64.

[15]   Caroline Walker Bynum, "Jesus as Mother and Abbot as Mother: Some Themes in Twelfth-Century Cistercian Writing," ch. 4 in her *Jesus as Mother: Studies in the Spirituality of the High Middle Ages* (Berkeley, CA: University of California Press, 1982), pp. 110–69.

[16]   Stanley Hauerwas, "Priesthood and Power: What It Means to Be a Father," unpublished ms.

into the general dance."[17] In the general dance human beings come to participate in God's own, particular life.

The Trinity is the paradigm or perfect case of otherness as an exchange of gift and gratitude, that from which all other cases of gift take their (analogically but not historically or empirically) derivative meaning.[18] The technical name for "gift" in Christian theology is "grace," and gift in that sense is especially appropriated to the Holy Spirit. What is grace? Is it pretty sunsets, serendipity, any kind of positive regard? It is the particular characteristics of God as Father, Son, and Spirit that define grace as a particular characteristic of this God. In Williams's phrase, it is first of all that "unconditional response to God's giving that God makes in the life of the Trinity,"[19] and secondarily, through God's turning to God's human creatures, it is God's incorporation also of them into that fellowship of gift and gratitude.

In the Trinity the Father is eternally sending the Son and receiving him back, the story of the Prodigal collapsed into a single, integral movement. Similarly the Son is always going out from the Father, and, precisely in going out, drawing near to the Father, since in going out the Son is gladly doing the Father's will. The Spirit is witnessing and celebrating and delighting in this eternal dance of love, clapping for the do-si-do of intimacy's joyous enactment, which the Cappadocians call the trinitarian perichoresis, dancing around.

"Perichoresis" also connotes moving through the same space, and the concept has something to say about how love and intimacy work for human beings and for God. For God, intimacy is possible on the basis of difference. Because the three persons are distinct from one another, God can "be" love; the relation of love can subsist among them. If they were one, instead of unified, it would not make sense to speak of God as "love," a designation that in context is communitarian through and through.[20]

Karl Barth describes that pattern as one of the blessing of an Other already in the intratrinitarian relations among Father, Son, and Spirit. "In God's own being and sphere [i.e., in God's own trinitarian life] there is a counterpart: a

[17]   "Tomorrow Shall Be My Dancing Day," in Hugh Keyte and Andrew Parrott,eds, *The Shorter New Oxford Book of Carols* (New York: Oxford University Press, 1993), no. 76, pp. 226–7.

[18]   Cf. John Milbank, "Can a Gift be Given? Prologemenon to a Future Trinitarian Metaphysic," *Modern Theology* 11 (1995): 119–41.

[19]   Rowan D. Williams, "The Body's Grace," in Charles Hefling, ed., *Our Selves, Our Souls and Bodies: Sexuality and the Household of God* (Boston: Cowley Publications, 1996), pp. 58–68; here, p. 59.

[20]   I John 4, the entire chapter, esp. v. 17.

genuine but harmonious self-encounter and self-discovery; a free co-exist-ence and co-operation; an open confrontation and reciprocity."[21] God lives out already *in se* a pattern of grace and gratitude. When Jesus gives thanks to the Father at the Last Supper, it is a glimpse into an intratrinitarian event, wherein the Father lives from giving, the Son from gratitude, the Spirit from delight. The Father offers Jesus bread and wine for his life; Jesus offers in return a *brukhah*, a blessing of gratitude for the Father's gifts. In identifying his body and blood with the bread and wine, Jesus offers thanks to the Father also for his life, which bread and wine support. He returns not only thanks for his life; he returns also his life itself, giving it back to the Father for the testimony and celebration of the Spirit. As it happens, the giving and blessing and feasting spills over also onto human beings at the Great Thanksgiving, the eucharist, that Jesus started there, inviting them bodily into God's intratrinitarian life.

The primary case of otherness, in Christian thought, is the Trinity. The second case we consider is otherness not within the Trinity but outside it. Again we turn first to Barth:

> Creation is the temporal analogue, taking place outside God, of that event in God Himself by which God is the Father of the Son. The world is not God's Son, is not "begotten" of God; but it is *created*. But what God does as the Creator can in the Christian sense only be seen and understood as a reflection, as a shadowing forth of this inner divine relationship between God the Father and the Son.[22]

Creation, Barth continues, is therefore strictly grace; a free and unmerited benefit from the One who loves in freedom – in freedom because for that One love is already complete:[23]

> The mystery of creation on the Christian interpretation is not primarily – as the fools think in their hearts – the problem whether there is a God as the originator of the world . . . . But the first thing, the thing we begin with, is God the Father and the Son and the Holy Spirit. And from that standpoint the great Christian problem is propounded, whether it can really be the case that God wishes to be not only for Himself, but that outside Him there is the world, that we exist alongside and outside Him. That is a riddle. If we make even a slight effort . .

---

[21]   *Church Dogmatics*, III/1, 185.
[22]   Karl Barth, "God the Creator," in his *Dogmatics in Outline*, trans. G. T. Thomson (London: SCM Press, 1949), p. 52.
[23]   *Church Dogmatics*, II/1, thesis of §28; II/2, thesis of §32.

. to conceive [God] as He reveals Himself to us, we must be astonished at the fact that there are ourselves and the world alongside and outside Him. God has no need of us, He has no need of the world and heaven and earth at all. He is rich in Himself, He has fullness of life; all glory, all beauty, all goodness and holiness reside in Him. He is sufficient unto Himself, He is God, blessed in Himself. To what end, then, the world? Here in fact there is *everything*, here in the living God. How can there be something alongside God, of which He has no need? This is the riddle of creation.[24]

Thus while it is not a matter of any external necessity that God create, nor even a matter of any internal compulsion, it is deeply *characteristic* of God to create, to give to another – because to give to an other is God's very life in the community of the Trinity.[25] It would have been enough for God to enjoy companionship in the Trinity, but God desired companionship also with human beings.[26] To speak in this way of God's triune *character* seeks to get beyond the horns of necessity and arbitrariness. In denying necessity Christians deny that creation has a source anywhere other than God's good pleasure, God's loving freedom; in denying arbitrariness they deny speculation about a god who would not have created; such a god would have had a different character from the God of Israel. The creation of the world and the trinitarian life befit each other as a characteristic act of One who blesses an Other, who receives that blessing, and who delights in their mutual blessing.[27]

Creation permits the possibility of marriage because creation allows the possibility of God's eternal life of grace and gratitude, of God's unconditional response to God's self-giving *also in finitude* – in space and time. Thus it is, too, that marriage can represent the Trinity in space and time. Space grants creaturely possibility to love. Finite creatures cannot love perichoretically, as God does, as if by interpenetration. Rather, their spatial boundaries first make love possible for them. Embrace would not be possible if human beings passed

[24]   Barth, *Dogmatics in Outline*, pp. 53–4, translation slightly modified.

[25]   Although creation is a gift of God, creation is not itself God, so that it is a self-communication of God that is not yet a *self-gift* in the way that the Trinity is. See Thomas Aquinas, *Summa Theologiae* I.20.

[26]   The pattern by which it would have been enough for God to have companionship in the Trinity is one that makes many Jews uncomfortable, but in putting it that way – it would have been enough – I mean to recall the refrain of the Passover liturgy by which each of God's blessings is greeted with "dayeinu," "it would have been enough."

[27]   This way of putting the matter was inspired by a similar formulation in Kendall Soulen, "YHWH the Triune God," *Modern Theology* 15 (1999): 25–54. See also Soulen, *The God of Israel and Christian Theology* (Minneapolis, MN: Fortress, 1996), esp. passages indexed under "consummation."

ghostlike through each other. Time, too, grants creaturely possibility to love. As Barth says, creation is the temporal analogue of the relation between the Father and the Son. Human conversation cannot take place simultaneously, but only in sequence. It takes time. It follows the divine Word at a distance. So, too, does human love. The formation of Christian households and corresponding monastic vows of stability honor the ties of love to place. The bonds of marriage and corresponding monastic vows of constancy honor the ties of love to time. Creaturely love involves making space, and taking time.[28] As God loves human beings, God does not begrudge them space and time, but grants them out of the divine expanse and patience. As Robert Jenson elegantly puts it, "God can, if he chooses, accommodate other persons in his life without distorting that life. God, to state it as boldly as possible, is *roomy*."[29] That goes also for God's time, which does not negate but includes created time, for beside God's time there is "nothing so capacious."[30] Human time participates in the triune life as creatures participate in a sort of availability analogous to that which the trinitarian persons enjoy for one another.[31] Marriage bears an analogy to the trinitarian life in that it grants ungrudging if not unlimited space and time to human love.

For material creatures, however, distinction takes place in space and time. Space and time are indexes of creaturely finitude. Creatures occupy this space for this time. Spatially, finitude means physical self-enclosedness. There cannot be the sort of occupying the same space, or circumincession, that marks the divine persons. Indeed, for material creatures, intimacy depends on physical boundaries. You cannot hug someone unless the two bodies have skins to press up against each other. Temporally, finitude means having a beginning and an end. You cannot hug someone unless your bodies adjoin at the same time. A sexual orientation is in part a special appreciation for the particular delights of spatial finitudes, or bodily forms. So in creation, the divine distinction becomes a distinction in space and time, or difference. We live in different places and at different times. This difference is not yet a fault. It is the appropriate condition of creaturely intimacy. It allows for such goods as the spatial intimacy of lovers and the temporal intimacy of generations. It allows for such goods as conversation, which requires both proximity in space and succession in time.

That bit of metaphysics accords with some modern uses of the Cappadocian

[28]   For more on taking time as a theological and ethical concept, see Williams, "The Body's Grace," p. 63.
[29]   Robert W. Jenson, *Systematic Theology*, vol. I, *The Triune God* (New York: Oxford University Press, 1997), p. 226.
[30]   Jenson, *Systematic Theology*, vol. I, p. 236.
[31]   I developed this way of putting the matter in conversation with William Young.

doctrine of perichoresis. It also conforms rather well, happily enough, with affectional human relationships in the Bible. For human beings are everywhere described in terms of spatial and temporal finitude, their love (of whatever sort) enabled by those conditions. (If their love is also limited by those conditions, that is a topic I save for chapter 12.) Thus "a man leaves his father and his mother and cleaves to his wife";[32] normally, that is, their friendship requires (minimally!) that they go to live in the same place. So, too, Joseph is reunited with his brothers in Egypt, saying "'Come near to me, I pray you.' And they came near. And he said, 'I am your brother Joseph, whom you sold into Egypt. And now do not be distressed, or angry with yourselves, because you sold me here.'"[33] The story of Ruth and Naomi is encapsulated in famous lines that stress geographic and temporal conditions for togetherness; having the same God and being of the same people requires being in the same place, and death names the temporal boundary. So (as we have seen) Ruth says to Naomi, "Entreat me not to leave you or to return from following you; for where you go I will go, and where you lodge I will lodge; your people shall be my people, and your God my God; where you die I will die, and there will I be buried. May the Lord do so to me and more also if even death parts me from you."[34] Again, David rejoices at meeting Jonathan after a separation: "David rose from beside the stone heap and fell on his face to the ground, and bowed three times; and they kissed one another, and wept with one another, until David exceeded himself."[35] Or David mourns for his son Absalom after he dies: "O my son Absalom, my son, my son Absalom! Would that I had died instead of you, O Absalom, my son, my son."[36] The theme of distance grows more urgent when the people Israel suffer exiles in Egypt and Babylon, and its threat to love becomes explicit in the Song of Songs, where it is asserted that "love is as strong as death."[37]

The pattern so far is this. In the Trinity, otherness is a condition for the possibility of love. God can be love, because God exists in the relationships among Father, Son, and Holy Spirit, not just two others, but also a third, a second difference, that their love might not be without celebration and blessing and witness. In creation, God enables distant but appropriate

---

[32]   Gen. 3:23.
[33]   Gen. 45:4–5.
[34]   Ruth 1:16–17.
[35]   I Sam. 21:41.
[36]   II Sam. 18:33.
[37]   Song 8:6.

correlates to the trinitarian love-in-freedom also for human love, structured by space and time. In creation the divine intimacy can become physical nearness and temporal duration. God grants the creature a body and a history. God enables lovers to make a household and a marriage. In Eden God gave Adam and Eve a place and in their lifespan he allotted them time.[38] In the New Jerusalem God will consummate time and place by calling them to share in God's own life, and calling it a wedding feast.

Because God is triune, God can bless human beings. Because God blesses the other in God, God can bless the other without. Because God reaches out to another already within, God is not contained by the Trinity's inner life, but can reach out also to creatures. Because God reaches into another already within, God is not trapped beyond the world, but can reach in also to creatures. Because God is the one who loves in *freedom*, God can be the one who loves in freedom *also for them*. God can make time and take place. God has time and room enough to show hospitality. God can have a history and a body. God can make a garden and walk in it. God can choose Israel and be with her like a jealous lover. God can do this to bring creatures into the trinitarian fellowship. God can elevate creatures from Eden to glory, so that creation is not static, but always already God-moved, so that creation is not all, but more is in store even for Eden. Creation might be complete by itself, but God wills to consummate it, to bring it into fulfillment by drawing it into "that unconditional response to God's giving that God's self makes in the life of the Trinity,"[39] adopting human beings into the Holy Spirit's celebration of the wedding of the Lamb.

For the consummation of creation God chooses Israel. We see this in the promise to Abraham, at Sinai, in Amos and Hosea, and in the Song of Songs. To Abraham God makes many promises, which, quasi-sacramentally, do not terminate only in created goods, but work by anagogy to prefigure the goods God has in store for Israel in the heavenly Jerusalem. God blesses Abraham with land and life and to make him the father of many nations. At Sinai God declares love and choice jealously in the third commandment: "I the Lord your God am a jealous God."[40] The warning implicit is the warning not of a judge but of a lover; sin and redemption come in the context of God's

---

[38] For an argument about how allotted time is a created *good*, rather than a defect, see Barth's long consideration of creaturely time in the *Church Dogmatics*, III/2, 437–640.
[39] Williams, "The Body's Grace," p. 59.
[40] Ex. 20:5. Cf., among many other passages, Ex. 34:14: "you shall worship no other God, for the Lord, whose name is Jealous, is a jealous God" (NRSV).—Name christologies often take it that God's Name is Christ (as in the Lord's Prayer). Interpreted christologically, would that passage mean that the Father is jealous for (not of) the Son, since it is the Son who marries the Church?

implacable desire for consummation. In the judgment of the prophets, too, redemption is for consummation. "You have ravished my heart,"[41] God declares of Israel; "I will allure her."[42] In the Song of Songs the anagogy is complete: this is the life that God has begun and will consummate with his chosen people Israel.[43] If this part of the story is heard only as prefiguring the drama of sin and redemption in Jesus, Christians neglect to identify God by God's final intention; they neglect to identify God by consummation where consummation is most densely plotted and most richly begun. Israel actually possesses polity with God, community with God[44] – possesses while yearning. Israel is the very stuff of anagogy, which sees in the Bible the types (technically, anagogues) of heavenly realities, the New Jerusalem.

This yearning is deeply erotic; or better: as Christ assumes flesh and redeems it, he also assumes fleshly eros and transfigures it, so that the yearning for the New Jerusalem becomes spiritual without ceasing to be erotic. But does eschatological yearning, participant in the trinitarian gift and gratitude that excite and satisfy it, really suffice – without ending in children?

Procreation Pressed

It has been argued that human beings are created in God's image in that as God creates, human beings procreate. Human beings are made in God's image as God wills and acts, so the objection continues, rather than as God is *in se*. And God wills and acts to create. Therefore human beings are in the image of God just as they procreate, after all. So Aquinas says that we are in the image of God as ones who have the power of our own reason and act, or free will.[45] And yet we are not in God's image, but depart from it, when we will evil. According

---

[41] Song 4:9a.

[42] Hos. 2:14.

[43] For more, see Denys Turner, *Eros and Allegory: Medieval Exegesis of the Song of Songs*, Cistercian Studies Series, 156 (Kalamazoo, MI: Cistercian Publications, 1995).

[44] See Soulen, *The God of Israel*, on consummation; Michael Wyschogrod, "Israel, the Church, and Election," in John M. Oesterreicher, ed., *Brothers in Hope* (New York: Herder & Herder, 1970), pp. 79–87, and *The Body of Faith: Judaism as Corporeal Election* (Minneapolis, MN: Fortress, 1983); David Novak, *The Election of Israel* (New York: Cambridge University Press, 1995); Eugene F. Rogers, Jr, "Selections from Thomas Aquinas's *Commentary on Romans* [9–11]," translation of excerpts with an introduction, in Stephen E. Fowl, ed., *The Theological Interpretation of Scripture: Classic and Contemporary Readings* (Oxford: Blackwell, 1997), pp. 320–37.

[45] *ST*, prologue to I-II.

to this objection, procreation is therefore normative for sex, and parent–parent–child is a human vestige, or left-over image, of the Trinity.

The objection is wrong-headed for a number of reasons. First let me clear up some of the less important ones, before returning to the main theme, which is that the human being does not *need* procreation to fulfill the image of God any more than God *needs* creation to be the Trinity.

1   Augustine considers the human being as in the image of the Trinity in terms of internal structures, indeed in the capacities to will and act, but not in their particular use, and certainly not in terms of their use for procreation. Furthermore, Augustine, as we have seen, does consider the image parent–parent–child for the Trinity, and *rejects* it.[46] Similarly, Richard of St Victor considers the image Father–Son–Grandson for the Trinity, and rejects that too.[47] The deeper point is that the Holy Spirit's role is *not* to provide the Father and the Son with a child or grandchild – nor to be reduced to their love itself – but it is to be an independent witness, celebrator, delighter in their love. A child can do that for a couple – but not only a child. The tradition has therefore resisted the identification of the Spirit with procreation as a reduction of the glory of God.

2   The objection makes Jesus a deficient human being, and separates celibacy from marriage, as we considered in the chapters on Barth.

3   Too easy, the critic will say: procreation is not required of celibates; it is only required (as in *Humanae Vitae*) that every sex act not be intentionally closed to procreation.[48] In any case, procreation is not, naturally or faithfully, the result of every sex act, and the proper use of human reason and will involves prudence about circumstances – without being closed to the possibility of children, even accidental ones. Well then, the critic will say, procreation is necessary only for *couples*. It is properly a good of *marriage*, so that as long as the *marriage* is open to children (but not necessarily every sex act of that marriage), then sex is licit.

But procreation is simply not a good that belongs to the couple as such, much less to every sex act. Rather it belongs to the *species*. Procreation is a good of the species, because the species is what procreation exists to promote. But if

---

[46]   Augustine, *De Trinitate* XII. 6–7, §§8–9.

[47]   Richard of St Victor, *De Trinitate* VI. 10.

[48]   Gay and lesbian couples who are Catholic might invoke the principle of double effect to argue that the infertility of their unions is precisely not *intentional*, but a foreseen yet unintended side-effect.

procreation is the good of the species, then not every human being must accomplish it (so celibacy is allowed); and not every sex act must accomplish it (so marriages of the postmenopausal or infertile, or, arguably, of gay and lesbian people, are licit); and not even every fertile couple need accomplish it; rather, the species as a whole must accomplish it. "Arguably, our survival as a species is more dependent on farmers than it is on actuaries or used car salesmen, more on MD's than on PhD's (certainly in religious studies!). What is not clear is whether there are any moral implications to these facts and, if so, what they are."[49] There need only be enough procreation to keep the species flourishing, and then procreation as the good of the species is fulfilled. And that need, fortunately or unfortunately, is in no danger of going unmet. Genesis 1:28 famously says "Go forth and multiply." It is not usually remembered that the command has an explicit end: "and fill the earth." The earth is now more or less full. But even those worried about the prospect of population *decline* would do well to remember that already in the fourth century, when the world was much more thinly inhabited than it is today, John Chrysostom could write, "As for procreation, it is not required absolutely by marriage. . . . The proof of this lies in the numerous marriages that cannot have children. This is why the first reason of marriage is to order sexual life, especially now that the human race has filled the entire earth."[50] Speaking precisely of the good of the *species* leaves room for those considerations. Sex before God is for sanctification, for God's catching us up into God's triune life. Sex is for procreation just as procreation promotes that end. The chief end of sex is not to make children of human beings, but to make children of God. As Chrysostom says, "If you desire children, you can get much better children now, a nobler childbirth and better help in your old age. if you give birth by spiritual labor."[51] And Christians best imitate God's relation to them as children not when they bear and beget them, but when they *adopt* them. "The union of the human being to God . . . is by the grace of adoption," says Thomas Aquinas.[52] "To all who received him . . . he gave power to become children of God, who were born, not of blood nor

[49]   Louis E. Newman, "Constructing a Jewish Sexual Ethic: A Rejoinder to David Novak and Judith Plaskow," in Saul Olyan and Martha C. Nussbaum, eds, *Sexual Orientation and Human Rights in American Religious Discourse* (New York: Oxford University Press, 1998), pp. 46–53; here, p. 49.

[50]   As translated in Evdokimov, *The Sacrament of Love*, p. 120, citing simply *On Marriage*. See John Chrysostom, "Sermon on Marriage," in *On Marriage and Family Life*, trans. Catharine P. Roth and David Anderson (Crestwood, NY: St Vladimir's Seminary Press, 1997), p. 85.

[51]   Chrysostom, "Sermon on Marriage," pp. 85–6.

[52]   III.3.1 *ad* 1, III.50c.

of the will of the flesh nor of the will of a man, but of God," says the gospel of John.[53]

Creation then is not God's will as such. Creation is grace. God's will is, by creation, graciously and unnecessarily and prodigally to signify God's glory. Marriages gay or straight, childbearing or childless, can signify God's glory, just because they involve the election of love.

Most important, however – and here we return to the chapter's theme – the objection makes creation necessary to God. To resemble creation, procreation must be recovered as a matter of non-necessity, of grace, of prayer. Even within a fertile marriage, "the nobility of the believing couple consists in drawing from sexuality something other than what links them to the animal world. . . . One cannot compel a woman to bring forth. Procreation can only be the *reflected creation of free beings* [when they have] prepared themselves by *prayer*."[54]

The gratuity of creation means that God is vulnerable not by external necessity or compulsive need, but by self-determination. God chooses to create; God chooses creaturely children. As we have seen, God woos Israel,[55] and Israel is allowed to ravish God.[56] In the love of Israel and the life of Jesus, God becomes vulnerable by choice. If Jesus prays freely to the Father, God's need is God's *wish*. As Barth says, God is the One who loves in *freedom*. Yet God's chosen vulnerability is also not out of character for God; God is not deprived even of the blessings of mutual dependence, since the life of the Trinity is itself one of grace and gratitude, so that Jesus can truly give thanks to the Father before breaking bread. Jesus's prayer for the disciples, like the creation as a whole, is God's *wish*; God's wish is grace, and God's faithfulness to that wish, grace on grace. Created space and time, and thus our bodies, precisely as finite, are structures of mutual dependence by which we may experience grace and gratitude. In loving Israel, in the life of Jesus, in the practice of the eucharist, called the Great Thanksgiving, God makes space and takes time for exchanges of mutual gift, for grace and gratitude.

The shock and wonder of God's self-determining love in creation has a better analogy, according to biblical metaphor, in the contingency of the love of one human being for another, than in procreation. The marriage covenant itself (human or divine) adds to love time and space for exchanges of mutual

---

53   Jn. 1:12.
54   Evdokimov, *The Sacrament of Love*, pp. 177, 178, my emphasis.
55   Hos. 2:14.
56   Song 4:9a.

gift, with procreation or without. Passages that speak of Israel as God's bride are distinct from those that speak of Israel as God's child, and do not speak of procreation. Jesus and Paul both speak of marriage without mentioning children. That they do so because they expect the imminent end of the world only heightens the point that marriage has an integral, eschatological end in the grace and gratitude of the trinitarian life, apart from childbearing. God's extension of the covenant to the Gentiles, just because it marks the eschaton at the (apparent? penultimate? ongoing?) end of the world, grows by baptism, which is a rite of adoption, not procreation,[57] and promises a future by resurrection, not childbirth. As Chrysostom wrote, "It is not unreasonable that those who disbelieve in the resurrection should grieve about having descendants, since this is the only consolation left to them. But we, who think that death is a sleep . . . what pardon would we merit if we mourned about such matters . . . ?"[58] When the baptized emerge from the water they rise with Christ "for adoption."[59] "[T]he Gospel makes us understand that it is not in the species but in Christ that [the human being] is eternal."[60] That is clear in Paul's metaphors too, where the Gentiles do not grow naturally on the Jewish vine, but by ingrafting (Rom. 11). The whole pattern of adoption, ingrafting, and resurrection, which goes to the very heart of God's extension of the covenant to the Gentiles, transfigures procreation, insisting that all human beings (that is, Jew and Gentile) find fulfillment in sanctification, that is, in God. The mutual self-giving of the marriage covenant, divine or human, has an integral end not in multiplication *as such*, but in the mutual self-giving of the Trinity – an end to which children may contribute.

For children, as an extraordinary case of other people generally, can help in sanctification, in making us better, and in consummation, in fulfilling our lives; if they do so, that, too, is grace. Procreation can be grace, as creation is

---

[57]   "Baptism is . . . the grace of adoption," Cyril of Alexandria, *Patrologia Graeca* 33.1081B, quoted in Jean Daniélou, *The Bible and the Liturgy*, no trans. (Notre Dame, IN: University of Notre Dame Press, 1956), p. 43.

[58]   John Chrysostom, *Against the Opponents of the Monastic Life* III.16, in David G. Hunter, ed. and trans., *A Comparison between a King and a Monk and against the Opponents of the Monastic Life: Two Treatises by John Chrysostom*, Studies in the Bible and Early Christianity, vol. 13 (Lewiston, NY: The Edwin Mellen Press, 1988), p. 162.

[59]   *Apostolic Constitutions* VII, 43, in Daniélou, *The Bible and the Liturgy*, p. 44.

[60]   Evdokimov, *The Sacrament of Love*, pp. 119–20. In a supersessionist mode, Evdokimov could continue: "The economy of the Law ordained procreation to perpetuate the race, for the increase of the chosen people in view of the birth of the Messiah. In the economy of grace, however, the birth of the elect derives from the preaching of faith," p. 120.

grace; and since procreation is also natural, it is a good of the species – though certainly not of every sex act, and not necessarily, either, of every marriage. The inability of a human pair to procreate may be a misfortune, but not one that undermines the likeness of human beings to God. Children are ends in themselves; they are delights; but they are still created goods (perhaps the best created goods of all) and they are ordered to God. Infertility, gay or straight, need not lead to moral disorder, unless it leads to a sense of entitlement become obsessive and idolatrous. On the contrary, Christians lay more weight on God's *adoption* (*huiothesia*) of them as children in baptism. God "predestined us in love for adoption as sons (children who inherit) through Jesus Christ unto himself."[61] Furthermore, since God is creator and human beings are creatures, the fulfillment of human community *cannot* be in more creaturely children; the fulfillment of human community is in sharing the trinitarian community of God.

The last resort of those arguing against same-sex partnerships on the grounds of procreation is that they differ from the opposite-sex infertile in that the latter can still have children "by miracle." To liberal ears, as we saw in chapter 1, that sounds like the worst sort of special pleading. When all else fails, appeal to miracle. It is a miracle, furthermore, that embodies a double standard: opposite-sex couples may appeal to miracle, and same-sex couples may not. Yet as Andrew Sullivan observes, "[m]iracles by definition may happen to anybody."[62]

But let us take appeals to miracle in the best light. The Bible does know of miraculous cases of opposite-sex procreation. In the most famous one, that of Abraham and Sarah, however, Abraham tries surrogate motherhood with Hagar,[63] and God undercuts the importance of Sarah's child, Isaac, by asking Abraham to give him up.[64] Both of those circumstances undermine the idea that it is the procreation of Abraham and Sarah that justifies their marriage.

But the Bible records two other cases of miraculous procreation that are just as important in salvation history, if not more so. In each case the production of a human being is single-sex. At the beginning, God produces Eve out of a man alone. And at the incarnation, God produces Jesus out of a woman alone. These two single-sex miracles are no mere curiosities in the biblical

61 Eph. 1:5.
62 Andrew Sullivan, "Alone Again, Naturally: The Catholic Church and the Homosexual," in *The New Republic*, November 28, 1994, pp. 47, 50, 52, 54–5; here, p. 54.
63 Gen. 16.
64 Gen. 22.

narrative; they are, as I have noted, of unequaled prominence. Nor is it a bizarre innovation so to associate them, but one of long theological standing. Anselm of Canterbury, for example, pairs them in his celebrated theory of the atonement, *Why God Became Human*.[65] If the appeal is to miracle, one ought not to exclude the single-sex ones. One ought rather to hold open the doors of hospitality to the unrelated stranger and so imitate the saving action of God.

In Jesus Christ, God *adopts* Gentiles to be God's children, as Israel is God's child already.[66] It is perhaps to honor that adoption that Jesus has no children of his own. One can think of many reasons why it might have been appropriate for Jesus not to beget children, but certainly the standard comment, that Jesus knew he would die, is insufficient reason; 33 was a normal rather than particularly early age at which a father might die in antiquity. Rather than honor the command to procreate, or even the command to honor his father and mother, Jesus explicitly, emphatically, and even offensively relativizes those commandments by relating them first of all to God. "Did you not know I must be in my Father's house?" he asks, perhaps hurtfully.[67] "Who are my mother and my brothers?" he asks.[68] "Whoever loves father or mother more than me is not worthy of me," he states,[69] or, as Luke has it, "If anyone comes to me and does not hate his own father and mother and wife and children and brothers and sisters, yes, and even his own life, he cannot be my disciple."[70] So Jesus is not a family-values kind of guy, and issues a sharp critique of family relationships that get in the way of the love of God.

The "family resemblance"[71] by which same-sex unions deserve to be called marriages is not primarily their resemblance to opposite-sex unions, although the family resemblance is close enough, with children or

---

[65]   Anselm of Canterbury, *Cur Deus homo*, book II, ch. 8; ET: *Why God Became Man*, in Eugene R. Fairweather, ed. and trans., *A Scholastic Miscellany: Anselm to Ockham*, Library of Christian Classics, vol. 10 (Philadelphia: Westminster Press, 1956), pp. 100–83; here, p. 153.

[66]   E.g., Rom. 8:15, 23, 9:4, Gal. 4:5, Eph. 1:5, Dt. 14:1, 32:6; cf. Jn. 1:12. "As Israel is God's child already" is meant to express a comparison, not a contrast. Paul uses adoption both of Gentiles at Rom. 8:15 and of Jews at 9:4. The point is the movement of the *Spirit* of adoption, 8:23.

[67]   Lk. 2:49.

[68]   Mk. 3:33.

[69]   Mt. 10:37.

[70]   Lk. 14:26.

[71]   Ludwig Wittgenstein, *Philosophical Investigations*, trans. G. E. M. Anscombe (New York: Macmillan, 1958), §§67, 32.

without.[72] The family resemblance by which same-sex unions deserve to be called marriages is the same resemblance by which Christians justify calling opposite-sex unions marriages: their resemblance to the marriage of Christ and the Church. By the theory of analogy, it is that prime analogate by participation in which Christians license other, secondary, earthly uses of the term.

Indeed, talk of children as a necessary goal of marriage risks idolatry. Here Eastern Orthodoxy's critique of Western Christianity is telling. So Paul Evdokimov writes, "Both the preservation of the species and selfish sexual pleasure reduce the partner to a mere tool and destroy [human] dignity."[73] Related stories of children central to Judaism and Christianity insist that children are not to be taken for granted, but as gifts of grace. In the binding of Isaac, Abraham shows that God's fulfillment of the promise to make him a father of many nations does not, somehow, depend on his only child, a pattern that Christianity takes up and repeats in the story of the crucifixion of God's Son. At the crucial moment, Abraham trusts in God to fulfill the promise, not Isaac; for Christians it is Christ's resurrection, not their progeny, that guarantees them a future. So far from holding that children sanctify marriage, some Christian thinkers have even interpreted the remarks of Paul ignoring childbearing in marriage at I Cor. 7:25–40 and of Jesus positively discouraging it at Mk. 13:17 and parallels as indicating that biological procreation not taken up into community with God simply carries forward the body of death.[74] We have seen Barth turn the tables when he comes to comment on the passage in Rom. 1:

Wherever the qualitative distinction between human beings and the final Omega is overlooked and misunderstood, that fetishism is bound to appear in which God is experienced in "birds and fourfooted things," and finally, or

---

[72]   David Novak denies that the resemblance is close enough; see his "Religious Communities, Secular Society, and Sexuality: One Jewish Opinion," in Olyan and Nussbaum, eds, *Sexual Orientation and Human Rights*, pp. 11–28; here, pp. 21–2. His respondent disagrees: "[The Jewish] tradition recognizes the legitimacy of divorce, not only in cases of infertility, but also when there is no longer love or commitment, joy, or stability in the relationship. The same reasoning explains (better than Novak's, I believe) why Judaism recognizes the legitimacy of marriages between those who are too old to have children. The point [the family resemblance] is not that all heterosexuals are presumed capable of procreation (or analogized to those who are), but rather that their marriages are fulfilling in other ways that make them sacred quite apart from the possibility of procreation." Newman, "Constructing a Jewish Sexual Ethic," p. 48.
[73]   Evdokimov, *The Sacrament of Love,* p. 43.
[74]   For a recent argument along those lines, with references to Maximus the Confessor and Gregory of Nyssa, see John D. Zizioulas, *Being as Communion: Studies in Personhood and the Church* (Crestwood, NY: St Vladimir's Seminary Press, 1985), pp. 50–65.

rather primarily, in "the likeness of the corruptible human being" – Personality, the Child, the Woman – and in the half-spiritual, half-material creations, exhibitions, and representation of the human being's creative ability – Family, Nation, State, Church, Fatherland.[75]

A nuptial sermon has had the audacity to admonish bride and groom that rings can signify not only faithful but also idolatrous commitment, so that wedding bands can make a cult of marriage much as the Israelites took rings of idolatry to make themselves a Golden Calf.[76] The goal of marriage is God, and community with God fulfills the human sexual nature for married and unmarried alike. For celibacy in community, like marriage, makes something before God precisely of the body.

Worried about the sort of idolatry that comes from too high a view of sex and marriage, a friend has complained that "all married couples need is to have a theologian telling them that they should not only expect great sex but *spiritually significant* sex, God help us."[77] A complementary view is that of the celibate Sebastian Moore: "The most dramatic, indeed comic, instance of cross-purposes between the Vatican and the married, is that the Vatican sees the problem as one of curbing desire, whereas the married know that the problem is to keep desire going, which means to keep it growing, which means deepening."[78] Both remarks are true. It is entirely beyond the power of human beings to render sex *spiritually* significant; that expectation would be idolatrous. It is entirely in character for *God*, however, to do just that; to deny it would be to despair of God's ability to make good on the creation of the human being as body and spirit. More important is the deepening of desire that Moore talks about; in marriage, it has the opportunity to become the more reliable means of sanctification that eros may trick lovers into: acts of faith, hope, and charity. Christian life stretches ahead (*epektasis*) into ever-greater love of God, because God expands desire for God as God fulfills it. The expansion is part of the fulfillment, because unexpanding desire for God is static and dies.[79] Marriage, too, allows desire to press ahead, now in space and time, so that it counts as sacrament. Desire does not press ahead into more of the same, but into what is better to desire. Marriage, we

[75] Karl Barth, *The Epistle to the Romans*, 6th edn, trans. Edwyn C. Hoskyns (New York: Oxford University Press, 1980), 50–1, reading "human being" for *Mensch*.
[76] Charles Hawes, unpublished typescript. Ex. 32:1–6 mentions earrings of both men and women; Gen. 35:4 and Jg. 8:24 connect them with idol worship.
[77] Personal correspondence.
[78] Sebastian Moore, *Jesus the Liberator of Desire* (New York: Crossroad, 1989), p. 104.
[79] Cf. Moore, *Jesus the Liberator of Desire*, pp. 89–93.

saw above, allows sex to mean *more*, about "how much we want our bodily selves to mean, rather than what emotional needs we're meeting."[80] "Who devalues the body?" Robert Jenson asks. "Those for whom its gestures make no commitments, or those for whom they can make irrevocable commitments? Those who find freedom in casual nakedness, or those who reserve this most visible word for those to whom they have something extraordinary to say?"[81] As we have seen, "[m]arriage is a place where our waywardness begins to be healed and our fear of commitment overcome"[82] – gay or straight, we might add, though the authors would not. Marriage and monasticism are both bodily practices through which God enters the soul and disarms it with delight, lightening the load of impediments to love as it, embodied, hurries forward to something more and better for the body to mean. God may seduce the married as the monk into greater and greater acts of charity, so that through their bodies God can nurture compassion, offer hospitality, witness to grace, build up the community, and show forth, in distant reflection, God's own holiness and glory. Lesbians and gay men may have much to teach Christians of all sorts about the famous words of Paul:

> If I speak in the tongues of humans and of angels, but have not love, I am a noisy gong or a clanging cymbal. And if I have prophetic powers, and understand all mysteries and all knowledge, and if I have all faith, so as to move mountains, but have not love, I am nothing. If I give away all I have, and if I deliver my body to be burned, but have not love, I gain nothing.[83]

God can use same-sex couples, too, as difficult schools for embodied virtue, where the partners may learn not in their minds only but through their bodies that:

> Love is patient and kind; love is not jealous or boastful; it is not arrogant or rude. Love does not insist on its own way; it is not irritable or resentful; it does not rejoice at wrong, but rejoices in the right. Love bears all things, believes all things, hopes all things, endures all things.[84]

By such love God draws human beings to signify the glory of God.

---

[80]   Williams, "The Body's Grace," p. 64.

[81]   Robert W. Jenson, *Visible Words: The Interpretation and Practice of the Christian Sacraments* (Philadelphia: Fortress, 1978), pp. 24–5.

[82]   "The Homosexual Movement: A Response by the Ramsey Colloquium," *First Things* 41 (March 1994), 15–20; here, p. 17.

[83]   I Cor. 13:1–3.

[84]   I Cor. 13:4–7.

The Significance of God's Glory

In the Westminster Catechism the first question asks, "What is the chief end of the human being?" And the answer follows, "To glorify God and enjoy God forever." Karl Barth, in the same, Calvinist tradition, writes:

> if we inquire into the *goal* of creation, the object of the whole, the object of heaven and earth and all creation, I can only say that it is to be the theatre of [God's] glory.... *Doxa, gloria* means quite simply to become manifest. God wills to be visible in the world; and to that extent creation is a significant action of God.[85]

That is what happens in a marriage, too. The partners will to be *visible in the world*. And to that extent, too, their marriage models not just the Trinity but *creation, too, as a significant action of God*. This is the true answer to the objection about modeling God's will and acts. Marriage is in microcosm a theater of God's glory, a place where human beings – not just the spouses, but also their neighbors – are allowed to witness creation as a significant action of God. So it is that God permits marriage to be a sign of God's will in creation, of its goodness and reflected glory.

Much hangs on Barth's phrase "significant action of God." There the word most in need of a gloss is "significant." In its relation to marriage it suggests the whole complex of what sex, as an element of creation, *means*. Thus Rowan Williams writes that "the moral question . . . ought to be: How much do we want our sexual activity to communicate?" Decisions about our sexual lives, he goes on to say, are "decisions about what we want our bodily life to say, how our bodies are to be brought into the whole project of 'making human sense' for ourselves and each other . . . how much we want our bodily selves to *mean*, rather than what emotional needs we're meeting or what laws we're satisfying."[86]

What, that is, shall sexual desire *signify*? Elsewhere Williams says, "Grace, for the Christian believer, is a transformation that depends in large part on knowing yourself to be seen in a certain way: as significant, as wanted."[87] Pope John Paul II has written in similar terms that sexuality is "a further discovery of the meaning of one's own body, a common and reciprocal discovery, just as the existence of man, whom 'God created male and female,' is common and

---

[85] Barth, *Dogmatics in Outline*, p. 58.
[86] Williams, "The Body's Grace," pp. 61, 64.
[87] Williams, "The Body's Grace," p. 59.

reciprocal from the beginning."[88] This commonness and reciprocity can find a signal instance in male and female, even if the light of Jesus does not allow Christians to reduce it to that.

Quoting John Paul, David Matzko McCarthy writes:

> if Christian communities are asked to recognize same sex unions, gay and lesbian couples will be called to give over their bodies, not only to each other but also to the Church as communicative signs. This donation of the body is the hermeneutical [meaning-bearing or significant] version of gaining one's life by losing it, the core of Christianity's understanding of giving oneself over to God's creative activity.[89]

What is the meaning of God's creative activity, according to Barth, as applied to the creation as a whole? It is, as we have seen, that "God wills to be visible in the world."

> Its goodness [the world's] incontestably consists in the fact that it may be the theatre of [God's] glory, and [the human being] the witness to this glory. . . . [The human being] is the witness; [the one] who is allowed to be where God is made glorious, is not a merely passive witness; the witness has to express what [he or she] has seen. That is [human] nature, that is what [the human being] is able to do, to be a witness of God's acts. . . . The covenant between God and [the human being] is the meaning and the glory, the ground and the goal of heaven and earth and the whole creation.[90]

How does that apply to marriage? The goodness of marriage, too, incontestably consists in the fact that it may be, by the grace of God, the theater of God's glory. The goodness of marriage, too, consists in that the human being – even, perhaps, the human partner, but more usually the believing community – may be, by the grace of God, the witness to this glory. Evdokimov sees the matter in similar terms:

> In the priestly prayer of Christ we hear, "I have glorified them . . . that they may be one in us as we are one." The [Eastern Orthodox] Service of Crowning of marriage announces that the spouses are "crowned with glory." This glory signifies the manifestation of the Spirit.[91]

---

[88] John Paul II, "Fatherhood and the Family," in James V. Schall, S. J., *Sacred in All Its Forms* (Boston: Daughters of St Paul, 1984), pp. 86–94.

[89] David Matzko McCarthy, "The Relationship of Bodies: Toward a Theological Hermeneutics of Same Sex Unions," *Theology and Sexuality* 8 (1998): 96–112; here, p. 108. The quotation from John Paul appears on p. 15.

[90] Barth, *Dogmatics in Outline*, pp. 58–9. Italics removed from the last line.

[91] Evdokimov, *The Sacrament of Love*, pp. 117–18.

The community as the witness, the community that is allowed to be in the presence of a marriage where God is made glorious, is no merely passive witness; it has to express what it has seen. (Thus it is that straight Christians are coming to express what they have seen in the lives of gay and lesbian couples.)[92] This then is human nature, this is what human community is able to do: to be a witness of God's acts in marriage as in a microcosm of creation. Marriage is the visibility, the publicness of bodies that mean, not for themselves alone, but for the Church, and what that visibility is of, is the glory of God.

David McCarthy offers an important qualification:

> Certainly, this account of the body can be accused of being idealistic and far removed from the reasons that two people may express in their desire for marriage. "We want to be married because we love each other." "I want to be married because I am tired of being lonely." . . . The set of reasons provided by a nuptial theology seems to produce an interpretive excess, reaching far beyond personal intentions. Critical questions can be raised. Does a couple need to intend to be an image of God . . . ? Is such an image ever achieved on an interpersonal level? In the end, these questions do not undercut the nuptial hermeneutics. The body is given more meaning than a person alone or a couple alone is able to sustain. The nuptial interpretation of the body lifts marriage beyond the design of the couple that is united. The body's agency comes to fulfilment through personal, bodily, and semiotic donation. As the body is given, the body is received. The desire of coming out is the desire of the body to enter and to be entered, to give away and to be given identity.[93]

The glory of God is self-subsistent. It does not lack for anything. In that marriage displays the glory of God, that is enough. For that reason, too, a marriage need not bear children, anymore than Samuel's father's did when he asked his wife, "Am I not more to you than ten children?"[94] Evdokimov notes that "[t]he account of the institution of marriage, found in the second chapter of Genesis, speaks of 'one flesh' without mentioning procreation at all"; rather, it refers to the statement: "It is not good for the human being to be alone."[95] Of course, the answer to loneliness produced from Adam's side is female; but Evdokimov undercuts the possible biologism of that circumstance by noting that in modern Arabic, "my side" means simply "inseparable

---

[92] To see this worked out as a principle of Catholic moral theology, see Stanley Hauerwas, "Virtue, Description, and Friendship [formerly: "Gay Friendship"]: A Thought Experiment in Catholic Moral Theology," *Irish Theological Quarterly* (1998): 170–84.
[93] McCarthy, "The Relationship of Bodies," pp. 107–8.
[94] I Sam. 1:8.
[95] Evdokimov, *The Sacrament of Love*, p. 120, quoting Genesis 2:18, 24.

companion."[96] Thus the covenant of God with Israel and with the Church is "notably nonbiological in its emphasis,"[97] and the metaphors for the love of God and Israel in the covenant do without children. That is enough significance for gay and lesbian couples, should they remain childless – which may have nothing to do with the desire of the partners to have children. Purpose enough that they show forth the glory of God.

How do they do this? It is sufficient for them to be: consider the lily of the field, how it grows.[98] It neither spins nor sews. It grows wild, without purpose, except to glorify God and give joy to human beings. In neither spinning nor sewing it is not procreative. In not sewing it is not even productive. Or better, it is productive of the glory of God. If it simply glorifies God, it suffices – indeed, it overflows. Or, as Williams puts it, there is a joy whose "material 'production' is an embodied person aware of grace."[99]

> Sing, O barren one, who did not bear;
> break forth into singing and cry aloud,
> you who have not been in travail!
> For the children of the desolate ones will be more
> than the children of her that is married, says the Lord.[100]

The chief end of the human being – the chief cause of joy and song – as the Westminster Catechism had it, is to glorify God and enjoy God forever – whether children, by the grace of God, are means and reason for glorifying and enjoying God, or not. As Gerard Manley Hopkins put it:

> All things counter, original, spare, strange;
> Whatever is fickle, freckled (who knows how?)
> With swift, slow; sweet, sour; adazzle, dim;
> He fathers-forth whose beauty is past change:
> Praise him.[101]

---

[96]   Evdokimov, *The Sacrament of Love*, p. 120.

[97]   Williams, "The Body's Grace," p. 67, quoting John Boswell, *Rediscovering Gay History: Archetypes of Gay Love in Christian History*, The Fifth Michael Harding Memorial Address (London: Gay Christian Movement, 1982), p. 13.

[98]   Mt. 7:26–9, Lk. 12:22–31.

[99]   Williams, "The Body's Grace," p. 66.

[100] Is. 54:1.

[101] "Pied Beauty," *Poems of Gerard Manley Hopkins*, 3rd edn (New York: Oxford University Press, 1961), p. 74, quoted to similar purpose in Peter S. Hawkins, "Counter, Original, Spare, Strange," in Hefling, ed., *Our Selves, Our Souls and Bodies*, pp. 76–86; here, p. 86.

What does the glory of God mean? Why is God glorious? For love – for the covenant between God and the human being. The covenant between God and the human being is the meaning and the glory, the ground and goal of marriage, as an emblem and microcosm of the whole creation. As Barth says famously elsewhere, creation is the external ground of the covenant, and the covenant is the internal ground of creation. Thus, too, marriage is in microcosm an external sign, manifestation, or making visible of the covenant, and the covenant is the internal ground of marriage. This is not a strained or arcane interpretation of Barth. On the contrary, as we have seen, "Because the election of God is real, there is such a thing as love and marriage."

In this eschatological celebration human beings are taken up into the love by which the Father loves the Son, taken up into "that unconditional response to God's self-giving that God's self makes in the life of the Trinity," so that it becomes manifest to the community and in the public participating in the Spirit's work that "God loves us as God loves God."[102]

---

[102]   Williams, "The Body's Grace," p. 59.

Chapter 10

EROS AND PHILANTHROPY

Philanthropy, the Eros of the Triune God

Christian language represents the love of God for God both as love between a father and a son, and as like a wedding feast. How does one relate to the other?

Ambivalent or polysemous language for God is not a strange thing in Christian talk, but normal already in descriptions of God's love for Israel. Thus God is routinely depicted as both Israel's father[1] and lover.[2] Rather than trying to sort out, rationalize, or explain away that mix of metaphors, Christians recognize them as the sort of "stammering" that human language undergoes in trying to repeat the truths of revelation. Indeed, that stammering becomes a rigorous, technical concept in the hands of theologians, the doctrine of analogy.[3] As Victor Preller puts it, "the [theological] appropriation of language is an equivocation pure and simple, although its appropriateness can be seen. Such analogical appropriations of language from one context to another may be quite illuminating, although they have their own intrinsic dangers. . . . A great deal of epistemological nonsense has been generated by the failure to see that such analogies are *appropriate equivocations*."[4]

A more constructive answer arises from the way in which analogies properly work from the top down. If Christians try to decide whether God's love is erotic or paternal, they will get into false dichotomies as sterile as

---

[1]   E.g., Dt. 32:6.
[2]   E.g., Ex. 20:5, Song 4:9a, Hos. 2:14.
[3]   For "stammering" as a term of art, see Catherine Pickstock, *After Writing: On the Liturgical Consummation of Philosophy* (Oxford: Blackwell, 1998), pp. 178, 181, 190, 198, 215.
[4]   Victor Preller, *Divine Science and the Science of God: A Reformulation of Thomas Aquinas* (Princeton, NJ: Princeton University Press, 1967), p. 243.

Nygren's *Eros and Agape*.[5] But if they allow the paternal and the erotic, the maternal and the kenotic, the love of friends and the love of enemies all to descend from the love that God enacts in the trinitarian life – from the top down – then the problems dissolve. Eros and the others all appear as derivative, deficient, partial loves dependent for their power on the empowering grace of the Spirit, who is the love of God in person. But how do human beings see the love that God enacts in the trinitarian life?

The love that God enacts in the trinitarian life appears to human beings when one of the Trinity is made human, and the New Testament records some of his interactions with the other persons. Each of the accounts to follow needs three characters to complete the action.[6] It is a principle of Christian trinitarian discourse that the works of the Trinity toward the outside – creation, redemption, sanctification – are indivisible, but that the relations among the persons belong to the Trinity apart from creation. Because crucial scenes from the life of Jesus involve interactions among the three divine persons, they give Christians a glimpse into God's life *in se*.

At the baptism, the voice of the Father identifies the Son as his beloved – *agapetos* – while the Holy Spirit in the form of a dove alights on him: "Now when all the people were baptized, and when Jesus also had been baptized and was praying, the heaven was opened, and the Holy Spirit descended upon him in bodily form, as a dove, and a voice came from heaven, 'Thou art my Son, my beloved; with thee I am well pleased.'"[7] At the transfiguration, similarly, the Son is again identified as the beloved of the Father, while traditional exegesis and Eastern iconography see the Spirit in the cloud and in the pregnant word "overshadowed": "A cloud came and overshadowed them; . . . And a voice came out of the cloud, saying, 'This is my son, my beloved; listen to him.'"[8] And in Paul's account of the resurrection, as we will see in more detail when we consider the effects of sin, that love is shown to be stronger than death, because the Spirit reunites the Father and the Son in a trinitarian answer to the Song of Songs.[9] Just where God is revealed as Trinity, therefore, God is also revealed as a certain sort of love: the love that is well pleased with Jesus, and that vindicates him even after a criminal's contaminating death.

---

[5]   Anders Nygren, *Eros and Agape*, trans. Philip S. Watson (New York: Harper & Row, 1969).

[6]   For a standard Orthodox use of these passages, see Kallistos Ware, "The Trinity," in *The Orthodox Way* (Crestwood, NY: St Vladimir's Seminary Press, 1979).

[7]   Luke 3:21, Mk. 1:10–11, Mt. 3:16–17.

[8]   Mk. 9:7, Luke 9:34–5, Mt. 17:5.

[9]   Rom. 8:11.

The Father is well pleased with the Son for a reason. The Father is well pleased because the Father enjoys and delights in the Son's enactment of the love in space and time of the whole Trinity for the human being – the Father loves the Son for his *philanthropia*. And there is more than a little of eros in that philanthropia, in the love of God for the human being.

Furthermore, the Father does not love the Son *only* because of what the Son accomplishes on earth; rather, the love of the Father for the Son in the trinitarian life is the condition for the possibility of his good pleasure at baptism, transfiguration, and resurrection. So, too, the gratitude and return of gift in the love of the Son for the Father in the trinitarian life is the condition for the possiblity of the Son's carrying out his love for human beings to the end. When the Father raises the Son, it is in vindication of a love that the Scriptures express like this:

> "The kingdom of heaven may be compared to a king who gave a marriage feast to his son."[10]

> "Why do [others] fast, but your disciples do not fast?" And Jesus said to them, "Can the wedding guests fast while the bridegroom is with them?"[11]

> "Then the kingdom of heaven shall be compared to ten maidens who took their lamps and went to meet the bridegroom."[12]

> "No longer do I call you servants . . . but I have called you friends."[13]

> "I will betroth you to me forever. . . . I will betroth you to me in faithfulness; and you shall know [who I am]."[14]

The images are too closely intertwined to come neatly apart. The love that is stronger than death is the love of the lovers in the Song of Songs and the love of the God of Israel for the people of Israel, the love of Christ the bridegroom for the mostly Gentile Church his bride. The Spirit does not perform a merely binding role in the resurrection, does not merely snap Father and Son back into communion. Rather it gathers into the resurrection those also who have, by marriage, become one flesh with the Son. The Spirit alone

[10] Mt. 22:2 (parallel Luke 14:16–24).
[11] Mk. 2:18–19.
[12] Mt. 25:1 Lk. 12:35, Mk. 13:34.
[13] Jn. 15:15.
[14] Hos. 2:19a, 20.

suffices to witness the love of the Father and the Son, but it gathers more witnesses, more guests for the wedding of the Lamb,[15] wedding guests who are taken up by the Spirit into the love of the Father who welcomes home the Son with the bride he met in the far country.[16] The good pleasure of the Father vindicates the eros of the Son.

Christians must norm their use of the word "love" by the love by which Jesus pleases the Father. The love by which Jesus pleases the Father is a love that pleases him already in the trinitarian life, and which human beings see directed also toward them in the *philanthropia*, a love which the Scriptures describe as erotic. It is not a genital or a sexual love; it is not a homosexual love in any interesting sense. It is an eros that (like monasticism and marriage) ends in goodness, righteousness, holiness, and the fulfillment of the trinitarian purpose. That does not make the love not erotic; it makes the erotic a subset of the love of the Son for human beings and the love for which the Father loves the Son, the love in which the Holy Spirit delights and – with the gracious inclusion of human beings – celebrates as a wedding. The love by which God loves God satisfies the desire of every living thing,[17] making human erotic love an acceptable subset or analogate of itself. The love by which the Father loves the Son is not defined by and also not separate from the love by which the Father eternally begets the Son.

Grace is the sharing in Christ's belovedness, which is, Christians believe, what happens to satisfy the desire of every living thing; every creature wants to be significant, wanted.[18] Thus they participate already in advance in the love of creation that the Son would embody. This desire cannot be human without bodily concomitants. Of these, "[s]exuality is a particularly insistent reminder of this radical availability," and although it has been vitiated by sin, "Christian faith involves an affirmation of radical availability."[19]

---

[15] Rev. 19:7.

[16] The prodigal son "took his journey into a far country," Lk. 15:13, which Karl Barth exploits for the title of the most beautiful christological section of the *Church Dogmatics*, "The Way of the Son of God into the Far Country."

[17] Ps. 145:16.

[18] In Sebastian Moore, *Jesus the Liberator of Desire* (New York: Crossroad, 1989), the entire exposition is devoted to this thesis. And cf. Rowan D. Williams: "Grace, for the Christian believer, is a transformation that depends in large part on knowing yourself to be seen in a certain way: as significant, as wanted," "The Body's Grace," in Charles Hefling, ed., *Our Selves, Our Souls and Bodies: Sexuality and the Household of God* (Boston: Cowley Publications, 1996), pp. 58–68; here, p. 59.

[19] Thomas E. Breidenthal, "Sanctifying Nearness," in Hefling, ed., *Our Selves, Our Souls and Bodies*, pp. 45–57; here, p. 56; see also Breidenthal, *Christian Households: The Sanctification of Nearness* (Boston: Cowley Publications, 1997).

Thus Christians have been free with erotic and romantic metaphors, and the eschatology that marries Christians foremost to God before each other could lead to the greatest romantic freedom of expression even, or especially, in such celibates as Augustine. We see in the first quotation that Augustine did not have to have read Freud to mix the yearnings of the spouse and the child that the Bible refuses to separate:

Let me leave them outside, breathing into the dust, and filling their eyes with earth, and let me enter into my chamber and sing my songs of love to Thee, groaning with inexpressible groaning in my distant wandering, and remembering Jerusalem with my heart stretching upwards in longing for it: Jerusalem my Fatherland, Jerusalem who is my mother: and Thou Ruler over it, Giver of Light, Father, Guard, Husband, pure and deep Delight and constant Joy. . . . (Augustine, *Confessions*)[20]

I had not yet fallen in love, but I was in love with love . . . . To love and to have my love returned was my heart's desire. (Augustine, *Confessions*)[21]

I have learnt to love you late, Beauty at once so ancient and so new! I have learnt to love you late! . . . The beautiful things of this world kept me far from you and yet, if they had not been in you, they would have had no being at all. You called me; you cried aloud to me; you broke my barrier of deafness. You shone upon me; your radiance enveloped me; you put my blindness to flight. You shed your fragrance about me; I drew breath and now I gasp for your sweet odour. I tasted you, and now I hunger and thirst for you. You touched me, and I am inflamed with love of your peace. (Augustine, *Confessions*)[22]

[20] Book 12, ch. 16, adopting for the first phrases the more evocative translation of Peter Brown in *Augustine of Hippo* (Berkeley, CA: University of California Press, 1967), p. 157. For a standard translation see Augustine, *Confessions*, trans. R. S. Pine-Coffin (New York: Penguin Books, 1961), p. 293.

[21] Book 3, ch. 1. The Latin is worth savoring: "Nondum amabam, et amare amabam . . . amare et amari dulce mihi erat." The translation, again better than those of standard editions, appears in Peter Brown, *Augustine of Hippo*, p. 171.

[22] Book 10, ch. 27; Pine-Coffin translation. Again I offer the sparer original: "Sero te amavi, pulchritudo tam antiqua et tam nova! sero te amavi! Et ecce intus eras et ego foris et ibi te quaerebam; et in ista formosa quae fecisti deformis irruebam. Mecum eras et tecum non eram. Ea me tenebant longe a te, quae si in te non essent, non essent. Vocasti et clamasti et rupisti surditatem meam. Coruscasti, splenduisti et fugasti caecitatem meam. Fragrasti et duxi spiritum et anhelo tibi. Gustavi et esurio et sitio. Tetigisti me et exarsi in pacem tuam."

> Take mee to you, imprison mee, for I
> Except you'enthrall mee, never shall be free,
> Nor ever chast, except you ravish mee.
>   (John Donne)[23]

The concept which lies ready to our hand here . . . is that of beauty. If we can and must say that God is beautiful, to say this is to say how He enlightens and convinces and persuades us. It is to describe not merely the naked fact of His revelation or its power, but the shape and form in which it is a fact and is power. It is to say that God has this superior force, this power of attraction, which speaks for itself, which wins and conquers, in the fact that He is beautiful, divinely beautiful in His own way, in a way that is His alone, beautiful as the unattainable primal beauty, yet really beautiful. He does not have it, therefore, merely as a fact or a power. Or rather, He has it as a fact and a power in such a way that He acts as the One who gives pleasure, creates desire and rewards with enjoyment. And He does it because He is pleasant, desirable, full of enjoyment, because He is the One who is pleasant, desirable, full of enjoyment, because first and last He alone is that which is pleasant, desirable and full of enjoyment. God loves us as the One who is worthy of love as God. This is what we mean when we say that God is beautiful. (Karl Barth, *Church Dogmatics*)[24]

Because the election of God is real, there is such a thing as love and marriage. (Karl Barth, *Church Dogmatics*)[25]

So God loves Israel with an erotic love, because (a Christian will say) Israel is the flesh of Jesus,[26] God's own flesh, and Israel is the whole of the people, into whom others will be grafted, who will become in Jesus God's own bride. So God loves the Church with an erotic love, because the Church is the body of Christ, and the Church is the people, grafted into Israel, who is Christ's bride. How can the Church be the body and the bride of Christ? Because in marriage they become one flesh. God is love, therefore, in a very specific way. It is not specific as eros or agape or maternity or friendship: it is specific as it is made concrete in the biblical narratives.

God is love as God is well pleased with the Beloved in baptism, transfig-

---

[23]   *Divine Poems* XIV, "Batter my heart, three person'd God," in H. J. C. Grierson, ed., *The Poems of John Donne* (London: Oxford University Press, 1933), p. 299.

[24]   II/1, 650–1.

[25]   III/1, 318.

[26]   In an odd but elegant theologoumenon, Robert Jenson proposes that not only Jesus but Israel as a whole is humanity become internal to God; see Robert W. Jenson, *Systematic Theology*, vol. 1 (New York: Oxford University Press, 1997), pp. 63–89, *passim*.

uration, and resurrection. In the Beloved God sees God in pursuit of us human beings, approving the marriage of God with us. It is God's own erotic love of us human beings that God approves when God loves the Beloved. By the erotic love that joins God to human flesh, God takes us human beings up into the love by which God loves God. The love by which God in Trinity first loves God may or may not be far removed from eros; the answer depends upon how Platonic one's doctrine of the Trinity is. But the love by which God brings human beings into the love by which God loves God – the love of the covenant – is primarily described in erotic terms.

Christians learn from Scripture and tradition, therefore, and not from human experience, that their erotic love has a place in God's plan: they learn that it is a secondary, deficient, and perhaps all-too-sinful analogate of the love by which God loves them, and by which God brings them up into the love by which God loves God. Eros may or may not be a good description of the love by which God loves God: but it is the principle description of the love by which God loves human beings. The love by which God loves human beings is eros, if eros is a love that yearns for union with the other, yearns for the flesh of the other, is made vulnerable and passionate for the other. God's *philanthropia* is the love of a lover as well as the love of a father.

It is no part of divinity to need and yearn, but God chooses and takes on need with the flesh, as part of God's humanity, God's body which is in Jesus. God's erotic love already in the Hebrew Scriptures, Christians would say, anticipates and prefigures – it types – the love of the human being that God would become. It is the need and humanity in advance of God's love, the down payment and guarantee of God's *philanthropia*.

Christ is the image of the Father, and human beings are made male and female in the image of God. That Christ is the image of the Father means that no strict complementarity theory will do, according to which no human being represents the image unless he or she is joined with a member of the opposite sex. If Christ is the complete image, then the image need not be a dyad. But the images, Christ, and the creation male and female, are also not unconnected. The incarnate Logos represents, carries out, and embodies God's election of the human being for God's delight, and in spite of sin. The incarnate Logos represents, carries out, and embodies the *coniunctio*, the yoking together, the marriage of God and the human being. Christ incarnate is the image of the Father *as the lover of humankind*. Human beings as male and female are in the image of God also *as lovers of humankind*. The image picks out the typical form of human erotic love *to inscribe in their bodies the claim that God has on them as jealous lover*, the God whose very name, according to Exodus, is "Jealous."[27] The image picks out the typical form of human erotic love *because human beings are in God's image just as they love one another as God loves them*. In God's story it becomes clear that the eros of God for human beings is neither due to a defect in God that the love must fill up, nor subject to the inconstancy and promiscuity of eros under conditions of sin. For eros does not move from us up to God, so that because we know eros, we know God, but it moves from God down to us, so that because we read the stories of God's yearning and God's constancy, God's covenant fidelity and God's covenant promise, we learn for the first time what eros is for and what it means. *Eros, therefore, does not reveal God, but God unveils eros.* God causes eros to mean, to signify, what it means. God causes eros to mean covenant. God causes eros to be the energy of virtue. What it signifies is not satisfaction, except incidentally, but sanctification. What it means is life with God, holiness. "Because God elects the human being, there is such a thing as love and marriage." It is no accident, therefore, that God makes a covenant with Israel, and that Ruth makes a covenant with Naomi, Jonathan with David,[28] Hosea with Gomer, and covenant becomes the primary conceptuality for marriage in Puritanism.[29] But as biblical examples indicate, heterosexual marriage does not exhaust covenant. Its whole trinitarian and salvation-historical basis make it a fluid concept, able to assume even same-sex marriages into its trinitarian pattern.

By the image God also calls human beings to love Christ in the neighbor. A chastened, virtuous eros is first of all charity, a love by which the desire for the other is always desire for the other's good. Under conditions of sin, however, this good eros, or eros-become-charity, which Augustine calls eschatologically *delectatio victrix*,[30] the delight that will be victor in heaven, proves unstable, susceptible to flickering, temptation, divorce from the good of the other, a remnant, a poignant reminder of what charity might be like.

---

[27]   Ex. 34:14.

[28]   I Sam. 18:3, 20:42.

[29]   Max L. Stackhouse offers an elegant description of covenant marriage in Puritan traditions, a description from which same-sex covenants would also follow, since, as he correctly sees from the biblical evidence, lack of fecundity does not exclude opposite-sex couples. Although Stackhouse excludes same-sex couples against his own logic, the essay can still be read with profit; see Max L. Stackhouse, "The Prophetic Stand of the Ecumenical Churches on Homosexuality," in Saul Olyan and Martha C. Nussbaum, eds, *Sexual Orientation and Human Rights in American Religious Discourse* (New York: Oxford University Press, 1998), pp. 119–33, with a response by Kathryn Tanner, pp. 161–8.

[30]   For comment see Eugene TeSelle, *Augustine the Theologian* (New York: Herder & Herder, 1970), p. 328; more recently, Carol Harrison, *Beauty and Revelation in the Thought of Saint Augustine* (Oxford: Clarendon Press, 1992), pp. 257–9.

So Christians have enemies and seek to love them. So, too, they experience sharp pangs of attraction to the bodies of others, whether or not that special, desirous appreciation of the beauty God created in their bodies is for anyone's obvious good. It is a way, a particular, embodied way, and hopefully a pleasant, promising way, in which human beings cannot escape from the neighbor, and from the neighbor's claim. The bodies of the desired do not leave even the most devoted misanthrope alone. Rather, inscribed in him or her, inescapably, is the claim of the neighbor, even if wounds and cries may have ceased to move compassion. Eros is both inscribed in the image and the last stand of God in human beings, that they might never entirely escape the image of God in their neighbors, however much their powerlessness and vulnerability before that image may distort them into anger, adultery, and murder. God created human beings embodied not only to their peril, but also for their salvation; it is through the body that the neighbor, and through the neighbor Christ, by the Spirit, does not leave human beings alone. As the Church and the eucharist are both the body of Christ because they locate places where Christ is physically accessible, so the body is the locus or reflex whereby human beings are accessible and vulnerable to others as God has become accessible and vulnerable to them. Love of neighbor is embodied because the body locates the accessibility of the other.

Concupiscence and Philanthropy in the Human Being

Properly speaking, concupiscence, or the eros appropriate to material human beings, is both that by which human beings fall and that by which they are redeemed: concupiscence is a place where they become vulnerable to the bodily neighbor.[31] In that God constrains them from their very source to imitate the love that God has for them, God's desire for human beings echoes in the human desire for human beings, for God desires that God and human beings should have desire for human beings in common. Theologically, "concupiscence" names sexual appetites, and especially sinful sexual appetites, only by a certain narrowing. More broadly it names the incompleteness or yearning or desire that human beings suffer – or enjoy – on account of being material creatures. As spatio-temporal beings, human beings cannot dispose

[31] Karl Rahner, "The Theological Concept of Concupiscentia," in his *Theological Investigations*, vol. 1, trans. Cornelius Ernst (Baltimore: Helicon Press, 1961), pp. 347–82, with extensive notes to Thomas Aquinas.

of themselves all at once, in a single, ultimate action. Rather, when they choose, they choose incompletely. When they choose good, they experience partial temptation – whence concupiscence gets its bad reputation. But when human beings choose evil – when they sin – they cannot do that with entire disposal of their whole selves, either. They can experience regret. And regret under conditions of sin also comes of concupiscence. Thus concupiscence is the condition for the possibility of repentance. This bodily aspect of the human make-up, concupiscence, is the very root of human salvation, the source of compassion as well as eros, of repentance as well as temptation.

For Aquinas, concupiscence can be even more positive. He considers the human being as created in grace, bracketing the effect of sin, and identifies concupiscence as the bodily appetite for the good – the embodiment of love (*amor*). It is the root bodily energy or passion that the virtues perfect, and the condition for the possibility of delight (*delectatio*) in material creatures.[32] It is the bodily correlate, therefore, of their orientation toward the good and their possibility of joy. It is what the Holy Spirit has to work with when it writes the law of love on the heart. It is what grace elevates when it orients the human creature toward the good that is God. It is the bodily energy for the taking up of which God created human beings in the first place. And it is the bodily energy in the final consummation of which God's glory saturates the human being with endless joy. It is that by which the human being witnesses to the glory of God in the created body. Whatever God wants with a human body, gay or straight, partnered or vowed, God does not pass by but takes up concupiscence. Concupiscence is God's way into human creatures, and the human creature's way into God.

In a different conceptual system, a similar insight also explains why the ascetic desert fathers could regard the body as a means of saving the soul. Although Peter Brown stresses that food asceticism predominated over sexual asceticism, he notes that nevertheless "sexual desire was now treated as effectively coextensive with human nature,"[33] corresponding to medieval concupiscence. That desire, too, could be a means of transfiguration:

> In the *Sayings of the Fathers*, the memories of the great monks of Nitria and Scetis collected in the mid-fifth century, in the *Lausiac History* of Palladius, and in the lives and rulings of Pachomius and his successors, we can sense the huge weight

---

[32] I-II.30. Other passions, the irascible ones, come into play in cases when some obstacle must be overcome to attain the good.

[33] Peter Brown, *The Body and Society: Men, Women, and Sexual Renunciation in Early Christianity* (New York: Columbia University Press, 1988), p. 230.

that the myth of Paradise placed on the frail bodies of the ascetics. It is precisely the bleak and insistent physicality of ascetic anecdotes that shocks the modern reader. They have led scholars to speak of "Contempt of the human condition and hatred of the body" as the principal motive that led the monks to undergo so much physical privation. Far from confirming this view, the mood prevalent among the Desert Fathers implicitly contradicts it. The ascetics imposed severe restraints on their bodies because they were convinced that they could sweep the body into a desperate venture . . . [T]he imagined transfiguration of the few great ascetics, on earth, spoke to them of the eventual transformation of their own bodies on the day of the Resurrection.[34]

The same underlying insight also explains why the medievals thought that God could save creation only by becoming a human being, and not by becoming an angel.[35] In the Middle Ages, angels were tremendously useful. For Aristotelians like Thomas Aquinas (differently than for the desert ascetics),[36] angels functioned as a sort of theological science fiction. They provided a heuristic rubric, much as aliens now do, under which to isolate the essentially human by considering hypothetical cases. Rational creatures made of matter were human. If they were not made of matter, such rational creatures were angels.[37]

Angels therefore differed from human beings in several interesting respects. Species were differentiated by form, individuals within a species by the material formed. Without matter, each angel must therefore be of a different species.[38] Similarly, angels might have a location, but not take up space;[39] how many could dance on the head of a pin could, therefore, be an interesting (if legendary) question. Theologically the most important consequence was this: if angels had no matter, they had no concupiscence; and if they had no concupiscence, they could be neither tempted nor regretful.[40] They could choose,[41] but only all at once, once and for all. In choosing they either confirmed themselves in original righteousness, or fell without hope of

---

[34] Brown, *The Body and Society*, p. 222.

[35] E.g., Anselm of Canterbury, *Why God Became Man*, book II, ch. 21.

[36] Although the desert ascetics also took the body as a locus of sanctification by asceticism, they had a more positive view of angels than the medievals. See, for example, Brown's chapter 16, "'These Are Our Angels': Syria," in *The Body and Society*, pp. 323–38; and Patricia Cox Miller, "Desert Asceticism and 'The Body from Nowhere,'" *Journal of Early Christian Studies* 2 (1994): 137–53.

[37] *ST* I.50.2.

[38] *ST* I.50.4.

[39] Cf. *ST* I.52–53.

[40] *ST* I.50.5, I.59.4: angels are not concupiscible.

[41] *ST* I.59.4: angels have free will.

repentance.[42] Thus the angels envied the newly baptized their repentance.[43] Strictly speaking, there was no salvation for angels, because they had no matter, no concupiscence, no bodily desire. They had rational desire, but reason would not stop a fall. Only a body could do that.

Angelology teaches us why it is crucial for all Christians to recognize the importance – the salvific importance – of their bodily desires. This does not by any means imply that Christians must act on sexual desires genitally for salvation's sake. That would be Freud instead of Aquinas. But neither marriage nor celibacy can proceed without taking up sexual desire into honest ascetic practice. "To mortify *Eros* by mortifying the flesh is to dangerously desiccate the human being."[44] Sexuality cannot be passed by; it must be assumed, transfigured. "Beware of downgrading sex in your quest for God. Beware of Neoplatonism. It is not quite Christian."[45] As the ancient Christian slogan has it, what is not assumed is not redeemed. Indeed, medieval angelology teaches us that if there is no bodily desire to assume, there is nothing to redeem. The body is the way of the creature into the Triune God. Because in Jesus, God takes on a body to pave him the Way.

This is why gay and lesbian Christians, whether they practice their participation in Christ's body as partners in a marriage or in a monastery, cannot simply deny but must use (directly or indirectly) their bodily desires.

So much for angelology. What about christology? Are not gay and lesbian Christians called to take up the cross when they follow the way? Should they not renounce their desire, as the alcoholic must give up alcohol?

Christ, "as a human being, the way stretched out for us into God,"[46] leads human desire through asceticism and death, but not the death of desire. In Mark his last words are words of agonized desire: "My God, my God, why have you forsaken me?"[47] Sebastian Moore offers a christology of desire:

> The crucifixion of Jesus with its pneumatic sequel is the final liberation of desire into the divine union that all desire is groping toward. . . .
>
>   It is because we do not understand desire but equate it with egoism, that we

[42]   *ST* I.62.4–5, 63.5–6.

[43]   Jean Daniélou, *The Bible and the Liturgy*, no trans. (Notre Dame, IN: University of Notre Dame Press, 1956), p. 199.

[44]   Paul Evdokimov, *The Sacrament of Love*, trans. Anthony P. Gythiel and Victoria Steadman (Crestwood, NY: St Vladimirs Seminary Press, 1985), p. 109, my emphasis.

[45]   Moore, *Jesus the Liberator of Desire*, p. 100.

[46]   *ST* I.2 proemium.

[47]   Mk. 15:34.

see the cross of Jesus as opposed to it. Real desire is what the cross empowers, bringing us to the death that its liberation entails. The death is the death of our present ego, whose perpetuation is the work of egoism posing as desire.

Real desire, what I really want and have always wanted, is to be more and more myself in the mystery in which I am. . . . Desire is love trying to happen. . . . It draws into its fulfilling meaning all the appetites of our physical being. It turns the need for shelter into the sacrament that is a house. It turns the need for food and drink into – well, Babette's Feast! And it turns sexual passions into – ah, there we have a problem. The sentence ends with "marriage," and this is true. But the biggest ethical gap in the Christian tradition is the failure to say anything much as to *how* that taking up of sexual passion into authentic desire, of which marriage is the institutionalizing, happens.

. . . To begin with, it is odd that we have no easy, comfortable common word for it. "Sexual desire" is very stilted. [C]olloquialisms for it . . . all belong to . . . the shadow language. But there is nothing in between, in the world of "*Buon appetito!*"[48]

For gay and lesbian couples, as for all Christians, it is possible, as we saw in Evdokimov, that "the most ascetic act is not renunciation of self but total self-acceptance."[49] There is plenty of death to ego, and plenty of cross to bear, in partnerships of whatever orientation.

Andrew Sullivan develops the theme of false renunciation and counterfeit crosses by contrasting (rather than comparing) sexuality and alcoholism:

Alcoholism does not ultimately work as an analogy because it does not reach to the core of the human condition in the way that homosexuality, following the logic of the Church's arguments, does. If alcoholism is overcome by a renunciation of alcoholic acts, then recovery allows the human being to realize his or her full potential, a part of which, according to the Church, is the supreme act of self-giving in a life of matrimonial love. [Such self-giving, we have seen, imitates and participates, by the grace of the Holy Spirit making human witnesses, in the trinitarian life God created human beings to share.] But if homosexuality is overcome by a renunciation of homosexual emotional and sexual union, the opposite is achieved: the human being is liberated into sacrifice and pain, barred from the matrimonial love that the Church holds to be intrinsic, for most people [those who do not have an authentic religious vocation, which for Catholic students of vocation is not *ipso facto* the same as a homosexual vocation], to the state of human flourishing. Their renunciation of such love also is not guided toward some ulterior or greater goal – as the celibacy of the religious orders [and the chastity of the married] is designed to

[48] Moore, *Jesus the Liberator of Desire*, p. 93.
[49] Evdokimov, *The Sacrament of Love*, p. 100.

intensify their devotion to God. Rather, the loveless homosexual destiny is precisely toward nothing, a negation of human fulfillment.[50]

The destiny toward nothing is strictly a destiny toward or through no created thing, the destiny of an angel. As Evdokimov writes, "Every solution that seeks to 'unsex' the human being is an attempt on the creative will of God."[51] The renunciation of homosexual desires, like the renunciation of heterosexual desires, confuses human beings with – desiccates them into – angels. It gives God nothing by which to redeem them, no hook in the flesh by which to capture them and pull them up. Sullivan's title, "Alone Again, Naturally," describes a well-known theological construct – the angel alone in its species, unredeemable because it has no bodily desire for God to assume.

The problem is not that gay and lesbian couples are denied satisfaction, although that is bad enough. The problem is that they are denied true asceticism. True asceticism imitates the suffering of God for love – God's true love, God's human love, God's will to liberate human beings for love. The movement of eros is first of all a reflection, in their very bodies, of the love God has for human beings. Their whole selves, "our selves, our souls and bodies," the Anglican marriage has it, bear the image of the desiring God. Their corresponding desire exists for covenant, holiness, life with God, and even when ruined by sin can partake enough of God's desiring image to keep them from becoming entirely cut off. Gay and lesbian people are left out of this precisely if they are told that their desires are for sin. Then they may reject the very reflex in them of the desiring God. The very spring of love for neighbor is denied. For Sullivan, "a theological austerity became the essential complement to an emotional emptiness. And as the emptiness deepened, the austerity sharpened."[52]

It is true that God may turn homosexual desire, as God may turn heterosexual desire, directly to the love of God; this we learn from the celibate mystics. But precisely then it does not lose its bodily character, and it increases, not its austerity, but its susceptibility to the turning to neighbor. "The greatest sign of Anthony's recovery of the state of Adam was . . . the quintessentially fourth-century gift of sociability. He came to radiate such magnetic charm, and openness to all . . . [that he] was instantly recognizable as someone whose heart had achieved total transparency to others."[53]

---

[50] Andrew Sullivan, "Alone Again, Naturally: The Catholic Church and the Homosexual," *The New Republic*, November 28, 1994, pp. 47, 50, 52, 54–5; here, p. 54.

[51] Evdokimov, *The Sacrament of Love,* p. 109.

[52] Sullivan, "Alone Again, Naturally," p. 50.

[53] Brown, *The Body and Society*, pp. 225–6, citing Athanasius, *Life of Anthony* 67.

For that transformation to take place, even the celibate must accept his or her desire as a gift from God, good in itself, and not a natural disorder, worthy of return to God and neighbor. Should desire "skip" a human, created good, in favor of a divine one, that must perfect nature and not reject it, or Christians become Manichees. Gay and lesbian people are left out of the mirroring and response to God's love if and only if their bodily desires are left out of it. Are they left out of it in celibacy? By no means! But only if their bodily desires are taken up, assumed into the love of God for us and us for God, not if those desires are rejected, repressed, and called sin. And yet if they are not to be rejected, repressed, and called sin, it cannot be wrong for other people, not called to celibacy, not called to direct their bodily desires immediately to God, but mediately through covenant with another person, to make that covenant with the bodies God inscribed with God's own desire for the partner. Under conditions of holiness, under the tutelage and rule, that is, of the Spirit gathering human beings into the love of the Father and the Son, the love of a committed sexual partner for the other can express the love of God for the partner, since God does love us with that love and has inscribed that love in us as God's image, the image of the marriage of God and the human being in the Son.

One might suppose that such an assessment of divine and human eros prevails in Eastern Orthodoxy and to a lesser extent in Roman Catholicism, but that Protestant Churches resist it. Yet in a more attenuated sense Protestant Churches have also done theological anthropology out of God's intention to consummate human desire, the execution of God's creation of the human being as significant, desired, wanted. Protestants have usually expressed God's desire for human beings in the doctrine of justification. Because of his notorious personal and theological difficulties holding justification together with sanctification and fidelity, Paul Tillich is a dangerous theologian to cite in support of that claim, but his sermon "You Are Accepted," perhaps the most famous Protestant sermon in the 20th century, still renders unmistakable how Protestantism characteristically interprets justification in the romantic terms of the reunion of the separated in God.[54] Indeed, Lutheranism has been interpreted as

---

[54] Paul Tillich, "You Are Accepted," in *The Shaking of the Foundations* (New York: Charles Scribner's Sons, 1948), esp. p. 162. Carter Heyward, in a paper to the American Academy of Religion Annual Meeting (Anaheim, California, 1985) has argued effectively that the problem with Tillich was that for him "the ground of our being" – earthly human desires – "is so far removed from the Ground of Being" (one of his terms for God). It would be part and parcel of that syndrome that "You Are Accepted" manages to proceed without significant reference to the incarnation.

a theological movement having its reason for existence in the proposal that the doctrine of justification should serve as a rule norming all other doctrines. Using "gospel" as a gloss on "justification," Robert Jenson puts it this way:

> According to the Reformation insight and discovery, the gospel is a wholly unconditional promise of the human fulfillment of its hearers, made by the narrative of Jesus' death and resurrection.[55]

In a secondary and derivative way, erotic love is also a wholly unconditional promise of the human fulfillment of those experiencing it, but its claim to unconditionality is compromised, outside of Eden, by the fickleness of sin and the inevitability of death, and it is close enough to justification to offer it falsely, as an alternative to God, and end in idolatry. Perversions of love can turn gospel into law by allowing love no time or freedom or reciprocity for one to be transformed by the perceptions of another.[56] No doubt they were wedding rings, a sermon observes, that were melted down to make the Golden Calf. Furthermore,

> Nothing will stop sex being tragic and comic. It is above all the area of our lives where we can be rejected in our bodily entirety, where we can venture into the "exposed spontaneity" that Nagel talks about and find ourselves looking foolish or even repellent, so that the perception of ourselves we are offered is negating and damaging (homosexuals, I think, know rather a lot about this).[57]

Such human deficiencies in participation in divine love make up part of the reason *why* the love that is stronger than death, the love that raised Jesus, and that is thereby never fickle but always faithful, taking infinite time, is that from which ordinary eros distantly and defectively derives, is that which redeems it and brings it home. True love, or

> [t]he gospel, rightly spoken, involves no ifs, ands, buts, or maybes of any sort. It does not say, "If you do your best to live a good life, God will fulfill that life,"

---

[55]   Robert W. Jenson and Eric W. Gritsch, *Lutheranism: The Theological Movement and Its Confessional Writings* (Philadelphia: Fortress, 1976), p. 42.

[56]   According to this analysis, freedom is lacking in "sexual encounters bound to specific methods of sexual arousal – like sado-masochism"; reciprocity is lacking in rape, pedophilia, and bestiality; time in promiscuity and adultery. See Williams, "The Body's Grace," p. 61, and Thomas Nagel, "Sexual Perversion," in his *Mortal Questions* (New York: Cambridge University Press, 1979), pp. 39–52, esp. pp. 48–51.

[57]   Williams, "The Body's Grace," p. 62, citing Nagel, "Sexual Perversion," pp. 48–51.

or, "If you fight on the right side of the issues of your time . . . ," or, "If you repent . . . ," or, "If you believe. . . ." It does not even say, "If you *want* to do good/repent/believe. . . ." The gospel says, "Because the Crucified lives as Lord, your destiny is good."[58]

By the grace of God a marriage participates bodily in that same pattern. The love of God expressed in the gospel is that by and in which Christian marriage (gay or straight) has its rationale. It is only as participant therein that marriage makes sense. But therein it may make sense, in fact, to say, in parallel fashion, not "if you are rich," or "if you are well," or "if you are HIV-negative," or "if things get better," but rather rejecting the conditions explicitly: "for better or worse, for richer or poorer, in sickness and in health." Marriage says, not "if these things happen," but, "Because I love you."

> If law-communication imposes an "If . . . then . . ." structure on life, a promise grants the pattern "Because . . . therefore. . . . " "Because I love you," I say to my daughter, "I will further your ambitions."[59]

The pattern that begins "Because I love you" and ends with a promise is one that is saved from utter generality, and one that only begins to make specifically Christian sense, when it begins with God's trinitarian life of gift and gratitude, and continues with the incorporation of creation into that life when the resurrection takes place within it. That pattern is also the pattern, when it involves human bodies, that takes eros up into itself. Its carrying out may be ascetic and belong to sanctification; but justification belongs to the acceptance of the other as wanted, as desired by God unconditionally.

It is a deep understanding of the doctrine of justification, therefore, that causes Williams to write lines we have seen before in this book:

> Grace, for the Christian believer, is a transformation that depends in large part on knowing yourself to be seen in a certain way: as significant, as wanted. The whole story of creation, incarnation, and our incorporation into the fellowship of Christ's body tells us that God desires us, *as if we were God*, as if we were that unconditional response to God's giving that God's self makes in the life of the Trinity. We are created so that we may be caught up in this, so that we may grow into the wholehearted love of God by learning that God loves us as God loves God.

[58] Jenson and Gritsch, *Lutheranism*, p. 42.
[59] Jenson and Gritsch, *Lutheranism*, p. 44.

To conclude, as Williams does, that "[t]he life of the Christian community has as its rationale – if not invariably its practical reality – the task of teaching us to so order our relations that human beings may see themselves as desired, as occasions of joy," is just the erotic counterpart of the Protestant thesis that the doctrine of justification ought to rule the language of the Church. That doctrine, too, aims to teach human beings that God loves them as God loves God. The grace of justification, too, is a transformation that occurs by being seen a certain way, as wanted, as desired, a grace in which God can cause marriage to participate.

Chapter 11

THE SHAPE OF THE BODY AND THE SHAPE OF GRACE

Williams's essay bears the title "The Body's Grace." It expresses the claim that grace, like some sexual love, works a change in a human being by causing her to reperceive herself as loved by Another. As we have just seen,

> [g]race, for the Christian believer, is a transformation that depends in large part on knowing yourself to be seen in a certain way: as significant, as wanted.
>
> The whole story of creation, incarnation, and our incorporation into the fellowship of Christ's body tells us that God desires us, *as if we were God*, as if we were that unconditional response to God's giving that God's self makes in the life of the Trinity. We are created so that we may be caught up in this; so that we may grow into the wholehearted love of God by learning that God loves us as God loves God.
>
> The life of the Christian community has as its rationale – if not invariably its practical reality – the task of teaching us so to order our relations that human beings may see themselves as desired, as the occasion of joy.[1]

A critic might raise related objections to the concept of the body's grace – one about grace and one about the body.[2] (1) Despite the stirring trinitarian ring, the concept of the body's grace trades on too vague a concept of grace, reducing it to any kind of transforming, positive regard, of which God's grace becomes a mere example. (2) The concept of the body's grace psychologizes

---

[1] Rowan D. Williams, "The Body's Grace," in Charles Hefling, ed., *Our Selves, Our Souls and Bodies: Sexuality and the Household of God* (Boston: Cowley Press, 1996), pp. 58–68; here, p. 59.

[2] I have developed these objections from personal correspondence with other readers of the essay.

the body, because a concept only takes the body seriously as a body if it takes account of real bodily differences.

A shorter answer to those objections has to do with how justice constructs bodies and grace. Bodies, as we have seen, are one of the ways in which Christians ought to take particulars seriously: God chose the Jews; the incarnation took place in a particular place and time; the sacraments locate Christ again in space and time; the priest represents Christ still another way in space and time; particular bodily things – this bread and this wine – do matter. And so, to sum up, it really does matter whether someone has a penis or a vagina. There is more to the "insert tab A in slot B" argument than meets the ear of most revisionists. Christians believe other things that are just that bodily.

The question is, *which* bodily things ought Christians to believe? Are some bodily forms, like gay and lesbian relationships, irredeemable, or can God sanctify them? Which bodily forms we revere has a lot to do with what sort of society we are, what our external boundaries and internal organs are in the *social* body.[3] And here the question depends upon what vision of justice we want to uphold. Societies that distinguish sharply between men and women have justice; it is different from the justice that obtains in an individualist society.

Justice among the baptized must be specified by the formula, "In Christ there is no Jew or Greek, slave or free, male and female." The center of biblical embodiment is circumcision. The important thing about Jesus's birth in space and time was that his mother was Jewish, and so was he. God's covenant with the Jews is specific, and only by being grafted into it do Gentiles have a leg to stand on. But the one center of the bodily, circumcision, is relativized in that saying of Paul's by another, the body of Christ. If the bodily distinction of circumcision is overcome, then gay/straight is nothing, especially if sexual license is the worry about both gay and Gentile Christians. Indeed, to the peril of the Church, it was unbelieving Jews, not gay and lesbian people, whom Paul assimilated to Sodom and Gomorrah.[4] Jewish and Christian societies have constructed Gentile and Jewish bodies according to better and worse notions of justice.[5] Paul overturns those patterns. Paul (at his best) causes bodies to be

---

[3]   See Mary Douglas, *Purity and Danger* (London: Routledge, 1966), chapter 2, last. For a use of Douglas to address the homosexuality issue, see Jeffrey Stout, "Moral Abominations," chapter 7 in *Ethics after Babel: The Languages of Morals and Their Discontents* (Boston: Beacon, 1988), pp. 145–62. Most recently, see Dale B. Martin, *The Corinthian Body* (New Haven, CT: Yale University Press, 1995).

[4]   Rom. 9:29.

[5]   See Howard Eilberg-Schwartz, ed., *People of the Body: Jews and Judaism from an Embodied Perspective* (Albany, NY: State University of New York Press, 1992).

constructed not according to human justice, but according to God's justification, because he believes in a God who justifies *Gentiles*, and justifies them
uncircumcised.

A longer answer to the question of the body's grace requires us to revisit the
theological procedure of realistic analogy. According to the doctrine of
analogy, related realities generate related meanings.[6] So in the standard
medieval example, dating to Aristotle, both food and urine can be "healthy,"
because food *contributes* to health, and urine *indicates* health. The two relations
are not the same, but they are real, and the notion of a healthy *person* stands
in the center to give sense to all appropriate uses. The healthy person is the
"primary analogate," the one that gives sense to the others, which theologians
call secondary analogates.

The theory of analogy offers a solution to the problem of human language
about God generally. Take the statement "God is good." If the primary
analogate of "good" is *human* goodness, then it is hard to see how the word
can apply properly to God. Human goodness is so unreliable that applying it
to God is equivocal, not appropriate. On the other hand, if *God's* goodness
is the primary analogate, then "good" applies properly to God in the first place,
and to human beings only derivatively, deficiently, and secondarily.[7]

The objection to a grace of the body is then this: it sounds as if it takes an
all-too-general category, transformative, positive regard, as the primary
analogate, of which God's grace is not the defining example, but a mere
illustration, if the most impressive. To be theologically adequate, grace must
be defined first of all as what God does, and the grace of the body related to
that. But that is just what Williams does:

> [T]he body's grace itself only makes human sense if we have a language of grace
> in the first place; and that depends on having a language of creation and
> redemption. To be formed in our humanity by the loving delight of another

[6] To readers disturbed to see references to social construction in one paragraph and
reality in the next, suffice it to say that Christian theologians have seen that debate before:
it is realists versus nominalists all over again. For application, see John Boswell, "Revolutions, Universals, and Sexual Categories," in Martin Duberman, Martha Vicinus, and
George Chauncey, eds, *Hidden from History: Reclaiming the Gay and Lesbian Past* (New York:
New American Library, 1989), pp. 17–36.

[7] E.g., *ST* I.13.3, 5–6, and Janet Martin Soskice, *Metaphor and Religious Language*
(Oxford: Clarendon Press, 1985) esp. the final chapter. See also her essay "Can a Feminist
Call God 'Father'?" in Alvin F. Kimel, ed., *Speaking the Christian God* (Grand Rapids, MI:
Eerdman's, 1992).

is an experience whose contours we can identify most clearly and hopefully if we have also learned or are learning about being the object of the causeless, loving delight of God, being the object of God's love for God through incorporation into the community of God's Spirit and the taking-on of the identity of God's Child.[8]

The references to God's Spirit and Child are crucial. For if *God* defines what grace is, then grace, as we saw in chapter 9, is simply an impersonal name for the Holy Spirit: "The gift of the Holy Spirit is nothing but the Holy Spirit."[9] That Spirit is identified in the Christian community and as the Spirit of the Christ identified in turn by the biblical stories. Without saying so, Williams makes the word "grace" an analogy in the strict theological sense, where the gracious life of God in Trinity supplies the primary analogate. The grace of the body only makes sense by reference to the grace of God identified in a community that tells certain stories of God's creation and redemption. Only thus can it emerge that the body is one of God's ways of catching human beings up into God's own life, and therefore a possible means, derivative and at second or third hand, of grace. The body's grace, should it occur, is not a movement of the body up to God, but a movement of the Spirit down – so that a human body will *not be left out* of salvation.

The word "body" also has to work analogously because Christian theology is committed to speaking in a number of ways about that central body, the body of Christ. The body of Christ is at once the body assumed by the second person of the Triune God, and thus God's body. The body of Christ was also a specifically identifiable, historical human body. The body of Christ is the Church, and the body of Christ is the consecrated bread of the eucharist. Christ's body, to sum up, names a place where God locates God's own self, a place where God has chosen to become vulnerable to human touch and taste and hurt, "God with us." Technically, Christians should say that the body of Christ is the primary analogate of the word "body" in their discourse, the use from which others derive their sense.

Salvation is itself bodily. It depends, for Gentile Christians, upon the crucifixion of God's body, and it depends on their human bodies' getting taken up into God's body. For Christians, bodies are no more or less than a means by which God catches hold of and sanctifies human beings. In short, bodies are made to be saved. Union with God does not take place otherwise than by incorporating their physical bodies into God's. What does that mean?

---

8   Williams, "The Body's Grace," p. 65.
9   Augustine, *De Trinitate* XV.19.

At the fraction, or breaking of the bread, of the eucharist, the Trinity also breaks open to let human beings, through their bodies, into God's triune life. The broken bread is the broken body of Christ, which is the broken body of the Triune God, the body by the breaking of which on the cross the Son was forsaken by the Father and the Trinity risked its unity, the persons threatening to come apart. Better: for humanity's sake the persons *promise* to come apart, their unity restored in the same way that human unity with them begins, in the Holy Spirit. Paul writes; "If the Spirit of the One who raised Christ from the dead dwells in you, the One who raised Christ from the dead will give life to your mortal bodies also through the Spirit that dwells in you."[10] That is the body's grace *par excellence*, the transfiguration of the body by the indwelling of the Spirit who just is grace, the Spirit trinitarianly defined as the *Spirit* of the *One* who raised *Christ*, where Christ is defined in turn as the one who was crucified. The body's grace is first of all what identifies the Trinity by the crucifixion and reunites it in the resurrection.

At the eucharist, secondarily, the fraction breaks open the Trinity to let the body in. The Trinity is entered by the body of a believer through the broken body of the Lord, and the body of the Lord is also broken to enter into the bodies of believers. This co-enveloping or interpenetration of bodies just is the trinitarian life embodied, broken open, entered into – which could not take place with unembodied human beings.

Human bodies, like human reason, are not left out of the Spirit's work and love's communion, but taken up into it on the pattern of the assumption of flesh by the Logos. Even: as older atonement theories talked about the flesh as bait and hook, so God can use eros, too, as bait and hook for a life of commitment and care that takes eros up into agape. As Gregory of Nyssa writes, "[a]gape which is aroused is called eros."[11] Yet eros still belongs among what remains of God's plan not to leave human bodies out of consummation when we abstract bodies from their purpose to incorporate human beings into God's life. Sexual desire, especially as portrayed by such celibates as St John of the Cross, prefigures the eucharist, in which, for Christians, God desires to enter into human bodies and to be desired bodily by them. The eucharist also begins to consummate their life in God, since in it they partake of the trinitarian communion – they pray to the Father,

---

[10]   Rom. 8:11. I owe my attention to this verse to David Yeago.

[11]   Gregory of Nyssa, *Commentary on the Song of Songs*, homily 13, trans. Casimir McCambley (Brookline, MA: Hellenic College Press, 1987), p. 234; for commentary, see Paul Evdokimov, *The Sacrament of Love*, trans. Anthony P. Gythiel and Victoria Steadman (Crestwood, NY: St Vladimir's Seminary Press, 1985), p. 82.

invoke the Spirit, and commune bodily (the only way they can?) with the Son.

Eros, for Christians, ought to be a remainder concept left over from the eucharist; sex, like the eucharist, is a participation, analogous and derivative, in a marriage of sacrifice for others and therefore a thanksgiving for involving us in their involvements (among them children or care of the sick). Taken up into the eucharistic community in a marriage that upbuilds it, eros returns home, performing its task of pointing to the trinitarian community when it issues in fruits of the Spirit that satisfy only as they sanctify. It does so particularly in a wedding centered on the eucharist, since the kingdom of heaven is like a wedding feast;[12] in a wedding feast the Spirit catches the people up into its own proper work of witnessing, blessing, sanctifying, celebrating, and enjoying the love between the Father and the Son, using the people like the pair as a means to the ascesis of living with others. A wedding feast too emparables, enacts, and furthers the unity of God as it catches human beings up into the love by which God loves God, seducing them into love of another even after they leave the feast, a movement prepared by the Son's commitment to the Father – the Father to whom the Son draws near precisely by going out into the far country of godforsakenness.

Thus gay and lesbian marriages can, like straight marriages, take bodies seriously in a handful of ways:

1   Since the true body, or the primary analogate of "body" in Christian discourse, is the body of Christ, any body is taken seriously that extends and deepens the eucharistic entry into God's body. Marriage, gay or straight, receives its sacramental character not independently but from the welcoming of the one flesh, in soteriological ways a new body, into the eucharistic community.[13]

The male–female version of the one flesh can be especially apt for representing the union of Christ with his bride, the Church, but not everyone need represent this union in the same way. The analogy is flexible enough already that both celibates and the married can represent it. Gay and lesbian couples also need not threaten the aptness of the relation between Christ and the Church, but can be taken up into it. As the Fatherhood of God is not male, so priests need not be male to be called "Father." Similarly,

---

[12]   E.g., Mt. 9:15, 22:2.

[13]   Note for sacrament-counters: this statement does not make marriage an *independent* sacrament, but one that depends upon the eucharist.

the frequent identification of the human race with the figure of Mary in Roman Catholic and Eastern Orthodox traditions can lead to taking the race as a whole as ontologically female, yet not everyone must be female for the typology to work.[14] Whether male or female, priests are (as human) brides to Christ's groom and (as ordained) father to the Church's children. Religious discourse works in a much richer and subtler fashion than by supposing that one has to instantiate physically what one honors or even represents figurally. What matters is mirroring the election and fidelity of God to God's people, so that "there is such a thing as love and marriage." So, too, gay and lesbian Christians need have no quarrel with the special aptness of the Genesis account of male and female and their procreation as normative for the *species*, as long as not everyone has to instantiate it to be in God's image.

To say otherwise is to limit the freedom of God in an unbiblical manner. The first chapter of Matthew picks out several stories that lead up to Mary as the supreme example – she who represents the race as a whole – of departures from "normative" marriage and childbirth. Matthew picks out the stories by naming women – only four of them – in the entire genealogy of Jesus. Those women are Tamar, Ruth, Rahab, and "the wife of Uriah," a designation emphasizing that Bathsheba was married to Uriah when David had sex with her.[15] After the death of her husband and the refusal of his brothers to give her sons as required by the law of levirate marriage, Tamar dresses as a prostitute and seduces her father-in-law by the side of the road, bearing twins.[16] Not only is one of the twins an ancestor of Christ, but they represent the elected and rejected together in him, according to typological exegesis of double election. Rahab, a Gentile, is also a prostitute; she shows "hospitality" to spies of Israel against her home town of Jericho.[17] Not only is the resulting son an ancestor of Jesus, but the spies save Rahab by telling her to hang from her house a "scarlet cord," employing the sign that Matthew, in a recollection of the

[14]   Human beings are ontologically female by identification with Mary in Evdokimov, *The Sacrament of Love*, pp. 34–5. For an even more recent example see Hans Urs von Balthasar, *Theodramatik: Die Personen des Spiels* , 4 vols in 5 (Einsiedeln: Johannes, 1973–83). For a critique of such notions, see Marilyn Chapin Massey, *Feminine Soul: The Fate of an Ideal* (Boston: Beacon, 1985).

[15]   Mt. 1:1–16. It is possible to learn much about the women of Matthew's genealogy, however one evaluates the title thesis, from Jane Schaberg, *The Illegitimacy of Jesus: A Feminist Theological Interpretation of the Infancy Narratives* (San Francisco: Harper & Row, 1987), pp. 20–32.

[16]   Gen. 38.

[17]   Joshua 2.

sacrifice of atonement on Yom Kippur, will take as Messianic.[18] After the death of her husband, Ruth, a Gentile, pledges herself to Naomi, her mother-in-law, and bears a son "to her";[19] she does this by seducing Boaz, her husband's next of kin, on the threshing floor, following Naomi's instructions to get him drunk and uncover his "feet," a Hebrew euphemism for "genitals."[20] Not only is the resulting son an ancestor of Jesus, but Boaz is called Ruth's *goel*, not only her next of kin, but the next of kin who is her "redeemer." Bathsheba, finally, was also presumably a Gentile, since she was married to Uriah the Hittite. Not only did David commit adultery with her, but he had Uriah killed when her pregnancy could not be passed off as her husband's.[21] Her second son with David was Solomon, he of the 700 wives and 300 concubines,[22] another ancestor of Jesus.

In picking out those resourceful women with their irregular pregnancies, Matthew portrays God as capable – even delighting in – the use of irregular sexual unions for God's own purposes. God not only chooses an unwed mother to bear Jesus, but, as one of my students put it, "it runs in the family." God's purpose in this case was human redemption itself. Here, too, God saves Gentiles "in excess of nature." "Taking the body seriously" must leave room for the way in which the Bible shows *God* taking the body seriously in the history of salvation. Many accounts of sexual relations outside of traditional marriage do not actually leave room for the scandals God delights in using to lead up to the incarnation. They tend to rule out a category of providence or divine freedom or the blowing of the Holy Spirit that could make any more of the virgin birth than a case of unwed motherhood.

2   Any body is taken seriously in which the eucharistic community is built up. Weddings, gay or straight, build up the eucharistic community both by contributing the institutional stability of marriage, and because weddings represent the trinitarian life. In a wedding, third parties guarantee, celebrate,

---

[18]   Joshua 2:22, Mt. 27:28. Apart from the dating of Matthew, Mishna Yoma records ceremonies performed in the temple before the writing down of either document. For a persuasive and original reading of Matthew as portraying Jesus as a Yom Kippur rather than a Passover sacrifice, see Linda Strohmier, "'His Blood Be on Us and on Our Children . . .': A Study of the Atonement Theme in Matthew's Passion Account," M.Div. thesis for General Theological Seminary, New York, 1984. The point of the title is that if the blood is the blood of atonement, then it brings forgiveness with it – and Matthew expects the reader to recognize that.

[19]   Ruth 4:17.

[20]   Ruth 3.

[21]   II Sam. 11.

[22]   I Kings 11:3.

witness, bless, testify to, and delight in the love of two. When Jesus says the kingdom of heaven is like a wedding feast, and theologians say that the role of the Spirit is to guarantee, celebrate, witness, bless, testify to, and delight in the love of the Father and the Son, they are speaking of the same reality. The Spirit incorporates the wedding guests into the public of love. It bears repeating that Augustine rejects the triad father – mother – child as an analogy for the Trinity, while the analogy of the Spirit to the guests at a wedding has implicit support in the parables of Jesus[23] – the second passage issuing a dire warning about the those who do not celebrate the wedding, who refuse the Spirit's work,[24] which takes up the earlier, even direr warning that blasphemy against the Holy Spirit is the unforgivable sin.[25]

3   Any body is taken seriously in which the Holy Spirit dwells so as to raise it from the dead. Anticipation of that resurrection is the bodily sanctification that marriage, as a form of ascetic practice, carries out. Human beings imitate God when they take time and make space for each other – this is asceticism – as God takes time and space for Israel and in Jesus; in so doing they honor the body that exists over time and in space. Sartre notoriously opined that "hell is other people"; so is holiness. Indeed, in Eastern Orthodoxy the crowns placed over the heads of bride and groom are crowns of martyrdom. This leaves room for the fading of sexual urgency in marriage (gay or straight) and its being taken up into other forms of care for the partner and the community. So it is, too, that "in heaven they neither marry nor are given in marriage."[26] The *pas de deux* with which a romance may begin is taken up into the trinitarian circle, "that man / May come unto the general dance."[27]

4   Any body is taken seriously in which a human being begins to fulfill the chief end for which she or he was made, which, according to the first answer of the Westminster Catechism, is to "glorify God and enjoy him forever." Sanctification and the eucharist and wedding feasts certainly glorify God. Properly understood, they enjoy God, too. And if human beings were so created to enjoy God, then the joy of sex, under sanctifying circumstances, cannot be unfitting. Sexual attraction is explicitly or implicitly concerned with real bodies. Gay and lesbian people care about bodies – otherwise many of

---

[23]   Mt. 9:15, 22:2.

[24]   Mt. 22:11–13.

[25]   Mt. 12:31. Cf. Rev. 13:6.

[26]   Mk. 12:18–25.

[27]   "Tomorrow Shall Be My Dancing Day," English traditional carol, in Hugh Keyte and Andrew Parrott, eds, *The Shorter New Oxford Book of Carols* (New York: Oxford University Press, 1993), no. 76.

them would take the easier route and settle for those of the opposite sex. There is *something* right about having tabs and slots, but the very language "reduces love to an instrumental and utilitarian sexuality."[28] Only because God gives tabs and slots more to be about – namely God – than insert-tab-A-in-slot-B, it also comes not amiss that God should give it to some to admire others with tabs. Even Augustine was able to speculate about the placement of nipples on a man's chest: "they articulate the space of the chest, and they prove that beauty is a value in itself, not tied inevitably to utility in the human body."[29] Or better: the utility is for bodies made aware of grace, the utility of joy.

Williams puts it this way:

> Same-sex love annoyingly poses the question of what the meaning of desire is – in itself, not considered as instrumental to some other process, such as the peopling of the world. We are brought up against the possibility not only of pain and humiliation without any clear payoff, but, just as worryingly, of nonfunctional joy – of joy, to put it less starkly, whose material "production" is an embodied person aware of grace.[30]

Just because a body is pleasing to me I become vulnerable, and God has made human beings so as to be vulnerable in one another's bodily presence. The embodiment of God's creation is borne in upon me and will not leave me alone.[31] Neither monogamy nor celibacy cause these interventions of God through bodily forms of the neighbor to go away.[32]

Perhaps this is a place to reiterate how gay and lesbian desire, contrary to popular belief, can contribute to the Christian articulation of what celibacy is for. Celibacy, too, raises the question of nonfunctional joy. It raises the question of how, for married and monastic alike, "[s]exuality is surpassed by its own symbolics."[33] Both Jesus and Paul speak of sexual desire and fulfillment without mentioning children. They may do so because "as a symbol of unity," sexuality "transcends itself toward the spiritual integrity of the one being."[34] If sex is for *God*, then the task of celibacy is to bear witness to that fact

---

[28]   Evdokimov, *The Sacrament of Love*, p. 169.
[29]   Gary Wills, *Under God* (New York: Simon & Schuster, 1990), p. 293, citing Augustine, *The City of God* 22.24.
[30]   Williams, "The Body's Grace," p. 66.
[31]   Thomas E. Breidenthal, "Sanctifying Nearness," in Hefling, ed., *Our Selves, Our Souls and Bodies*, pp. 45–57.
[32]   Cf. Williams, "The Body's Grace," p. 65.
[33]   Evdokimov, *The Sacrament of Love*, p. 169.
[34]   Evdokimov, *The Sacrament of Love*, p. 169.

immediately, whereas the task of people in sanctifying sexual relationships of whatever orientation is to bear witness to that through the faithful mediation of a human partner. "It is perhaps because of our need to keep that perspective clear before us," that the body's grace depends on the loving delight of God, and that

> the community needs some who are called beyond or aside from the ordinary patterns of sexual relation to put their identities direct into the hands of God in the single life. *This is not an alternative to the discovery of the body's grace.* All those taking up the single vocation . . . must know something about desiring and being desired if their single vocation is not to be sterile and evasive. Their decision (as risky as the commitment to sexual fidelity) is to see if they can find themselves, their bodily selves, in a life dependent simply upon trust in the generous delight of God.[35]

5   Any body is taken seriously which is *ruled* by the *Spirit*. For the shape of grace is the rule of the Spirit.

That thesis addresses the further objection that if grace is properly to be described as "grace" it must occur in morally licit circumstances; the Bible and the tradition determine morally licit circumstances; and therefore it begs the question to deploy a concept of grace against received traditional morality. The body's grace, says this objection, is antinomian.

Reliance on the Spirit rather than on concrete forms of the created order, or the previously revealed order (such as that of circumcision), is not antinomian. On the contrary, the Spirit's work is also and precisely that of fidelity, or of keeping faith between the Father and the Son. Fidelity is a work proper to the Spirit, particularly "the Spirit of the One who raised Christ Jesus from the dead," the *vinculum caritatis*, the one who "restores" the bond between Father and Son, and works (much less successfully?) to restore unity also among human beings, even through the witnesses of a wedding to restore unity in a couple.

The 20th century mystic Adrienne von Speyr suggests a name for the Spirit bridging the gap that opens between spirit and letter and makes appeals to the Spirit seem antinomian to Western Christian ears. She calls the Spirit "the Rule," as in the Benedictine rule,[36] or, though she neglects to say so, the Torah – a structure that liberates people for sanctification. Similarly, Paul describes the formation and regulation of the community in terms of "the Spirit's law."

---

[35]   Williams, "The Body's Grace," p. 65, my emphasis.
[36]   Adrienne von Speyr, *The Word Becomes Flesh*, trans. Lucia Wiedenhoever and Alexander Dru (San Francisco: Ignatius, 1994).

In a dense piling up of modifiers, it becomes "the law of the Spirit" – "the law of the Spirit of life" – "the law of the Spirit of life in Christ Jesus."[37] The Spirit loves the law enough to write it on fleshy hearts.[38] To rely on the Spirit is the only way, not only to keep, but to "*delight* in the law of the Lord,"[39] since it is proper to the Spirit to delight in the love of the Father for the Son. Taken up into the delight of the Spirit in witnessing, vindicating, celebrating, and furthering the fidelity of the Father and the Son, human beings also, in the community the Spirit gathers, become free to witness, vindicate, celebrate, and further analogous forms of covenant among themselves. There can be no question of antinomianism where the Spirit is rightly invoked, since the Spirit is the Rule of faith-keeping.

Gay and lesbian relationships must exhibit not only the spiritual fruits of faith, hope, and charity, but must also exhibit them in sacramental form. Just as marriage gives form or rule to the sanctifying possibilities of heterosexual sex, so gay and lesbian people need sacramental forms, or inspired rules. Perhaps Boswell's ceremonies provide them, perhaps not.[40] In any case they are not celebrated in the modern West. Gay and lesbian relationships must wait upon a churchly form – call it sacramental if you think of marriage as a sacrament – to give their holiness ecclesial shape, just as heterosexual relationships had to wait centuries for the Church to integrate them fully into its life with heterosexual marriage forms.[41] Conservatives are right to complain about what you might call unformed love: Christians must mine Scripture and tradition under the Spirit, who will rule new rules for them.

I do not mean to say that only the Church can justify same-sex love. Evdokimov is right to say, "Marriage does not justify love: it is its grace."[42] In calling for marriage, same-sex couples are calling for God to crown grace with grace. In calling for grace, they are praying the Spirit to rest where it has alighted. In praying the Spirit to rest, they are invoking a rule of life.

[37]   Rom. 8:1–2.

[38]   Heb. 8:10.

[39]   Ps. 1:2.

[40]   John Boswell, *Same-Sex Unions in Premodern Europe* (New York: Villard Books, 1994).

[41]   See John Meyendorff, *Marriage: An Orthodox Perspective*, 2nd edn (Crestwood, NY: St Vladimir's Seminary Press, 1975), pp. 18–34; and Alvian N. Smirensky, "The Evolution of the Present Rite of Marriage and Parallel Canonical Developments," *St Vladimir's Seminary Quarterly* 8 (1964): 38–47.

[42]   Evdokimov, *The Sacrament of Love*, p. 187.

Chapter 12

HOSTILITY AND HOSPITALITY

Sin and Redemption, or Deathbed Wedding

So far we have proceeded without an explicit doctrine of sin. I hope to supply one that recovers the meaning of the *felix culpa* of the Easter vigil, the cry "O happy fault! that merited such and so great a Redeemer." It seems to affirm that God enjoys a sense of irony sufficient to delight in taking the worst that human beings have to offer and turning the plot of the story just there.[1] I take up the theme of the eucharist no more as a "mere" wedding feast, an eschatological banquet; this time it is the Last Supper, a deathbed wedding. I interpret it as God's constancy in hospitality just in the face of rejection and violence. It gives us a chance to revisit the rape of Sodom, the un-hospitality, the un-eucharist, and God's great reversal of it in using the Gentiles' very violence to adopt them. I propose that gay and lesbian Christians should not overlook but reclaim that story, imitating God's sense of irony by imitating God's own practice of adoption.[2]

Under conditions of sin, the plot thickens, or more exactly a subplot opens. Space can become separation and time can lead to divorce. Can grace and gratitude survive in finitude? Here they have limits. Difference becomes distance that can strain love and end it. Duration can become a burden, and

---

[1] Thomas Aquinas quotes it to this effect at *Summa Theologiae* III.1.3 *ad* 3 *in fin*. See also James Alison, *The Joy of Being Wrong: Original Sin through Easter Eyes*, with an introduction by Sebastian Moore (New York: Crossroad, 1998). I take it that "the joy of being wrong" is a rendition of *felix culpa*.

[2] Jn. 1:12. For different constructive uses of Sodom, see Mark D. Jordan, "The Responsibilities of a Theology of Sodomy," in his *Invention of Sodomy in Christian Theology* (Chicago: University of Chicago Press, 1997), pp. 159–76. See also Graham Ward, *Hetropolis: The City and the Postmodern Body of Christ* (New York: Routledge, forthcoming), and Brian Doyle, "The Sin of Sodom," *Theology and Sexuality* 9 (1998): 84–100.

death can cut it short. "Till death do us part": a promise becomes a threat. The Song of Songs asserts, "Love is as strong as death."[3] Is it? Otherness becomes the wall of hostility. Can God tear it down? God has begun to bring free creatures into the trinitarian fellowship. Will God complete what God began?

"This is my body," Jesus says, "given for you."[4] God takes a body and lets death have it, lets hostility have its way with it. In the breaking of the bread, Jesus's body also is broken. And since Jesus's body is God's, we can even say that God's body is broken. But in the death of Jesus, not only the body, but the trinitarian fellowship itself of God is broken, in that one of the Trinity dies; the Son says to the father, " My God, my God, why have you forsaken me?"[5] and the Father loses the Son to death. Yet since both the breaking of the body and the breaking of the trinitarian fellowship are overcome in the trinitarian event of Jesus's bodily resurrection, the breaking turns out to be more a promise than a threat, and less a breaking than a breaking open. So the Psalm that begins with the words "My God, my God, why have you forsaken me?" ends up open to the Gentiles with these: "All the ends of the earth shall remember and turn to the Lord; and all the families of the nations shall worship before thee."[6] In the breaking of bread, too, the body of God opens up – to let us in, to admit us to the trinitarian communion at its point of greatest vulnerability, at its time of greatest risk. The eucharist – the Great Thanksgiving – is the intratrinitarian exchange of grace and gratitude carried out in the face of death and shared with those who are subject to it.

Jesus gives thanks to the Father for his grace, and he shares the grace of the Father, and the opportunity for gratitude, also with us in his death. Is love stronger than death? The story is not over, but God would complete what God began even on the night in which he was betrayed. On that night human beings come to participate in the unconditional response to God's self-giving that the Son makes to the Father even unto death. A vain attempt, perhaps – a deathbed wedding. "The days will come, when the bridegroom is taken away from them, and they will fast in that day."[7]

That risk or apparent risk of God's is deeply implicated in what it means to be human. Whether the risk is real or apparent depends, humanly, on whether the human being perceiving it is looking at it prospectively or eschatologically. The unity of the Trinity exists eschatologically, when all human beings will

---

3   Song 8:6.
4   Lk. 22:28.
5   Mk. 15:34, quoting Ps. 22:1.
6   Ps. 22:27, RSV, following the Hebrew. I owe the observation to William Young.
7   Mk. 2:20.

be incorporated into the general dance. Until then they – and therefore God identified with their cause – will be dramatically at risk, even if the Christian assurance of things hoped for is eschatologically certain.

Christians may regard the stories of Jesus in the New Testament as God's argument or Logos that "love is as strong as death." The Word descends from trinitarian realms where no space and time can threaten love, and assumes with human flesh the susceptibility to separation and death. In so doing the Trinity risks its unity. The drama is: *is* love stronger than death? Will the incarnation separate the Son from the Father permanently?

To ask that question is not to imply that finite existence is bad after all. Jesus uses space and time for his divine work. In space and time, the Word incarnate accommodates himself to material creation by doing "human things divinely and divine things humanly," as Maximus the Confessor summed it up.[8] That is, the Word made flesh does a human thing, bound by time, such as dying, with an effect that only God can grant, atonement for sin. Or the Word does a divine thing, such as healing the sick, by means of a human act, touching.[9] Such acts of love toward human beings – dying, touching, speaking – as conditioned by space and time become the evidence for the doctrine that God has condescended to be God with us, has assumed flesh like ours. God becomes next to us, our neighbor, finite in first-century Galilee, susceptible to death.

Creaturely distance does, I have hinted, allow for the possibility of separation. Human intimacy can be cut off by separation in time, especially by death. And human intimacy can also be cut off by separation in space, as the one flesh of separated lovers can also die. The sting of death, or its power

---

[8] See Maximus the Confessor, *Opuscule* 7. I owe the phrasing to David Yeago; for exposition, see his "Jesus of Nazareth and Cosmic Redemption: The Relevance of St Maximus the Confessor," *Modern Theology* 12 (1996): 163–93. For a slightly different English translation, see *Opuscule* 7, in Andrew Louth, ed. and trans., *Maximus the Confessor*, The Early Church Fathers (New York: Routledge, 1996), pp. 180–91: "being by nature God, he acts humanly, willingly accepting the experience of suffering for our sake . . . human by nature, he acts divinely and naturally exhibits the evidence of his divinity," p. 188; cf. the phrase, "the same acting 'at once divinely and humanly,'" where Maximus quotes Cyril of Alexandria, *Commentary on St John's Gospel*, book 4, ch. 2, on Jn. 6:53, in P. E. Pusey, *In D. Joannis Evangelium*, 3 vols (Oxford: Clarendon Press, 1872), vol. I, p. 530.

[9] Cf. Athanasius, *On the Incarnation of the Word*, ch. 18, in Edward R. Hardy, ed., *Christology of the Later Fathers*, Library of Christian Classics (Philadelphia: Westminster Press, 1954), p. 72 and *Orations against the Arians*, book III, ch. 32, in Richard A. Norris, Jr, ed. and trans., *The Christological Controversy*, Sources of Early Christian Thought (Philadelphia: Fortress, 1980), p. 90.

to separate or divorce human intimacy, is sin. So created difference is good; but under conditions of sin, it becomes an occasion of separation that cries out for redemption.

So the question persists, can love overcome death? Can the divine intimacy survive conditions of creation, and the conditions of sin? Can sin separate the Father from the Son and the Spirit in half? Can sin finally disrupt the dance into "ashes, ashes, we all fall down"?

The answer to that question explains why the resurrection is a trinitarian event. The resurrection preserves the intimacy of the Trinity under conditions of created space and time, and, more important, even in the *face* of sin and death. Indeed, by a marvelous exchange the death becomes a sign of the relationship and of the escape from sin, prompting the centurion to exclaim, "certainly this man was innocent,"[10] or even "Truly this man was the Son of God!"[11]

So in Paul we read: "If the Spirit of the One who raised Jesus from the dead dwells in you, the One who raised Christ Jesus from the dead will give life to your mortal bodies also through his Spirit which dwells in you."[12] The resurrection is described in trinitarian terms.[13]

The object of the resurrection, Jesus, is named. "Which Jesus" is implicitly identified in terms of his death and resurrection. In him, later theologians would say, God died. Here, too, the 19th century divide between the Jesus of history (who was crucified) and the Christ of faith (who rose into the faith of believers) is denied. For it is none other than the one who died who is raised. In this the Son acts in character with his intratrinitarian role: he goes forth on his Father's mission until the end, and finds in his going forth a return; both his going forth and his return constitute a constant acceptance and a constant giving back of the love he receives from the Father.

The subject of the resurrection is identified in terms of the Jesus who died; the subject is "the One who raised Jesus." That is the one Jesus called "Father." In this the Father, too, acts in character with his intratrinitarian role: he gives, and he continues giving even in the face of evil; and he vindicates his love and his promises even in the face of resistance.

According to Paul's account, the resurrection's witness and celebrator is not

---

[10]   Luke 23:47.
[11]   Mark 15:39, Mt. 27:54.
[12]   Rom. 8:11.
[13]   I owe my attention to this verse to David Yeago, *The Faith of the Christian Church* (Columbia, SC: Lutheran Theological Southern Seminary, 1992), p. 119. Cf. also Robert Jenson's treatment in *The Triune Identity* (Philadelphia: Fortress, 1982), p. 44.

first of all the community of the disciples or the women who followed Jesus, but the Spirit, who is also identified in its terms. In v. 9 it is alternately "the Spirit of God" and "the Spirit of Christ." Here the Spirit is the Spirit of life in the resurrection: it is "the Spirit of the One who raised Jesus" – who witnesses and celebrates the resurrection in a particular way: by giving life to human mortal bodies also by dwelling in them. In this, too, the Spirit acts in character with its intratrinitarian role: it raises up from among us human beings witnesses and sharers and concelebrators of the love it celebrates between the Father and the Son; in the Spirit human beings come to do what it does in the life of the Trinity, namely, glorify the Father who breathes it and the Son it rests upon. Through the Spirit human beings are taken up, assumed into the work of the person who comes out from the Father and goes to the Son, and who returns from the Son to the Father. In the circulation of the trinitarian dance, the Spirit takes human beings by the arm and insinuates them into the general dance, and this means here the general resurrection of the body.

As the witness and advocate of the love between the Father and the Son, the Spirit finds that the crucifixion stretches that love, as it were, to the very point of breaking.[14] Is the life and love of the Triune God so capacious as to accommodate that? Yet like the witness at a wedding, whose office it is not only to celebrate the marriage but to safeguard and uphold it, the Spirit has still its role to play. "If the Spirit of the One who raised Jesus from the dead dwells in you, the One who raised Christ Jesus from the dead will give life to your mortal bodies also through the Spirit that dwells in you." The Spirit is the Giver of Life; the Father raises the Son, the Son arises, and the Spirit restores their bond, this time with a difference: having been admitted to the trinitarian exchange of grace and gratitude, which is the trinitarian communion and eucharist, in the breaking open of Christ's body, human beings participate, too, in the reintegration and resurrection of that body, and as the Spirit flows between the Father and the Son it now flows – detours perhaps – also through Gentiles. There is now no part of the world godforsaken, because the Spirit did not forsake the Son, in whom alone the Father sees those created in his image, and in whom alone the Father sees sin. It is in the Spirit, the Giver of Life, which flows through mortal bodies also, that love is stronger than death.

The Father loved Jesus enough, and the Church his spouse enough, to raise him from the dead rather than allow his love to go unrewarded and his righteousness unvindicated. "Why do you look for the living among the

---

[14] Cf. D. Lyle Dabney, *Die Kenosis des Geistes: Kontinuität zwischen Schöpfung und Erlösung im Werk des Heiligen Geistes* (Neukirchen-Vluyn: Neukirchner Verlag, 1997).

dead?" ask the two angels in Luke.[15] If the wages of sin is death, the secret of life is righteousness; and the one who is righteousness is life and cannot stay dead.[16]

In creation, too, God's love, the love between the Father and the Son witnessed, celebrated, and participated by the Spirit, is stronger than death. In creation, too, under conditions of finitude, God is able to make that unconditional response to God's self-giving that God makes eternally in the life of the Trinity. In sinful flesh, too, under conditions of falseness, God is able to make that unconditional response to God's self-giving that God makes eternally in the life of the Trinity. The intimacy of the Trinity stretches, opens, but is preserved when the Father raises the Son from the dead, the Spirit brooding over this second, God-restoring creation as over the first, world-founding one. The Spirit not only binds, but also personally shares and delights in the love of the Father and the Son so as to pull human beings also into that suffering and triumphant love.

The love stronger than death is therefore no abstract power, for Christians, but a particular person, and that is why it is to their peril that the Spirit should be resisted or denied. The Spirit that blesses the love between the Father and the Son remains a source of blessing even in the face of death. In the process the other to God within God, the Spirit, overcomes the other to God that God is not, or evil. The other that is curse is overwhelmed in the other that is blessing in person. The dialectical inclusion by which God determines the lost cause of the human being for God's own cause, by which God determines the sad lot of the human being for God's own lot, by which God chooses God for this way and work, changes everything for the cause and lot and way of the human other.

In Eastern Orthodoxy, marriage derives its sacramentality from the eucharist celebrated during the Eastern matrimonial rite. For the community welcomes a new creation, the one flesh, into its midst, as the parties feed each other bread dipped into hot wine. It is this feast into which the community invites the wedding couple, which is also the feast that the couple in turn sponsors for the community. In it there is mutual blessing: one lover blesses the other; together they bless the community; and together the community blesses them. The inviting and welcoming cross reciprocally back and forth.

---

[15]   Lk. 24:5.

[16]   I take that to be a consequence of Hans Frei's quasi-ontological argument for the resurrection in "Jesus Identified in His Resurrection," ch. 13 in Frei, *The Identity of Jesus Christ: The Hermeneutical Bases of Dogmatic Theology* (Philadelphia: Fortress, 1975), pp. 139–52, esp. pp. 147–9 on the angels' question at Lk. 24:5.

Alexander Schmemann develops the eucharist as overarching blessing:

> [T]he unique position of man in the universe is that he alone is to *bless* God for the food and the life he receives from Him. He alone is to respond to God's blessing with his blessing. The significant fact about the life in the Garden is that man is to *name* things. . . . [I]n the Bible a name . . . reveals the very essence of a thing . . . as God's gift. . . .
>
> To name a thing, in other terms, is to bless God for it and in it. And in the Bible to bless God is not a "religious" or a "cultic" act, but the very *way of life*. God blessed the world, blessed the man, blessed the seventh day (that is, time), and this means that He filled all that exists with His love and goodness, made all this "very good." So the only *natural* (and not "supernatural") reaction of man, to whom God gave this blessed and sanctified world, is to bless God in return, to thank Him, to *see* the world as God sees it – and in this act of gratitude and adoration – to know, name, and possess the world. . . . [The human being is] first of all "*homo adorans*." . . . He stands in the center of the world and unifies it in his act of blessing God, of both receiving the world from God and offering it to God – and by filling the world with this eucharist, he transforms his life, the one that he receives from the world, into life in God, into communion.
>
> The world was created as the "matter," the material of one all-embracing eucharist . . . [17]

Yet, and this is grace on grace, the eucharist is the sacrament of blessing not only as the consummation of creation, but also as redemption from sin. For with sin, the freedom lost is the freedom to be blessed and to bless; the thing ruined is primarily the gift of God's body, and yet God does not give up the plan to feast us, even under conditions of sin, for God wants to complete what God began. Herbert's poem has Love ask whether the companion lacked anything at the feast: "'A guest,' I answer'd, 'worthy to be here:' / Love said, 'You shall be he.'"[18] That makes sin a subplot, complication in the eucharistic plot – is that all?

The eucharistic reversal is perhaps too familiar to shock. In her famous account of Judges 19, Phyllis Trible has recovered its risk and terror. Judges 19 offers a story of violated hospitality and rape that echoes the one of Sodom and Gomorrah. We read: "So the man seized his concubine, and put her out to them; and they knew her, and abused her all night until the morning."

---

[17] Alexander Schmemann, *For the Life of the World* (New York: National Student Christian Association, 1963), pp. 4–5.

[18] George Herbert, "Love" (III), in T. E. Hutchinson, ed., *The Works of George Herbert* (Oxford: Clarendon Press, 1941), pp. 188–9.

Having found her lying on the doorstep, "he took a knife, and laying hold of his concubine he divided her, limb by limb, into twelve pieces, and sent her throughout all the territory of Israel."[19]

God's story, the Logos, must reabsorb such stories into itself, renarrating them as ones in which freedom is restored.[20] The body has become a place not of life but of death, and the body God offers in Jesus is treated not with blessing but with violence. Even procreation perpetuates the body of death.[21] In the person of the Logos, the Story *par excellence*, God retells the story of trinitarian love by turning the curses of others back into blessing for them. The body they crucify in the great un-eucharist becomes, at the Last Supper, a gift once again and in advance. The crucifixion is an anti-philoxenia, an un-hospitality. But God retells the story so that human beings recover the freedom they lost, the freedom for gift and gratitude, the freedom to bless God for God's blessings.

Although Trible's explicit thesis about that passage from Judges 19 is that it calls readers to repentance, her implicit thesis is christological. In a few scattered phrases she subtly *retells* the story, the more powerfully because she calls no attention to the procedure. "Truly, the hour is at hand, and the woman is betrayed into the hands of sinners," she comments, citing Mark 14:41. "At the end of the section," she continues, "safety within the house has lost to danger without. Yet only the concubine suffers the loss. No one within comes to her aid." Like the disciples of Jesus, "[t]hey have all fallen away in the darkness of night."[22] Several pages later eucharistic lines appear: "Her body has been broken and given to many. Lesser power has no woman than this, that her life is laid down by a man."[23] It is stories as terrible as these of which the eucharist practices God's retelling.

An awareness of the emblematic theological significance of adoption can help Christians, gay and straight, to recover the emblematic biblical and theological significance of the story of Sodom and Gomorrah. In part I, I wrote that liberal Christians ought not merely to read biblical stories out of the Bible. As the theological significance that the creation story had for such traditional

---

[19] Judges 19:25b, 29.

[20] I owe my attention to renarration to David Hart.

[21] John D. Zizioulas, *Being as Communion: Studies in Personhood and the Church* (Crestwood, NY: St Vladimir's Seminary Press, 1985), pp. 50–65.

[22] Phyllis Trible, "An Unnamed Woman: The Extravagance of Violence," in her *Texts of Terror* (Philadelphia: Fortress, 1984), pp. 65–91; here, p. 76. The disciples fall away at Mark 14:26–42.

[23] Trible, "An Unnamed Woman," p. 81, recalling Jn. 16:13.

exegetes as Augustine could be recovered only after Christians cease to read it as natural science, so the theological significance that the Sodom and Gomorrah story had for Jesus can be recovered only after Christians cease to read it as about homosexuality. If there is any importance to the common maleness of the visitors and of the rapists, it is that it marks the Sodomites, like the idolaters of Romans 1, as stereotypical Gentiles.

Genesis and most other biblical books taking up the story count the sin of the Sodomites as inhospitality: "Do nothing to these men, *for they have come under my roof.*"[24] Hospitality – a strange one that suffers in rabbinic exegesis by comparison with Abraham's – is also the only reason the text gives for Lot's offering his daughters instead: his duty as host trumps his duty as father. Perhaps the offer is a distant echo of the child sacrifice that the stories of Isaac and Jesus acknowledge, take up, sublimate, and transfigure. Genesis is not concerned with men and women, but with men and angels. The Sodomites seek to know the visitors as "men," because, unlike Abraham, they do not know the visitors as angels.

Second, although for the Bible inhospitality is the controlling moral species, the action of the Sodomites also counts as rape. The story in Judges resembles in shape, tone, and even wording the story of Sodom.[25] Here, too, a host is asked to produce his male visitor for rape, this time by Benjaminites. But when the visitor recounts the story in a call for vengeance, he does not ascribe sexual intent to them: he says, "they meant to kill me."[26] The Bible agrees with modern analysis surprisingly in this: rape is not about sexual interest, but about doing *violence*, even death, to the neighbor.

Finally, the threat to destroy the city comes three times before, not after, the rape:[27] Sodom and Gomorrah are not destroyed because of that incident, but were slated for destruction already. In a famous scene, Abraham had pleaded and bargained for the Sodomites with God.[28] The rape is only their last rejection of mercy, their "up yours" to God precisely when the covenant of blessing with Abraham has gotten under way.

The angels come as ministers of grace and mercy, which the inhabitants reject with violence. Thus in several biblical uses of the story, the reference

---

[24] Gen. 19:8. "Seeing that this man has come into my house, do not do this vile thing," Jg 19:23. "[N]o one shall sojourn in [a city like Sodom]," Jer. 49:18. "[N]o son of a human being shall sojourn in her," Jer. 50:40.

[25] Jg 19:22.

[26] Jg 19:5.

[27] Gen. 13:10–13, 14:21–4; 18:16–33.

[28] Gen. 18:22–33.

is to rejection of grace.[29] In remaining cases it serves as an all–purpose word for Gentile ungodliness, which is "ungodliness" in the strict sense, symptomatic of their lack of relation to the God of Israel,[30] or Israelite wickedness with no mention of sexual sin except adultery as emblematic of infidelity to the Lord.[31] Even conservatives on homosexuality, as we saw in chapter 1, now tend to agree with Ezekiel about the sin of Sodom: "Behold, this was the sin of your sister Sodom: she and her daughters had pride, surfeit of food, and prosperous ease, but did not aid the poor and needy."[32] "Abominations," listed before, go unspecified, while Jerusalem's are said to be worse.[33] But no one calls sexual sinners "Jerusalemites." Jude 7, which in some English translations refers to "unnatural lust," refers in Greek to "strange," that is, angelic, "flesh," where the word for "strange" is *heteros*, as in heterosexual, and depends upon a Jewish tradition of women having sex with angels.[34] In no account is there any mention of same-sex sin. Rather the Sodomites would take by force the strange grace of God.

Jesus himself understands the text as one about inhospitality, comparing cities that refuse to receive his disciples to Sodom and Gomorrah,[35] while Paul uses it to warn those who would limit the hospitality of God's community.[36]

In discussion of the story it goes almost unrecognized that in Gen. 18 Abraham had just offered hospitality to three angels who appeared to him at the oaks of Mamre.[37] Since the story moves back and forth ("stammeringly"), between counting three angels and two angels and the Lord, Orthodox

---

[29]   Dt. 29:23, Amos 4:11 ("You did not return to me"), Matt. 10:14–15, Lk. 10:10–12, 17:29.

[30]   Is. 13:19, Zeph. 2:9, 2 Pet. 2:6.

[31]   Dt. 32:32, Is. 3:9, Jer. 23:14, Lam. 4:6, Ezek. 16:46–8, Zeph. 2:9, Rom. 9:29.

[32]   Ezek. 16:49.

[33]   Ezek. 16:48.

[34]   The passage in Jude begins by referring to "the angels that did not keep their own position but left their proper dwellings," apparently to have sex with human women, as in Gen. 6:4. For argument, see Derrick Sherwin Bailey, *Homosexuality and the Western Christian Tradition* (London: Green, 1955), pp. 11–16; John Boswell, *Christianity, Social Tolerance, and Homosexuality: Gay People in Western Europe from the Beginning of the Christian Era to the Fourteenth Century* (Chicago: University of Chicago Press, 1980), p. 97; Robin Scroggs, *The New Testament and Homosexuality: Contextual Background for Contemporary Debate* (Philadelphia: Fortress, 1983), p. 100, n. 3; J. N. D. Kelley, *The Epistles of Peter and of Jude* (New York: Harper & Row, 1969), pp. 258–9.

[35]   Matt. 10:14–15, Luke 10:10–12.

[36]   Rom. 9:29.

[37]   Gen. 18:1. But see, recently, Doyle, "The Sin of Sodom."

iconography takes this hospitality, "the Philoxenia," as not just any meal, but as an icon of the Holy Trinity – that is, of the feasting and hospitality that constitute God's very life.[38] Nor is the episode one of just any meal at which Abraham offered bread and a sacrifice.[39] The angels have come to foretell the birth of Isaac,[40] the beginning of God's fulfillment of the promise to Abraham that by his name all the nations of the earth would bless themselves, or would share in God's hospitable goodness. Thus the Orthodox take the Philoxenia as also emblematic of the sharing of the Gentiles in the hospitality of the God of Israel at the eucharist. It stands in giant mosaic over the altar at Ravenna, depicting the eucharist as proleptic participation in God's trinitarian life.

The angels that promise the blessing to Abraham are the very same angels that come to Lot later in the next chapter.[41] As far as I am aware, no commentator in the sexuality debates has noticed that the Sodom and

---

[38]   For the tradition of taking the three visitors as the persons of the Trinity, see, for example, Cyril of Alexandria, *Contra Julianum* I.20 (*PG* 66:532ff), Prokopius of Gaza, *Commentary on Genesis*, at vv. 18:1–3 (*PG* 87:364BC), Augustine, *Contra Maximinum Arianorum episcopum*, bk. II, ch. 7 (*PL* 42, 809: "et ipse Abraham tres vidit, unum adoravit; nonne unus erat hospes in tribus qui venit ad patrem Abraham") and *De trinitate*, bk. II, ch. 34 (*PL* 42, 868). Hilary of Poitiers disagreed, saying that only one of the guests was the Lord, *De trinitate*, bk. IV, ch. 27 (*PL* 10, 117). Art historical commentary tends to focus on examples in Italy: San Vitale at Ravenna, Santa Maria Maggiore, Old St Peter's, and the catacombs of the Via Latina in Rome and San Marco in Venice. See *The Oxford Dictionary of Byzantium*, 6 vols, ed. Alexander P. Kazhdan, et al. (New York: Oxford University Press, 1991), *s.v.* "Philoxenia of Abraham," 3:1664; *Lexikon der christlichen Ikonographie*, 8 vols, ed. E. Kirschbaum and W. Braunfels (Rome, Feiburg, Vienna: Herder, 1968–76), *s.vv.* "Abraham," 1: 21–3 and "Dreifaltigkeit," 1: 532; and Otto G. von Simson, *Sacred Fortress: Byzantine Art and Statecraft in Ravenna* (Princeton, NJ: Princeton University Press, 1987), p. 25 (on San Vitale). But see also Manolis Chatzidakis, *Icons of Patmos: Questions of Byzantine and Post-Byzantine Painting* (Athens: National Bank of Greece, 1985), p. 64 (on the hospitality of Abraham on *panghiaria*, or patens used to contain the "Virgin's share" of holy bread); Anastasios Kallis, "Philoxenia," in Kallis, ed., *Philoxenia: Prof. Dr Bernhard Kötting gewidmet von seinen griechischen Schülern* (Munich: Aschendorff, 1980), pp. v–vi; D. Mouriki, "Ἡ παράσταση τῆς φιλοξενίας τοῦ Αβραάμ σε μία εἰκόνα τοῦ Βυζαντινοῦ Μουσε ίου," *ΔΧΑΕ* 3 (1962–63): 87–112, and George Soroka, "Are Iconographic Depictions of the Trinity in Accord with Eastern Orthodox Church Teaching? Scriptural Antecedents for Icons Depicting the Trinity with Emphasis on the Validity of the Hospitality of Abraham Icon," BA thesis, Drew University, 1994. The famous icon by Andrei Rublev abstracts almost entirely from the biblical details.

[39]   Gen. 18:5, 8.

[40]   Gen. 18:9–10.

[41]   Gen. 18–19 is a continuous narrative. The angels, although counted sometimes as three and sometimes as two angels and the Lord, are the same.

Gomorrah story provides a contrast to the promise of Isaac. In the first case, Abraham shares hospitality with the Trinity and receives the promise of a covenant. In the contrasting case, the Sodomites greet the visitors with violence. Their story has the same shape as the New Testament parable of the wicked tenants,[42] who rebuff multiple pleaders on the owner's behalf (parallel to Abraham's bargaining), and finally do violence to the owner's very son (representing Jesus), as the Sodomites threaten violence to the angels (even persons) of the Lord. The violence of the Sodomites is a type of the violence toward God that Jesus turns to good when the eucharist becomes no longer the Last Supper before the crucifixion's violent injustice but now the first hospitality of Abraham's visitors opened up to Gentile nations.

God intended to elevate human beings without having to descend into hell to rescue them from sin, but God has laughter enough to use even the human worst as the occasion for putting the plan through. God turns human inhospitality and murder – they take themselves too seriously – into the very matter of the feast, giving back to human beings what they would take by force. God gives back for feasting the bread and wine the Romans would break; God gives back for love the body the Sodomites would rape.

The Hospitality of Adoption

It is by representing the recipients of the Trinity's eucharistic hospitality that gay and lesbian Christians can remind the whole community that they are almost all Gentiles, whether they fit Paul's rhetorical stereotyping in Romans 1 or not. And it is by actually enacting the practice of hospitality toward the bodily neighbor, in households like Abraham's, empty of natural children, that infertile Christians, gay and straight, can remind all Christians, but especially Gentile ones, that they are not God's natural children, but adopted.[43] To do that is to teach the community how the eucharist reverses Sodom, how God makes Abraham the father of many nations, how Jesus returns violence with hospitality – vocation enough for a group in the Church.

The reversal of the Sodom and Gomorrah story by adoption shows up in many ways.

1   Hospitality to children does not conflict with natural procreation, but restores its gratuity. The election of God is of Abraham, who was promised

---

[42]   Mt. 21:33–46, Mk. 12:1–12, Lk. 20:9–19.
[43]   Jn. 1:12, Rom. 8:15, 8:23, Gal. 4:5, Eph. 1:5.

to be father of many nations. Thus it is characteristic – not necessary – of this covenant to issue in natural children. Michael Wyschogrod puts it this way: "If God continues to love the people of Israel – and it is the faith of Israel [as of Christians adhering to Romans 11] that he does – it is because he sees the face of his beloved Abraham in each and every one of his children as a man sees the face of his beloved in the children of his union with his beloved."[44] Better, marriage, like God's covenant with Abraham, "promises" to issue in children. Insofar as marriage represents God's creation, these children are understood as natural to it. Insofar as marriage represents God's covenant with Abraham, however, these children are understood as in some sense unnecessary and the gift of grace elevating nature. Thus Isaac was the unexpected – impossible – miraculous child of Sarah's old age, an impossible gift not of nature but of grace. And thus, too, Abraham had faith in the covenant even when faced with chosen childlessness at the sacrifice of Isaac.[45]

2   The sacrifice and "resurrection" of Isaac, furthermore, prefigure the death and resurrection of another beloved son of the covenant, Jesus Christ. Jesus Christ, Barth says, is the electing God and the elect human being in one. Like the circumcised Isaac, Jesus Christ is for Christians the Son and the embodiment of the covenant in his very flesh. It is not two covenants but one, the covenant with Abraham carried forward, so that Abraham becomes the father of *many* nations, not just of the nation of Isaac, who was renamed Israel. In Christ these other nations participate in the covenant with Abraham not as Abraham's natural children, but by *adoption*. Gentiles gain inheritance rights that Jews retain.[46] Because the covenant with Abraham is of *many* nations, there is such a thing as love and marriage raising *adopted* children.

3   Because the covenant with Abraham is not only real, but, according to Christians, really embodied in Jesus Christ, there is such a thing as celibacy and marriage to God issuing in *baptized* children. Jesus Christ, as Barth puts it, is the electing God and the elect human being in one. He is the bridegroom of the Church, but also in him the *coniunctio*, the joining together, or even marriage, of God and humanity is embodied. Jesus Christ has no children of his own, natural or adopted, but he causes human beings to become children of God by the Spirit of adoption in baptism.[47] "To all who received him . . .

---

[44]   Michael Wyschogrod, *The Body of Faith: Judaism as Corporeal Election* (Minneapolis, MN: Fortress, 1983), p. 64. Of course God's seeing the face of Abraham in the Jews need not be any more biological than God's seeing Christ in the neighbor, but Wyschogrod does tend to take biology seriously.

[45]   Even Wyschogrod recognizes this, *The Body of Faith,* pp. 20–1.

[46]   Rom. 8:15, 23; Paul can also apply *huiothesia* to Israel, Rom. 9:4.

[47]   Rom. 8:23.

he gave power to become children of God, who were born, not of blood nor of the will of the flesh nor of the will of a man, but of God."[48]

4   In Jesus, God takes on the identity of one who is, humanly speaking, a fatherless child. Joseph is at best his adoptive father. Although the Gospel of John does not have a birth narrative, the passage just quoted about "not of blood nor of the will of the flesh nor of the will of a man, but of God," applied to believers, implicitly analogizes them to the humanly fatherless status of Jesus.[49] Ezekiel brings together images of abandonment, adoption, marriage, and baptism for the people of God:

> "And as for your birth, on the day you were born your navel string was not cut, nor were you washed with water to cleanse you, nor rubbed with salt, nor swathed with bands. No eye pitied you, to do any of these things to you out of compassion for you; but you were cast out on the open field . . . .
>
> "When I passed by you again and looked upon you, behold, you were the age for love; and I spread my skirt over you, and covered your nakedness: yea, I plighted my troth to you and entered into a covenant with you, says the Lord God, and you became mine. Then I bathed you with water and washed off your blood from you, and anointed you with oil."[50]

The practice of adoption by Christian households, gay and straight, can bear witness to the fatherlessness of Jesus, the hospitality of Joseph, and even to the Virgin birth. Adoption imitates the adoptive love of God in making human beings God's heirs, and the adoptive love of Joseph in making Jesus his son. Inasmuch as Christians adopt the least of them, they adopt Jesus. The Magnificat, too, is an act of surprising hospitality in a woman who was not old and barren, but young and virgin, and whose pregnancy would cause scandal rather than delight. The Holy Family has more of adoption in it than nature. Those who adopt shall be as kings and queens: "Kings shall be your foster fathers, and their queens your nursing mothers."[51]

5   It follows from the theory of analogy that the relation of parent and child exists primarily, properly, and paradigmatically between God and God's only begotten child Jesus; secondarily and by participation between God and human beings partaking in the identity of God's child by the indwelling of the "Spirit of adoption";[52] tertiarily between God's vicar, the priest or pastor who may be called "Father," and the members of her or his flock by baptism. The

[48]   Jn. 1:12.
[49]   Cf. Jn. 8:19–20.
[50]   Ezek. 16:4–9.
[51]   Is. 49:23.
[52]   Rom. 8:23.

relation of parents and their natural or adopted children represents the relation of the Father and the Son not only distantly, by reason of their finitude, but also only *at fourth remove* as a matter of analogy. And because most Christians are Gentiles, their relation to the Fatherhood of the God of Israel is by adoption, represented by baptism, rather than by natural birth, represented by circumcision. And therefore for the very great majority of Christians – those who, like the Sodomites, are Gentiles – adopted children are *better* representative of their relationship to God as God's children "in excess of nature" than natural ones are. If adoption is technically a *misericordia aliena*, a strange mercy,[53] it recalls the strange mercy that God showers *para phusin* upon the Gentiles and the "alien righteousness" with which God regards the elect.[54]

6   In the first part, I mentioned oblation, or the practice of leaving unwanted children at the doorstep of vowed same-sex communities, which seems to have been a distinctively Christian innovation. In Protestant communions that have lost the practice of monasticism, it is infertile couples of the same or opposite sexes who can now take up that important Christian exercise of hospitality toward the neighbor, the stranger to whom one is unrelated by blood, just as God in Jesus brings the Gentiles into the promises of Abraham, to whom they are unrelated by blood. As Abraham becomes father of many nations, so same-sex communities, monastic or married, may become parents of many oblates.

7   When Paul refers in Romans 9 to the story of Sodom, he does so for a very good reason. The Sodomites are Gentiles who have rejected God's invitation to hospitality, and they misuse the angels instead of returning it. Romans 1 characterizes the attitude of the Gentiles toward God as one of subtracting from God's hospitality, and for that reason God condemns them to act contrary to nature. But part of Paul's reversal, as we saw in part I, is that God also is said to act "contrary to nature," *para phusin*, in bringing the Gentiles into the covenant with Israel, grafting wild branches onto a domestic olive tree.[55]

---

[53]   John Boswell, *The Kindness of Strangers: The Abandonment of Children in Western Europe from Late Antiquity to the Renaissance* (New York: Vintage Books, 1990), pp. xiv, 49, 95, 120, 131, *et al.*

[54]   *Iustitia aliena* is a technical term in Luther, esp. in the later Galatians commentary. *Iustitia aliena* arises from God's *misericordia*: "Est quidem iustitia possessio nostra, quia nobis donata est ex misericordia, tamen est aliena a nobis, quia non meruimus eam." *Weimarer Ausgabe* 39/I, 109.2.

[55]   Rom. 11:24 – as I have learned from Richard Hays's article, "Relations Natural and Unnatural: A Response to John Boswell's Exegesis of Romans 1," *Journal of Religious Ethics* 14 (1986): 184–215, which uses it quite differently. For a reply to Hays, see Dale B. Martin, "Heterosexism and the Interpretation of Romans 1:18–32," *Biblical Interpretation* 3 (1995): 332–55, cited above.

That shocking phrase, the same one Paul uses in Romans 1 to condemn homosexual behavior, governs the earlier passage theologically. In Rom. 1 as in Rom. 11 Paul is talking of the nature – and more importantly the salvation – not of human beings generally, but of Jews and Gentiles. In Rom. 1 acting contrary to nature characterizes idolatrous *Gentiles*, and the great amazement that drives Paul's ministry is that God pours out the Spirit also on *those* people, an amazement Paul expresses in Rom. 11 by characterizing God's saving action as itself contrary to nature. It is more than a vinicultural metaphor to express how God grafts Gentiles regarded as wild, idolatrous, and unfruitful onto the domestic vine of Israel – close enough already, perhaps, to justify the grafting of another group sometimes regarded as promiscuous, idolatrous, and infertile into the domestic practices of marriage.

Romans 11 presents the reader with another of Paul's rhetorical sting operations.[56] It is a reversal of guilt by association. God becomes "guilty" of acting contrary to nature by choosing solidarity with the Gentiles, whose identifying characteristic it is to act contrary to nature. "Nature" must become logically subsequent to soteriology, to God's concrete history with Jews and Gentiles, which means also that we must reconceptualize nature not in terms of a predetermined end, immanent to a general human nature, or *telos* (such as procreation), but in terms of a God-determined end, or eschaton,[57] such as the mutual blessing of God's own trinitarian life. In good Barthian fashion we learn about nature, such as it is, from what God does with it: and if God appears to be capable of using sexual orientations too, both heterosexual and homosexual, just in their concrete, messy details, just in their complicated relations to the larger Christian community that they both upbuild and both betray, for God's saving purposes, then that is of a piece with God's surprising salvation of the Gentiles. Like the claim that the Spirit of Christ is joining the Gentiles to the vine in baptism, the claim that the same Spirit is building up the body of Christ by joining together gay and lesbian couples is a pneumatological one, a claim, that is, about what the Spirit is doing new in the Church, one that will one day, if not soon, be empirically verifiable in the Church's life.

8   Finally, married couples, gay or straight, that neither bear children nor adopt may not be showing inhospitality. They may be bearing witness to the Christian claim that the survival of the species does not depend finally upon human beings, but upon God. Childless couples, like ones who adopt, may undercut the sense of entitlement that now bedevils aggressive reproductive

---

[56]   I owe the phrase, but not its application, to Richard Hays.
[57]   As I have learned from David Novak.

technologies. And they may be bearing witness to the Christian conviction that God does not ensure the survival of the species by sufficient procreation in any case, but by resurrection. As Chrysostom wrote, "Now that resurrection is at our gates, and we do not speak of death, but advance toward another life better than the present, the desire for posterity is superfluous."[58] And Cyril of Alexandria finds a sign of the resurrection in the fact that the marriage at Cana was consummated, according to John 2:1, "on the third day," because "that which was smitten by corruption and death [Christ] bound up on the third day: that is . . . in the last ages, when for us made human, He made all our nature whole, raising it from the dead in Himself."[59] Resurrection carries forward the pattern by which God chooses younger sons and unwed mothers, preferring eschatology over teleology. The married (gay or straight) may signify the eschatological community not only by participating in the love of God for the community, not only by participating in the witness of the Spirit to the glory of love, and not even only by exemplifying the taking up of eros into compassion and the sanctification of concupiscible passion become ascetical community, but also by trusting to the general resurrection for their bodily survival. Certainly the Church lacks for serious testimony to the bodily resurrection these days. Theologians doubt it and students, who have confused it with a disembodied immortality of the soul, encounter the traditional doctrine with disgust. What would the Church – especially Protestant Churches lacking monasticism – make of couples whose childlessness takes the resurrection seriously and embodies it in an unmistakable sign?

The Eucharist and Forgiveness

In using as I did Trible's eucharistic solution to the rape of the concubine in Judges 19, I picked out and raised to prominence suggestions that she makes fleetingly and sometimes with irony. She means to suggest, and not to emphasize. She hopes to gain more by a rhetoric of understatement against a theology of the cross that, by an irony of its own, takes the place of moral

---

[58] John Chrysostom, "Sermon on Marriage," in Chrysostom, *On Marriage and Family Life*, trans. Catharine P. Roth and David Anderson (Crestwood, NY: St Vladimir's Seminary Press, 1997), p. 85.

[59] Cyril of Alexandria, *Commentary on the Gospel According to S. John*, 2 vols, trans. P. E. Pusey and T. Randell, Library of the Fathers of the Holy Catholic Church (London: Rivingtons and Oxford: J. Parker, 1874–85; Microfilm edn, Chicago: University of Chicago Library, 1969), bk. 2, ch. 1, on Jn. 2:11, p. 157.

seriousness and repentance. Facile references to the cross and the eucharist can domesticate and prettify violence, too easily dispensing sublimation and forgiveness, overlooking the necessity of judgment and change of life, turning redemption to cosmic child abuse.[60] Yet if the cross and eucharist do not turn judgment into blessing, then the story is not retold. The only solution, if the cross brings forgiveness, is that the resurrection brings judgment.

In the Jewish tradition of atonement, practiced person to person in the ten days between Rosh Hashanah, the New Year, and Yom Kippur, the Day of Atonement, when the gates of atonement are closed, God forgives the sins committed against God – but *not* the sins that one human being commits against another: for those one must ask forgiveness of the one wronged.[61] A crime such as the one depicted in Judges seems to trap both the victim and the criminals in their fates. She cannot return to life, and therefore they cannot repent before her. They foreclose the possibility of new life not only for her but for themselves. Rowan Williams suggests that the resurrection of Jesus has part of its meaning within such traditions; the suggestion is especially apt if Matthew represents the crucifixion as a Yom Kippur sacrifice.[62]

> [T]he primary stage in preaching the resurrection [is] to *recognize one's victim as one's hope*. . . . The Jesus who is preached as the sole source of salvation is the particular victim of that court.[63] If any insight may be generalized out of this saying, it is that salvation does not bypass the history and memory of guilt, but rather builds upon and from it. . . . I am not saved by forgetting or cancelling my memory of concrete guilt. . . . And so I must look to my partner: to the victim who alone can be the source of renewal and transformation.[64]

So the eucharist is not the domestication of violence and easy forgiveness. Under the sign of the resurrection, it *enables* Jesus to meet his victimizers face to face. The one whom they had betrayed, denied, abandoned, condemned,

---

[60]   See Joanne Carlson Brown and Carole R. Bohn, *Christianity, Patriarchy, and Abuse: A Feminist Critique* (Cleveland, OH: Pilgrim, 1989), and William T. Cavanaugh, *Torture and the Eucharist: Theology, Politics, and the Body of Christ*, Challenges in Contemporary Theology (Oxford: Blackwell, 1998).

[61]   *Mishnah Yoma* 8.9.

[62]   Linda Strohmier, "'His Blood Be on Us and on our Children . . .': A Study of the Atonement Theme in Matthew's Passion Account," M.Div. thesis for General Theological Seminary, New York, 1984.

[63]   Acts 4:12.

[64]   Rowan D. Williams, "The Judgement of Judgement: Easter in Jerusalem," in his *Resurrection: Interpreting the Easter Gospel* (London: Darton, Longman & Todd, 1982), pp. 11–12.

and crucified, is back again, walking the streets, before their faces. The victim will not stay dead. The story of the victim's terror becomes the story of the victimizers' terror. The unnamed woman, the holocaust victim meets and judges the executioners. Opponents in this and other churchly debates meet one another again. Jesus meets and judges them.

He judges them with – forgiveness. They must live differently – and they may, because the resurrection restores their victim as the one in whom alone there is judgment, and therefore hope. This confrontation might also become part of eucharistic practice, if we took seriously Jesus's suggestion that we go and be reconciled with our brother before we place a gift upon the altar. Why? Because bringing gifts to the altar participates in the eschatological movement toward the feast where we shall meet our victims face to face.[65]

Here, too, is where original sin comes in – under the influence of the forgiveness mediated among the community by Christ. As James Alison puts it, when Christians pose the question of original sin,

> we are asking about the first people to be like us. We are doing so out of a grateful acceptance of their likeness to us and because of an awareness that we are able to accept that likeness on our way to becoming something else, and indeed that our learning to accept that likeness may actually help us construct a forgiveness that includes them. The question is not so much how "Adam's" sin affects us, as how Christ's forgiveness (which we are charged to make real) affects Adam. To put this another way: there is no properly theological approach to "our first parents" that is not a discourse of love concerning the first people to need the sort of constructive forgiveness that we first discovered ourselves to need.[66]

Opponents on both sides of the sexuality debates could ponder that more deeply. It puts into perspective all attempts to see a besetting sin of the community as the most emblematic one – whether one sees homosexual couples as emblematic of idolatry, or opposition to them as emblematic of hatred. Christian sexuality will not be healed until each side considers its opponents in "grateful acceptance of their likeness to us . . . on our way to becoming something else, and indeed that our learning to accept that likeness

---

[65] Richard Hays once made this point by stopping his celebration of a eucharist at Yale Divinity School just before the consecration. The Bible on the altar there had been defaced by someone highlighting with a marker passages about homosexual acts. Hays required everyone to go request personal forgiveness from those present, if (from either side) they differed from them sinfully on those matters, before they partook of the elements.

[66] Alison, *The Joy of Being Wrong*, p. 243.

may actually help us." The eschatological banquet, like or unlike its eucharistic anticipations, does not take place without the reconciliation of enemies.

> Thou preparest a table before me
>   in the presence of mine enemies;
> thou anointest my head with oil,
>   my cup overflows.
> Surely goodness and mercy shall follow me
>   all the days of my life;
> and I shall dwell in the house of the Lord
>   forever.[67]

---

[67]   Ps. 23:5–6.

Chapter 13

THE NARRATIVE OF PROVIDENCE AND A CHARGE FOR A WEDDING

The community of the forgiven that Alison describes forms a public, a polity that, like the one with which we began this essay, remembers its forgiveness in baptism. That public is the Rule of the Spirit embodied, since the Spirit is the public of the Father and the Son. What that community does in public – its liturgy – is also done before the Father and the Son. Its liturgy both narrates the drama of sin and forgiveness that reverses the inhospitality of Sodom, and incorporates the adopted people into the eucharistic hospitality of God.

To be properly trinitarian and scriptural, this image must be public, for several reasons. First, the love of the Father for the Son always has a public in the New Testament. When the Father declares his pleasure in the Son at his baptism, the dove is present in the Spirit's role as witness, as public, as condition for the possibility of any further human public to witness the declaration. When the Father declares his pleasure in the Son at his transfiguration, the saints are present, Moses and Elijah, saints sanctified and gathered by the Spirit. When the Son returns the Spirit to the Father at the crucifixion, the Spirit transforms the crowd into a community of witnesses by moving the centurion to say, "Surely this man was the Son of God." In Paul's account of the resurrection, as we have seen, the Spirit creates a community, a public, of those who begin even now to share in the resurrection life. After the ascension, the Spirit gathers a public, a witnessing community, to testify to Christ's abiding presence, to the persistence of the love of God for the human being. When Christians come before courts, Paul assures them, the Spirit who is the condition for the possibility of witness to God will move even their testimony. That is the work of the Spirit, that is why Christians confess, "Credo in ecclesiam": because the believing community, the body of Christ animated by the Spirit, is also the dwelling of God. Without the Spirit, the love of the Father for the Son would be without a witness, without a celebration, and in that way deficient.

Marriages have an important public no matter how the union is celebrated. Friends, churches, children, other couples, and the single are among those in whom households build up community and upon whom marriages rely as the witnesses and guarantors of their commitment. But the witness and guaranty of the community, as well as its celebration and delight, are especially open and explicit, especially public, in the wedding feast. In celebrating, witnessing, guarantying, blessing, delighting in, and feasting the covenanted love of a human couple, a community may, by the Spirit's economic work, be caught up into the Spirit's proper work of doing these things for the love of the Father and the Son, which it eternally celebrates, witnesses, guaranties, blesses, delights in, and feasts in the Trinity's general dance. Thus a married life extensively, and a wedding feast intensively, becomes a mimesis of God, an acting out of God's loving image in Christ.

That returns us to the question of what human bodies are to *mean*. Marriages and weddings are not the only imitation of God that acts out God's image. Any act of charity toward the neighbor does that. The vowed life, which, as Williams suggests, attempts to devote the body to the love of God directly, without intermediaries, does that too, and is proved by its fruit: the celibates above all teach us that the love of God reaches and takes hold of our bodies. But married lives, and the weddings that mark them, do make particularly emblematic, or sacramental, moments of the image that God creates, redeems, and consummates. Married lives and the weddings that mark them sacramentalize the saying of Barth's, that creation is the external ground of the covenant, the covenant the internal ground of creation. Married lives and the weddings that mark them insist that that thesis applies even, and especially, to human bodies. Bodies are the external ground for the desiring love of God, and the desiring love of God is the internal ground for human bodies. And the ascesis of marriage, which according to Evdokimov's reading of the tradition is the same as the ascesis of celibacy, is the sanctification wrought by living with inescapable others, who like the Spirit will not leave us alone, who complete over time what eros tricked, or swept, or caught us up into. But the ascesis of marriage, in which the Spirit acts as the Law or Torah of the Spirit of Christ, is a law in which a couple may continue to delight. The work of the Spirit, of the delight that will be victor, of eros assumed into agape, is much more than romantic love and covenanted marriage but is active in every act of charity toward the neighbor and the self.

Yet if Christians want to see the Rule enacted who is the Spirit, if they want to see the body of the Spirit, or the shape of grace, they need to look to the liturgy – especially liturgies that tell stories of lives ruled by the Spirit, or inspired by the Rule. For if the shape of grace is the Rule of the Spirit, the shape of her Rule is narrative.

Sexuality as Narrated Providence in Eastern Orthodoxy

The liturgy teaches best of all that the lives of believers need inspiration by the Rule, or that nature needs reconceptualization as part of God's *oikonomia*. Consider this Orthodox prayer:

> O Lord our God, who didst grant unto us all those things necessary for salvation and didst bid us to love one another and to forgive each other our failings, bless and consecrate, kind Lord and lover of good, these thy servants who love each other with a love of the Spirit and have come into this thy holy church to be blessed and consecrated. . . . [B]estow . . . also on these, O Christ our God, . . . all those things needed for salvation and eternal life.[1]

Whatever this ceremony means, it manifests the economy of bringing *nature* to *salvation*. Similarly, in the Orthodox Order of Crowning, as the marriage proper is called, Jesus's presence at the marriage of Cana is ascribed to the "saving providence" of "the Lord our God."[2] In the order of second marriage, too, the appeal is to God's providence: "O Master, Lord our God, who showest pity upon all human beings, and whose providence is over all thy works."[3] In all those cases, the appeal to God's providence emerges from a catena of biblical and saintly examples, so that the economy of salvation of the couple before the congregation is incorporated into the economy of biblical salvation history. Consider the Order of Betrothal:

> For thou, O Lord, hast declared that a pledge should be given and confirmed in all things. By a ring was power given unto Joseph in Egypt; by a ring was

---

[1] *Grottaferrata gamma*, B, II, translated in John Boswell, *Same-Sex Unions in Premodern Europe* (New York: Villard Books, 1994), p. 296.
[2] *Service Book of the Holy Orthodox-Catholic Apostolic Church*, 6th rev. edn, trans. Isabel Florence Hapgood (Englewood, NJ: Antiochene Orthodox Christian Archdiocese of North America, 1983), p. 299.
[3] *Service Book*, p. 304.

Daniel glorified in the land of Babylon; by a ring was the uprightness of Tamar revealed [!]; by a ring did our heavenly Father show forth his bounty upon his Son; for he saith: Put a ring on his hand, and bring hither the fatted calf, and kill it, and eat, and make merry.[4]

(Note well: it is the prodigal – one might by application say, the gay son – that receives the ring!) And the Order of Second Marriage is wittiest:

O thou who knowest the frailty of human nature, in that thou art our Maker and Creator; who didst pardon Rahab the harlot, and accept the contrition of the Publican: remember not the sins of ignorance from our youth up. For if thou wilt consider iniquity, O Lord, Lord, who shall stand before thee? Or what flesh shall be justified in thy sight? For thou only art righteous, sinless, holy, plenteous in mercy, of great compassion, and repentest thee of the evils of human beings. Do thou, O Master, who hast brought together in wedlock thy servants, N. and N., unite them to one another in love: vouchsafe unto them the contrition of the Publican, the tears of the Harlot, the confession of the Thief; that, repenting with their whole heart, and doing thy command-ments in peace and oneness of mind, they may be deemed worthy also of thy heavenly kingdom.[5]

If that can go for remarriage after divorce, how much more for almost any wedding now in our complicated society, where very few, straight or gay, save sex for marriage. What couple should *not* invoke the contrition of the Publican, the tears of the Harlot, the confession of the Thief, by the time they marry?

One might object that such narratives about God's providential rule are best understood as the way in which God acts through evil to bring about good rather than as establishing a pattern for behavioral norms. Those who put forward patterns for behavioral norms, on the other hand, tend not to take account of biblical stories in which God seems unconcerned with the ethics of the characters, or at least the editorial redaction records no moral judgment one way or the other. It would be hard to argue for divine disapproval of Tamar's subterfuge, for example; still less of Mary's bearing a child not begotten by Joseph. The "low estate" of the Magnificat refers not to barrenness, as usual, but to her apparently illegitimate pregnancy. The reason I turn to *liturgically worked* biblical texts is precisely to overcome the dichotomy between behavioral norms and providential action, between letter and spirit. In the liturgy the Spirit who rules is invoked and present. In the liturgy the

---

4   *Service Book*, pp. 292–3.
5   *Service Book*, p. 304.

Church *does* take up biblical narratives and put them to moral use, integrating divine providence and behavioral norms holding together spirit and letter. Thus the liturgies quoted neither overlook nor prettify Rahab the harlot, but invoke her for a particular purpose. In that way they serve as the proper model for the *integration* of behavioral norms and providential narratives. They invoke the latter to qualify and inculcate the former. Better: the liturgy casts the people *inside* the providential narratives as the context where alone their behavior can begin to make sense before God. It is in such a context that gay and lesbian couples must also place their lives, to make room for going on when they inevitably fail to measure up to their models and vows. It is that context that Eastern Orthodoxy calls, in a delightfully delicate word, the *economy* of salvation. It is the economy of salvation that allows the Holy Spirit to be itself a Rule or Law that gives life.

The pattern to be recovered from the liturgies is this: *everything* is given to human beings for use in God's economy of salvation, or, less starkly, nothing is left out; and the economy of salvation is identified by incorporating the community into the biblical narratives. This pattern goes for *nature itself*, as we have seen, in that God conforms nature itself to the economy of salvation in grafting the Gentiles onto the Jewish vine. Not only that: the original nature, which Paul has God contravening for the salvation of the Gentiles, is not so much natural in any general, metaphysical sense of the term, as covenantal. What is natural is that God should love the Jews especially. What is unnatural is that God should incorporate the Gentiles into that love. The same reasoning might well go for straight and gay. What is natural is that God should love bearers of children, especially bearers of Jewish children: Abraham and Sarah. But God also incorporates into that love Gentiles like Zipporah and Ruth, the childless like the eunuchs, and delights in irregular pregnancies, like the ones Matthew singles out as leading to the birth of Jesus, for God's providential purposes.

Gay and lesbian unions can build up the Church as well as straight marriages do, with or without children in both cases. Certainly lesbian and gay relationships can exhibit an egoism *à deux*, but they need not, any more than straight ones do. Still, marriage forms that included gay and lesbian couples would make clear that their unions, too, are from and for the larger community – indeed, if the kingdom of God is like a wedding feast, then it is thus that they represent the Trinity. That leads to my final offering – the charge for a wedding.[6]

---

[6] In fact, I read it at a heterosexual wedding but wrote it with both that couple and these considerations in mind.

Charge for a Wedding

Dearly beloved: we have come together in the presence of God to witness and bless the joining together of these God's human creatures, [N and N], in Holy Matrimony. Marriage signifies the mystery of the love that God bears to human beings, in that God desires, befriends, and keeps faith with us. That love is mysterious to us in that, unlike us, God *just is* love,[7] an interior community, never lonely, already rich. That love is open to us in that God desires, befriends, and keeps faith in God's very self, as these two desire, befriend, and keep faith with each other. And God's Spirit internally witnesses and blesses and keeps faith with the love in God[8] as today we externally witness and bless the love of these two human creatures in God's image. Today the celebration, blessing, and witnessing of this wedding catch us up into a parable of the inner love and life of God.[9]

In desire God says to us, "You have ravished my heart."[10] God declares of Israel, "I will allure her."[11] As Jacob worked twice seven years for Rachel;[12] as Ruth seduced Boaz upon the threshing floor;[13] as the soul of Jonathan was knit to the soul of David;[14] as these two of God's human creatures desire each other, so God desires us. Grace like desire transforms us by showing us to be perceived in a certain way: as significant, as desired.[15]

In the friendship of the best sort, says Aristotle, the friends make each other better.[16] As Naomi became to Ruth a teacher, and Ruth became to Naomi more than seven sons;[17] as Jonathan prepared David for kingship;[18] as these two befriend each other; so, too, God says, "No longer do I call you servants . . . but I have called you friends."[19] In friendship God does not merely con-

---

[7]   1 Jn. 4:8b.

[8]   Mt. 3:17, Mk. 1:9–11, Lk. 3:21–2, Jn. 1:31–4.

[9]   Mt. 9:15, 22:2.

[10]   Song 4:9a.

[11]   Hos. 2:14.

[12]   Gen. 29.

[13]   Ruth 3.

[14]   I Sam. 18:1.

[15]   Rowan D. Williams, "The Body's Grace," in Charles Hefling, ed., *Our Selves, Our Souls and Bodies* (Boston: Cowley Publications, 1996), pp. 58–68; here, pp. 59, 65, near quotation.

[16]   *Nichomachean Ethics*, IX.12, 1172a11–14.

[17]   Ruth 2:2, 22, 3:1–4, 4:15.

[18]   1 Sam. 18–23, esp. 23:17.

[19]   Jn. 15:15.

descend to be God with us, but God elevates us to be with God. Marriage's friendship, too, may elevate you so that your "love is patient and kind."[20]

In faith we grant time to desire's risk and friendship's work. Faith sustains the will to let ourselves be formed by the perceptions of another.[21] As Jonathan promised David that "the Lord shall be between you and me, between your posterity and mine forever";[22] as Ruth pledged to follow Naomi till death did them part;[23] so God, too, counts the cost of love for Israel and declares: "I will betroth you to me forever. . . . I will betroth you to me in faithfulness; and you shall know [who I am]."[24]

"Beloved, let us love one another; for love is of God, and whoever loves is born of God and knows God."[25] We are created – and we marry – so that the desire of a spouse, divine or human, may show us to ourselves as occasions of joy.[26] We are created – and we marry – so that the friendship of a spouse, divine or human, may make us worthy of that showing. We are created – and we marry – so that the faithfulness of a spouse, divine or human, may teach us who we are. We are created – and we marry – so that on this wedding day we may be caught up into those things, so that we may grow into the wholehearted love of God by seeing how God loves us as God loves God.[27]

20 1 Cor. 13:4ff.
21 Williams, "The Body's Grace," p. 62, near quotation.
22 I Sam. 20:42.
23 Ruth 1:16–17.
24 Hos. 2:19a, 20.
25 1 Jn. 4:7.
26 Williams, "The Body's Grace," p. 59, near quotation.
27 Williams, "The Body's Grace," p. 59, near quotation.

BIBLIOGRAPHY

For a book ranging as widely as this one, no bibliography could be exhaustive. Items appear only if they have actually influenced the argument. Sources especially recommended for further reading are marked with an asterisk.

Abelove, Henry, Michele Aina Barale, and David M. Halperin, eds. *The Lesbian and Gay Studies Reader*. New York: Routledge, 1993.

Adams, Marilyn McCord. "Hurricane Spirit, Toppling Taboos." In *Our Selves, Our Souls and Bodies: Sexuality and the Household of God*, edited by Charles Hefling. Boston: Cowley Publications, 1996.

—— "Yes to Bless." Paper delivered to the conference "Beyond Inclusion." All Saints' Episcopal Church, Pasadena, CA, April 1997.

Aillet, Marc. *Lire la bible avec St Thomas: Le Passage de la lettre à la res dans la Somme théologique*. Fribourg: Éditions universitaires, 1993.

Alexander, Marilyn Bennet, and James Preston. *We Were Baptized Too: Claiming God's Grace for Lesbians and Gays*. With an introduction by Archbishop Desmond Tutu. Louisville, KY: Westminster / John Knox, 1996.

Alison, James. *The Joy of Being Wrong: Original Sin through Easter Eyes*. With an introduction by Sebastian Moore. New York: Crossroad, 1998.

★—— "Theology Amongst the Stones and Dust." In *Theology and Sexuality*. Forthcoming.

Anderson, George H., T. Austin Murphy, and Joseph A. Burgess, eds. *Justification by Faith: Lutherans and Catholics in Dialogue*, VII. Minneapolis, MN: Augsburg Press, 1985.

Anselm of Canterbury. *Cur Deus homo*. ET: "Why God Became Man." In *A Scholastic Miscellany: Anselm to Ockham*, edited and translated by Eugene R. Fairweather. Library of Christian Classics, vol. 10. Philadelphia: Westminster Press, 1956.

Aquinas: see Thomas Aquinas.

Aristotle. *Nichomachean Ethics*.

Athanasius. *On the Incarnation of the Word*. In *Christology of the Later Fathers*, edited by Edward R. Hardy. Library of Christian Classics. Philadelphia: Westminster Press, 1954.

—— *Orations against the Arians*. In *The Christological Controversy*, edited and translated by Richard A. Norris, Jr. Sources of Early Christian Thought. Philadelphia: Fortress, 1980.

Augustine. *The City of God*, translated by Henry Betenson. With an introduction by John O'Meara. New York: Penguin, 1984.

—— *Confessions*, translated by R. S. Pine-Coffin. New York: Penguin, 1961.

—— *The Good of Marriage*. Partially translated in *Marriage in the Early Church*, edited and translated by David G. Hunter. Sources of Early Christian Thought. Minneapolis MN: Augsburg Fortress, 1992.

—— *The Trinity*, translated by Stephen McKenna. The Fathers of the Church. Washington, DC: Catholic University of America Press, 1961.

Bailey, Derrick Sherwin. *Homosexuality and the Western Christian Tradition*. London: Green, 1955.

Balthasar, Hans Urs von. *Theodramatik: Die Personen des Spiels*. 2 vols. Einsiedeln: Johannes, 1973–83.

Barth, Karl. *Dogmatics in Outline*, translated by G. T. Thomson. London: SCM Press, 1949.

—— Introduction to *The Essence of Christianity*, by Ludwig Feuerbach. New York: Harper Torchbooks, 1957.

—— *Die Kirchliche Dogmatik*. 4 vols in 13. Zurich: Evangelischer Verlag/Zollikon, 1932–70. ET: *The Church Dogmatics*, 4 vols in 13, translated by G. W. Bromiley et al. Edinburgh: T. & T. Clark, 1936–75.

—— *Kurze Erklärung des Römerbriefes*. Munich: Christian Kaiser, 1956. ET: *A Shorter Commentary on Romans*, translator unknown. Richmond, VA: John Knox, 1959.

—— *Letters 1961–1968*, edited by Jürgen Fangmeier and Hinrich Stoevesandt, and translated by Geoffrey W. Bromiley. Grand Rapids, MI: Eerdmans, 1981.

—— *Der Römerbrief*, 5. Abdrück der neuen Bearbeitung. Munich: Christian Kaiser, 1929. ET: *The Epistle to the Romans*, translated by Edwyn C. Hoskyns. 6th edn. New York: Oxford University Press, 1980.

—— *The Word of God and the Word of Man*, translated by Douglas Horton. London: Hodder & Stoughton, 1928.

Bawer, Bruce. *Beyond Queer: Challenging Gay Left Orthodoxy*. New York: The Free Press, 1996.

—— *A Place at the Table: The Gay Individual in American Society*. Boston: Poseidon Press, 1993.

Beeck, Frans Jozef van. "Fantasy, the Capital Sins, the Enneagram, and Self-Acceptance: An Essay in Ascetical Theology." *Pro Ecclesia* 3 (1994): 179–96.

Boisvert, Donald L. "Queering the Sacred: Notes for a Typology of Gay Spirituality." Paper delivered to the American Academy of Religion Annual Meeting, November 1997.

Boswell, John. *Christianity, Social Tolerance, and Homosexuality: Gay People in Western Europe from the Beginning of the Christian Era to the Fourteenth Century*. Chicago: University of Chicago Press, 1980.

—— Introduction to *Uncommon Calling: A Gay Man's Struggle to Serve the Church*, by Chris Glaser. San Francisco: Harper & Row, 1988.

—— *The Kindness of Strangers: The Abandonment of Children in Western Europe from Late Antiquity to the Renaissance*. New York: Vintage Books, 1990.

—— *Rediscovering Gay History: Archetypes of Gay Love in Christian History*. The Fifth Michael Harding Memorial Address. London: Gay Christian Movement, 1982.

—— "Revolutions, Universals, and Sexual Categories." In *Hidden from History: Reclaiming the Gay and Lesbian Past*, edited by Martin Duberman, Martha Vicinus, and George Chauncey. New York: New American Library, 1989.

—— *Same-Sex Unions in Premodern Europe*. New York: Villard Books, 1994.

Bowlin, John. *Contingency and Fortune in Aquinas's Ethics*. New York: Cambridge University Press, 1999.

Brakke, David. *Athanasius and the Politics of Asceticism*. Oxford: Clarendon Press, 1995.

Brawley, Robert L., ed. *Biblical Ethics and Homosexuality*. Louisville, KY: Westminster / John Knox, 1996.

Breidenthal, Thomas E. *Christian Households: The Sanctification of Nearness*. Boston: Cowley Publications, 1997.

★—— "Sanctifying Nearness." In *Our Selves, Our Souls and Bodies: Sexuality and the Household of God*, edited by Charles Hefling. Boston: Cowley Publications, 1996.

Briggs, Sheila. "Schleiermacher and the Construction of the Gendered Self." In *Schleiermacher and Feminism: Sources, Evaluations, and Responses*, edited by Iain Nicol. Schleiermacher: Studies-and-Translations, vol. 12. Lewiston, NY: The Edwin Mellen Press, 1992.

Brockway, Alan, et al. *The Theology of the Churches and the Jewish People*. Geneva: WCC Publications, 1988.

Brooten, Bernadette J. *Love Between Women: Early Christian Responses to Female Homoeroticism*. The Chicago Series on Sexuality, History, and Society. Chicago: University of Chicago Press, 1996.

Brown, Joanne Carlson, and Carole R. Bohn. *Christianity, Patriarchy, and Abuse: A Feminist Critique*. Cleveland, OH: Pilgrim, 1989.

Brown, Peter. *Augustine of Hippo*. Berkeley, CA: University of California Press, 1967.

—— *The Body and Society: Men, Women, and Sexual Renunciation in Early Christianity*. New York: Columbia University Press, 1988.

Browning, Frank. *The Culture of Desire: Paradox and Perversity in Gay Lives Today*. New York: Vintage Books, 1994.

Buber, Martin. *I and Thou*, translated by Walter Kaufmann. New York: Charles Scribner's Sons, 1970.

Buckley, James J. Review of *Thomas Aquinas and Karl Barth: Sacred Doctrine and the Natural Knowledge of God*, by Eugene F. Rogers, Jr. *The Thomist* 61 (1997): 320–35.

Burrell, David. *Knowing the Unknowable God*. Notre Dame, IN: Notre Dame University Press, 1986.

Busch, Eberhard. *Karl Barth: His Life from Letters and Autobiographical Texts*. Philadelphia: Fortress, 1976.

—— *Unter dem Bogen des einen Bundes: Karl Barth und die Juden 1933–1945*. Neukirchen-Vluyn: Neukirchner Verlag, 1996.

Bynum, Caroline Walker. "Jesus as Mother and Abbot as Mother: Some Themes in Twelfth-Century Cistercian Writing." In *Jesus as Mother: Studies in the Spirituality of the High Middle Ages*. Berkeley, CA: University of California Press, 1982.

Calhoun, Robert M. *Evangelicals and Conservatives in the Early South, 1740–1861.* Columbia, SC: University of South Carolina Press, 1988.

Cavanaugh, William T. *Torture and the Eucharist: Theology, Politics, and the Body of Christ.* Challenges in Contemporary Theology. Oxford: Blackwell, 1998.

Chenu, Marie-Dominique. *La Théologie comme science au XIIIe siècle.* 3rd edn. Bibliothèque thomiste, 33. Paris: J. Vrin, 1957.

Cherry, Kittredge, and Zalmon Sherwood. *Equal Rites: Lesbian and Gay Worship, Ceremonies, and Celebrations.* Louisville, KY: Westminster / John Knox, 1995.

Christy, David. *Cotton Is King: Slavery in the Light of Political Economy.* Reprinted in *Cotton Is King and Pro-Slavery Arguments, Comprising the Writings of Hammond, Harper, Christy, Stringfellow, Hodge, Bledsoe, and Cartwright, on this Important Subject,* edited by E. N. Elliott. Augusta, GA: Pritchard, Abbott & Loomis, 1860.

Chrysostom, John. *Dialogue sur la sacerdoce, Discours sur le mariage, Lettre à une Jeune veuve,* translated by Fernand Martin. Paris: Garnier Frères, 1933.

★—— *Homily I on Marriage.* Partially translated as "Sermon on Marriage." In *On Marriage and Family Life,* translated by Catharine P. Roth and David Anderson. Crestwood, NY: St Vladimir's Seminary Press, 1997.

★—— *Homily III on Marriage.* Partially translated as "How to Choose a Wife." In *On Marriage and Family Life,* translated by Catharine P. Roth and David Anderson. Crestwood, NY: St Vladimir's Seminary Press, 1997.

Congregation for the Doctrine of the Faith. "Instruction on the Ecclesial Vocation of the Theologian." *Origins: CNS Documentary Service* 20 (1990): 120–6.

—— "Letter to the Bishops of the Catholic Church on the Pastoral Care of Homosexual Persons." Reprinted in *The Vatican and Homosexuality,* edited by Jeannine Gramick and Pat Furey. New York: Crossroad, 1988.

Constantelos, Demetrios J. *Marriage, Sexuality, and Celibacy: A Greek Orthodox Perspective.* Minneapolis, MN: Light and Life Publishing, 1975.

Corbin, Michel. *Le Chemin de la théologie chez Thomas d'Aquin.* Bibliothèque des archives de philosophie, 16. Paris: Beauchesne, 1974.

★Countryman, L. William. *Dirt, Greed, and Sex: Sexual Ethics in the New Testament and Their Implications for Today.* Philadelphia: Fortress, 1988.

Courtine, Jean-François. "La Métaphysique dans l'horizon scholastique." Pt. I of *Suárez et le système de la métaphysique.* Paris: Presses Universitaires de France, 1990.

Crites, Stephen. "The Spatial Dimensions of Narrative TruthTelling." In *Scriptural Authority and Narrative Interpretation,* edited by Garrett Green. Philadelphia: Fortress, 1987.

Cunningham, Mary Kathleen. *What Is Theological Exegesis? Interpretation and Use of Scripture in Barth's Doctrine of Election.* Valley Forge, PA: Trinity Press International, 1995.

Curb, Rosemary, and Nancy Manahan, eds. *Breaking Silence: Lesbian Nuns on Convent Sexuality.* London: Columbus Books, 1985.

Dabney, D. Lyle. *Die Kenosis des Geistes: Kontinuität zwischen Schöpfung und Erlösung im Werk des Heiligen Geistes.* Neukirchen-Vluyn: Neukirchner Verlag, 1997.

Daniélou, Jean. *The Bible and the Liturgy*, translator unknown. Notre Dame, IN: University of Notre Dame Press, 1956.

Denman, Rose Mary. *Let My People In: A Lesbian Minister Tells of Her Struggles to Live Openly and Maintain Her Ministry*. New York: William Morrow, 1990.

Domanyi, Thomas. *Der Römerbriefkommentar des Thomas von Aquin: Ein Beitrag zur Untersuchung seiner Auslegungsmethoden*. Basler und Berner Studien zur historischen und systematischen Theologie, vol. 39. Bern: Peter Lang, 1979.

Donne, John. "Batter my heart, three person'd God." In *The Poems of John Donne*, edited by H. J. C. GriersonLondon: Oxford University Press, 1933.

Douglas, Mary. "The Gender of the Beloved." *The Heythrop Journal* 36 (1995): 397–408.

—— *How Institutions Think*. Syracuse, NY: Syracuse University, 1986.

—— *Natural Symbols: Explorations in Cosmology*. New York: Routledge, 1996.

—— *Purity and Danger: An Analysis of the Concepts of Pollution and Taboo*. London: Routledge, 1966.

Durkin, Mary G. *Feast of Love: Pope John Paul II on Human Intimacy*. Chicago: Loyola University Press, 1983.

Eilberg-Schwartz, Howard, ed. *People of the Body: Jews and Judaism from an Embodied Perspective*. Albany, NY: State University of New York Press, 1992.

Elm, Susanna. *"Virgins of God": The Making of Asceticism in Late Antiquity*. Oxford Classical Monographs. Oxford: Clarendon Press, 1994.

Eskridge, William N., Jr. *The Case for Same-Sex Marriage: From Sexual Liberty to Civilized Commitment*. New York: The Free Press, 1996.

*Evdokimov, Paul. *Sacrement de l'amour: Le Mystère conjugale à le lumière de la tradition orthodoxe*. Paris: Éditions de l'Épi, 1952. ET: *The Sacrament of Love: The Nuptial Mystery in the Light of the Orthodox Tradition*, translated by Anthony P. Gythiel and Victoria Steadman. Crestwood, NY: St Vladimir's Seminary Press, 1985.

—— *Woman and the Salvation of the World: A Christian Anthropology on the Charisms of Woman*, translated by Anthony P. Gythiel. Crestwood, NY: St Vladimir's Seminary Press, 1994.

Farley, Margaret. *Personal Commitments*. San Francisco: Harper & Row, 1986.

Feuerbach, Ludwig. *The Essence of Christianity*, translated by George Eliot. With an introduction by Karl Barth. New York: Harper Torchbooks, 1957.

Fiorenza, Elisabeth Schüssler. *In Memory of Her: A Feminist Theological Reconstruction of Christian Origins*. New York: Crossroad, 1983.

Fowl, Stephen. "How to Read the Spirit and How the Spirit Reads." In *Engaging Scripture*. Oxford: Blackwell, 1998.

Frederickson, George M. *The Black Image in the White Mind: The Debate on Afro-American Character and Destiny 1817–1914*. New York: Harper & Row, 1971.

Freehling, William W. "The Direct Defense of Slavery, 1833–1836." Pt. III of *Prelude to Civil War: The Nullification Controversy in South Carolina, 1816–1836*. New York: Harper Torchbooks, 1968.

—— "The Indirect Defense of Slavery, 1816–1833." Pt. II of *Prelude to Civil War: The Nullification Controversy in South Carolina, 1816–1836*. New York: Harper Torchbooks, 1968.

Frei, Hans W. "Eberhard Busch's Biography of Karl Barth." In *Types of Christian Theology*, edited by George Hunsinger and William C. Placher. New Haven, CT: Yale University Press, 1992.

—— *The Eclipse of Biblical Narrative: A Study of Eighteenth and Nineteenth Century Hermeneutics.* New Haven, CT: Yale University Press, 1974.

—— "Jesus Identified in His Resurrection." In *The Identity of Jesus Christ: The Hermeneutical Bases of Dogmatic Theology*. Philadelphia: Fortress, 1975.

—— "The 'Literal Reading' of Biblical Narrative in the Christian Tradition: Does It Stretch or Will It Break?" In *Theology and Narrative: Selected Essays*, edited by George Hunsinger and William C. Placher. New York: Oxford University Press, 1993.

—— "Of the Resurrection of Christ." In *Theology and Narrative: Selected Essays*, edited by George Hunsinger and William C. Placher. New York: Oxford University Press, 1993.

—— "Theological Reflections on the Accounts of Jesus' Death and Resurrection." In *Theology and Narrative: Selected Essays*, edited by George Hunsinger and William C. Placher. New York: Oxford University Press, 1993.

Gaillardetz, Richard R. *Teaching with Authority: A Theology of the Magisterium in the Church.* Collegeville, MN: The Liturgical Press, 1997.

Geertz, Clifford. "Ethos, World View, and the Analysis of Sacred Symbols." In *The Interpretation of Cultures*. New York: Basic Books, 1973.

Genovese, Eugene D. *A Consuming Fire: The Fall of the Confederacy in the Mind of the White Christian South.* Athens, GA: University of Georgia Press, 1999.

—— "Slavery Ordained of God": *The Southern Slaveholders' View of Biblical History and Modern Politics.* 24th Annual Robert Fortenbaugh Memorial Lecture. Gettysburg, PA: Gettysburg College, 1985.

Gibbon, William J., ed. *Seven Great Encyclicals.* New York: Paulist Press, 1963.

Gilman, Sander. "The Jewish Body: A Foot-Note." In *People of the Body: Jews and Judaism from an Embodied Perspective*, edited by Howard Eilberg-Schwartz. Albany, NY: State University of New York Press, 1992.

Glaser, Chris. *Uncommon Calling: A Gay Man's Struggle to Serve the Church.* San Francisco: Harper & Row, 1988.

Gomes, Peter J. "The Bible and Homosexuality: The Last Prejudice." In *The Good Book: Reading the Bible with Mind and Heart*. New York: Avon, 1996.

Gottlieb, Robert, and Peter Wiley. "The Priesthood and the Black." In *America's Saints*. New York: G. P. Putnam's Sons, 1984.

Gregory of Nyssa. *Commentary on the Song of Songs*, translated by Casimir McCambley. Brookline, MA: Hellenic College Press, 1987.

Guenter-Gleason, Patricia E. *On Schleiermacher and Gender Politics.* Harvard Theological Studies. Boston: Trinity Press International, 1997.

Hall, Pamela M. *Narrative and the Natural Law: An Interpretation of Thomistic Ethics.* Notre Dame, IN: Notre Dame University Press, 1994.

Hannigan, James. *Homosexuality: Test Case for Christian Ethics.* New York: Paulist Press, 1988.

Hardy, James Earl. *B-Boy Blues.* Boston: Alyson Publications, 1994.

Harper, Chancellor. "Slavery in the Light of Social Ethics." Reprinted in *Cotton Is King and ProSlavery Arguments, Comprising the Writings of Hammond, Harper, Christy, Stringfellow, Hodge, Bledsoe, and Cartwright, on this Important Subject*, edited by E. N. Elliott. Augusta, GA: Pritchard, Abbott & Loomis, 1860.

Harrison, Carol. *Beauty and Revelation in the Thought of Saint Augustine.* Oxford: Clarendon Press, 1992.

Harrowitz, Nancy A., and Barbara Hyams, eds. *Jews and Gender: Responses to Otto Weininger.* Philadelphia: Temple University Press, 1995.

Hauerwas, Stanley. "Priesthood and Power: What It Means to Be a Father." Unpublished ms.

*——— "Virtue, Description, and Friendship [formerly "Gay Friendship"]: A Thought Experiment in Catholic Moral Theology." *Irish Theological Quarterly* (1998): 170–84.

Hawkins, Peter S. "Counter, Original, Spare, Strange." In *Our Selves, Our Souls and Bodies: Sexuality and the Household of God*, edited by Charles Hefling. Boston: Cowley Publications, 1996.

Hays, Richard. "Homosexuality." In *Moral World of the New Testament: Community, Cross, New Creation: An Introduction to New Testament Ethics.* San Francisco: HarperSanFrancisco, 1996.

——— "Relations Natural and Unnatural: A Response to John Boswell's Exegesis of Romans 1." *Journal of Religious Ethics* 14 (1986): 184–215.

Hayter, Mary. *The New Eve in Christ: The Use and Abuse of the Bible in the Debate about Women in the Church.* London: SPCK, 1987.

Hefling, Charles, ed. *Our Selves, Our Souls and Bodies: Sexuality and the Household of God.* Boston: Cowley Publications, 1996.

Heitz, Sergius, ed. *Der orthodoxe Gottesdienst.* Vol. 1, *Göttliche Liturgie und Sakramente.* Mainz: MatthiasGrünewald, 1965.

Helminiak, Daniel A. "Ethics, Biblical and Denominational: A Response to Mark Smith." *Journal of the American Academy of Religion* 65 (1997): 855–60.

Herbert, George. "Love" (III). In *The Works of George Herbert*, edited by T. E. Hutchinson. Oxford: Clarendon Press, 1941.

Heyward, Carter. *Our Passion for Justice: Images of Power, Sexuality, and Liberation.* New York: Pilgrim, 1984.

——— *Speaking of Christ: A Lesbian Feminist Voice.* New York: Pilgrim, 1989.

——— *Staying Power: Reflections on Gender, Justice, and Compassion.* Cleveland, OH: Pilgrim, 1995.

——— *Touching Our Strength: The Erotic as the Power and the Love of God.* San Francisco: Harper & Row, 1989.

Hodes, Martha Elizabeth. *White Women, Black Men: Illicit Sex in the Nineteenth-Century South.* New Haven, CT: Yale University Press, 1997.

Hood, Robert E. "Ham's Children in America." In *Begrimed and Black: Christian Traditions on Blacks and Blackness.* Minneapolis, MN: Augsburg Fortress, 1994.

Hopkins, Gerard Manley. *Poems of Gerard Manley Hopkins.* 3rd edn. New York: Oxford University Press, 1961.

Horner, Thomas M. *Jonathan Loved David: Homosexuality in Biblical Times.* Philadelphia: Westminster Press, 1978.

Hunsinger, George, ed. *Karl Barth and Radical Politics.* Philadelphia: Westminster Press, 1976.

Hunter, James Davison. *Culture Wars: The Struggle to Define America.* New York: Basic Books, 1991.

Inglis, John. "Philosophical Autonomy and the Historiography of Mediaeval Philosophy." *British Journal for the History of Philosophy* 5 (1997): 21–53.

Irwin, Terrence. *Aristotle's First Principles.* New York: Oxford University Press, 1988.

Jenson, Robert W. "Predestination." In *Christian Dogmatics*, edited by Robert W. Jenson and Carl E. Braaten. Philadelphia: Fortress, 1984.

—— *Systematic Theology.* Vol. 1, *The Triune God.* New York: Oxford University Press, 1997.

—— *The Triune Identity.* Philadelphia: Fortress, 1982.

—— *Unbaptized God: The Basic Flaw in Ecumenical Theology.* Minneapolis, MN: Augsburg Fortress, 1992.

—— *Visible Words: The Interpretation and Practice of the Christian Sacraments.* Philadelphia: Fortress, 1978.

—— "You Wonder Where the Spirit Went." *Pro Ecclesia* 2 (1993): 296–304.

Jenson, Robert W., and Eric W. Gritsch. *Lutheranism: The Theological Movement and Its Confessional Writings.* Philadelphia: Fortress, 1976.

John Paul II, Pope. "Ad tuendam fidem." *Origins* 28 (1998): 113, 115–16.

Johnson, James Weldon. "The Creation." In *God's Trombones.* New York: Penguin, 1955.

Johnson, Luke Timothy. "Disputed Questions: Debate and Discernment, Scripture and the Spirit." *Commonweal* (January 28, 1994): 11–13.

Jordan, Mark D. *The Invention of Sodomy in Christian Theology.* Chicago: University of Chicago Press, 1997.

Julian of Norwich. *Showings*, translated by Edmund Colledge and John Walsh. New York: Paulist Press, 1978.

Kallis, Anastasios. "Philoxenia." In *Philoxenia: Prof. Dr Bernhard Kötting gewidmet von seinen griechischen Schülern*, edited by Anastasios Kallis. Munich: Aschendorff, 1980.

Katz, Jonathan Ned. *Gay/Lesbian Almanac: A New Documentary.* New York: Harper & Row, 1983.

Kellenbach, Katharina von. *Anti-Judaism in Feminist Religious Writings.* American Academy of Religion Cultural Criticism Series, no. 1. Atlanta, GA: Scholars Press, 1994.

Kelley, J. N. D. *The Epistles of Peter and of Jude.* New York: Harper & Row, 1969.

Khodre, George. "A Great Mystery: Reflections on the Meaning of Marriage," translated by A. M. Moorehouse. *St Vladimir's Theological Quarterly* 8 (1964): 31–7.

Kirk, Marshall, and Hunter Madsen. *After the Ball.* New York: Plume Books, 1990.

Klappert, Bertold. "Auf dem Weg der Gerechtigkeit ist Liebe: Gemeinschaftsgerechte Lebensformen in der Perspektive des Reiches Gottes und Seiner Gerechtigkeit.

Erwägungen zum Diskussionspapier 'Sexualität und Lebensformen sowie Trauung und Segnung.'" In *"Und hätte die Liebe nicht": Texte vom Mülheimer Symposion zum rheinischen Diskussionspapier "Sexualität und Lebensformen sowie Trauung und Segnung,"* edited by Evangelischen Kirche im Rheinland. Düsseldorf: Presseverband der Evangelischen Kirche im Rheinland, eV, 1997.

—— *Israel und die Kirche: Erwägungen zur Israellehre Karl Barths.* Munich: Christian Kaiser, 1980.

Kramer, Larry. "Sex and Sensibility." *The Advocate* 734 (May 27, 1997): 59–66.

LeVay, Simon. *Queer Science: The Use and Abuse of Research into Homosexuality.* Cambridge, MA: MIT Press, 1996.

Levenson, Jon D. *Creation and the Persistence of Evil: The Jewish Drama of Divine Omnipotence.* 2nd edn. Princeton, NJ: Princeton University Press, 1988.

Lexikon der christlichen Ikonographie, 8 vols, edited by E. Kirschbaum and W. Braunfels. Rome, Feiburg, Vienna: Herder, 1968–76.

Lindbeck, George. "The Church." In *Keeping the Faith: Essays to Mark the Centenary of Lux Mundi,* edited by Geoffrey Wainwright. Philadelphia: Fortress, 1988.

—— "Response to Michael Wyschogrod's 'Letter to a Friend.'" *Modern Theology* 11 (1995): 206–7.

Lovelace, Richard F. *Homosexuality and the Church.* Old Tappan, NJ: Revell, 1978.

Lubac, Henri de. *Exégèse médiévale: Les Quatre sens de l'écriture.* 4 vols. Paris: Aubier, 1959–64.

MacIntyre, Alasdair. *First Principles, Final Ends and Contemporary Philosophical Issues.* The Aquinas Lecture, 1990. Milwaukee, WI: Marquette University Press, 1990.

—— *Whose Justice? Which Rationality?* Notre Dame, IN: Notre Dame University Press, 1988.

Marenbon, John. "The Theoretical and Practical Autonomy of Philosophy as a Discipline in the Middle Ages." *Acta Philosophica Fennica* 48 (1990): 262–74.

Marquardt, Friedrich-Wilhelm. *Das christliche Bekenntnis zu Jesus, dem Juden: Eine Christologie.* Bd. 1. Munich: Christian Kaiser, 1990.

—— *Die Entdeckung des Judentums für die christliche Theologie: Israel im Denken Karl Barths.* Munich: Christian Kaiser, 1967.

—— *Die Gegenwart des Auferstandenen bei seinem Volk Israel.* Munich: Christian Kaiser, 1983.

—— *Die Juden im Römerbrief.* Zurich: Theologischer Verlag, 1971.

—— *Von Elend und Heimsuchung der Theologie: Prolegomena zur Dogmatik.* Munich: Christian Kaiser, 1992.

Marshall, Bruce D. "Absorbing the World: Christianity and the Universe of Truths." In *Theology and Dialogue: Essays in Conversation with George Lindbeck,* edited by Bruce D. Marshall. Notre Dame, IN: Notre Dame University Press, 1990.

★—— "Can Lutherans Have Episcopal Bishops? Reflections on a Refusal of Communion." *The Lutheran Forum* 32, 1 (1998): 36–41.

★—— "Theology of the Jewish People." In *The Cambridge Companion to Christian Doctrine,* edited by Colin E. Gunton. New York: Cambridge University Press, 1997.

Martin, Dale B. *The Corinthian Body*. New Haven, CT: Yale University Press, 1995.

—— "Heterosexism and the Interpretation of Romans 1:18–32." *Biblical Interpretation* 3 (1995): 332–55.

—— "The Life and Times of Galatians 3:28: 'No Male and Female.'" Paper delivered at the University of Oslo, September 1998.

Massey, Marilyn Chapin. *Feminine Soul: The Fate of an Ideal*. Boston: Beacon, 1985.

Maximus the Confessor. *Opuscule 7*. In *Maximus the Confessor*, edited and translated by Andrew Louth. The Early Church Fathers. New York: Routledge, 1996.

★McCarthy, David Matzko "Homosexuality and the Practices of Marriage." *Modern Theology* 13 (1997): 371–97.

—— "Marriage, Equality, and Homosexuality." Unpublished ms.

★—— "The Relationship of Bodies: Toward a Theological Hermeneutics of Same Sex Unions." *Theology and Sexuality* 8 (1998): 96–112.

McConkie, Bruce R. *Mormon Doctrine*. 2nd edn. Salt Lake City, UT: Bookcraft, 1966.

McCormack, Bruce. *Karl Barth's Critically Realistic Dialectical Theology*. Oxford: Clarendon Press, 1995.

McNeill, John. *The Church and the Homosexual*. 4th edn. Boston: Beacon, 1993.

—— *Freedom, Glorious Freedom: The Spiritual Journey to the Fullness of Life for Gays, Lesbians, and Everybody Else*. Boston: Beacon, 1995.

—— *Taking a Chance on God: Liberating Theology for Gays, Lesbians, and Their Lovers, Families, and Friends*. Boston: Beacon, 1996.

McWhorter, Ladelle. "The Queer Concept of Minority: Homosexual Citizens in American Public Discourse." Unpublished ms.

★Meyendorff, John. *Marriage: An Orthodox Perspective*. 2nd edn. Crestwood, NY: St Vladimir's Seminary Press, 1975.

Milbank, John. "Can a Gift Be Given? Prologemenon to a Future Trinitarian Metaphysic." *Modern Theology* 11 (1995): 119–41.

—— "The Second Difference: For a Trinitarianism without Reserve." *Modern Theology* 3 (1986): 213–33.

—— *Theology and Social Theory: Beyond Secular Reason*. Oxford: Blackwell, 1990.

Miller, James E. "Pederasty and Romans 1:27: A Response to Mark Smith." *Journal of the American Academy of Religion* 65 (1997): 861–6.

Miller, Patricia Cox. "Desert Asceticism and 'The Body from Nowhere.'" *Journal of Early Christian Studies* 2 (1994): 137–53.

Molinsky, Waldemar. *Theologie der Ehe in der Geschichte*. Aschaffenburg: Pattloch, 1976.

Moltmann-Wendel, Elisabeth, and Jürgen Moltmann. *Humanity in God*. New York: Pilgrim, 1983.

★Moore, Sebastian. *The Inner Loneliness*. New York: Crossroad, 1982.

★—— *Jesus the Liberator of Desire*. New York: Crossroad, 1989.

★Nagel, Thomas. "Sexual Perversion." In *Mortal Questions*. New York: Cambridge University Press, 1979.

Nelson, Daniel Mark. *The Priority of Prudence: Virtue and Natural Law in Thomas Aquinas and the Implications for Modern Ethics.* University Park, PA: Pennsylvania State University Press, 1992.

Newman, Louis E. "Constructing a Jewish Sexual Ethic: A Rejoinder to David Novak and Judith Plaskow." In *Sexual Orientation and Human Rights in American Religious Discourse,* edited by Saul Olyan and Martha C. Nussbaum. New York: Oxford University Press, 1998.

Novak, David. "Before Revelation: The Rabbis, Paul, and Karl Barth." *The Journal of Religion* 71 (1991): 50–67.

——— *The Election of Israel: The Idea of the Chosen People.* New York: Cambridge University Press, 1995.

——— *Jewish Social Ethics.* New York: Oxford University Press, 1992.

——— *Judaism and Natural Law.* New York: Oxford University Press, 1998.

——— "Religious Communities, Secular Society, and Sexuality: One Jewish Opinion." In *Sexual Orientation and Human Rights in American Religious Discourse,* edited by Saul Olyan and Martha C. Nussbaum. New York: Oxford University Press, 1998.

Nugent, Robert, ed. *A Challenge to Love: Gay and Lesbian Catholics in the Church.* With an introduction by Bishop Walter F. Sullivan. New York: Crossroad, 1984.

Nugent, Robert, and Jeannine Gramick, eds. *Building Bridges: Gay and Lesbian Reality and the Catholic Church.* Mystic, CT: Twenty-Third Publications, 1992.

Nygren, Anders. *Eros and Agape,* translated by Philip S. Watson. New York: Harper & Row, 1969.

*O'Donovan, Oliver. "Homosexuality in the Church: Can There Be a Fruitful Theological Debate?" In *The Way Forward? Christian Voices on Homosexuality and the Church,* edited by Timothy Bradshaw. London: Hodder & Stoughton, 1997.

Outka, Gene. "Following at a Distance." In *Scriptural Authority and Narrative Interpretation,* edited by Garrett Green. Philadelphia: Fortress, 1987.

Oxford Dictionary of Byzantium, 6 vols, edited by Alexander P. Kazhdan et al. New York: Oxford University Press, 1991.

Pennington, M. Basil. "Vocation Discernment and the Homosexual." In *A Challenge to Love: Gay and Lesbian Catholics in the Church,* edited by Robert Nugent. New York: Crossroad, 1984.

Pesch, Otto Hermann. "Exegese des Alten Testamentes bei Thomas." In *Das Gesetz: ST I-II.90–105. Die Deutsche Thomas-Ausgabe,* vol. 13, edited by Otto Hermann Pesch. Graz: Styria, 1977.

——— "Paul as Professor of Theology: The Image of the Apostle in St Thomas's Theology." *The Thomist* 38 (1977): 584–605.

——— *Die Theologie der Rechtfertigung bei Martin Luther und Thomas von Aquin: Versuch eines systematisch-theologischen Dialogs.* 2nd edn. Mainz: Matthias Grünewald, 1985.

——— *Thomas von Aquin: Grenze und Größe mittelalterlicher Theologie.* Mainz: Matthias Grünewald, 1988.

Peterson, Thomas Virgil. *Ham and Japeth: The Mythic World of Whites in the Antebellum South.* ATLA Monograph Series. Metuchen, NJ: Scarecrow Press and The American Theological Library Association, 1978.

Pickstock, Catherine. *After Writing: On the Liturgical Consummation of Philosophy*. Oxford: Blackwell, 1998.

Plekon, Michael. "Paul Evdokimov: A Theologian Within and Beyond the Church and the World." *Modern Theology* 12 (1996): 85–107.

Plunkett-Dowling, Regina. "A Paradox of Grace: The Gospel Call to Homosexuals." *Sojourners* 20 (July 1991): 26–8.

Pope, Stephen. "Scientific and Natural Law Analyses of Homosexuality: A Methodological Study." *Journal of Religious Ethics* 25 (1997): 89–126.

Preller, Victor. *Divine Science and the Science of God: A Reformulation of Thomas Aquinas*. Princeton, NJ: Princeton University Press, 1967.

Pronk, Pim. *Against Nature? Types of Moral Argumentation Regarding Homosexuality*, translated by John Vriend. Grand Rapids, MI: William B. Eerdmans, 1993.

Rad, Gerhard von. *Old Testament Theology*, translated by D. M. G. Stalker. 2 vols. New York: Harper & Row, 1962.

Rahner, Karl. *Foundations of Christian Faith: An Introduction to the Idea of Christianity*, translated by William V. Dych. New York: Crossroad, 1992.

——— "Magisterium and Theology." In *Theological Investigations*, vol. 18, translated by Edward Quinn. New York: Crossroad, 1983.

——— "On Bad Arguments in Moral Theology." In *Theological Investigations*, vol. 18, translated by Edward Quinn. New York: Crossroad, 1983.

——— "Pseudo-Problems in Ecumenical Discussion." In *Theological Investigations*, vol. 18, translated by Edward Quinn. New York: Crossroad, 1983.

——— "The Theological Concept of Concupiscentia." In *Theological Investigations*, vol. 1, translated by Cornelius Ernst. Baltimore: Helicon Press, 1961.

Rahner, Karl, and Heinrich Fries. *Unity of the Churches: An Actual Possibility*. New York: Paulist Press, 1985.

Ramsey Colloquium. "The Homosexual Movement: A Response by the Ramsey Colloquium." *First Things* 41 (March 1994): 15–20.

Richard of St Victor. *The Twelve Patriarchs, The Mystical Ark, Book Three of the Trinity*, translated and with an introduction by Grover A. Zinn. Classics of Western Spirituality. New York: Paulist Press, 1979.

Ritzer, Korbinan. *Formen, Riten, und religiöses Brauchtum der Eheschließung in den christlichen Kirchen des 1. Jahrhunderts*. Münster Westfalen: Aschendorff, 1962.

Rogers, Eugene F., Jr. "Aquinas and Barth in Convergence on Romans 1?" *Modern Theology* 12 (January 1996): 57–84.

——— "Good Works and the Assurance of Salvation in Three Traditions: *Fides Praevisa*, the Practical Syllogism, and Merit." *The Scottish Journal of Theology* 50 (1997): 131–56.

——— "How the Virtues of the Interpreter Presuppose and Perfect Hermeneutics: The Case of Thomas Aquinas." *The Journal of Religion* 76 (1996): 64–81.

——— "The Narrative of Natural Law in Aquinas's Commentary on Romans 1." *Theological Studies* 59 (1998): 254–76.

★——— "Sanctification, Homosexuality, and God's Triune Life." With a response by Kathryn E. Tanner. In *Sexual Orientation and Human Rights in American Religious*

Discourse, edited by Saul M. Olyan and Martha C. Nussbaum. New York: Oxford University Press, 1998.

—— "Selections from Thomas Aquinas's *Commentary on Romans* [9–11]." Translation of excerpts with an introduction. In *The Theological Interpretation of Scripture: Classic and Contemporary Readings*, edited by Stephen E. Fowl. Oxford: Blackwell, 1997.

—— *Thomas Aquinas and Karl Barth: Sacred Doctrine and the Natural Knowledge of God.* Notre Dame, IN: Notre Dame University Press, 1995.

—— "Thomas Aquinas on Natural Law and the Virtues in Biblical Context: Homosexuality as a Test Case." *Journal of Religious Ethics* 27 (1999): 29–56.

Roth, Catharine P. Introduction to *On Marriage and Family Life*, by John Chrysostom. Translated by Catharine P. Roth and David Anderson. Crestwood, NY: St Vladimir's Seminary Press, 1997.

Ruether, Rosemary Radford. *Sexism and God-Talk.* Boston: Beacon, 1983.

Rulla, L. M. *Anthropology of the Christian Vocation*, vol. 1. Rome: Gregorian University Press, 1986.

Satlow, Michael L. *Tasting the Dish: Rabbinic Rhetorics of Sexuality.* Atlanta, GA: Scholars Press, 1995.

—— "'Try To Be a Man': The Rabbinic Construction of Masculinity." *Harvard Theological Review* 89 (1996): 19–41.

Schaberg, Jane. *The Illegitimacy of Jesus: A Feminist Theological Interpretation of the Infancy Narratives.* San Francisco: Harper & Row, 1987.

Schleiermacher, Friedrich. *Die Weihnachtsfeier: Ein Gespräch*, edited by G. Wehnung. Basel: B. Schwage, 1953. ET: *Christmas Eve: Dialogue on the Incarnation*, translated and with an introduction and notes by Terrence N. Tice. Richmond, VA: John Knox, 1967.

*★Schmemann, Alexander. *For the Life of the World.* New York: National Student Christian Association, 1963.

Schmidt, Thomas E. *Straight and Narrow? Compassion and Clarity in the Homosexuality Debate.* Downer's Grove, IL: InterVarsity Press, 1995.

Scroggs, Robin. *The New Testament and Homosexuality: Contextual Background for Contemporary Debate.* Philadelphia: Fortress, 1983.

—— "Paul and the Eschatalogical Woman." *Journal of the American Academy of Religion* 40 (1972): 283–303.

Sedgwick, Eve Kosofsky. *Epistemology of the Closet.* Berkeley, CA: University of California Press, 1990.

Seow, Choon-Leong, ed. *Homosexuality and Christian Community.* Louisville, KY: Westminster / John Knox, 1996.

Service Book of the Holy Orthodox-Catholic Apostolic Church, translated by Isabel Florence Hapgood. 6th edn. Englewood, NJ: Antiochene Orthodox Christian Archdiocese of North America, 1983.

Siker, Jeffrey S. "Gentile Wheat and Homosexual Christians: New Testament Directions for the Heterosexual Church." In *Biblical Ethics and Homosexuality: Listening to Scripture*, edited by Robert L. Brawley. Louisville, KY: Westminster / John Knox, 1996.

*—— "Homosexual Christians, the Bible, and Gentile Inclusion: Confessions of a Repenting Heterosexist." In *Homosexuality in the Church: Both Sides of the Debate,* edited by Jeffrey S. Siker. Louisville, KY: Westminster / John Knox, 1994.

—— ed. *Homosexuality in the Church: Both Sides of the Debate.* Louisville, KY: Westminster / John Knox 1994.

Simson, Otto G. von. *Sacred Fortress: Byzantine Art and Statecraft in Ravenna.* Princeton, NJ: Princeton University Press, 1987.

Smirensky, Alvian N. "The Evolution of the Present Rite of Marriage and Parallel Canonical Developments." *St Vladimir's Seminary Quarterly* 8 (1964): 38–47.

Smith, Mark D. "Ancient Bisexuality and the Interpretation of Romans 1:26–27." *Journal of the American Academy of Religion* 64 (1996): 223–56.

Sokolowski, Robert. "Reading the Scriptures." Ch. 10 in *The God of Faith and Reason: Foundations of Christian Theology.* Notre Dame, IN: University of Notre Dame Press, 1982.

Sonderegger, Katherine. *That Jesus Christ Was Born a Jew: Karl Barth's "Doctrine of Israel."* University Park, PA: Pennsylvania State University Press, 1992.

Soskice, Janet Martin. "Can a Feminist Call God 'Father'?" In *Speaking the Christian God,* edited by Alvin F. Kimel. Grand Rapids, MI: Eerdman's, 1992.

—— *Metaphor and Religious Language.* Oxford: Clarendon Press, 1985.

Soulen, Kendall. *The God of Israel and Christian Theology.* Minneapolis, MN: Fortress, 1996.

—— "YHWH the Triune God." *Modern Theology* 15 (1999): 25–54.

Speyr, Adrienne von. *The Word Becomes Flesh: Meditations on John 15,* translated by Lucia Wiedenhœver and Alexander Dru. San Francisco: Ignatius Press, 1994.

Stackhouse, Max L. "The Prophetic Stand of the Ecumenical Churches on Homosexuality." With a response by Kathryn Tanner. In *Sexual Orientation and Human Rights in American Religious Discourse,* edited by Saul Olyan and Martha C. Nussbaum. New York: Oxford University Press, 1998.

Steinmetz, David C. "The Superiority of Pre-Critical Exegesis." In *The Theological Interpretation of Scripture: Classic and Contemporary Readings,* edited by Stephen E. Fowl. Oxford: Blackwell, 1997.

Stendahl, Krister. *The Bible and the Role of Women: A Case Study in Hermeneutics.* Philadelphia: Fortress, 1966.

Stout, Jeffrey. "Moral Abominations." In *Ethics after Babel: The Languages of Morals and Their Discontents.* Boston: Beacon, 1988.

—— "Truth, Natural Law, and Ethical Theory." In *Natural Law Theory: Contemporary Essays,* edited by Robert P. George. Oxford: Clarendon Press, 1992.

*Stowers, Stanley K. *A Rereading of Romans: Justice, Jews, and Gentiles.* New Haven, CT: Yale University Press, 1994.

Strohmier, Linda. "'His Blood Be on Us and on Our Children . . .': A Study of the Atonement Theme in Matthew's Passion Account." M.Div. thesis, General Theological Seminary, New York, 1984.

Stuart, Elizabeth, ed. *Chosen: Gay Catholic Priests Tell Their Stories*. London: Geoffrey Chapman, 1993.

★Sullivan, Andrew. "Alone Again, Naturally: The Catholic Church and the Homosexual." *The New Republic* (November 28, 1994): 47, 50, 52, 54–5.

—— *Virtually Normal: An Argument about Homosexuality*. New York: Alfred A. Knopf, 1995.

—— ed. *Same-Sex Marriage, Pro and Con: A Reader*. New York: Vintage Books, 1997.

Sullivan, Francis. *Creative Fidelity: Weighing and Interpreting Documents of the Magisterium*. New York: Paulist Press, 1996.

—— *Magisterium: Teaching Authority in the Catholic Church*. New York: Paulist Press, 1985.

Swartley, Willard M. *Slavery, Sabbath, War, and Women: Case Issues in Biblical Interpretation*. Scottsdale, PA: Herald Press, 1983.

★"Symposium on 'Jewish Christians and the Torah.'" *Modern Theology* 11, 2 (April 1995): 163–241.

Tanner, Kathryn E. *The Politics of God: Christian Theologies and Social Justice*. Minneapolis, MN: Fortress, 1992.

—— "Response to Max Stackhouse and Eugene Rogers." In *Sexual Orientation and Human Rights in American Religious Discourse*, edited by Saul M. Olyan and Martha C. Nussbaum. New York: Oxford University Press, 1998.

—— "Theology and the Plain Sense." In *Scriptural Authority and Narrative Interpretation*, edited by Garrett Green. Philadelphia: Fortress, 1987.

TeSelle, Eugene. *Augustine the Theologian*. New York: Herder & Herder, 1970.

Thomas Aquinas. *De duobus praeceptis charitatis*. In *S. Thomae Aquinatis opera omnia ut sunt in indice thomistico*, vol 6, edited by Robert Busa. Stuttgart-Bad Cannstatt: Friedrich Frommann Verlag-Günther Holzboog KG, 1980.

—— *De modo studendi*. In *S. Thomae Aquinatis opera omnia ut sunt in indice thomistico*, vol. 6, edited by Robert Busa. Stuttgart-Bad Cannstatt: Friedrich Frommann Verlag-Günther Holzboog KG, 1980.

—— *De potentia*. In *S. Thomae Aquinatis opera omnia ut sunt in indice thomistico*, vol. 3, edited by Robert Busa. Stuttgart-Bad Cannstatt: Friedrich Frommann Verlag-Günther Holzboog KG, 1980.

—— *In Gal. Super epistolam ad Galatas lectura*, edited by Raphael Cai. In *S. Thomae Aquinatis doctoris angelici Super epistolas S. Pauli lectura*. 8th edn. 2 vols. Turin: Marietti, 1953. ET: *Commentary on Saint Paul's Epistle to the Galatians*, translated by F. R. Larcher. Aquinas Scripture Series, vol. 1. Albany, NY: Magi Books, 1966.

—— *In Io. Super evangelium S. Ioannis lectura*, edited by Raphael Cai. 5th rev. edn. Turin and Rome: Marietti, 1952.

—— *In Rom. Super epistolam ad Romanos lectura*, edited by Raphael Cai. In *S. Thomae Aquinatis doctoris angelici Super epistolas S. Pauli lectura*. 8th rev. edn. 2 vols. Turin: Marietti, 1953. French translation: *Commentaires de S. Thomas d'Aquin: Sur toutes les épitres de S. Paul*, edited and translated by Abbé Bralé. Paris: Vivès, 1869–74. German translation: *Des heiligen Thomas von Aquin Kommentar zum Römerbrief*, edited and translated by Helmut Fahsel. Freiberg im Briesgau: Herder, 1927.

—— *In Sent. In quattuor libros sententiarum*, 1252–56. In *S. Thomae Aquinatis opera omnia ut sunt in indice thomistico*, vol. 1, edited by Robert Busa. Stuttgart-Bad Cannstatt: Friedrich Frommann Verlag-Günther Holzboog KG, 1980.

—— *Quaestiones Quodlibetales*. In *S. Thomae Aquinatis opera omnia ut sunt in indice thomistico*, vol. 6, edited by Robert Busa. Stuttgart-Bad Cannstatt: Friedrich Frommann Verlag-Günther Holzboog KG, 1980.

—— *CG. Summa Contra Gentiles*, 1259–64. In *S. Thomae Aquinatis opera omnia ut sunt in indice thomistico*, vol. 2, edited by Robert Busa. Stuttgart-Bad Cannstatt: Friedrich Frommann Verlag-Günther Holzboog KG, 1980.

—— *ST. Summa Theologiae*, 1266–73. Leonine ed, edited by Pietro Caramello. 5 vols. Turin and Rome: Marietti, 1952.

—— *Super epistolam ad Ephesios lectura*, edited by Raphael Cai. In *S. Thomae Aquinatis doctoris angelici Super epistolas S. Pauli lectura*. 8th rev. edn. 2 vols. Turin and Rome: Marietti, 1953.

Thompson, Earnest Trice. *Presbyterians in the South*. Vol. 1,*1607–1861*. Presbyterian Historical Society Publication Series, 13. Richmond, VA: John Knox, 1963.

Tillich, Paul. "You Are Accepted." In *The Shaking of the Foundations*. New York: Charles Scribner's Sons, 1948.

Tise, Larry E. *Proslavery: A History of the Defense of Slavery in America, 1701–1840*. Athens, GA: University of Georgia Press, 1987.

"Tomorrow Shall Be My Dancing Day." In *The Shorter New Oxford Book of Carols*, edited by Hugh Keyte and Andrew Parrott. New York: Oxford University Press, 1993, no. 76.

Trible, Phyllis. "A Love Story Gone Awry." In *God and the Rhetoric of Sexuality*. Philadelphia: Fortress, 1978.

—— "An Unnamed Woman: The Extravagance of Violence." In *Texts of Terror*. Philadelphia: Fortress, 1984.

Turner, Denys. *Eros and Allegory: Medieval Exegesis of the Song of Songs*. Cistercian Studies Series, 156. Kalamazoo, MI: Cistercian Publications, 1995.

Valantasis, Richard. "Constructions of Power in Asceticism." *Journal of the American Academy of Religion* 63 (1995): 775–822.

Vatican Council II. *Dei Verbum*. In *The Documents of Vatican II*, edited by Walter M. Abbott. New York: Guild Press, 1966.

Ward, Graham. "The Erotics of Redemption—After Karl Barth." *Theology and Sexuality* 8 (1998): 52–72.

Ware, Kallistos. "The Trinity." In *The Orthodox Way*. Crestwood, NY: St Vladimir's Seminary Press, 1979.

Welker, Michael. "Barth und Hegel: Zur Erkenntnis eines methodischen Verfahrens bei Barth." *Evangelische Theologie* 43 (1983): 307–28.

Westberg, Daniel. *Right Practical Reason: Aristotle, Action, and Prudence in Aquinas*. Oxford: Clarendon Press, 1994.

White, Edmund. "What Century Is This, Anyway?" *The Advocate*, 762 (June 23, 1999): 55–6, 58.

★Williams, Rowan D. "The Body's Grace." 10th Michael Harding Memorial Address.

London: Institute for the Study of Christianity and Sexuality, 1989. Reprinted in *Our Selves, Our Souls and Bodies: Sexuality and the Household of God*, edited by Charles Hefling. Boston: Cowley Publications, 1996.

—— "Bread in the Wilderness: The Monastic Ideal in Thomas Merton and Paul Evdokimov." In *Monastic Traditions East and West: One Yet Two*, edited by M. Basil Pennington. Spencer, MA: Cistercian Publications, 1976.

★—— "Knowing Myself in Christ." In *The Way Forward? Christian Voices on Homosexuality and the Church*, edited by Timothy Bradshaw. London: Hodder & Stoughton, 1997.

—— *Resurrection: Interpreting the Easter Gospel*. London: Darton, Longman & Todd, 1982.

Williamson, Clark M. *A Guest in the House of Israel: Post-Holocaust Church Theology*. Louisville, KY: Westminster / John Knox, 1993.

Wills, Gary. *Under God*. New York: Simon & Schuster, 1990.

Wittgenstein, Ludwig. *Philosophical Investigations*, translated by G. E. M. Anscombe. New York: Macmillan, 1958.

Wypijewski, JoAnn. "The Secret Sharer: Sex, Race, and Denial in an American Small Town." *Harper's Magazine* 297, 1778 (1998): 35–54.

Wyschogrod, Michael. *The Body of Faith: Judaism as Corporeal Election*. Minneapolis, MN: Fortress, 1983. Reprinted as *The Body of Faith: God in the People Israel*. San Francisco: Harper & Row, 1989.

—— "Israel, the Church, and Election." In *Brothers in Hope*, edited by John M. Oesterreicher. New York: Herder & Herder, 1970.

—— "A Jewish Perspective on Karl Barth." In *How Karl Barth Changed My Mind*, edited by Donald K. McKim. Grand Rapids, MI: Eerdmans, 1986.

—— "Why Was and Is the Theology of Karl Barth of Interest to a Jewish Theologian?" In *Footnotes to a Theology: The Karl Barth Colloquium of 1972*, edited by Martin Rumscheidt. Studies in Religion Supplements. Waterloo, Ont.: Corporation for the Publication of Academic Studies in Religion in Canada, 1974.

★Yeago, David S. "The *Concordat*, Ecumenism, and Evangelical–Catholic Politics." *The Lutheran Forum* 32, 1 (1998): 42–6.

—— *The Faith of the Christian Church*. Columbia, SC: Lutheran Theological Southern Seminary, 1992.

—— "Jesus of Nazareth and Cosmic Redemption: The Relevance of St Maximus the Confessor." *Modern Theology* 12 (1996): 163–93.

★Zion, William B. *Eros and Transformation: An Eastern Orthodox Perspective*. New York: University Press of America, 1992.

Zizioulas, John D. *Being as Communion: Studies in Personhood and the Church*. Crestwood, NY: St Vladimir's Seminary Press, 1985.

INDEX OF NAMES
AND TOPICS

INDEX OF SCRIPTURAL CITATIONS